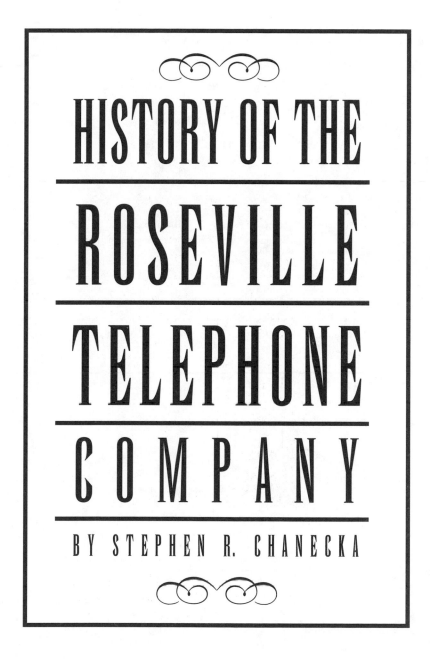

# HISTORY OF THE
# ROSEVILLE
# TELEPHONE
# COMPANY

BY STEPHEN R. CHANECKA

International Standard Book Number: 0-9645508-0-6

Library of Congress Catalog Card Number: 95-67588

Published by

Roseville Telephone Company
200 Vernon Street
Roseville, California 95678

First published 1995

Designed by Page Design, Inc., Sacramento, California

Manufactured in the United States
by Griffin Printing, Sacramento, California

## How To Order:

Single copies may be ordered by mailing $20 plus $3.50 for shipping/handling to the company or by calling (916) 786-1117. Discounts available for ordering 5 or more books.

Roseville Telephone
P.O. Box 969
Roseville, CA 95678
Attn: History Book

# Table Of Contents

# Introduction

In recent years, many people have suggested to me that Roseville Telephone do a book about the company's history. They said that since most of the employees and retirees who helped build the company are still around, it would be worthwhile to document how Roseville Telephone grew from a tiny, local telephone exchange into a highly-successful and sophisticated telecommunications corporation. They said a book would be of particular interest and value to the company's retirees, employees and shareholders. Also, they said a book about Roseville Telephone would be an important contribution to the history of the Roseville area as well as to the history of independent telephony.

After weighing the idea for some time and discussing it with the Board of Directors and others, we decided to commission Sacramento financial writer Steve Chanecka to write the book. In the years since he came to Sacramento in 1977, Steve had written several articles about Roseville Telephone and we were confident he understood the company and could do a good job on this project.

Over 18 months, Steve interviewed more than 150 retirees and others who were affiliated with Roseville Telephone and spent hundreds of hours poring over archival material at the company and at libraries. His research uncovered much new information about the company's early years. After completing his extensive research, Steve had to organize and categorize reams of information to identify what material should be included in the book. Then he had to write the copy in a logical and readable style. I believe Steve's efforts produced a first-class book, one we can all be proud of, and I thank him for his outstanding effort.

Since 1953 when I joined Roseville Telephone, I've always considered it a family company, with every employee important to its success, from the president to the janitor. It was my job over the years to make sure we all worked together, and that everyone was treated fairly. It took us all working together as a team to be successful and, as long as we continue to work together, no competitors can beat us. As far as I'm concerned, Roseville Telephone Company is not only the best telephone company in California, it's the best anywhere.

I want to thank all the employees and the members of the Board of Directors who through the years have contributed to our success. Our current board, including my brother, Tom Doyle — a director since 1952 — Ralph Hoeper, John Roberts, Brian Strom and myself, is hard at work preparing to guide the company into the next century.

I also want to thank my family — my wife Carmen and children, Carol and Mike. They have put up with me through good times and bad times. Without their support, my job would have been much more difficult.

I'm confident that our new executive leadership, with Brian Strom at the helm joined by Al Johnson and Mike Campbell, will keep Roseville Telephone strong, progressive and independent. This company has never been for sale and it will not change in the future.

The years ahead will be every bit as exciting for the Roseville Telephone Company as the last 40. With the significant growth occurring in the region, including expansion at Hewlett-Packard and NEC, new medical complexes built by Kaiser-Permanente and Sutter Health and Del Webb's beautiful Sun City Roseville development, to name only a few, Roseville Telephone is ideally positioned to prosper and grow with the area.

I've said it many times in the past and I'll say it again, "You ain't seen nothing yet!"


*Robert L. Doyle*
Chairman of the Board


April, 1995

# Foreword

## HISTORY OF THE ROSEVILLE TELEPHONE COMPANY

Roseville Telephone Company and its long-time president, Robert L. Doyle, intrigued me from the first time I met him in the late summer of 1977. "This company is different," I remember thinking. Little did I realize at the time how unusual it was.

During that first visit, Doyle expounded at considerable length about what a great company Roseville Telephone was and why it was so superior. "The employees make it great," he said emphatically. His own role, he added with characteristic understatement, was and is to "hire people smarter than me and let them do their jobs." Doyle pictured himself as the orchestra leader, a conductor who knows how all the parts fit into the score, but can't play an instrument.

His method of "big picture" management worked. For more than 40 years he has successfully steered Roseville Telephone into an increasingly complex telecommunications industry even though his knowledge of the technology behind it has always been minimal at best.

Although Roseville Telephone celebrated its 80th year in 1994, in truth the company as it is today began to take shape on Jan. 23, 1954, when the Board of Directors elected Bob Doyle its new president, succeeding his father, William J. Doyle, who had held that position for most of the first 40 years.

The company Bob Doyle took over in 1954 had for four decades been a cash cow that placed a much higher priority on delivering steady and ample dividends to its few founding shareholders than on delivering quality telephone service to its customers in the northeast Sacramento suburban areas encompassing Roseville and Citrus Heights. As brothers Bob and Tom Doyle are quick to point out, in the early 1950s Roseville Telephone was "the most hated telephone company in the United States."

In its first 40 years, Roseville Telephone had managed to accumulate total assets of only slightly over $500,000, an amazingly tiny investment considering it was a public monopoly. It was the original families' reluctance to reinvest their profits in plant and equipment over the years — as opposed to paying themselves fat dividends — that led the California Public Utilities Commission in the early 1950s to threaten the owners of Roseville Telephone with losing their company unless customers received better service ... and soon.

This was the situation when Bob Doyle, a farmer, joined the company in 1953 "as the janitor," he likes to say, with the mission of finding somebody to "straighten out this god damn company." When starting out, he never imagined he would be that person.

What has transpired since is a tale unlike few in corporate annals. Roseville Telephone has evolved from a small-town, antiquated telephone utility serving about 3,000 telephones in 1953 into a sophisticated, high-tech, $100-million-a-year company serving in excess of 250,000 telephones with 94,676 access lines at the end of 1994. Company assets grew from less than $500,000 in 1953 to about $250 million. Profits in 1953 were less than $20,000; in 1993, net income exceeded $22 million. In the early '50s, Roseville Telephone was among the smallest of the 5,000 telephone companies in existence. Today, it is the 24th largest telephone company in the nation and the third biggest in California, after giants Pacific Bell and GTE. And for purists in the industry, Roseville Telephone is the largest "true" independent telephone company in the nation, i.e., a telephone company that doesn't also hold other types of utility properties or have operations in other states.

Roseville Telephone's territory includes only 83 square miles, but this territory has been among the fastest growing areas in California for the last 40 years. Also, it doesn't have the natural barriers to growth, such as mountains, canyons, rivers and forests. Nearly every square inch of the company's service territory can be built upon.

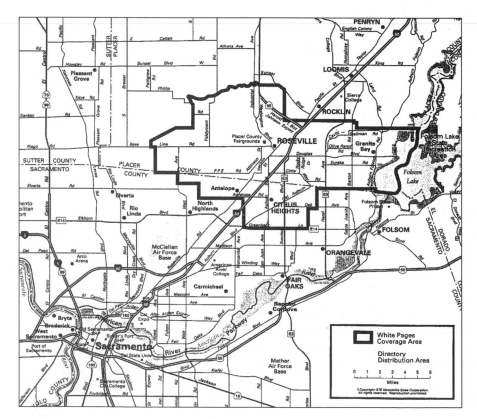

The spectacular success of the past 40 years has enriched the founding families. The extended Doyle family, which in 1954 owned more than 50 percent of Roseville Telephone, today owns less than 10 percent of the stock. But the value of the Doyle family stake has grown to be worth many millions.

Perhaps the most heartening aspect of the phenomenal success story that is Roseville Telephone is how Bob Doyle's personal approach to selling stock and watching closely over those shares has created significant wealth for hundreds of retired and current employees and thousands of investors in Roseville and greater Sacramento. An estimated 90 percent of the shares are held locally, including 10 percent by the employees' retirement plan. Roseville Telephone has never been listed on any stock exchange and the company has sold its own shares from 1953 through its last sale in 1983. It has never used a stockbroker to sell shares. Bob Doyle has been the company's stockbroker and there probably wasn't a day during those 30 years that he wasn't somewhat involved in selling the stock. Bob Doyle knows who owns the company. That wouldn't be the case if the shares were sold through brokers and listed on major stock exchanges.

This huge local ownership stake would make it exceedingly difficult, if not virtually impossible, for a larger company to acquire Roseville Telephone. That's not to say that just about every large telephone company hasn't shown interest! Bob Doyle's personal involvement with the major shareholders and his dogged commitment to remain independent has kept any potential acquirers at a distance, a far distance.

As one retiree noted, through the decades Bob Doyle looked cross-eyed at anybody who sold Roseville Telephone stock. It was not something an employee did unless an emergency warranted the sale. "Damn him," the retiree said of Doyle, "for all those years we couldn't sell the stock because he would have known. We were so afraid to sell the stock that the son of a bitch literally forced us to become rich along the way."

The rewards of the company's success have not been limited to shareholders and employees. The Roseville/Citrus Heights communities have benefited greatly. For example, the Roseville Telephone Foundation, which is funded by contributions from employees, in 1994 raised more than $80,000 for area charities. And the recently-opened Roseville Telephone Museum is a major attraction that not only contributes to the quality of the city's arts, but over time will bring in significant tourist dollars as well.

The *History Of The Roseville Telephone Company* is really two stories. The first is a rather brief account of the company's first 40 years, when the company certainly took as much from the community as it gave. The second is a meaty account about a seemingly unsophisticated farmer — a self-proclaimed "fat ass kid out of Roseville High" — who was able to use the qualities of common sense, vision, judgment and loyalty to forge a company that today is the envy of its community and the giant telecommunications industry. And as lengthy an account as this book is, it only skirts the accomplishments, humor, fun and hard work that represent the full story of Roseville Telephone, its employees and its irrepressible leader. That would take another several thousand pages at least.

It's obvious that my first impressions of Bob Doyle and Roseville Telephone have been borne out by extensive research into its past and present, and the hundreds of hours I've spent talking with past and present employees and associates of the company. This is a "different company" indeed.

# ACKNOWLEDGMENTS

Writing a book is not an individual effort even if one person is called the author. It's a joint effort that touches many people. In my case, I owe gratitude to a host of good people, starting with Bob Doyle who gave me as much time as I desired to delve into the past and present affairs of the company. His secretary, Virginia Amick, is one of the truly exceptional employees at Roseville Telephone. Unfailingly, she assisted me in any way she could, as did her compatriots in the Executive Office, Ophelia Martinez, Sandy Frazer and Lila Mettler.

A.A. "Al" Johnson, the company's Executive Vice President and Chief Operating Officer, contributed greatly to my understanding of the telephone industry through interviews. He also lent me several books which were invaluable in my gaining a better understanding of telephony.

Other employees assisted in the effort, including Robert Parsons, Stewart Brown, Dennis Cordeiro, Kate Mitchell, Mimi Longway and Steve Venturi. I also appreciate the assistance offered by President-CEO Brian Strom and his administrative assistant, Darla Yetter. For more than a year, anything I asked for was taken care of, pronto. That's the way things are done at Roseville Telephone.

One of the first persons to offer aid in this project was Roseville historian Leonard "Duke" Davis. He was particularly useful in helping me learn about the origins of Roseville and its early telephone history. He also provided most of the old photos that are used in the book.

Kimberly Bickel, of Page Design, made the arduous task of designing a book this size interesting and fun. I thank her for her extra efforts to get the job done well and on time.

Another person to mention here is my editor, Bob Carney, who has been improving my writing for the nearly 20 years I've worked for him and with him. My respect for his expertise continues to grow.

Finally, I want to make special mention of my family, my wife Pam and our young children, Marty and Lauren. There were long stretches in writing this book that I needed extended blocks of free time necessary to pull together an undertaking of this magnitude. For their extra inconveniences during my absences, I especially thank them. They know how much I love them.

*Stephen R. Chanecka*
April 1995

# A Homegrown Success Story

## EARLY ROSEVILLE, A RAILROAD TOWN

*"Lucky Jack" Doyle was known for his unswerving belief that the Roseville area would grow and prosper ... in 1896, Doyle bought the bottom floor of the Odd Fellows Hall on Pacific for $10!*

Roseville's location a step from California's capital city and a stride from the majestic Sierra Nevada range was ideal when the push came to build a transcontinental railroad. Fertile, wide-open California beckoned the adventurous and ambitious among the settled populations of the East and Midwest. The western migration led to the growth of Junction, as Roseville was called in its earliest days.

In 1863, Sacramento merchants Charles Crocker, Leland Stanford, Collis P. Huntington and Mark Hopkins (the Big Four) began building a railroad from Sacramento to Omaha, Neb. At Promontory, Utah, the "golden spike" was driven into the rails to join the Big Four's Central Pacific and the Union Pacific, which had been racing west from Omaha. Four decades later, this transcontinental railroad fueled Roseville's growth and prosperity as a major railroad center.

Before the turn of the century, Rocklin had established itself as the major railroad depot for trains chugging up or rolling down the steep Sierra grade. It wasn't until the Southern Pacific (successor to the Central Pacific) chose to expand its switching yards, maintenance facilities and produce-handling facilities in the first decade of the new century and put them in Roseville that it replaced Rocklin as a railroad center

Pacific Fruit Express' decision to build the world's largest ice-making factory in Roseville helped establish its preeminence. PFE, a subsidiary of Southern Pacific, moved its icing capabilities from Sacramento. This vast facility could make 300 tons of ice daily and store 17,000 tons of ice. It cost $250,000 in 1908-1909 and enabled more of the increasingly productive farmers of California to ship fruit and vegetables to the population centers to the East.

*Automatic Electric candlestick telephone (1905) with 11-digit Strowger dial.*

## DOYLES BECOME A LEADING ROSEVILLE FAMILY

SP's decision to grow in Roseville, the last stop before heading up the long, steep grade of the Sierra Nevada, anchored the area's economy for decades.

In 1860, a 20-year-old farmer named John "Jack" Doyle came to California via ship around Cape Horn from New Brunswick, Canada. He arrived in search of good land for livestock and farming. Although there is no record of why Jack Doyle decided to make "Junction" his home, it didn't take the aggressive, hard-drinking Doyle long to become one of the area's leading businessmen and farmers. It was Doyle who first acquired the acreage along Folsom Road in Roseville that was for decades the family's farm and which became the Roseville Square shopping center.

In May 1871, the Placer County assessor's rolls listed John Doyle as the owner of two large parcels, one 50 acres and the other 80 acres. The value listed for the 130 acres was $4 per acre, or $520. Improvements on the property included a house, barn, fence and vines.

Three years later Doyle married Clara B. Mertes, a member of the pioneer Mertes family of the Sylvan District in present day Citrus Heights. That union produced two children, William John Doyle and Winifred Doyle. Winifred would later marry W.J. Kaseberg, one of Northern California's leading ranchers and a descendant of the Donner Party.

"Lucky Jack" Doyle, as he was called, was a shrewd businessman. He took advantage of business cycles in Roseville to acquire property and acreage at bargain-basement prices. One such purchase was completed in 1896 when Doyle bought the bottom floor of the Odd Fellows Building on Pacific Street for $10. The Doyles didn't own the entire building until nearly 50 years later when son W.J. Doyle acquired the second floor, too. Jack Doyle was known for his unswerving belief that the Roseville area would grow and prosper. He had no doubt of it. His attitude was shared by his son who also took advantage of his faith in the growth to build substantial holdings in the area during his 81 years. The Doyles' success in real estate and business was primarily the result of their knowledge of the land. Few residents of Roseville, then or now, understand its character and potential as well as the Doyles.

Jack Doyle's faith in the Roseville area paid off in the early 1900s when Roseville grew to become a railroad center. The population exploded and commerce expanded rapidly. He died in

*Branstetter Store and Hall, erected by W.J. Branstetter at the corner of Pacific and Washington streets in the early 1820s. To the right of the two-storied Branstetter Hall Building are the storage sheds for Mr. Branstetter's lumber business. Later, the lumber business was taken over by the vast Towle outfit. (1905)*

Courtesy of Leonard M. Davis Historical Collection

1910, one year after Roseville was incorporated as a city. Had he lived longer, it's likely Jack Doyle would have been among the founders of the original local telephone company.

## SUNSET/PACIFIC T&T GIVES UP TURF TO HOME TELEPHONE CO.

Although there were a few area farmers that had some type of telephone service in the 1880s, the first telephone reported operating in Roseville was owned by merchant W.J. Branstetter, who had a "speaking tube" in his store on Pacific Street in June 1891. This was more than a decade after telephones first appeared in Sacramento.

Telephony was slow to take hold in Roseville throughout the remainder of the 19th century, but by 1897 local business interests were successful in getting the independent Capital Telephone and Telegraph Company of Sacramento to extend a line between Sacramento and Roseville. Located at the Sawtelle Store on Pacific Street, Roseville now had a direct connection to Sacramento and Folsom. As of 1901, however, Capital reported that it had only two Roseville subscribers. Conversely, Placerville had 52 installed telephones at the time. Other nearby towns were like Roseville and had few telephones. In 1901, Capital T&T had six subscribers in Auburn, three in Penryn, seven in Newcastle, four in Rocklin, three in Orangevale, six in Folsom and only one in Fair Oaks.

Only a year later in 1902, Capital Telephone gave up the struggle and merged with the larger, more established Sunset Telephone and Telegraph Company (a Bell affiliate), which was formed in 1883 as successor to earlier telephone concerns — the Sacramento Telephonic Exchange and the Sacramento District Telegraph Company. In the late 1800s and early 1900s, competing telephone companies generally did not interconnect. In other words, one couldn't telephone another party on a competing system. Eventually, this problem led to single, unified telephone systems in virtually all areas of the country. It was too expensive to maintain competing companies.

On New Year's Eve of 1906, Sunset combined with the Pacific States Telephone and Telegraph Co. to form Pacific Telephone and Telegraph Co., the forerunner of today's giant Pacific Telesis and its subsidiary, Pacific Bell. Sunset apparently retained its name in Roseville, however. In the same year, Roseville was enjoying a boom thanks to Southern Pacific's relocating its major rail yard operations from Rocklin to Roseville. In the next three years, Roseville's population would jump from 400 to more than 2,000 residents. Among them, of course, were key railroad personnel who relied upon communications to keep the trains running on time.

In 1906, the local chamber of commerce sent a delegation to Sunset Co. to inquire about opening a Roseville telephone exchange. Told that a minimum of 12 subscribers were required to justify its own exchange, chamber officials assured Sunset management that 14 subscribers in Roseville were ready to establish service. Soon thereafter, a new 50-line magneto switchboard was installed at the Sawtelle store. Service, however, remained poor, and businesses and residents did not flock to sign up. Sunset/Pacific had a difficult time expanding its Roseville business.

*Neher Saloon (later bakery) Building, Roseville, California.*

Courtesy of Leonard M. Davis Historical Collection

The *Roseville Register* newspaper lamented the poor service in its May 23, 1908, edition. Under the subhead of "Our Telephone Service," the newspaper was careful to say that the local Sunset Co. operator, Miss Georgie Douglass, "a faithful and obliging operator," was not at fault but that "...if the Sunset Co. were careful and desirous of serving the public we would have no complaint to make. A thorough and improved service was promised over three months ago and there has been no change whatever. The people who have local telephones would be $1.50 per month better off if they would take them out for all the service they are outside the town system."

Complaints about Sunset/ Pacific's service continued the next few years. Not only did Sunset/Pacific not serve its Roseville subscribers to their satisfaction, but nationwide the Bell-affiliated companies, of which Sunset was one, were concentrating on serving the urbanized areas, leaving small towns and rural areas to the independent telephone companies. There was more money to be made in the big cities so small towns such as Roseville didn't get much attention.

In its Nov. 10, 1910, pages, the *Roseville Register* reported that a local business group, led by Gottlieb M. Hanisch, on Oct. 27, 1910, had acquired the "right, title and interest" in the Pacific Telephone Co. (Sunset in Roseville), which the *Register* added, "has been giving unsatisfactory service in the past two or three years." Ironically, in late 1909, the Pacific company had tentatively been granted the franchise for the new city of Roseville, but the company balked at one of the conditions — that the city be allowed to take over the telephone franchise at its option after 15 years. With Pacific bowing out, the way was paved for local ownership of the franchise.

Hanisch was named president of the new organization, called the Roseville Home Telephone Co. The other officers of the Home Telephone Co. were J.A. Hill, vice president; L.L. King, secretary, and William Sawtelle, treasurer. Joining Hanisch, Hill and King as original directors were F.A. Lewis and Westman Dickinson, who was the company's first general manager. Other owners were F.H. Crosby, C.T. McCracken, F.A. Pendell and W.D. Gould. The group raised $2,850 in founding capital at $10 per share. Home Telephone bought out Sunset/Pacific's 26-subscriber service and telephone equipment for $1,100.

The *Register* also reported that the new company had already initiated longer hours, from 7 a.m. to 9 p.m., and would offer 24-hour service beginning New Years Day 1911. It also reported that Home Telephone Co. had ordered 125 new telephones, adding that "residents of Roseville should give this new home company all the encouragement they possibly can, for it means a better service and a better system."

Improved service had to come of the new Home Telephone Co.'s efforts, the *Register* editorialized. "We have been struggling along with poor service for three or four years and instead of being the benefit it should have been to the town, it has been a nuisance. Think of having to call Sacramento, 18 miles away, to call Rocklin, 4 miles away. Many a time patrons have had to wait an hour to get a 15-cent message to Auburn. In fact, the service has been most aggravating. We trust and hope the new company will be able to meet all the demands and that the people will appreciate the service rendered."

Only a month later, Home Telephone Co. started to spend money and put up seven miles of pole lines in order to serve more sections of Roseville. Subscribers flocked to sign on to the new telephone company and by year-end 1910, nearly 200 residents were scheduled to receive service, up from only 26 earlier in the year. In 1910, Roseville's population was 2,608 and the town was prospering.

Also in December 1910, the new Board of Directors accepted a proposal by President G.M. Hanisch to construct a new telephone exchange building on Lincoln Street between Vernon and Atlantic streets. The new structure was to be located next to the two-story G.M. Hanisch Building, built in 1907, at the southeast corner of Lincoln and Atlantic streets. That Lincoln/Vernon/Atlantic streets location would remain the hub of the telephone business in Roseville to the present day.

The decision to move the new company from the A.B. McRae Building on Pacific Street made sense because the main telephone cable from Pacific Telephone interconnected with Roseville's lines at Lincoln and Atlantic streets. The new building was a simple, one-story, two-room, 14-foot-by-24-foot corrugated iron and frame structure. It housed a one-position switchboard. Accordingly, in January 1911, Roseville's town trustees granted the local telephone franchise to Home Telephone Co. and by the end of the year 120 telephones were in service.

*Gottlieb M. Hanisch was Roseville's first Volunteer Fire Chief and first president of the Roseville Home Telephone Co. and its successor, Roseville Telephone Company.*

In 1912, Home Telephone Co. petitioned the Railroad Commission of California, which began regulating telephone companies in 1911, for an increase in rates charged "farmer-line" subscribers. Home Telephone wanted to raise the rates on its 13 farmer-line subscribers from $.25 per month to $.50 per month. This increase would generate $39 in additional annual revenue and help the company "receive an adequate income." The request was denied. The commission sympathized with Home Telephone because it "gives a more comprehensive service and is likewise more expensive in operation from the standpoint of service, plant and equipment" than its predecessor, Pacific Telephone. But the decision also said the difficulties which were the basis of the application were "primarily traceable" to operating conditions. "There is no reason why unreasonable burdens due to the operating conditions of public utilities should arbitrarily be shifted to rate payers and it is incumbent on the telephone companies to correct such difficulties in order that they may not be a factor in any alleged necessity for increased rates."

By 1913, probably because the telephone business was more difficult and less profitable than anticipated, the original group of businessmen had decided to disband, resulting in the reorganization of the Home Telephone Co. and an infusion of new money. It was at this point that Jack Doyle's son, William J. Doyle, became an owner in the telephone enterprise.

The business straits faced by Roseville Home Telephone Co. were common during the early days of independent telephony, according to Charles A. Pleasance, author of *The Spirit of Independent Telephony*. "One of the chief problems faced by Independent telephone companies from the start was finding capital. Many were small and unknown in the financial community; and although they were usually begun with local money, they continually needed infusions of cash. The nature of these businesses, often not appreciated by their founders, was that growth had to be accommodated and obsolete equipment had to be replaced."

According to reports filed with the Railroad Commission, at the end of 1913, W.J. Doyle owned 372 shares out of the 735 shares outstanding, an ownership position of just over 50 percent. Gottlieb Hanisch owned 117 shares and was the second largest stockholder. Druggist F.A. Lewis with 110 shares was the third largest shareholder. The remaining shares were held by 13 other shareholders. Hanisch remained president after the reorganization and Doyle was appointed vice president.

"From what I remember him saying, he bailed them out," recalled W.J.'s son, Bob Doyle. "That's the reason he became president later, because he owned over 50 percent of the stock. When he came in, they were up to their asses in alligators, so he drained the pond..."

When he first invested in the telephone business, Doyle was a 38-year-old bachelor farmer of some prominence. And given that his father had died three years earlier, it's likely that W.J. Doyle had capital to invest. Young Doyle's timing was good as well. In 1913, the "Kingsbury Commitment" was adopted, dramatically changing the relationship between independent telephone companies and the large and fast-growing Bell-affiliated telephone companies.

This edict, which was a commitment, but not a law, essentially prohibited Bell companies and independents from competing for the same territories, thus assuring local telephone monopolies. It said Bell would not compete with independents if they were already established and vice versa. Under the "commitment," Bell also granted independent telephone companies access to its long-distance services. At this time, independents competed favorably against the Bell companies for local exchange business, but the independents' lack of a viable long-distance alternative gave Bell the crucial advantage.

No doubt about it, Doyle had good timing. He had bought into a business that now was assured of a monopoly plus guaranteed access to long distance.

In 1913, according to reports filed with the Railroad Commission, the Roseville Home Telephone Co. had 73 miles of wire strung on 251 poles serving 288 subscribers. The company charged monthly rates of $.25 for farmer-line service, $1.50 for four-party service, $2.25 for two-party service and $3 for single-party service.

*Pacific Street, c. 1906-07,*
*Roseville, California.*
Courtesy of Leonard M. Davis Historical Collection

Revenue from local service in 1913 totaled $5,835 and toll service via Pacific Telephone's facilities amounted to $2,495 for total revenue of $8,330. The expenses in 1913 were topped by $3,242 in wages for the five operators. Minor expenses were listed for lights, water, rent, printing, taxes, insurance, freight and draying. All the toll revenue, less commissions, collected went back to Pacific Telephone. Net earnings amounted to nearly $2,000.

In December 1912, Walter Hanisch, the 29-year-old son of Gottlieb, returned from Polytechnic College in Oakland at his father's behest to become the lineman for Home Telephone Co. The younger Hanisch and the elder Doyle would guide the destiny of Roseville's telephone business for the next 40 years.

## ROSEVILLE TELEPHONE BUYS OUT HOME TELEPHONE CO.

Owners in the reorganized Home Telephone Co. developed essentially a swap stock strategy to effect a legal ownership change from Roseville Home Telephone Co. to the newly-formed Roseville Telephone Company. It was a straight-forward business deal that was relatively easily accomplished, but it required approval from the Railroad Commission and the city of Roseville. These legal maneuvers gave corporate birth to the Roseville Telephone Company.

On April 1, 1914, the Roseville Telephone Company was incorporated, consisting of directors from the existing Home Telephone Co. Then Home Telephone Co. requested approval of the purchase by Roseville Telephone of Home Telephone Co.'s assets. When this approval from the Railroad Commission was received on May 7, 1914, the two companies then adopted the necessary resolutions

FRANK C. JORDAN, SECRETARY OF STATE                    FRANK H. CORY, DEPUTY

# STATE OF CALIFORNIA

## DEPARTMENT OF STATE

I, FRANK C. JORDAN, Secretary of State of the State of California, do hereby certify that I have carefully compared the annexed copy of Articles of Incorporation of

ROSEVILLE TELEPHONE COMPANY

with the certified copy of the original now on file in my office, and that the same is a correct transcript therefrom, and of the whole thereof. I further certify that this authentication is in due form and by the proper officer.

In Witness Whereof, I have hereunto set my hand and have caused the Great Seal of the State of California to be affixed hereto this 20th day of June A.D. 191 4.

Frank C. Jordan
Secretary of State.

By Frank Cory
Deputy.

to legally transfer the assets of the telephone company. These resolutions were adopted on June 19, 1914, the day Roseville Home Telephone Company officially became Roseville Telephone Company.

The first resolution passed by the Home Telephone Co. stated its intentions to transfer all its assets to the new company in return for stock in the new company:

"That the Roseville Home Telephone Company, a corporation, shall subscribe to $11,000 of the capital stock of the Roseville Telephone Company, a corporation intended to be formed with an authorized capital stock of $25,000, divided into 2,500 shares of the par value of $10 each, and in payment for the stock so subscribed, said Roseville Home Telephone Co. shall sell, assign, transfer and convey to C.A. Baker, the treasurer of the intended corporation, all telephone lines and plant, all equipment and instruments, all agreements, rights, franchises, interests and all other property of every kind and character of said Roseville Home Telephone Company, at a valuation of $11,000, as fixed by the Railroad Commission of the State of California and in full payment for said stock, said property to be transferred by said Baker to Roseville Telephone Company when formed and in the manner and upon terms specified and required by said Railroad Commission in its order of May 7th, 1914. In case said Roseville Telephone Company shall not be formed or if it shall not comply with the orders and terms of said Commission authorizing the transfer, then said Baker shall re-convey said property to the Roseville Home Telephone Co."

*Early construction crew for Roseville Home Telephone Co.*

Courtesy of Leonard M. Davis Historical Collection

This resolution was passed by the board of the reorganized Roseville Home Telephone Co., which at this time was the same as the original board of the new Roseville Telephone Company. The five directors were G.M. Hanisch, C.T. McCracken, F.A. Lewis, Lena A. Etzel and W.J. Doyle.

This same group on June 19, 1914, also approved a resolution allowing the Roseville Home Telephone Company to sell all its property to the new company. The resolution stated:

"We, the undersigned, being the owners of and holding of record two thirds and over of the issued capital stock of the Roseville Home Telephone Co., a corporation, hereby consent to the foregoing sale of all the property, franchises and interest of said Roseville Home Telephone Co. in accordance with the terms of the foregoing subscription to stock and transfer of property."

At the same meeting, these same directors exercised their role as directors of the Roseville Telephone Company by agreeing to subscribe to one share each of the new corporation. This allowed them to legally conduct a meeting. The resolution is as follows:

"We, the undersigned, hereby subscribe to one share each of the capital stock of the Roseville Telephone Company, a corporation about to be formed by us as directors, such capital stock of said corporation to be $25,000, divided into 2,500 shares of the par value of ten dollars each, and we agree to pay for our respective shares the sum of ten dollars for each share on demand.

"We designate and appoint C.A. Baker, as treasurer of the intended corporation.

"We accept the subscription of the Roseville Home Telephone Company to $11,000 in shares of stock of the proposed corporation in accordance with the order of the Railroad Commission of the State of California, rendered on the 7th day of May, 1914, the subscription of the said Roseville Home Telephone Company being hereunto annexed.

"Witness our hands the 19th day of June, 1914."

The Roseville Telephone Company was now officially born. It had a capitalization of $11,050, of which 1,100 shares was distributed pro-rata to stockholders in the predecessor company and five shares, one each, to the original five shareholders of Roseville Telephone Company.

# The Early Years, 1914-1920

. . . . . . . . . . . . . . . . . . . . . . .

BILL DOYLE BUYS SHARES IN THE FUTURE

*Roseville Telephone paid its owners 10 percent annual cash dividends, a generous return on their investment, particularly in those years when interest rates were low, typically in the 2-3 percent range.*

With fresh capital from new shareholders fueling the goal of providing the residents of Roseville with better telephone service, the new Roseville Telephone Company immediately began investing in plant and equipment. By August 1914, the new company had requested Railroad Commission authorization to sell another 100 shares at $10 each "for the purpose of paying for labor and material used for additions and betterments to its plant in the sum of $703.73, and for other additions and betterments to be made in the sum of approximately $300.00." This increased the total capitalization to $12,000, representing 1,200 shares at the end of 1914. In addition, there were 52 treasury shares.

From 1913, when W.J. Doyle bought in as majority owner of the reorganized Roseville Home Telephone Co. until the end of 1914 when the company was the Roseville Telephone Company, Doyle invested $2,860. He increased his stake from 372 shares to 658. Although Doyle continued to be the majority shareholder, Gottlieb Hanisch remained president of Roseville Telephone until his death at 73 in October 1917. Doyle became president at that time and would remain so until retiring in January 1954.

Through the early years, the growing company needed additional capital for improvements and additions to its plant and equipment. When new shares were sold, Doyle kept adding to his position to remain the majority owner. Doyle's farming interests, which included vineyards, cattle, sheep and turkeys, apparently produced sufficient income to pay his bills and allow him to acquire more shares in the telephone company, and a wife, too. He married Hazel Wright in 1916 and the first of their five children was born in 1918.

In 1915, the company sold 100 shares — the 52 treasury shares it was holding plus 48 new shares to fund expansion. Doyle bought 35 of them for $350 to increase his ownership to 693 shares out of 1,298 outstanding. In 1916, Doyle bought another 135 shares of the 195 new shares sold by the company as it continued to expand. At this point, Doyle owned 828 shares, or 53.4 percent of

. . . . . . . . .

*F.A. Lewis, Roseville's first druggist, was a founding director of the Roseville Telephone Company who stayed on the Board of Directors until his death in 1957.*

the shares outstanding. The following year, 1917, the company's growth required the sale of another 555 shares to raise more than $5,000. Again, Doyle stepped up to purchase 189 shares to raise his ownership to 1,017 shares, slightly under 50 percent of the 2,048 shares outstanding at the close of 1917. His ownership would remain at this level until 1922, the next time the company sold shares.

From the beginning, however, Doyle devoted almost no time to company operations. He presided over the monthly Board of Directors' meetings and signed checks, showing little interest in the day-to-day affairs of the company. But he knew the telephone company was a good investment, and kept adding shares. In 1914, the Roseville Telephone Co. began paying its shareholders regular dividends. The first year the dividend amounted to 9 percent of the invested capital. For many years thereafter, Roseville Telephone paid its owners 10 percent annual cash dividends, a generous return on their investment, particularly in those years when interest rates were low, typically in the 2-3 percent range.

## GOTTLIEB HANISCH: PHONES AND FIRES

*The Roseville Volunteer Fire Department in 1910 with Fire Chief Gottlieb M. Hanisch at far right.*
Courtesy of Leonard M. Davis Historical Collection

After Doyle, the leading Roseville Telephone Company. shareholder was undoubtedly Gottlieb M. Hanisch. Hanisch was not only the primary force behind the founding of the Roseville Home Telephone Co., his business and civic interests were wide and varied. Born in 1844 in Klagenfurt, Austria, he

came to San Francisco with his family in 1850. There Gottlieb was schooled and trained in the building trades. His family moved to a ranch east of Roseville in 1867.

Hanisch primarily farmed until the railroad boom of the late 1800s sparked his desire to pursue the plumbing and contracting trades. Over a 10-year period in the early 1900s, the barely five-foot Hanisch erected several important buildings in Roseville, including the G.M. Hanisch Building, which served as headquarters for his extensive business activities. Hanisch was also one of the founding members of the Roseville Corporation, a group of prominent local capitalists who financed and oversaw construction of several commercial buildings in Roseville, including the Post Office Block (later known as Red Men's Hall) on Lincoln Street. The Roseville Telephone office was adjacent to the Hanisch Building.

His other great interest, one to be passed down to his son Walter and grandson David, was his passion for fighting fires. Gottlieb was Roseville's first Chief of the Volunteer Fire Department in 1907. He served until 1915 when he resigned, in protest over the Roseville Board of Trustees' denial of his request that volunteer firefighters be paid $.50 an hour when fighting fires.

Gottlieb Hanisch's ability to remain president of the Roseville Telephone Co. despite holding far fewer shares than Doyle attested to Hanisch's stature in the business community and the fact that he was more than 30 years Doyle's senior. It's also likely that Doyle didn't mind playing second fiddle to Hanisch because Doyle was quite unpretentious. Titles meant nothing to Bill Doyle. He was secure in his 50 percent-plus ownership of the company.

The other large shareholders in Roseville Telephone in its first year of operation were druggist F.A. Lewis, with slightly over 9 percent of the stock, and Walter Hanisch with more than 8 percent.

Lewis remained a board member longer than any of the founders, including Bill Doyle. He served both Home Telephone Co. and Roseville Telephone as a vice president. Lewis was still a director of Roseville Telephone when Bill Doyle stepped down in early 1954. Through the years, Lewis' drug business would thrive in downtown Roseville. His final store was just a few doors down from the present headquarters of Roseville Telephone.

Charles A. Baker, who was the original corporate secretary, owned a haberdashery across the street from the telephone company office. A native of England, Baker opened up his shop upon arrival to Roseville in 1909 and was known for his austere British demeanor and his frugality. Although he was involved with the telephone company from its very beginning, the parsimonious Baker never owned a telephone in his home. He had no use for modern conveniences — he didn't have a refrigerator nor did he have heat in his home on Brookview Avenue overlooking Dry Creek in downtown Roseville. Foods were kept cool in a basement room where the Baker and guests would retreat during the hot summer months. Baker sold his shop in December 1923. The Bakers were very private people, according to his nephew Robert Lake of Roseville. They kept to themselves or socialized mostly with the Hanisches and Etzels.

Another member of the original Board of Directors was Lena A. Etzel, a former school teacher who was married to Chris Etzel, a Roseville carpenter/contractor. Mrs. Etzel was on the board because she handled the family's finances and was generally "more literate" than her husband, according to her granddaughters, Betty Benedetti and Marguerite Smart. "She could spell and write and I think my grandfather felt that she would be better on a board," said Betty Benedetti. "And for the times, she was kind of a woman's libber."

*Lena A. Etzel, a founding director of the Roseville Telephone Company who stayed on the Board of Directors until her death in 1930.*

The Etzels moved to Roseville in 1908 from Rescue in El Dorado County. Chris Etzel was a dirt farmer and blacksmith there, but Lena longed to be in a city environment and threatened to go herself to such a place if he didn't join her. Thus, they decided on moving to Roseville where Etzel's building skills could be of service in the fast-growing railroad town. Lena Etzel was involved in Roseville cultural activities and remained on the Board of Directors until her death in 1930.

Charles T. McCracken, also a board member and one of the original founders of Home Telephone Co., was born in Illinois. He was a school teacher for two years and a railroad fireman and locomotive engineer for 10 years before moving to California in 1906 at age 32. Described as "one of the substantial business owners in Roseville" by W.B. Lardner and M.J. Brock in their 1924 book, *History of Placer and Nevada Counties*, McCracken owned a drayage, feed and fuel business in Roseville from 1906 through 1917. From 1918 through 1923, McCracken was assistant manager of Roseville Telephone Company, according to the Lardner/Brock book.

In 1924, McCracken founded a gas service station affiliated with Shell Oil and left the Roseville Telephone Board of Directors. He was not associated with the telephone company after 1923. McCracken died in 1949.

## WALTER HANISCH NAMED MANAGER IN 1914

In 1914, Walter Hanisch was named manager of Roseville Telephone. As manager, he ran the day-to-day affairs and reported monthly to the Board of Directors. His tenure continued for more than 40 years.

As far as the public was concerned, Walter Hanisch *was* the Roseville Telephone Company. He ran the business affairs, dealt with the regulatory Railroad Commission, and was the chief maintenance and "fix-it" man for the company until the 1940s. Until the 1950s, Hanisch ran a tiny telephone exchange that he kept small and provincial. Under Hanisch, the area close to Roseville's downtown area was given service, often just barely adequate, but prospective customers outside the city limits would just have to wait ... and wait, in many cases years and years, to get telephone service.

Walter, born in November 1883, was the oldest of seven children of Gottlieb and Emily (Saunder) Hanisch. After attending Roseville Grammar School, he worked for his father and also had stints with Pacific Gas and Electric and Pacific Fruit Express before permanently joining the Roseville Home Telephone Co. as a lineman in December 1912. He had already worked part-time with Home Telephone, but was in Oakland taking engineering courses when his father summoned him home to work full-time at the telephone company. In the century's first decade, Walter also worked as an electrician, as evidenced by an advertisement in the Dec. 31, 1909, *Roseville Register*.

Walter joined his father on Roseville's volunteer fire brigade in 1907 and was to have a lifelong association in the fire department. For many years Walter was Fire Chief for Roseville. The telephone company was on top of all fires, since the first person that had to be notified was Walter Hanisch.

## WORLD WAR I AND SLOW GROWTH

The Roseville Telephone Company grew steadily during World War I. Although the 1914-1918 war curtailed supplies and services to America, war was a boon to the railroad industry, which carried the material to meet the demands of a world at war. From 1910 to 1920, Roseville nearly doubled in population — to 4,477 residents — largely at the expense of Rocklin. Rocklin underwent a drastic decline from 1,026 residents in 1910 to only 643 residents by 1920. The loss of the railroad and related businesses hit that community hard.

In fact, Roseville was by far the fastest-growing town in the immediate area. In the decade between 1910 and 1920, Auburn's population dropped from 2,376 to 2,285. Lincoln's population dropped from 1,402 in 1910 to 1,325 and Colfax declined from 621 to 573. Sacramento County was growing then, however, jumping from 67,806 in 1910 to 91,029 in 1920.

In 1914, there were five churches in Roseville — Methodist, Roman Catholic, Baptist, Presbyterian and Episcopal. Almost as conspicuous and probably more important, however, were the fraternal orders that dominated the railroad town culture. In 1914, established orders in Roseville included the Masons, Odd Fellows, Eagles, Moose, Knights of Pythias, Woodmen, Rebekahs, Pythian Sisters and the Eastern Star. There were also a number of fraternal societies that were connected only with railroad employees.

*Lincoln Street looking northward from Vernon Street. Today Roseville Telephone's administration building occupies the entire Lincoln Street frontage on the left and most of the block on the right.*

Courtesy of Leonard M. Davis Historical Collection

Roseville Telephone's growth mirrored the community's. In 1915, when Roseville's population was estimated to be 3,500, the company had 83 miles of wire on 291 poles serving 460 telephones. This was a substantial increase from a few years earlier. It was clear that investment in more wire, poles and additional telephones resulted in additional subscribers as well. In 1915, the company's first full year, more than $4,000 was invested in new fixed plant. That was nearly half a year's revenue. Total revenue in 1915 jumped to $9,130 and the net operating income after taxes was $2,512. After paying out $1,247 in dividends and investing $1,692 in "construction, equipment and betterments," the company's retained earnings account dwindled by $858 for the year.

In 1916, the pattern continued as annual revenue exceeded $10,000 for the first time, reaching $11,209. Operating income rose to $2,980, and aided by an additional $1.35 in bank interest, total income rose to $2,981. After dividends of $1,434 and other miscellaneous purchases, $1,287 was added to the corporate surplus account. In the same year, the telephone company increased its wire mileage to 100 miles on 391 poles serving 550 telephones.

In this year the company also had a skirmish with the Railroad Commission over appropriate horizontal and vertical clearances for its wires on poles throughout the system. In a hearing before the commission's staff, manager Walter Hanisch pleaded that the $1,000 expense to re-do roughly half of the company's outside plant and bring it into compliance would be a financial burden on the company. The commission, however, noting that Roseville Telephone "made no special effort" to comply with the statute, didn't accept Hanisch's plea that the company was "a small one and not in good financial condition." The commission also pointed out that the company paid its shareholders more than $1,200 in dividends in 1915. Hanisch's request that the company be given five years to comply with the statute was denied. Instead, the company was given two years to comply. The commission admitted, however, that "the petitioner is a small company and is uncertain as to exactly what it must do to comply with the statute. The commission will send an inspector to assist petitioner in reaching a conclusion as to the work that must be done." This pattern of Roseville Telephone crying "poverty" to the regulatory authorities would continue for nearly 40 more years.

*Automatic Electric type 21 candlestick telephone with dial (1918).*

In 1917, revenue rose to $12,627 and operating income climbed to $2,687. Surplus reserves were such that the company purchased $2,600 in Liberty Loan bonds to aid the war effort. As a community, Roseville was committed to buying $40,000 of the first issue of Liberty Bonds. Actual purchases were double that.

In 1917, telephones in use grew only slightly to 560 and no new wire or poles were added. The company did note in its annual report to the Railroad Commission that it had changed about 75 percent of its subscribers "from code ringing to harmonic ringing."

In this year the company for the first time delineated its subscriber base and the rates paid by them. There were 13 farmer-line customers paying $.25 per month. The company's five operators enjoyed discount service at $.75 per month. There were four "rural" customers paying $1.25 per month. Resident subscribers on four-party lines paying $1.50 a month numbered 435 with another 35 customers, presumably on the outskirts of town, paying $1.75 for the same residential service. As has historically been the case in telephony, businesses paid the highest rates with 25 area businesses paying $2.25 per month for two-party service. Another 40 businesses paid $3 per month for single-party service.

In those years, and for decades thereafter in Roseville and surrounding areas, telephone lines were rationed according to priority uses. This meant that even if an individual desired one- or two-party service and was willing to pay the extra amount, the telephone company didn't necessarily grant the request. Additional service required that the company invest in expanded outside plant (cables, poles, aerial wire, etc.) and for decades at Roseville Telephone, there was no hurry to invest in outside plant. Under Walter Hanisch's direction, with the agreement of shareholders accustomed to receiving fat dividends each year, the growth would be steady, but slow. Growth would only happen as the company could afford it after paying 10 percent annual dividends. It would be almost 40 years before the company borrowed outside funds to fuel growth.

In October 1917, Gottlieb Hanisch died at the age of 73. Upon his death, W.J. Doyle was elected president of Roseville Telephone and F.A. Lewis became vice president. Charles Baker filled Hanisch's seat on the Board of Directors, a position he was to hold for nearly four more decades.

In 1918, growth leveled off. Revenue actually fell slightly to $12,555 and operating income, impacted by a sizable increase in taxes, fell to $2,145. It was the first year taxes exceeded $1,000. The company paid $1,093 in taxes, more than double the previous year's $431 tax bill. Net income that year declined to $1,860. After paying $2,048 in dividends, $1 per share, and investing $835 in central office equipment, new telephones and new pole lines, the cash surplus at the end of 1918 declined to $3,123. Another $1,400 went to war bonds, bringing the total to $4,000. Roseville Telephone was playing its part as the war ended in November 1918.

Total assets of the company amounted to $28,939 and the company was now serving 654 telephones from its magneto switchboard. The company had 200 lines with all but two working at the end of 1918. There were nine employees, two men and seven women, six of them operators.

In October 1918, Roseville was hit by a wave of the Spanish influenza and schools, churches, public halls and theaters were closed. Women in the community, led by the Woman's Improvement Club, converted a local boarding house into what was called "Community Hospital." The women did all the scrubbing, washing and nursing for those afflicted and out of 75 patients struck by the Spanish flu epidemic, only one patient died.

The year 1919 was another flat one for Roseville Telephone Company. Revenue inched up a few dollars to $12,573, but expenses climbed. Net income after taxes amounted to only $761. The situation was so bleak that the Board of Directors decided to cut the dividend in half, paying a 5 percent dividend compared to the 10 percent of the previous several years. The surplus again declined, this time by $527. Subscriber stations grew to 660 at the end of 1919, a paltry gain of six from the end of 1918. Employees at the end of the year declined to eight, two men and six women, five of them operators. Business, it appeared, was going backward.

But the final year of the 20th century's second decade wasn't all bad for Bill Doyle and the Roseville Telephone Company. On Feb. 11, 1919, Hazel Doyle gave birth to their second son, Robert L. Doyle. Years later this infant would reshape his father's company and bring it to prominence in telephony.

# The Roaring '20s

COMPANY SHOWS RENEWED GROWTH IN 1920s

*It was the best of all worlds ... Roseville Telephone enjoyed growing revenue, higher profit and fat dividends with still enough left over to invest in new plant and equipment while adding to its cash surplus. And all this was accomplished without borrowing a penny — what a business!*

Having suffered through flat results in the years just after World War I, Walter Hanisch and the Board of Directors decided it was appropriate to petition the Railroad Commission for a general rate increase. As has been the case historically in dealings with regulatory bodies, utilities such as Roseville Telephone ask for major increases, understanding that they will likely not receive all they request. This appeared to be the case in 1920 when the company asked the commission for the authority "to increase its rates on all classes of telephone exchange service." The petition said that the rates in effect at that time are "not sufficient to pay a reasonable return upon the investment in the exchange plant, and hence an increase of the present rates is necessary."

Not surprisingly, the commission's findings did not agree with the company's submission. Several of the rate hike requests were either denied altogether or pared back. The company did win a number of rate hikes, however, including an increase of $1.20 per year to provide farmer-line residence service. The annual fee went up to $4.20 from $.25 per month, or $3 per year.

The improvement in rates enabled the company to resume the growth pattern of its early years. The new decade started with $15,703 in revenue, an increase of more than $3,000 over the previous year, and an operating net income of $2,305 in 1920. The company reported 700 telephones in service, operating through an expanded switchboard, which was enlarged by 50 new lines during 1920, bringing the total to 250.

The remainder of the 1920s produced steady, if uneventful, growth. The business aspects followed the traditional patterns of a growth company. As new residents moved into the company's territory, requiring new telephones and the fixed plant to serve the new customers, the company would have to fund the expansion. Throughout its first 40 years, Roseville Telephone's method of financing its growth was relatively straightforward. Investments in new plant and equipment were financed from cash generated by net operating income plus its reserve account for depreciation less any moneys paid out in dividends. Each year the company depreciated its fixed plant and equipment, charging this expense against income. The cash reserve was used to fund new plant and equipment, the theory being, of course, that equipment wears out over time and must be replaced by newer equipment. All equipment is assigned a "lifetime" in years and depreciated accordingly. In Roseville Telephone's case, this depreciation reserve was watched closely by the Railroad Commission to ensure that enough funds were being put aside to enable the telephone utility to keep its plant modern and capable of providing adequate service to its customers.

In years of rapid growth, the cash provided from income and the money in the depreciation reserve are often not sufficient to fund the capital improvements necessary to prepare for future growth. The shortfall is made up by the sale of new shares of stock — new investment in the company — or by borrowing money. Roseville Telephone Company was an extremely conservative company in its early years, and the prospect of borrowing large sums of money did not appeal to its Board of Directors and shareholders. When capital was required, Roseville Telephone's shareholders typically bought more shares of common stock, which injected new funds into the company. This occurred three times in the first part of the 1920s as the company made steady new investments in its plant and equipment to serve a Roseville population that jumped to 6,425 in 1930 from 4,477 in 1920. In the first half of the 1920s, Roseville Telephone was a going concern, indeed.

In many respects, the decade of the '20s held true to the preceding one, i.e. heady growth for the first half followed by a stagnant second half. The late 1920s exhibited a tightening of the financial belt as Roseville Telephone — without knowing it — was preparing for the most severe downturn in the history of the United States, the Great Depression of the 1930s.

The first six years were excellent for the company, aided by the rate increase of 1920 and a growing population. In 1921, Pacific Fruit Express once again enlarged its Roseville plant by installing huge electric motors, increasing its ice-making storage capacity. New businesses were moving to Roseville, including Dorman Furniture, a Sacramento store that opened a branch in Roseville. It was also in 1921 that Roseville First National Bank opened for business. It would later be acquired by the Bank of Italy, which was later re-named Bank of America. According to advertisements in local newspapers, a brand new Ford Model T touring car sold for $440 while the rugged Willy's Knight motor car, that era's Jeep, cost a cool $1,895. A Sacramento-based real estate company, Trainer Desmond Co., was advertising house lots in Citrus Heights from $125 to $225 each.

Roseville Telephone's revenue grew to $18,761 in 1921, up about $3,000 from the previous year and $6,000 from only two years earlier. Net operating income was $2,692. In that year, $1,155 was invested in new plant and equipment and the customary 10 percent dividend was paid, which equalled $2,048, or $1 a share for each outstanding share. The company had 11 employees, which included eight operators. There were 760 telephones in service.

In 1922, revenue went down slightly, as did net income, to only $1,295. But the capital investment grew as the company spent $3,285 to increase the central office's switchboard capabilities, adding a third position for an operator, and to buy new telephones and add wire lines to carry the telephone signals. Telephones in use rose to 800 and the employees totaled 12 at the end of the year. One new man was added to help on construction.

In that same year, plans were drawn up to build new quarters for the company. This new structure would be next door to the existing telephone office and be much larger. It required new capital to fund its construction and the new equipment that would be installed. In 1922-23 the company nearly doubled its stock outstanding, from 2,048 shares held by 15 stockholders after the last stock offering in 1917 to 3,876 shares at the end of 1923 held by 11 shareholders.

W.J. Doyle continued to invest heavily in the telephone company and in 1922-23 more than doubled his ownership from 1,017 shares to 2,157 shares, requiring a cash investment of $11,400. Doyle's total investment in Roseville Telephone was now $21,570, a princely sum for the times. He now owned more than 55 percent of the shares.

*Roseville Telephone Company's "new" office shortly after completion in the winter of 1922.*

Courtesy of Leonard M. Davis Historical Collection

One of the newcomers among the shareholders was Hale M. Trevey, a prominent engineer with the Southern Pacific and an investor. He bought 300 shares and would later increase his ownership and become a director. Trevey, a native of Memphis, Tennessee, was schooled in Missouri and became a railroad engineer in 1903. He moved to Roseville in 1907. Trevey was also a shareholder in the Railroad Bank of Roseville and the Roseville Banking Company.

The other shareholders and their ownership at the end of 1923 included: Charles A. Baker (325), Walter Hanisch (275), F.A. Lewis (237), Christian and Lena Etzel (226), the G.M. Hanisch Estate (204), Roy and Minnie Etzel (102), Marrion Lewis (13) and P.L. Campbell (11). Previous shareholders who sold their positions to other stockholders during the years from 1917 through 1923 included Charles T. McCracken and Effie J. McCracken, Edith (Hanisch) Engvall, W.D. Gould, Emily Hanisch and Harriett Lewis. Charles T. McCracken, a founder of the Home Telephone Company, director of Roseville

Telephone and its assistant manager from 1918-1923, sold his shares to Trevey, who replaced him as a director.

The year 1923 was an important year for Roseville Telephone. Not only did it receive a significant infusion of capital from its shareholders, but its financial performance set records. Revenue reached $21,566 and operating income totaled $4,597. Profit from the sale of war bonds added another $412, giving the company gross income of $5,009. Employee totals dropped to 11.

Investments in capital equipment soared to $12,496 in 1923. A new convertible switchboard and related equipment cost $7,249. With three operator positions, it had the capability of serving 260 lines. There were approximately 900 telephones in use at the end of 1923. Although the new 20-foot-by-60-foot office was built in 1922, it was in 1923 that the new central office exchange became fully operational. This relatively modest office, while a signature of progress in 1922-23 when it opened for business, would remain Roseville Telephone Company's only office for another quarter-century. The outdated office reflected the company's stand-pat posture during the next three decades.

The company spent more than $3,000 on new wire and cable in 1923. Wire mileage was reported annually to the Railroad Commission, which kept tabs on how much wire and cable the utility owned. The company had to report this in the following categories: pole miles, miles of cable (which included multiple wires inside the cable), miles of wire in (inside) cable, miles of aerial wire (referred to as "open wire") and finally total miles of all wire. For example, at the end of 1923, Roseville Telephone listed 10 miles of pole line (the total distance of pole lines in the service territory), only one-half mile of cable, 50 miles of wire in cable (100 separate circuit pairs enclosed inside a half mile of sheathed cable equalling 50 total cable miles), and 150 miles of aerial wire, which suggested that there were approximately 15 individual wires strung on the company's 10-mile pole route. Total wire mileage for the company in 1923 amounted to 200 miles. One could track Roseville Telephone Company's progress, or lack thereof, by the annual changes in wire mileage reports.

In that year, majority owner W.J. Doyle proved once again that farming, not the telephone company, was his main occupation. It was in December of 1923 that Doyle spent $40,000 to acquire 870 acres of the Lucy Murray ranch four miles west of Roseville. This parcel plus his fine ranch on Folsom Road reaffirmed Doyle's position as one of the area's prominent farmers.

Roseville Telephone's financial fortunes continued on the upswing in 1924 as revenue jumped to $25,202 and operating income reached $6,072. More than $5,000 was invested in new plant and equipment with the bulk of that going to purchasing new telephones and additional wire to serve the 100 new customers who joined the system during the year. At the end of 1924, the company reported serving 900 telephones. Also, on the last day of 1924, a fourth operator position was added to the "convertible" switchboard. It would be the last operator position added for more than 20 years.

An additional $3,390 was invested by existing shareholders in 1924 to buy shares in the company. The biggest purchase was made by Hale M. Trevey, who added 180 shares, giving him 480, or 11.4 percent of the 4,215 shares out-standing. Baker increased his ownership to 390 shares, or over 9 percent. Both Etzel families added somewhat to their holdings as did a small holder, Harriet Lewis. Doyle didn't buy any stock in 1924 and his ownership dropped slightly to 51.2 percent. Apparently, his purchase of 870 acres of ranch land the previous year had him temporarily "tapped out" of cash.

## COMPANY'S ROLE IN FIGHTING FIRES

It's a wonder Roseville Telephone didn't burn down in those early years since, according to news accounts of the period, it appears that just about every other local business did! Fires in the early years of the 20th century were rather commonplace compared to today's standards. The old wooden buildings didn't mix well with the rough-hewn nature of the bawdy railroad community. Carelessness with smoke and drink were the cause of many a blaze back then. Take 1924, for example.

In February, fire gutted the old wooden portion of the the Barker Hotel and properties across the alley from the hotel. It was listed as a "major Roseville fire" by the Brill family's *Roseville Tribune*, the successor to the 1923 merger of the *Roseville Register* and *Roseville Tribune* newspapers. A fire in May 1924 demolished the Liberty Bakery on Church Street. On June 26, the block on Lincoln Street that included J.R. O'Neil's Hardware Store, C.S. Wilson's Men's Store and Thompson's Saloon went up in flames. A day later, the Fiddyment family's warehouse on Tahoe Avenue burned to the ground.

In August, the two-story Phillips Building on the corner of Vernon and Washington was devoured by fire and in November, Herring's wooden building on Lincoln went up in smoke taking with it the Mint Cafe, Roseville Billiards Parlor and Krieger's Log Cabin Bakery.

In those early days before modern fire departments and sophisticated fire detection systems became the norm, the telephone company was integrally involved in getting the word out to volunteer firemen and the rest of the community that a fire was in progress. And fire fighting was a top priority of the Hanisches, from Gottlieb to his son, Walter, to his grandson, David. The three were among Roseville's most active fire fighters. As mentioned earlier, Gottlieb Hanisch became Roseville's first volunteer fire chief in 1907 when he organized 19 other local men, including his son Walter, to establish the force. For many years later on, Walter would be volunteer fire chief and his son, David, was an ardent firefighter who became assistant fire chief.

In the early years of fire fighting, the volunteer crew used a horse-drawn water carriage and the bucket brigades — volunteer firemen throwing buckets of

*Vernon Street looking westward in 1925. Right foreground is "Fiddyment Block," the current site of Roseville Telephone's administration offices.*

Courtesy of Leonard M. Davis Historical Collection

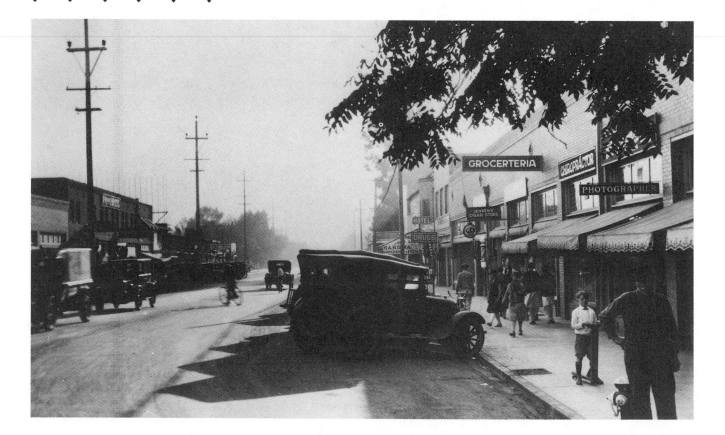

water on the fire. Then there were hose carts, pulled by men and paid for by public subscription among local citizens.

"The first fire alarm was a triangular steel tube, similar to lumber camp dinner gongs," explained Walter Hanisch in a *Roseville Press-Tribune* article in 1954. "Then we used church bells and then the Southern Pacific fire whistle. The first automobile used by the fire department was a Studebaker chemical truck bought in 1917. The first pumper was bought in 1922 and the second in 1924."

When there was a fire in Roseville, the first people to be called were the operators at the telephone company. They would immediately sound the alarm to alert the community that there was a fire. Volunteer firemen would call the operators to learn where the fire was and the operators would also call them.

In the years before police car radios, the telephone company operated a "light and bell" police call system. When alerted to an incident requiring police action, the operators would send the signal to activate a flashing light. When a patrolman saw the light flashing, he'd call the police station.

Roseville Telephone's operators were the first people to know about major fires or crimes occurring in Roseville and it stayed that way until the dial system was installed in 1953.

## 1925: A PIVOTAL YEAR FOR THE COMPANY

In the mid-decade, prospects couldn't be brighter. Revenue and income at the company again reached new highs in 1925. Operating income hit $7,736 on revenue of $27,637. Adding interest received, gross income bettered $8,000 for the first time. After paying dividends totalling $4,215 and investing $8,304 in more capacity to the switchboard, buying new telephones and more wire and cable, the company was still able to contribute $3,149 to its surplus account, which stood at $9,292 at the end of 1925.

It was the best of all worlds, it seemed, since the company's owners enjoyed growing revenue, higher profit, fat dividends with still enough left over to invest in new plant and equipment while adding to the cash surplus. And all this was accomplished without borrowing a penny — what a business!

The optimistic owners decided to invest more in the business. Led by W.J. Doyle, who invested another $4,880 to pick up 488 shares, seven of the remaining 10 shareholders added to their stakes in 1925. Only the G.M. Hanisch Estate, which hadn't purchased any new shares since the founding president's death in 1917, and small holder Marrion Lewis passed up the opportunity to increase their holdings.

One stockholder sold stock. F.A. (Frank) Lewis, a founder of the company, director and vice-president since Gottlieb Hanisch's death in 1917, sold 90

*Advertisement in the 1925 telephone directory.*

*F.A. Lewis Drugstore on Vernon Street was Roseville's first drug store, established in 1906. Lewis was a founder and long-time director of Roseville Telephone.*

Courtesy of Leonard M. Davis Historical Collection

shares, dropping his stake from 237 shares to 147. It's likely Lewis liquidated shares to raise cash to move his drug store business from the Sawtell Building, then adding a second story, back to a bigger building on Lincoln Street where he had first operated after moving from Rocklin in 1906. Or perhaps it was the new shaving cream, called "Kremeze," that Lewis had concocted in 1916 with his brother Fred that had finally drained their financial resources.

The total investment in the company reached $50,000 in 1925. Doyle, who had turned 50 in 1925, had invested $26,450 in the enterprise. The second largest shareholder was H.M. Trevey with 569 shares (11.3 percent) followed by C.A. Baker with 474 shares (9.5 percent). The manager, Walter Hanisch, was next with 364 shares, or 7.3 percent.

Other vital signs of the company were healthy, too. With the switchboard now expanded to four positions, Roseville Telephone Company had in service 340 circuits providing service for 1,081 telephones. It was the first year the customer base had exceeded 1,000.

The employee total remained flat at 12, with only two men, manager Walter Hanisch and an all-purpose construction/maintenance/installation man. There was one woman clerk in the business office and nine operators. One of the those operators was a 20-year-old Roseville native, Gladys Wortell, who in January 1925 began what was to become a 45-year career with the Roseville

Telephone Company. Her married names were Gladys Ellis and, after becoming widowed and remarrying, Gladys Ross. She remains the company's oldest retiree and is still a Roseville resident.

## AFTER THE POP, THE FIZZLE

Revenue climbed past $30,000 for the first time in 1926 as Roseville and the rest of the nation enjoyed the Roaring '20s. Times were good throughout the country, and when the economy was buoyant, almost by definition it meant good times for the railroads, too. Growing commerce and trade resulted in expanded shipping. With the railroad business healthy, it's no surprise Roseville was healthy, including its small, but growing local telephone company.

The company got a boost in 1926 when the 35 farmer-line subscribers in the rural Antelope district west of Roseville petitioned the Railroad Commission that they be served by Roseville Telephone rather than the tiny exchange operated there by Pacific Telephone. The Antelope area telephone subscribers wanted to hook into Roseville even though their rates would rise to $4.20 for residences and $8.40 for businesses from $3 and $6, respectively. The commission's decision approving the change noted that "Roseville service will better meet these subscribers' needs primarily on account of the longer hours of service."

*Southeast corner of Vernon and Atlantic streets in 1925, catercorner from Roseville Telephone's present-day administration building.*

Courtesy of Leonard M. Davis Historical Collection

In the same order, Roseville picked up small portions of Fairoaks (Fair Oaks) and Folsom which Pacific Telephone agreed to abandon. The Rio Linda territory, which had been part of the Antelope exchange, stayed with Pacific.

In 1926, Roseville Telephone continued its recent pattern of investing in itself. That year more than $9,000 was put into expanding the switchboard's capacity with more lines capable of serving more customers. By the end of the year the company reported it was serving 1,250 telephones and had 400 lines available on its four-position switchboard. Still, the total employee count remained at 12, nine of them operators.

Total revenue for the year rose to $31,185, up $3,548 from 1925, nearly a 13 percent increase. Operating income set another record, $8,691, and the surplus grew to $12,799. The company's directors were obviously satisfied with the improved financial results over the past few years and with Walter Hanisch's management of the company. The board was so pleased in 1926 that it raised Hanisch's pay to more than $60 a week for the first time. The other employees received raises as well. Two of the operators were paid in the range of $15 to $17.99 per week and the other seven earned in the $18 to $23.99 range. The chief operator made $24 to $35.99 and the sole male construction/maintenance worker earned in the range of $36 to $59.99 per week, probably toward the lower end. In 1926, operator wages totaled $7,546 for nine full-time operators.

By 1927, the first signs of economic slowing appeared. Although revenue increased to $32,625, this was up less than 5 percent from the previous year. Tight expense control — which would become a hallmark of Walter Hanisch's management style — enabled the company to again earn a record operating profit of $9,032. After several years of significant investment in new plant and equipment, Hanisch and the Board of Directors slashed spending in 1927 with

*Lincoln Street railroad crossing looking toward Vernon Street in February 1928. Roseville Telephone office was second building from the left after tracks. Present-day telephone facilities cover both sides of Lincoln Street up to Vernon Street on far side of railroad tracks.*

Courtesy of Leonard M. Davis Historical Collection

only $1,466 used to fund improvements to the switchboard and to buy more telephones. By the end of 1927, total telephones served by Roseville Telephone inched up to 1,279 from 1,250 a year earlier.

Although business was slowing, 1927 was the final year until the 1950s that the company would raise capital from investors. In 1927, 1,250 new shares were sold at $10 apiece. Doyle re-affirmed his faith in the company as he bought another $7,180 worth of stock to bring his holdings to 3,363 shares, or 53.8 percent of the 6,250 outstanding at the end of 1927. Walter Hanisch and H.M. Trevey bought 142 shares apiece while Baker augmented his position by 120 shares. Chris Etzel and his son, Roy, added to their holdings by acquiring 72 and 48 shares, respectively.

Revenue rose by less than $700 in 1928 compared to 1927 to a total of $33,322 and operating income dropped by more than $1,000, to $7,922. Telephones reported served by the company climbed by only six, to 1,285, in 1928. Capital investments amounted to only $950 as the board and manager Hanisch obviously were taking a "look-see" attitude about business conditions. Surprisingly, however, the company had 13 employees at year-end, with 10 operators vs. nine the year before. After several years of keeping the operator ranks at nine while telephone call volume rose, it's clear the frugal Hanisch had to give in and hire another operator in 1928.

Historically, 1929 is the year that America's excesses after World War I came due. The stock market crash in October 1929 was the cataclysmic event that historians say propelled America into the deepest economic decline it had ever seen, the Great Depression of the 1930s. Roseville Telephone had an early warning about the impending decline in 1928 when call volume and growth began moderating compared to the mid-decade period. Nonetheless, in 1929, the company's revenue rose to $34,342, up barely more than $1,000 from the previous year. Expenses, though, rose appreciably from the previous year and the operating income dropped to $7,078. However, the company did invest more than $5,000 in new plant and equipment in 1929, adding 100 more lines of capacity to the switchboard. For the first time, 15 years after its organization, total assets of the Roseville Telephone Company exceeded $100,000, ending the year at $101,009.10.

*Automatic Electric desk phone type 3 with dial (1925).*

Now there were 500 lines available in the switchboard's four positions although the company reported no gain in telephones in 1929. It still served 1,285 telephones, same as the previous year. Thanks to the increasing cash provided for capital investment by the depreciation reserve, the company was still able to fatten its surplus account in 1929, adding $931 to reach a total of $18,999.

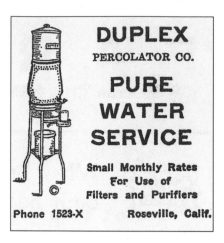

*Advertisement in the 1925
telephone directory.*

The railroad business in Roseville was healthy in 1929 as the Southern Pacific reported in a newspaper article that as of April 1929 there were 1,225 employees at its local railroad and Pacific Fruit Express operations. It reported its monthly payroll at $186,000 in 1929. That averages out to about $150 per month per employee, excellent pay for the time.

Although the 1920s were generally a positive period for Roseville Telephone, the company had received a taste of the dire conditions that were just around the corner.

# Depression Of 1930s Slows Growth To A Crawl

## COMPANY GIVES UP GROUND IN EARLY 1930s

*Expenditures for new plant and equipment amounted to only $795 in 1931, $344 in 1932 and $433 in 1933. In 1934 and 1935, the company did not spend any money on capital improvements and in 1936, it spent $47.*

The 1930s hardened and in many ways defined the personality of Roseville Telephone Company for years thereafter. As the decade began, Roseville Telephone was a relatively prosperous, growing company that gave its territory adequate service. Its direct service area consisted primarily of Roseville proper — the remainder of the company's 83-square mile territory was served by individual farmer lines which tied into Roseville Telephone's lines at the city limits.

Since its founding in 1914, the company had invested in plant and equipment to keep abreast of demand. But as the '30s set in, the attitude of the company's management and directors changed. These owners were born in the 1800s and had been through boom times and bust times. But they had experienced nothing like the Great Depression. It made these conservative men even more conservative. It seems their primary objective during this period, and for the remainder of their years, was to spend as little as possible on capital investments while ensuring that the fat 10 percent dividend was paid each year. The company's directors and owners succeeded in this strategy, but in the process alienated many customers and earned a reputation for niggardliness that would remain for many decades thereafter.

*Vernon Street in the mid-1930s looking eastward. The two-story building (left center) is the J.E. Beckwith residence. The H.T. Miller store is visible in the right center.*
Courtesy of Leonard M. Davis Historical Collection

Deteriorating economic conditions nationwide in 1930-31 were reflected in Roseville. Unemployment skyrocketed as the economic decline hit the railroads. As a "railroad town," Roseville suffered. It's logical to assume that in a declining economic period, the relative luxury of having telephone service could easily be done without. And those who needed telephone service as part of their jobs — for example the Southern Pacific's engineers and conductors — didn't need it if they were out of work. And that was the predicament in Roseville for most of the 1930s.

Even so, 1930 wasn't a bad year for the company. Revenue again rose, to $34,568, and operating income reversed its two-year slide, exceeding $8,000 once again. Bank interest of $830 helped matters, as did scaling back to nine operators from 10. The company spent more than $8,000 on fixed plant, the bulk of that being wire and cable totaling more than $7,000. By the end of the year wire mileage totaled 685 miles, more than triple that of five years earlier. Pole mileage had risen to 26 miles from 10, and the company now had six miles of cable which enclosed 600 miles of wire within its sheathing. Wires strung aerially came to 85 miles. The telephones served rose to 1,300, an increase of 25, or less than 2 percent, in the last two years!

But the financial performance of 1930 was not to be equalled again until 1937. In the years between, Roseville Telephone lost customers and saw revenue decline, hitting a low point in 1933. The same debacle was occurring at Bell companies. In 1931, the total telephones in operation at Bell companies declined by 292,000, the first time in its history there had been a decline. In 1932, the dropoff was more than 10 percent as Bell companies lost 1,650,000 telephones in service. At Western Electric, the manufacturing arm of AT&T, sales of equipment fell to $70 million in 1933 compared to $411 million in 1929 when Bell companies stopped ordering telephone equipment as the Depression took hold. More than 80 percent of Western Electric's workers were laid off in 1933.

Joining the trend of telephone companies everywhere, Roseville Telephone virtually halted all new investments during the early '30s. After plunking down more than $8,000 in 1930, expenditures for new plant and equipment amounted to only $795 in 1931, $344 in 1932 and $433 in 1933. In 1934 and 1935, the company did not spend *any* money to improve or enlarge its fixed plant and equipment. In 1936, the total capital investment was only $47.20. One can imagine what a debilitating period this must have been. It wasn't until 1937, after three years of rising revenue, that the company once again made any significant capital investment, spending $5,467.72, most of it to improve its switching equipment.

Gladys Ross, whose maiden name was Wortell, an operator from 1925, remembered those years. "It was a bad time, the Depression. We didn't go hungry, but people were poor, and I remember people were lined up at the bakery every morning trying to get in there to get one roll. And there was one lady that every morning used to bring sandwiches downtown and give them to the poor. So it was really a hard time. Everything was down ... well, of course, in those days nobody had too much of anything."

The company's financial performance tracked the decline in the national economy. In 1931, revenue dropped for the first time in the history of Roseville Telephone. Revenue was $34,111, down about $450 from the previous year. Operating income was $7,671 and with bank interest income of $820, gross income exceeded $8,000 again. By the end of the year, however, the company was serving 1,253 telephones, 47 fewer than a year earlier. The employee rolls stayed at 12, including nine operators. Despite the stagnating business climate, the company was able to add $973 to its surplus account, which now totaled $22,576.

In 1932, the Depression took hold nationwide and in Roseville. The telephone company's revenue dropped sharply to $30,392, a decline of 11 percent. The number of telephones served fell off by 148 to 1,105. Operating income dropped by more than $2,000 to $5,407 and the number of employees dropped back to 10. Two operators were laid off, leaving only seven. Nonetheless, the company was able to increase its surplus account by $10.30 for the year, even after paying its normal 10 percent cash dividend, amounting to $6,250 to its 11 shareholders. It certainly helped the company's cash flow that it spent only a few hundred dollars on capital improvements in that year.

School bell from Roseville's first school was used for many years as a signal at the Lincoln Street railroad crossing. It was also used as a fire bell.
Courtesy of Leonard M. Davis Historical Collection

Many historians and economists say 1933 was the low point of the Depression and that was true for Roseville Telephone. Revenue fell another $3,000, or 10 percent, to $27,356, less than the company collected in 1925. Careful management, however, enabled the company to minimize its profit deterioration, which ended up only $160 lower than the previous year. For the first time in many years, however, the surplus account declined, but by only $275. Company manager Walter Hanisch pared expenses by nearly $4,000 compared to 1932. Included in the cutbacks was Hanisch's own compensation, which was again reduced to less than $60 per week. There remained 10 employees. Telephones served increased by 29 telephones to 1,134.

The Depression almost claimed the largest independent telephone company in the nation, the giant Associated Telephone Utilities Co. It was a victim of stock manipulation by its executives in addition to the hard economic times that dramatically reduced demand for telephone service. The company operated in receivership from 1933 until 1935, when it emerged with a different name — General Telephone Corporation. Now known as GTE, it rebounded from its depths and went on to stay the biggest independent telephone company in the land.

Revenue at Roseville Telephone inched up in 1934 to $27,992, a gain of a little more than $600. Telephones in service rose to 1,180, an improvement of 46 from 1933. Again, Hanisch's fiscal knife was in evidence as expenses dropped a little less than $100 in 1934. The total employee count at the end of 1934 fell to nine, eight women and Hanisch. There remained seven operators and a woman clerk in the business office. Since the company had allocated zero budget for new plant and equipment in 1934, there was little need for a construction/ maintenance employee. The all-purpose Hanisch did it himself if the need arose. The result of this tight expense control was an improved operating profit, which again exceeded $7,000. And after paying the annual $6,250 in dividends, the company contributed to its surplus account, if by only $373. The worst was over and the dividends were paid on schedule throughout. Similarly, AT&T maintained its $9 annual dividend per share through the Depression despite the fact that earnings in a few of those years were barely half that.

Continued recovery, albeit slight, enabled Roseville Telephone to again increase revenue, closing 1935 at $28,934. While still well below the peak year of 1930, at least the revenue slide had been stanched and business appeared to be solidly on the upswing again. Operating income rose to $7,574 and the bank interest of $763 pushed gross income over $8,000 again. After paying the customary 10 percent dividend, the surplus account grew by $993.

*Chris Etzel, right, with son, Horace, in mid-'30s.*
Courtesy of Marguerite Smart

The ownership of Roseville Telephone changed in 1935, the first such change since 1927. The death of the company's second-largest shareholder and director, H.M. Trevey, precipitated the change. His 711 shares of stock were acquired by existing shareholders. Doyle picked up another 435 shares. This purchase brought his investment in the company to $37,980 with his 3,798 shares accounting for more than 60 percent ownership of Roseville Telephone. Walter Hanisch bought 119 of Trevey's shares, increasing his ownership to 625 shares, or 10 percent of the company. Charles Baker replaced Trevey as the second-largest shareholder by acquiring 77 of Trevey's shares, giving Baker 671 shares. The Etzels, father Chris and son Roy, bought 47 and 33 shares, respectively, to bring their totals to 409 and 275 shares. Together, the Etzels now had a slightly bigger stock ownership position than Baker. It was at this time that Chris Etzel joined the board, joining his son Roy, Baker, Lewis and Doyle. Roy Etzel had succeeded his mother Lena on the board in 1930 upon her death. This board would remain intact until 1949.

Conditions at the company in the mid-1930s were depressing, to say the least. Not only had the luster of the '20s worn off, but the lack of investment in the company was not lost on the all-purpose operators. Since the beginning, they were the mainstay of the company and did virtually everything, including sweeping floors, washing windows and keeping the place habitable in winter. In those days, the company's tiny office was heated by a coal-fired, pot belly stove.

"In the back room behind the switchboard, there was a small room where the Board of Directors used to meet," recalled Gladys Ross. "There was a bathroom right next to it. I used to go out there in the back at night when I was alone and shovel coal for the stove. I figured about two scuttles of coal would last all night. Then it didn't get so cold. It could be freezing in that building and I'm surprised the office never burned down because that stove was dangerous."

Although there would be an operator on duty 24 hours a day, in the wee hours of the morning there weren't many calls. To ensure that nothing was amiss, the operator on duty was supposed to call the AT&T operator in Marysville at regular intervals. If a call was missed, the Marysville operator would call the Roseville switchboard to make sure no foul play had occurred involving the operator. It would have been easy to nod off in those days.

## 1936 — RECOVERY IS UNDER WAY

Roseville Telephone's recovery accelerated in 1936 as revenue grew to $32,130, an increase of about $3,200 over 1935 and nearly $5,000 better than 1933. Operating income climbed back to more than $8,500. Interest income put it over $9,000. The surplus account grew by $1,860, its biggest jump since 1930. It now exceeded $25,000 for the first time. Telephones in use rose to 1,200, which included approximately 1,000 company-owned telephone stations and 200 owned by farmer-line families and businesses. The year was so good that another operator was hired and the total employee count returned to 10, including Hanisch and nine women, eight of them operators. Hanisch's salary went back above $60 a week.

By 1937, conditions were improving so much that the board authorized $5,468 for fixed plant improvements, including nearly $4,700 to improve the central office equipment. Revenue hit a record high of $34,937, slightly above 1930. Gross income again exceeded $9,000 and another operator was hired, bringing the employee count to 11 again, including nine operators. Hanisch earned $3,640 in "calary" (sic), according to the report filed with the Railroad

*Robert L. Doyle's 1938 graduation photo from Roseville High School. Fifteen years later, he would join the Roseville Telephone Company.*
Courtesy of Robert L. Doyle

*In 1938, baseball was Bob Doyle's (bottom right) favorite activity. This was his Newcastle Bears team in the Sierra Foothill League. Players clockwise from the top left are John Buechner, Ernie Fiene, Ralph Andrade, Jim Davidson, Richard McManus, Marrion Benedetti, Bob Doyle, Jerry Stennick, Tony Schuper, Frank Mohney, John Piches, and Laurie Davis with Bill Miller in front.*

Courtesy of Robert L. Doyle

Commission. The wire mileage report showed the company had 1,372 wire miles, including 12 miles of cable, 1,267 miles inside the cables and 105 aerial wire miles. Total wire mileage was approximately double that of 1930. Total telephones served jumped another 100 to a reported 1,300 at the end of the year. Also, the surplus account grew to $29,676 at the end of 1937, a sizable increase over the previous year, thanks to a series of accounting adjustments and income tax refunds that added a few thousand dollars to the surplus above the amount contributed from net income.

It was more of the same in 1938 as revenue climbed to more than $36,000. Operating income came under pressure from rising expenses and higher taxes — taxes had started to become a significant expense item by the mid-1930s — and came in under $7,000. Part of the expense increase came from the addition again of a construction/maintenance employee as the total employee count went to 12 again. The 10 female employees, including eight operators and two business clerks, earned in the $18-to-$23.99 range per week. Nearly $2,500 was contributed to surplus in 1938. Total telephones served dropped back to 1,267, a loss of 33 year-to-year.

Investment in new plant and equipment soared in 1938 to $24,156. More than $12,000 was invested in new telephones, presumably to replace older ones since there was actually a decrease in telephones in service during the year. More than $6,000 was also spent on new wire and cable and more than $4,000 was expended for "general" equipment which no doubt included a construction rig.

The year 1938 later was remembered as the year Walter D. (David) Hanisch came to work at the company, learning the business from his father. As a youngster David had been around the company a lot and was already well-versed in the operation when he became an employee. Dave Hanisch was the third generation of his family to be affiliated with Roseville Telephone. In his first year, the younger Hanisch worked eight hours a day, six days a week and earned $16 a week. "That's how I broke in," Dave Hanisch remembered. His tenure was to be the most controversial of any employee ever at the company.

At this point, nearly 25 years into Roseville Telephone's history, the leading figures were W.J. Doyle, the farmer who owned the majority of the stock; Walter Hanisch, the long-time, tight-fisted manager of the company, and his son David, who later would become assistant manager and, he hoped, the successor to his father as manager. The stage was being set for the eventual clash of the Hanisches and the Doyles over the future course of Roseville Telephone.

In 1939, the final year of a difficult decade, the company's revenue showed a moderate increase to $37,830 and operating income jumped to $8,712. The addition of young Hanisch brought the employee count to 13. The last time Roseville Telephone had 13 employees was 10 years earlier, in 1929. The capital investment that year was $6,846, which included $1,805 in the "land and building" category. The surplus rose slightly to $32,565.

The worst decade in the history of the country was over, and despite a few difficult years, the Roseville Telephone Company had survived and was stronger than ever as it entered the 1940s. Roseville's population remained flat in the 1930s, growing from 6,425 to only 6,653 in 10 years. It would be the last decade of economic stagnation in Roseville Telephone's territory. Beginning in 1940, the company and its service region would enjoy nearly unstoppable growth and prosperity.

## ROSEVILLE TELEPHONE: THE FIRST LINE OF DEFENSE

Although Bill Doyle was always a farmer and had no operational role in the day-to-day affairs of his telephone company, other than to co-sign checks, it's clear he valued his investment in the local utility. This was particularly true during the Depression.

"I remember the old man used to call the telephone company and his vineyards his first line of defense," Bob Doyle recalled. "During the Depression, the fact that he was a big farmer hurt my dad more than it helped him. When the Depression came, the more you owned, the worse off you were. The Bank of Italy, now the Bank of America, was taking farms over like they were going out of style because people couldn't make their payments. The Bank of Italy owned one hell of a lot of the farms around here.

"My dad also had a bunch of sheep and turkeys in addition to his grapes and livestock," Bob Doyle said. "He gave the sheep to my Uncle Will (Kaseberg) just to get rid of them. My dad had 4,000-5,000 head, and in those days that was quite a few sheep. He had these Basque sheepherders, and hell, he'd have to take them up in the mountains in the summertime and find pasture for the sheep, plus he had to worry about moving those guys, their cook houses and all their stuff. It was just too much."

Gladys Ross remembered the elder Doyle commenting on the telephone company's importance to him while working the farm and raising five children. "I remember Mr. Doyle, Bob's father, saying, 'If it hadn't been for the telephone company, we would have starved during the Depression.' So they (the Doyles) were relying on what they were getting in dividends."

Myron McIntyre, whose family moved to the Roseville area in the 1930s and became large turkey farmers, remembered Hazel Doyle as a strong, outspoken woman who didn't necessarily agree with her husband's heavy investment in the telephone company.

"She'd buy everything we had left because the Doyles were harvesting and picking grapes. She said there were always people working for them, and she didn't have enough food," McIntyre said. "And I remember one time she complained about her husband's interest in the telephone company. She said, 'That man made me so mad, he'd come home and tell me he'd spent all the money I'd made on the turkeys buying telephone stock.' I said, 'How much was it?' and she said, 'it was $10 a share.'"

Setting Mrs. Doyle's opinion aside, it's clear Bill Doyle's ownership in Roseville Telephone helped the family get through the 1930s. And like his own father, "Lucky Jack" Doyle, Bill Doyle showed the courage to invest when others were more cautious. During the 1930s, Doyle spent $4,350 to strengthen his ownership control in the company. This would seem to be a reasonable strategy since he collected dividends aggregating nearly $36,000 during the decade.

The dividends were equally important to the 10 other shareholders, too, because it would be apparent in later years that the consistency with which they received their dividends lulled them into complacency. Roseville Telephone's owners seemed to forget that the primary purpose of the telephone utility was to provide service to customers, not to simply earn big enough profits to pay its owners generous dividends.

# World War II Propels Roseville Telephone

## AMID THE BOOM, CLOUDS GATHER

*The war meant greatly increased toll traffic as Roseville subscribers called loved ones in other parts of the state and nation to check on their sons, brothers and husbands in the armed forces.*

The opening year of the new decade was a replay of the previous one — another year of modest growth for Roseville Telephone. Operating income surpassed $8,000 on record revenue of $39,112. The investment in new plant and equipment was $6,250 and the surplus account grew to $33,557. Times were good enough that Walter Hanisch hired another operator. There were now 14 employees, including nine operators, the highest total ever. The company also invested in another telephone company, the giant American Telephone & Telegraph Co., paying $921.30 for seven shares. The stock not only earned annual dividends, but gave access to AT&T's annual report so Roseville could follow what the Bell colossus was doing in the industry.

By 1941, the war in Europe was raging and the militaristic Japanese were overrunning their neighbors in Asia. It's likely that most Americans, including the aging Board of Directors and owners of Roseville Telephone, could sense that an incident of some kind would eventually drag the United States into the conflict. The country was on a war footing and there was a renewed vibrancy in manufacturing and transportation. Business conditions strengthened in anticipation of the need for supplies to fight a war involving the United States.

Roseville Telephone began preparing for increased call traffic that would probably occur if war broke out. Also, Hanisch and the Board of Directors knew that telephone equipment would become hard to get during war-time since military needs would come first. Domestic telephone companies would scramble to receive what was left over. So in 1941, the company invested more than $12,000 in new plant and equipment, including more than $4,000 in new telephones. The company also added 60 new lines to its switchboard capacity, which then contained 560 lines in its four positions, serving a total of 1,307 phones, including 178 farmer lines.

Total revenue jumped nearly $5,000 in 1941 to $43,992, and for the first time operating income surpassed $10,000, reaching $11,084. The employee count remained at 14 and the surplus account climbed to a healthy $37,726.

*In 1938, construction was under way to build the Sacramento Army Air Depot which later was renamed McClellan Field and in 1948 McClellan Air Force Base.*

Courtesy of McClellan Air Force Base History Office

If 1941 was a good year, 1942 was a great year for the 28-year-old Roseville Telephone Company. The United States entry into the war meant greatly increased toll traffic as Roseville subscribers called loved ones in other parts of the state and nation to check on their sons, brothers and husbands in the armed forces.

The company benefited greatly from the rapid buildup of McClellan Field, a huge Army Air Corps base that opened in 1939. Its location just west of the company's service territory meant that many of McClellan's civilian employees lived in the Roseville Telephone service territory. McClellan, which in 1948 became an Air Force base when the U.S. Air Force was officially founded, employed more than 17,000 service and civilian personnel at the height of the war and was a huge economic boon to the Sacramento region. Also, the Army Signal Corps depot at nearby Camp Kohler on the south side of Roseville Road brought nearly 5,000 servicemen to the area for training. It later became incorporated into McClellan AFB and served as the laundry center for the base.

Buoyed by the big jump in toll calls, the company's revenue soared to $52,314 in 1942. Although expenses were held under control — just under $30,000 — taxes totaling $12,714 kept operating income below the previous year, coming in just over $10,000. Interestingly, the company's tax burden more than doubled from 1941 to 1942, jumping more than $7,000 in a year. And in true patriotic fashion, Roseville Telephone invested $13,981 to buy U.S. war bonds in 1942. Now the company's two investments included AT&T and the U.S. government, just about the two biggest entities around in 1942.

The company's fixed plant investment policy remained fairly steady in 1942 with $5,795 going for new telephones, improving the switchboard, adding poles, wires and furniture. The surplus account finished the year at just over $40,000. The military called the company's two eligible male employees, leaving only Walter Hanisch, who was now 59 years old. The company got by with 13 employees, but increased traffic forced the hiring of a tenth operator.

In 1943, business continued to be excellent for Roseville Telephone. Revenue expanded to $56,623 and a lighter tax burden enabled the company to reach an operating profit of $12,571. Both were all-time highs. The company now served 1,500 telephones, including 190 on farmer lines. Revenue from toll calls in 1943 climbed $2,777, or over 20 percent, to more than $16,000. Clearly, more men were involved in the war now with huge conflicts waging around the globe.

The employee count finished the year at 14 with only nine operators, but in June of 1943 there were 17 employees, 11 of them operators. The general pay scales had increased, too, with the operators now earning in the range of $24 to $35.99 per week for some and $36 to $59.95 for the more experienced operators. Walter Hanisch's compensation increased as well. In 1943, he earned almost $75 a week.

The Board of Directors also decided that if giving raises to employees made sense, then maybe it was time to raise their own pay, too. And they did by increasing the annual dividend to $1.15 per share, up from $1. It was the first dividend increase since 1920. The company also increased its investment in U.S. war bonds by another $3,000, bringing the company's stake to nearly $17,000.

## AGING DIRECTORS GROW EVEN MORE CONSERVATIVE

Surprisingly, perhaps, the company's investment in plant and equipment remained modest in 1943. Only slightly more than $3,000 was put into new fixed plant. Part of the reason, of course, was the difficulty in getting equipment during the war, but it's likely the other reason had to do with the risk-averse Board of Directors. In 1943, W.J. Doyle was 68 years old. Hanisch had turned 60. Charles Baker and Chris Etzel were in their late 70s. Only Roy Etzel was under 60. This group was growing more conservative with age. Having survived the Great Depression, they were not about to become foolhardy by throwing lots of money into new plant and equipment. This board was clearly more interested in generating current income than investing for the future. Their stance was most likely guided by Hanisch, who may have been the most conservative of the bunch. He not only desired to keep investment to a minimum, but at his age the company was becoming unwieldy for him to manage. It was his desire to keep Roseville Telephone small, and in many respects he ran the company with an iron hand without interference from the directors. In Hanisch's mind, he answered to no one.

Hanisch was able to nurture his no-growth attitude partially because W.J. Doyle, although he owned 60 percent of the shares, had little interest in company operations. It was not uncommon for the elder Doyle to skip the monthly board meetings.

"Ever since I was a little kid, I always knew Walter because he'd come over and see my dad," Tom Doyle recalled. "They'd talk about things, but none of us knew anything about the company. My dad almost never went down there. He never even knew when the meetings were. They would call up and tell him there was a meeting tonight and he'd say, 'Do you need me?'"

In truth, the elder Doyle really didn't know anything about the telephone business, according to sons Bob and Tom. He knew only what Walter Hanisch reported at the board meetings. Those times Doyle would come into town to sign checks, he did it quickly so he could get to a card game, one of his favorite pastimes. His favorite games included pitch and hearts. Usually, Hanisch brought the checks out to the senior Doyle on the farm. Although they had a business relationship for more than 40 years, Walter Hanisch and Bill Doyle were not close personal friends. Hanisch was even more old-fashioned than the average 60-year-old and Doyle was strictly business when it came to the telephone company.

Bob Doyle remembered when Walter Hanisch would come out to the farm.

"Walter would come out in his little old pickup with the ladder on the driver's side. To get out, he'd have to crawl out the other side of the truck," Doyle said. "And it didn't matter if he came over for only a few minutes to get my dad to sign checks, he would lock that pickup even though there wasn't a thing in it. He didn't trust anybody."

In 1943, the Board of Directors had no reason to be unhappy. Business was flourishing, the surplus account — which the directors considered their protection against another major economic collapse — amounted to more than $45,000, and their dividend was increased. Why rock the boat? Let the company be a cash cow and the future be damned.

The next year was even better than 1943, by a whole lot, too. Toll revenue soared 55 percent to more than $25,000. This propelled total revenue to $68,132, nearly $12,000 higher than in 1943. Operating income, however,

*Vernon Street near Lincoln in the 1940s. Bank of America building is present-day site of Roseville Telephone's administration building.*
Courtesy of Leonard M. Davis Historical Collection

declined to just under $11,000 as taxes leaped to $18,311, up from $11,115 the previous year. The surplus reached $50,551.

The employee count rose to 15, including 11 operators who were working hard to keep up with the calls. The company spent $4,500 on new plant and equipment, but didn't make any significant expansion in its capacity to serve its territory. Residents who were moving into Citrus Heights, Antelope, Orangevale and certain parts of Roseville were denied telephone service because the company had not built the infrastructure to serve them. These unfilled orders for service — called held orders — were growing and would eventually become so severe a problem that the company could have been forced to sell.

Rather than spend money on expanding its fixed plant, the Board of Directors opted to authorize another dividend increase in 1944, to $1.20 per share. At that point, Doyle's dividends alone exceeded $4,500 annually. This life-long farmer had indeed found fertile ground. The board continued its patriotic duty, investing another $5,000 in war bonds during 1944.

The war years were also excellent for W.J. Doyle's grape operations, according to Bob Doyle. "With the limited supply of grapes because of the war, my father's grapes made nothing but money back then," Doyle recollected. "Where he was getting about $25 a ton in the pre-war years, he was getting over $100 a ton during the war. He did real well."

The final year of the war, 1945, was another record-breaker for Roseville Telephone. Toll revenue jumped more than $9,500 to nearly $35,000 in 1945, pushing total revenue to $79,924. Although taxes climbed to $22,117 and the company employed 18 workers in 1945, including 13 operators, Hanisch kept other expenses in check.

A total of 1,756 telephones were being served, including 200 farmer-line phones. Operating income hit $16,436, a good enough performance for the board to authorize an increase in its dividend for the third consecutive year, this time to $1.25 a share. For the first time, total assets of the company surpassed $150,000. And the company bought another $3,000 in war bonds.

Certainly the end of the war saw Roseville Telephone a prosperous utility that served its owners and management very well. Unfortunately, however, the company was gaining a reputation as a telephone company that didn't care about serving its territory, an indifferent monopoly that was increasingly becoming out of step with the growth trends of the region and nation. The seeds of discontent were being planted.

*Southern Pacific railroad yards and Vernon Street in 1942. Bill Doyle's ranch and vineyards are on the top left and middle.*
*Today, Interstate 80 goes through the middle of the old ranch and Roseville Square shopping center is situated on the old ranch land.*

Courtesy of Leonard M. Davis Historical Collection

# 1946-1951: Post-War Growth Strains Company

RETURNING WARRIORS WANT HOMES WITH PHONES

*As time marched forward, Roseville and its neighboring communities kept attracting new residents. But at the telephone company, time stood still.*

The post World War II period was a buoyant one. The victorious troops came home flush with optimism and intent on creating a better life for themselves and their loved ones. Many were afraid, but plunged ahead anyway by borrowing what seemed like vast sums of money to buy their first new home. After all, most of them had just faced death in the battlefield. They could certainly handle the risk of a loan. Among the amenities these returning vets wanted in their home was a telephone … a modern telephone.

It was during the post-war period that Roseville Telephone's "corporate culture" began to come into serious conflict with the realities of the growth occurring in greater Sacramento, including the company's 83-square-mile territory. Although Walter Hanisch and the Board of Directors would have preferred to maintain the slow growth pace of the past, increasing requests for new telephone service forced the company to step up its investment in new fixed plant and telephones to at least give the appearance of trying to satisfy the requests.

The central problem remained Hanisch's reluctance to extend service beyond the immediate confines of the city of Roseville. Although the service territory included most of Citrus Heights, portions of Orangevale, Fair Oaks and Antelope, for the 31-plus years of its existence, the company purposely kept its service limited to within only a few miles of its downtown Lincoln Street location. The rest of the territory was served by "farmer lines" that fanned out through the service area of Roseville Telephone. These farmer lines tied into Roseville's Telephone's "base area" at or near the city limits in

*Automatic Electric rotary dial business telephone (1947)*

order to be able to reach Roseville and the rest of the world via Roseville Telephone's tie-in with Pacific Telephone's cables.

"The company had those 83 square miles but instead of serving the whole area, they just served what was easy and the balance was served by farmer lines," Bob Doyle said. "These were people, usually farmers, who started their own line up. They put up their own poles, strung their own lines, and maintained them themselves. They put lines on trees, and everything else that didn't move, they hooked on to it. They paid Roseville Telephone a dollar a month for service, but they owned their own outside plant, as bad as it was."

Myron McIntyre remembered the farmer lines: "We put the wires on trees, on fence posts. On our second ranch, my brother and his neighbors built everything from what is now about the Target Store on Douglas Boulevard all the way to where Folsom Lake is. They rented the poles from PG&E, put crossarms up, did the whole thing. We owned our own telephones. We paid a switchboard fee, about a dollar a month at the time. The Johnson Ranch farmer line came right into the same place. Nobody owned a whole line, there was no such thing. I think there were about 70 homes we hooked up and I think there were 10 lines with seven on a line, or something like that. It was pretty loaded."

In fact, most farmer lines had 12-to-14 parties on them, even up to 16 parties on some farmer-line systems during the 1940s and 1950s. The only way households could tell whether a call was for them was by the distinctive ringing code of "longs and shorts." Each household on the line was assigned a certain combination of long and short rings and you only answered when it was yours. But if someone were on the telephone too long, one of the parties could get on and not so politely say, "Get the hell off. I want to make a call."

Post-war Roseville was a lively, if relatively backward place. "Of course it was still completely a railroad town," recalled Bob Doyle. "The engineers and conductors and such needed telephone service because their job depended on it, a lot of them. Back then, of course, they still had call boys to notify the railroad workers who didn't have a telephone when they were needed. A call boy would go out to worker's house riding a bike or whatever, and call them to let them know they'd been called out for such and such a time. But the SP frowned on that and would rather that their employees have a telephone. The conductors and such worked on rotation so if they missed their turn, they'd have to wait until they came up again. So he didn't get paid. It was a dog eat dog thing."

As a railroad town, Roseville had long been known for its night life, saloons and houses of ill repute. That didn't fade until the 1950s when then U.S. 40 (now Interstate 80) prompted new residents to flock into the area. But in a railroad town, that's the way life was.

"The town was going strong when I was born, there's no doubt about that," Bob Doyle said. "All these little towns, especially railroad towns. What happens in a railroad town? The guy who lives in Sparks comes down here and stays overnight and the guy here goes to Sparks and stays overnight. So these guys are out on the town ... they're looking around, let's put it that way. There were many local employees who didn't go on the road, the switchman and workers in the yards … they just stayed here and worked here. But the guys on the road, engineers, switchmen, conductors, brakemen, hell, their train took off and they had regular runs. They'd run down to wherever the hell they were going and then they'd lay over a night before coming back the other way. They got paid extra for room and board, so they'd eat in cheap restaurants and flop houses and save as much as they could.

"The guys that came here, they didn't have anything to do, so they'd go to the bars, hang around and raise hell. It was kind of a 'wild west' sort of town. Houses of prostitution, hell, we had them all over. In Roseville, we probably had at any given time five or six at least. Sacramento used to have a lot of them, too, of course. Life was different then."

For years, the Barker Hotel's pay telephone was a big money maker for Roseville Telephone. "You had to go and empty that booth at least once a week

*Before completion of the Seawell Underpass (1950), travelers and residents going north or south through Roseville were plagued with long delays (such as the one pictured below in the early 1930s) by railroad switching operations at the Lincoln Street crossing.*

Courtesy of Leonard M. Davis Historical Collection

because it would fill up with about $150 in nickels, dimes and quarters. That's a hell of a lot of nickels, dimes and quarters. In those days, a local call was a nickel."

Operators received frequent calls from men wanting taxis. "It was kind of hush hush," remembered Betty Dosher, an operator in the late '40s. "When the railroad men would call a taxi, they wouldn't tell us where they wanted to go. It was kind of an 'unmentioned' location."

Getting around Northern California by auto took a lot of time before 1950, especially if it meant going through Roseville. Bob Doyle remembered this period:

"Before the freeway came, you came in on Auburn Boulevard. It started in Sacramento, came through North Sacramento, followed the railroad tracks down and cut across by Haggin Oaks. Then it continued right on through Citrus Heights, Roseville, Rocklin, Loomis, Penryn, Newcastle and up to Auburn. It was the main drag.

"If you were going to Lincoln, Marysville or any place north, it was a real pain. In those days, the railroad didn't have the underpass. They did all their switching right in the middle of Roseville here. So if you came through and you wanted to go to Lincoln and they're making up a train there, well you sat there until they damned well got ready to let you through. They'd bump those cars and then it'd look like they were going to clear the tracks, and then they'd start back again. Rail cars are sitting there, and in the meantime, the autos are stacked up down here to the corner and around the corner. In those days, there was no air conditioning. You're sitting there just ringing wet with sweat, cussing the town of Roseville. If I would go someplace, they'd say 'Where you from?' and I'd say Roseville. They'd say, 'I know that goddamn town. That's where you have to stop while they make up the train.'

"This was a marshaling yard," Doyle continued. "This is where they made up all the trains before they went over the hump. We had the largest ice plant in the world and iced every train that came through. We re-iced all the refrigerator box cars. They'd pull the ice in and put the rock salt in. We had an ice deck there the length of a train. It makes a lot of noise, right in the middle of Roseville, but nobody paid any attention because everybody worked for the goddamned railroad. That's how you made your living. The only one who paid attention to it was the poor son of a bitch trying to go someplace."

The cars and trucks waited in lines right in front of the telephone company office. It made it hard on operators in the summer. Betty Dosher recalled those days.

"That was the highway that ran in front of the telephone company," she said. "We kept screen doors open for the breeze. I can remember those big old fruit trucks racing their engines and we'd get their fumes. And the noise was terrible, too. It made it hard to hear some of the time. That stopped in 1950 when they put the underpass in."

In Roseville, the operators knew everything going on. Doyle recounted a typical exchange between a caller and an operator. "Since the company was all manual, when a person called in, the operator would pick up the telephone and say, 'Number, please.' The number might be me 338J, for example, or whatever it was. And she'd say, 'Oh, Mr. Doyle isn't in right now. I just saw him walk in the store across the street.' In other words, everybody knew what everybody was doing, you might say. It was a small town and a small company."

As time marched forward, Roseville and its neighboring communities kept attracting new residents. But at the telephone company, time stood still. That's what its owners desired. The company's aversion to serving the areas outside immediate Roseville was simple to understand. It cost a lot of money to put up poles, string cable and wires, and purchase telephones to serve sparsely populated areas. Hanisch and the board didn't have the entrepreneurial drive or energy to mount a major expansion. Better to maintain the status quo and keep collecting hefty dividends.

By the post-war period, however, there was enough growth in the outlying areas that the company had no choice but to step up its investment in fixed plant. Even so, the company remained focused on increasing capacity in the existing area, close-in to Roseville. Ralph Hoeper, a current director of Roseville Telephone and owner of Foresthill Telephone, knew Walter and David Hanisch in the late 1940s. The young Hoeper had just gone to work at Foresthill Telephone.

"The Hanisches were sure that this big boom after the war was going to be short-lived and we were going into another big depression. So they weren't about to go in debt whatsoever," Hoeper said. "By god, according to the way the Hanisches saw it, people already had been waiting 10-15 years for telephone service and they can continue to wait. The Hanisches weren't going to borrow any money and then get caught in a bind. There's no question the Hanisches were trying, and they meant well, but they just were not doing enough to keep up with the demand and that was creating the problem."

Roseville Telephone wasn't alone in believing another depression would mar the 1950s. It was a commonly-held opinion among many of the nation's largest independents that a depression would occur in the early '50s, according to *Spirit of Independent Telephony*, Charles Pleasance's book. Those companies, like Roseville Telephone, were reluctant to increase capacity until they were certain there would be no major downturn. This resulted in increasingly poor service and mounting frustration.

Ron Amick, a retired Pacific Telephone executive who was raised down the street from the Doyles, recalled his impressions of the company in the mid '40s. "It was a little … when it worked … manual switchboard. I remember our first telephone number was 307R. And you had party lines all over the place. The wires were strung up and down the alleys. Oh, God, it was terrible. For years, you had to go through an operator and everybody knew the operators by first name and all that. We actually had our telephone installed quite a long time before the company ever hooked it up. It was in 1942-43 when we first got our telephone, but it didn't start working until about 1944-45. We had neighbors who had telephones that did work. See, it was a railroad town and a telephone was kind of important because the call boy didn't have to come call you, the crew. They could call you on the telephone, and so if you were an engineer or a fireman or something like that, most of them were able to get a telephone. It made it easier for the dispatcher to call you to pick up your train. That's when Roseville was only a railroad town. That was the whole thing that Roseville even existed for."

Roseville Telephone also had its priorities in telephone installations. Anybody involved with police and fire protection was on the top of the list as were engineers, conductors and other employees associated with the railroad. Whether ordinary residents received telephone service was primarily a function of how close they were to the company's pole lines. Other considerations were at times personal, according to employees and telephone users at the time. If you were to get on the bad side of Walter or David Hanisch, it might be a long time before you'd get a telephone. The Hanisches ran Roseville Telephone as their personal preserve, that was clear.

## PRESSURES FOR BETTER SERVICE

If Roseville Telephone had been simply a private business offering less than satisfactory service, no doubt over time competing companies would have come in and provided the service that the telephone company was not giving. But as a monopoly provider of an essential service to residents and businesses in a territory covering 83 square miles, Roseville Telephone was obligated by law to provide adequate service. In 1946, with the state's population mushrooming after World War II, the state renamed the Railroad Commission. It was now called the California Public Utilities Commission (CPUC) with the charge to regulate the state's fast-growing utility companies. Newly-named, the CPUC appeared more focused than ever on its mission and it wasn't long before it began to pressure Roseville Telephone to improve and expand its service.

The CPUC represented the kind of government bureaucracy, or interference if you will, that Walter Hanisch and the staid Board of Directors loathed. In 1946, for example, Roseville Telephone's annual report to the commission changed dramatically. For more than 30 years, the company had submitted its financials, ownership, wire mileage, employee data and other information to the Railroad Commission in a report that was never longer than 18 pages. The first annual report to the CPUC was 84 pages!

Moreover, the first few CPUC annual reports were actually Federal Communications Commission (FCC) annual reports that simply had "Public Utilities Commission of the State of California" pasted over the FCC headings on the cover page. Wherever the FCC was printed on the inside, it would be crossed out and "California Public Utilities Commission" would be stamped in blue ink. One can imagine how livid Walter Hanisch must have been when filling out the first one of these reports. "Damn government," was surely the mildest of his comments.

In the mid-'40s, there was no written evidence that the newly-named CPUC or the old Railroad Commission had formally threatened Roseville Telephone with reprisals if the company didn't begin to serve its existing customers better and increase efforts to serve its entire territory. That formal pressure from the CPUC would come later. But the prospect of possible interference did prompt Hanisch and the Board of Directors to step up capital spending in the late '40s.

Exactly how to grow was a hard decision for Roseville Telephone midway into the 1940s, however. Other telephone companies, both the Bell System and independent companies, were accelerating the replacement of their old systems with modern "dial service" that required an enormous initial investment in new switching equipment and telephones. Roseville Telephone in 1946 was not ready to make this commitment. Instead, it opted to enlarge and improve its existing system.

## HEADY GROWTH, INVESTMENT MARK
## 1946-1949 PERIOD

Business continued strong in the post-war years. Revenue jumped nearly 60 percent from $79,924 in 1945 to $125,567 by 1949. The increase was fueled primarily by a large increase in toll revenue, i.e. for calls going outside the Roseville service area. Toll revenue jumped nearly 90 percent from $34,829 in 1945 to $65,785 in 1949. Local exchange revenue from traffic within the exchange grew only moderately in comparison. Local growth depended on new installations, which in the case of Roseville Telephone remained modest in view of the demand.

In 1946, operating income rose to $21,579, making it by far the most profitable year in the company's 32-year existence. The years 1947-1949 generated relatively flat operating earnings of $21,766, $19,685 and $22,748, respectively. The improved financial performance prompted the board to raise the dividend another nickel to $1.30 per share in 1946. That $1.30 rate continued in 1947-1949.

Total telephones in service increased from 1,756 in 1945, including 200 farmer-line customers, to 2,668 at the end of 1949, which included 360 farmer-line telephones. The increase in farmer-line customers reflected the residential population growth close enough to hook into existing farmer lines. There were scores of other newcomers who were not close enough to farmer lines to receive service. They simply had to wait for Roseville Telephone to build infrastructure to reach them. Since that was not occurring in the 1940s, many frustrated and often irate prospective customers waited for years to get a telephone. Although Roseville Telephone dragged its feet in meeting the burgeoning demand, compared to its previous capital spending, the years 1946-1949 marked the first sustained period of relatively significant fixed plant investment. In 1946, the company expended $12,482 on improvements. The next year the company spent $26,403 to add more sections to the switchboard, bringing the circuit capacity to 800 by the end of 1947. And it was in the same year that total plant wire mileage increased to 1,678 from the 1,373 wire-mile figure of the previous few years. In 1948, $25,172 was invested in plant and equipment as wire mileage crept up to 1,705.

By 1948, the company had long outgrown its 25-year-old building. From only 18 employees in 1945, 13 of them operators, just three years later the work force had grown to 28. By 1948, there were 18 operators, four women in the business office and six men — the two Hanisches, Walter and son David, two linemen, a construction man and an installer. Actually, the men were all-purpose then and did whatever was required.

In response to the growth, Hanisch and the Board of Directors decided to build a new construction/maintenance shop on a small lot at the corner of Linda and Lincoln streets, only a hundred yards or so south of the main office. After spending nearly $65,000 on capital improvements during the three previous years, spending would leap to $74,939 in 1949 alone. Included in this spending was well over $30,000 for the land and new building, $13,000 for another 100-line section addition to the switchboard, about $20,000 for more than 100 miles of new wire, cable and poles, plus nearly $10,000 to purchase more than 300 new telephones.

While they were in the spending mode, probably at the suggestion of Charlie Baker, it was decided the officers of the company — including W.J. Doyle as president and Baker as corporate secretary — should be paid a modest salary over and above the $25 per month they received for attending Board of Directors meetings. It was agreed and Doyle got an additional $40 and Baker $50 per month.

Although there are no company records available that reflect the board minutes or opinions of the directors and owners in the late 1940s, it's clear that the stress level on Walter Hanisch and his aging Board of Directors must have been intense. In fact, it was in 1949 that Hanisch finally became a member of the board, replacing Chris Etzel who died at age 86 in June 1949. After nearly 40 years of running a tiny, very independent and private telephone company, explosive population growth in its service area and rapid changes in technology were forcing these older men to make major decisions about the future of the

*The Washington Boulevard (Seawell) underpass was dedicated on April 1, 1950. It enabled auto and truck traffic to bypass the lengthy delays that were common prior to then, as travelers waited at street crossings for long trains to exit the Southern Pacific railyards.*

Courtesy of Leonard M. Davis Historical Collection

Roseville Telephone Company. These decisions involved what seemed to them incredibly huge sums of money. They were not by nature risk-takers and their age may have made them even more averse to change.

## GROWTH FORCES SHAREHOLDERS TO LEND COMPANY MONEY

In 1949, for the first time in the company's history, the heavy investment in plant required that the company go into debt. Ever cautious and conservative, however, the board opted to borrow from its own members rather than go to an outside lender or to sell new shares. It's likely that they didn't know quite how to approach an outside lender, fearful they would get "snookered" by an unfavorable loan agreement.

According to the annual report filed with the CPUC in 1949, three loans of $10,000 apiece were made to Roseville Telephone that year. Each was a demand note paying 6 percent annual interest. The first to lend was Charles Baker, who made his loan on April 15, 1949. On June 15, Walter Hanisch lent the company $10,000, and on Sept. 1, the G.M. Hanisch Estate lent $10,000. So at the end of 1949, the company was in debt $30,000, the first time in its history it had debt on its balance sheet. There were probably only a handful, if any, of the nation's 1,500 telephone companies at that time that had gone 35 years without borrowing money. But that was Roseville Telephone.

More than loans were needed to fund the company's operations in 1949. It was during July and August of 1949 that the company sold its war bonds for more than $25,000. Clearly, these had to be antzy times for the old gentlemen of Roseville Telephone. Now in debt and having disposed of most of the company's liquid investments, they faced the new decade with even more growth and change staring them in the face.

## NEW DECADE BRINGS FASTER GROWTH

In 1950, Roseville Telephone was straining under the weight of continued heavy capital requirements necessitated by booming growth in its service territory. Roseville itself had grown by more than 2,000 residents from 1940 to 1950 and now had a population of 8,723. The entire Sacramento region was growing rapidly, thanks in part to the heavy military commitment to the Mather and McClellan Air Force bases and the U.S. Army Depot. In addition, the population explosion occurring in California was creating significant growth in the already bloated state bureaucracy. Probably the growth of McClellan had the most direct impact on Roseville's service territory because it is a neighbor.

At the company, the many years of static management were taking their toll. It is clear that Walter Hanisch, now 67 years old, was not up to running the company that was rapidly growing despite his efforts, subtle or not, to keep it small. Exacerbating the situation was the increasingly dominant role assumed by David Hanisch. It was clearly the intention of Walter Hanisch that his son succeed him as manager and there's no doubt that David expected that he would take over from his father. He was named assistant manager in 1952, but in the eyes of the employees, David Hanisch was running the company years before.

Betty Dosher joined the company on July 7, 1949, as one of Gladys Ellis' "girls" on the switchboard. Her impressions at the time were that Walter Hanisch did all he could to limit the growth of the company.

"The rumors were that Mr. Hanisch didn't want to grow," recalled Dosher. "I remember the business office was right out in front of us and one day this lady was arguing with Mr. Hanisch because she couldn't get a telephone. Her husband was in the military. Hanisch told her, 'I can't get the equipment,' but she wouldn't accept that answer. She yelled back, 'The government tells me you can.' I remember thinking, how does she know what the government said? But Hanisch used to argue. You just couldn't get a telephone easily in those days."

The operators had little to do with Walter or David Hanisch during those years. Anything the Hanisches wanted to convey to the operators, they did it through Gladys Ellis. As a 25-year employee of the company by 1950, Ellis knew Walter Hanisch's ways better than anyone alive today, excepting perhaps David Hanisch. The picture she paints of Walter was one of a serious man who grew up in an austere family. To him frugality was the closest thing to godliness. His overriding objective, it seemed to Gladys, was to refrain from spending money.

"I remember one night when Mr. Doyle came in to see Walter — they used to meet in the little room in the back of the building behind the operators — they appeared to be having an argument. Not long afterward Mr. Doyle came walking through ... we hardly noticed him most of the time ... and just as he entered the operators' area, he turned and yelled to Mr. Hanisch in the back, 'and give the goddamned operators a raise, too, Walter.' Walter never thought of giving raises. While we weren't paid much back then, it wasn't like Walter was trying to make money off of the company. I remember one time when he went to San Francisco on a business trip. The next day Walter came by the switchboard and kind of bragged to me, saying, 'I spent only 49 cents for lunch yesterday in San Francisco ... I had the blue plate special.' That was Walter."

Gladys attributed Walter Hanisch's stern personality to a hard childhood. "I have great respect for Walter Hanisch because his people were from the old country, I believe Austria, and his mother had died young. As the oldest, Walter virtually had to raise his brothers and sisters. I think he was very strict with the whole family. He didn't have it easy."

Gladys also remembered the elder Hanisch — or "Father" as the operators called him — as a hard worker, but one who had to do it all himself. He did not know how to delegate. "He believed he was responsible for everything and had to do everything," she added. "David was that way, too."

In her own way, Gladys was almost every bit the "company man" the Hanisches were. She was extremely loyal to Roseville Telephone and her girls knew it.

"Gladys was a company-minded boss," recalled Betty Dosher. "You didn't take sick time off if you weren't flat in bed. If you weren't feeling good, she'd say, 'Take an aspirin and come on in.' She was particularly strict about Mother's Day and Christmas, the two biggest days of the year. She'd put us on notice that no one gets Mother's Day off. Well, there were all of us mothers who would have loved to have had the day off. Even if Mother's Day was your day off, you didn't have it off. You had to work.

"The telephone company came first," Dosher continued, "but we loved Gladys. I can remember one time she called me into her office and said my paycheck was wrong. My check had been shorted two days' pay. She said, 'Do you want me to loan you the money, or just wait and have it put on the next time?' She was that way. She was really working for us, too. It got to be a joke, 'Take an aspirin and come on to work.' Gladys said that so much."

Bernice (Harris) Moser, also an operator in the early 1950s, seconded Dosher's opinion that Gladys kept tight reins on her operators. "We went to work until we absolutely would drag. Then we'd go home. You tried the aspirin first before you asked to go home, that was for sure. Gladys was very company-oriented and people my age were all what you call Depression babies. We didn't spend dimes we didn't need and I think it all carried over into anything that we were doing. I believe Gladys was very much that way, too."

David Hanisch, according to those who worked with him, shared his father's inability to delegate authority, although he carried this trait even further. David Hanisch not only didn't want anyone else doing what he considered important work, he didn't trust them to do it right, and was condescending in his treatment of those who worked for him. The Hanisches were not popular among the men who worked with them.

Ed Gardetto joined the company in February 1951 and worked for David Hanisch on the construction crew with the late Tommy Apostolos, who had joined the company about a month earlier. He remembers Walter Hanisch as being "gruff and grouchy" and very tight with the buck.

"One day, Tommy and I were installing telephones. Back then we had to collect the money while we installed them," Gardetto remembered. "The customer had to have the exact amount of money because Hanisch wouldn't give us any money for change and none of us had any money back then.

"So we got back to the shop late that night and Tommy gave Walter (Hanisch) the installation money we had collected that day. As Tommy was giving the money to Walter, a penny dropped on the floor and rolled under the line truck," Gardetto said. "He made Tommy get a flashlight and look for that penny. 'You stay until you find that penny,' he told us. That's the kind of guy he was. And Walter's personality was such that you didn't know whether he'd speak to you. I'd walk right by him and he wouldn't even say hello."

Bernice Moser remembered that Walter Hanisch seemed happiest when he could sit alone in the back room where the switching equipment was. "You could walk back there anytime and see Mr. Hanisch. If you had to get him for something because the cords were tangled or a repair was needed on the

switchboard, he would be in the back sitting on a chair. In front of him, he'd have a box, like an apple box, that would have all kinds of pieces in it. He'd rummage in this box or another box to find a certain wire or a certain bell that he needed to fix the equipment. I think he had two boxes of parts on the floor back there. That was Roseville Telephone's repair department back then. Stuff was just scattered all around … it looked like somebody's back garage.

*Horses were still common in parades in the late 1940s as this parade in August 1949 shows. The route went east on Vernon Street passing by Judah Street.*
Courtesy of Leonard M. Davis Historical Collection
Photo by Alan Ashe

"I remember when the cord that fits onto the plug would get worn and the wires would break loose because they hung down all the time where you plug them in," Moser continued. "Walter would come around if we told him a cord wouldn't ring for us, or we'd put one into a jack and it wouldn't connect with a customer. He'd say, 'Oh, I'll see about it.' Then he'd do something to fix it and say, 'Now try it.' I think he enjoyed tinkering."

He was a lot more than a tinkerer, according to David Hanisch. "My dad was also a ham radio operator, an amateur meteorologist and an astronomer. He built two telescopes ... it took him a year to grind the lens on one of them. When he started a project, he worked at it until it was finished. He was no tinkerer. He was more than that. My dad could have been a great engineer, if he had had the schooling."

The Hanisches' good qualities aside — and both father and son had their good qualities — it was obvious to the employees in those years that the Hanisches' management style and leadership would not carry Roseville Telephone to the next level of growth. The employees' lack of faith had more to do with the Hanisches' incurable aversion to spending money than with their unpopular management style.

Surprisingly, the employees had a better handle on Roseville Telephone's short-comings in the early 1950s than did the Board of Directors. After all, wasn't the company generating year-after-year of record profits? The dividend was grow-ing, too. How could there be any problems? Walter Hanisch would tell the directors the company was doing well, there weren't any problems, and the directors believed him.

The numbers supported the rosy reports offered by Hanisch. In 1950, revenue rose to an all-time high of $147,429 and operating income rose to $23,708, also a record. Telephones in service jumped to 2,903, including 378 farmer-line telephones. Employees had grown to 32, including two part-timers. Walter Hanisch's pay had increased to $93 a week, surpassed only by his son David, who was making $96 a week at the end of 1950. There were now 21 operators, including chief operator Gladys Ellis. That year the company had made another substantial investment in plant and equipment, spending in excess of $32,000.

The recent growth required more cash to finance it than the company was generating from earnings, however. In 1950, the company again needed to borrow from shareholders and their families. The first loan of $2,500 was granted by W.J. Doyle on Jan. 15, 1950. More than likely Doyle lent the money using his semi-annual dividend of $2,468.70 plus $31.30 out of pocket to fund the loan. The second loan was the biggest one to date, $12,000, made on Sept. 1, 1950, by Chantee Lewis, the son of long-time director F.A. (Frank) Lewis. Chantee Lewis was a career Navy man. It's not clear why he made the loan rather than his father.

## PREPARING TO GO DIAL

After 36 years in business, in 1950 the Roseville Telephone Company was in as uncomfortable a position as any start-up company on the verge of explosive growth. Its options must have been daunting to the Board of Directors, men born in the 1800s who were not accustomed to the world of high finance. The company had two choices to fund growth. One was to sell a substantial amount of new stock and/or to borrow more money than its owners would have ever dreamed possible only a few short years earlier. Neither choice was easy for the board.

Faced with the necessity of raising money, however, the directors devised a two-part strategy. It should be mentioned once again that there are no written records or witnesses to explain exactly why the company's board acted as it did during these years. One must re-create how these decisions were likely to have been made based upon the actions that occurred later on.

In 1951, the capital structure changed for the first time in 24 years. Since 1927 Roseville Telephone had not sold one share of stock to finance its operations and growth. Any changes in holdings were made by existing shareholders selling their shares to themselves or to family members.

In this year, however, the company unfurled a capitalization plan that smacked of Wall Street. The capitalization strategy involved the declaration of a 200 percent stock dividend, the exchange of new shares for stockholder debt, the exchange of shares for telephone switching equipment, new shares sold to existing shareholders, a big loan made by the controlling shareholder, and the addition of three new shareholders, bringing the total to 13 shareholders at the end of 1951. The deceased Chris Etzel's shares were absorbed by his son, Roy Etzel.

The exact timing of these major financial transactions is unknown, but it's likely it went something like this. In late February 1951, W.J. Doyle lent Roseville Telephone $17,352. Why that particular amount is unclear. Perhaps it was to pay for new equipment or the new building the company was building to replace its office built in 1922-23.

In May 1951, there were four simultaneous transactions that occurred, in the following order: First, the board paid a 200 percent stock dividend to holders of the existing 6,250 shares. This action created an additional 12,500 shares of common stock, bringing the total outstanding to 18,750. The second step involved exchanging 340 shares of stock for three positions of a Western Electric switchboard owned by David Hanisch. The exchange was made at his cost for the switching equipment, $3,400. It increased the operator positions on the board from six to nine.

"The board would not spend any money and I knew we needed more positions," Hanisch remembered. "So I found three positions of a Western Electric No. 12 that were coming out of Gilroy. I hired a truck, moved this big piece of

equipment, about 10-feet long as I recall, and hauled it to Roseville. Then I installed it. I spent my own money because the board wouldn't do it. They wouldn't buy anything."

The third step involved the exchange of 5,450 shares of stock for the $54,500 in loans made to the company by certain stockholders. These loans included the $44,500 in loans made in 1949 and 1950 plus $10,000 in additional loans, $5,000 each, that must have been made by Charles Baker and Roy Etzel in early 1951. In addition, it appears that Doyle and Chantee Lewis made a deal to exchange their debt positions, since Doyle purchased an additional 1,200 shares, equal to $12,000, the exact amount of Lewis' loan to the company made in late 1950, while Chantee Lewis ended up owning 250 shares worth $2,500, the exact amount of Doyle's loan to the company made in early 1950.

*Bill Doyle took time out from a typically busy day in about 1951 to pose with the "Doyle Brothers" farming partnership, from left to right, Jack, Bob and Tom Doyle. The photo was taken on the site of the company's present-day Industrial Avenue complex.*

Courtesy of Robert L. Doyle

The fourth step in the recapitalization was the sale of 1,940 new shares in Roseville Telephone, raising an additional $19,400. Roy Etzel apparently was a strong believer in the company's future, since he bought 1,140 shares of the 1,940 offered. Walter Hanisch picked up another 400 shares and David Hanisch acquired 300 shares for cash to add to the 340 shares he received in exchange for the switchboard positions. The other new shareholder was Walter Hanisch's brother, Oscar Hanisch, who bought 100 shares in 1951.

The financial maneuvers of 1951 changed the ownership makeup of the telephone company for the first time in 16 years. The biggest shareholder, W.J. Doyle, now owned 12,594 shares, or 47.6 percent of the shares of the company. It's assumed, however, that Doyle's $17,352 loan in early 1951 was convertible into common stock at his option. If so, Doyle's position would grow to 14,329 shares, or 50.8 percent of the 28,215 shares that would be outstanding if the debt were converted into common stock at $10 per share.

The other shareholders and their holdings were as follows: Roy Etzel (3,692), Charles Baker (3,513), Walter Hanisch (3,275), Hanisch Estate (1,612), David

Hanisch (640), F.A. Lewis (441), Elizabeth Lewis (261), Chantee Lewis (250), Marrion Smith (54), Walter Campbell (30) and Laura Neeley (18).

As a result of the financing strategy effected in 1951, the capitalization of Roseville Telephone rose from $62,500 (6,250 shares at $10) at the beginning of the year to $264,000 (26,400 shares at $10) at the end of the year.

No doubt a primary reason for dramatic repositioning of the capital structure of the company was the decision that Roseville Telephone needed to convert to a dial operation, which would cost an estimated $200,000. A capital investment of this size would require a loan far beyond the means of the existing shareholders, which meant approaching outside lenders. Any lender would base the decision to lend money upon the company's balance sheet, its current operating performance and its projected operating results after the investment. By virtue of the stock dividend — which was long overdue — and the other transactions, Roseville Telephone sported by far the strongest balance sheet in its history at the end of 1951.

Otherwise, 1951 was not an exceptional year. Operating income was in the same range it had been since 1946, amounting to $22,048 on record revenue of $159,693. Clearly, operating performance was diminishing under the heavy investments of recent years and the increased staffing required to handle the growing telephone traffic. Revenue gains were driven by increased usage and telephone station gains, each of which required growing investment from the company. Increased usage, or "traffic" in telephone parlance, required additional operators, while increases in infrastructure generated new customers, or station gains. In 1951, the company had 39 employees at year end, including three part-timers. The operator corps had climbed to 24, up four over the previous year as the company added another 100 lines to its switchboard, increasing capacity to 1,000.

Capital expenditures in 1951 jumped to $90,654, by far the highest in the company's history. The biggest item was the construction of a new headquarters office adjacent to its old office. This brick structure was built at a cost of nearly $38,000. Nearly $10,000 was used to purchase new telephones and the remainder of the capital spending went for additional poles, wire and cable and used vehicles.

The momentous decision to convert to dial was one Roseville Telephone could not afford *not* to make. Staying with the old common battery switchboard and magneto telephones in an area where demand for service was exploding would have been the death knell of the company. The old telephone system, while quaint and personal in its service, was extremely labor intensive. Since 1946, revenue at Roseville Telephone had climbed from about $90,000 to nearly $160,000 in 1951. But in the latter year 24 operators were needed to handle the business vs. only 13 in 1946. Not only did operators make a decent wage, but they took up a lot of space, too. In hard, logical business terms, telephone companies switched to dial systems in part to control labor costs. In that respect, spending $200,000 on a dial system that would temper the need for new operators made a lot more sense and this was undoubtedly a factor in Roseville Telephone's decision. Weighing the alternatives available, going dial was the sensible course of action.

As Roseville Telephone entered 1952, it was poised for more change than it had experienced in its 38-year history.

# 1952-1954: Ownership, Management Transition

## OLD STOCK, NEW BLOOD

*"When I joined the company in 1953, Roseville Telephone Company had to be the most hated telephone company in America."*
— Bob Doyle

By 1952, Roseville Telephone was facing pressures on many fronts. With the already fast-growing region poised to explode with new growth, Roseville Telephone was heading for a crisis and the Board of Directors knew it. With its members elderly and faced with the pressures from the community and the California Public Utilities Commission (CPUC) for better service, William J. Doyle, nearing 80 years old, knew it was time for a changing of the guard, but nonetheless was slow to act. New blood was needed both at the board level and the management level. But change didn't come easily or quickly.

The Board of Directors also finally determined it was time to recruit younger members to its ranks. In January 1952, Tom Doyle and A. Stanley "Stan" Anderson purchased 100 shares each and joined the Board of Directors, bringing the membership to seven. The other members were the senior Doyle, F.A. Lewis, Roy Etzel, Charles Baker and Walter Hanisch. At the time of his election to the board, Tom Doyle was part of the "Doyle Brothers" farming operation with his older brothers Jack and Bob. Anderson was a successful chicken rancher in nearby Rio Linda and a friend of Jack Doyle's.

"I bought 100 shares for $10 apiece from Walter Hanisch. He came down to the ranch one day and said they were going to sell some stock, so I said I'd buy 100 shares," Tom Doyle recollected. "Of course, my wife gave me hell because there we were sitting on lug boxes … I mean we didn't have furniture or anything, living out there on the ranch. So I told her, 'Look what I did!' In those days, $1,000 was a lot of money … especially when I didn't have any furniture or a damned thing. She wasn't happy about it."

When Tom Doyle joined the board, the members shared one overriding trait — they were extremely tight with money. "Those guys were something else.

*Thomas E. Doyle joined the Board of Directors in January 1952.*

Old Charlie Baker, he was as tight as the bark on a tree. I don't think there was ever a board meeting that he didn't tell me, 'What are you going to do with the money you get paid?' and I'd tell him I was going to save it, and he'd say, 'Good!' I got $25 a month, oh boy, what a deal! Those fellows were from the old school and figured they'd just run the company anyway they wanted to. Let's face it, they were making big bucks for those days. With the few phones they had, they weren't spending any money, so if it's all income and nothing going out, you're going to make money."

But the board couldn't ignore the fact that pressures were mounting to both expand and improve service. As Tom Doyle remembered, "Some of the old-timers were in favor of Stan and me coming on the board because they figured they'd better get some young guys on there. But there was a lot of dissension between Walter Hanisch and F. A. Lewis, one of the directors. Lewis had a drug store where the executive building is now and I used to go over there and talk to him. He'd say, 'We got to do this and we got to do that.' But it was a struggle to get the other members of the board to see that we had to deal with our problems. They had had it good for so long."

Roseville Telephone began 1952 by negotiating the largest financial transaction in its history, a $200,000 mortgage loan from Pacific Mutual Life Insurance Co. on Jan. 23, 1952. This was the beginning of a long — and sometimes rocky — relationship between Roseville Telephone and its principal lender. The interest rate was 4.75 percent over a 20-year term. The loan required Roseville Telephone to pledge virtually all its assets as security. It also included restrictive covenants requiring the company to maintain stated minimum levels of equity and retained earnings before cash dividends were allowed to be paid.

The gargantuan task of installing the dial equipment began sometime in 1952 when installers and engineers from Automatic Electric of Chicago, the manufacturers of the Strowger Automatic "step-by-step" switching system, came to Roseville to begin the process. No records exist to identify the precise date when the installation began. It is assumed, however, that installation must have begun in early-to-mid-1952 for at least two reasons: First, the Pacific Mutual loan was taken out in January, and second, in the company's subsequent application to the CPUC requesting an across-the-board rate increase to pay for the new equipment, the financial projections assumed the dial equipment would be operational for all of 1953. In fact, it did not go into service until late 1953. Obviously, there must have been delays.

"It was a big project and it took a lot of time to finish," said David Hanisch of the dial conversion. "In addition, we had to replace or convert the old phones to dial. With a small crew of three or four men, that took a time to accomplish. We had a lot of other work to do, too. It all took time."

Most likely, the delays were in part caused by unforeseen unavailability of the equipment, since many other telephone exchanges across the country were converting to dial in the early 1950s. It was a booming period for Automatic Electric and, as a relatively small customer, it's likely Roseville Telephone was not a top priority for installation at that time.

For the second consecutive year, the cash-strapped company raised capital by selling stock. In 1952, the company sold 3,700 new shares, raising $37,000. Seven new shareholders joined the ownership ranks. As might be expected, the new stockholders consisted of family and friends of existing shareholders. The new holders and their stock purchases were Joseph Drago (300), Lynn Hubbard (300), Chester Palmer (500), L.C. Anderson (130), Stan Anderson (100), Tom Doyle (100) and Marie Ruffin (200).

Drago was Bob Doyle's father-in-law. "Pappy" Hubbard was a Roseville fireman, part-time employee of Roseville Telephone, and a friend of David Hanisch. Palmer was the local Studebaker dealer. L.C. Anderson was a Roseville attorney who in December 1953 became a director of the company. He was also to become an important adviser to Bob Doyle. Of course, Stan Anderson and Tom Doyle were new directors. Ruffin owned a dress shop in Roseville and was Jack Doyle's wife's aunt. Ironically, Ruffin was also the aunt of David Hanisch's wife. As a group, the seven acquired 1,630 shares for $16,300.

The other 2,070 shares were acquired by W.J. Doyle. He was issued 1,735 shares to pay off the $17,352 loan he made the company the previous year. In addition, he purchased another 335 shares. At the end of 1952, the elder Doyle owned 14,664 shares, or 48.6 percent of the 30,180 shares outstanding. Although his position again fell under 50 percent, no one doubted that W.J. Doyle controlled the destiny of Roseville Telephone. There were now 20 shareholders.

Even as the installation of the new dial facilities proceeded, the growth of the company continued unabated. In 1952, total phones served by the company rose to 3,479 of which 2,814 were primary company-owned phones, the remainder being extensions and farmer lines. By this time, the telephone count was becoming more complicated since it included main telephone stations, a growing number of extensions in homes and businesses, plus the advent of the PBXs (private branch exchanges) which were themselves small switchboards to serve an individual business. In 1951, the company reported it served three PBX systems with 27 telephones attached to them.

As became clear early on to the author in researching the old financial records of the company, Walter Hanisch's skill in maintaining up-to-date and accurate accounts of total phones in service, wire mileage and similar statistics was limited. For instance, in 1951, the telephones-in-service figures were recalculated and revised downward, probably in response to inquiries from the CPUC.

Financially, 1952 was not a good year. Although revenue climbed to $175,539, another record, operating income dropped to $18,336, the lowest since 1945. This was quite a turnabout from the early and mid-1940s when the company earned fat profits. In 1945, for example, the company's operating income was

$16,559 on revenue of only $79,924. Seven years later, the revenue had climbed by nearly $100,000, but earnings had improved by less than $2,000.

In response to the weak financial performance and in view of the looming requirements for large capital outlays, no cash or stock dividend was paid in 1952. It stands as the only year in Roseville Telephone's long history that shareholders received no cash or stock dividend.

The operator count by the end of 1952 had grown to 26 and total employees mushroomed to 40, 32 women and eight men. There were now six women in the business office. David Hanisch, newly named as assistant manager, was the highest paid employee, earning $120 a week. He was also the plant superintendent. Walter Hanisch earned only $93 a week.

"The pay may seem like it was high, but in those days keeping service up was a 24-hour, seven-day a week job," explained David Hanisch. "For example, we owned a PBX at Southern Pacific that would go out occasionally. It didn't matter if it was 2 or 3 in the morning, I'd have to go fix it because SP controlled all its switching through that PBX. If it wasn't working, the trains weren't running. I was up a lot of nights making sure service was up."

Bob Heintz was the construction foreman, although, according to employees there at the time, David Hanisch directed every detail involving construction, installation and maintenance. Chief operator Gladys Ellis earned $87, but was working a 52-hour week.

Total payroll at the end of 1952 was $2,380 a week. The operators were the lowest-paid employees, ranging from $.90-$.97 an hour for the lowest paid to $1.20-$1.29 for the highest paid. The men who worked outside putting up lines, installing phones and such were working 46 hours a week and earning under $2 an hour. The top hourly rates in 1952 ranged from $2.10-$2.29.

The employees in 1952 remember those times as uncertain. As indicated in the previous chapter, operators were relatively insulated from the Hanisches by Gladys Ellis. Although she ran a tight, no-nonsense department, her "girls" loved her and would do anything for Gladys or the telephone company. The male employees, however, were not so lucky. They worked directly for the Hanisches. But in 1952 a job at Roseville Telephone meant reasonably good pay and likely job security. It didn't matter that the company had no employee benefits since most companies didn't have benefits then. And there was no union or other means of filing grievances at that time. If an employee didn't like the working conditions, he or she could leave and work somewhere else. Despite its poor reputation as a utility, plenty of early '50s area residents would have jumped at a job opportunity at Roseville Telephone.

*A. Stanley Anderson joined the Board of Directors in January 1952. He was a prominent chicken rancher from nearby Rio Linda.*

Bernice Moser joined the company as an operator in May 1952 after the company had already moved into its "new" quarters the previous year. The office was not glamorous.

"On one side was the Welcome Club and just down the street there was the Rainbow Club. There were always bars next to the telephone office, it seemed.

"In those days, nobody really locked a door, and the front of the telephone company looked like an old store," Moser remembered. "There were two doors, one leading into the business office and one into our operator area. In the summertime, it was hot so we finally bought our own fans. But we'd leave that door open and just have the screen door locked with just a regular little hook on it. Men would come out of the bars and want to come in there, or they would forget which door was to the bar and they'd come up and pound on our door, thinking it was a bar. At times we had to call the police to come and take them away and, of course, then I think we only had about two policemen in town, if we had that many.

"The office was always busy when I first started because on one side was the business office with a counter. The operator board was on the other side and along the wall was mostly just boxes ... it was just really a mess. The only place we had to sit down on our relief time was in back where there was a six-foot wall to separate it from the front part. In the area was an old couch and a couple of chairs. There were a few lockers but none of them had locks on them. There was one lavatory, " she recalled.

In the 1920s and 1930s, the office was heated by a coal stove and the night time operators had to shovel coal to keep the place warm enough to work. By the 1950s, it was heated by an old gas stove, but an unreliable one, according to Moser. "With Mr. Hanisch running it, he would go and get second-hand everything and put it in there. So there were times when we would smell gas and call someone to come and fix it. We also swept the floors, dusted ... we did everything. It was a dirty place with a wood floor, and the counter ... it was just a bunch of boards put together and painted a light green."

The operators sat in "positions" on the switchboard. As the company kept adding capacity to the switchboard, it kept getting longer and taller. "The jacks were up as far as you could reach," Moser said. "The shorter operators almost had to throw the plugs into the jacks. It was almost like flinging darts. But they got real good at it."

The timing of long distance calls wasn't as precise in the early '50s as they are today. "We timed calls by old watches Mr. Hanisch had tied with shoestrings up to the top of the board. The watch would hang in front of us in between two sections of the board. We would write on the back of our little toll ticket what time it was and then the disconnect time. That's the way we would figure it."

*Bernice (Harris) Moser, an operator for more than 30 years.*

Operators in the years before dial would also make "appointment calls," but not for the doctor and dentist. Bernice Moser explained:

"Back then we'd would call a town and leave word for that person to call back to the person here in Roseville at a certain time. This occurred when somebody in Roseville couldn't get ahold of a person they were calling. We called that an appointment call," she said. "They were really person-to-person calls. We did these a lot, as a courtesy to our customers."

The telephone operators truly were the information center before dial service. As Moser recounted, operators knew just about everything going on. "People would call and ask, 'What time does Dr. So and So open his office?' or 'Have you seen so and so's car go by?' We were the hub of Roseville as far as keeping everything going."

Roseville loved and revered its operators. Businesses and residents all over town would shower gifts on the operators during the holiday season. One company would send olive oil, another handkerchiefs. And, of course, boxes of candy came aplenty, as did flowers. The community appreciated its "Hello Girls."

## UNFLATTERING TALES OF CONDITIONS IN THE EARLY '50s

For the other employees who worked at the company in the early 1950s under the Hanisches, however, it was a job, period. The managerial shortcomings of the father-son team were many, according to the employees in those years, including the need to control everything, distrust of the employees, indifference to customers and a serious lack of communication.

The picture the employees paint of working at Roseville Telephone in the pre-Bob Doyle years is not a flattering one. And the following recollections of working conditions then were not unique to one or two disgruntled employees. All retirees interviewed who worked in those years had similar stories. Many more unflattering, but true tales from those years could be told if there were the space or desire. The following are included to give the reader a sense of why wholesale changes were needed at the telephone company in the early 1950s if it was going to survive. The following anecdotes are intended to re-create the atmosphere at Roseville Telephone in those years.

Janie Opich joined the company in mid-1953 as a supervisor in the business office, a few months before Bob Doyle came aboard. She recalls some of the difficulties she had at the time.

"The management didn't want to share any information with anybody. We had to do a monthly statement and the information I needed on the outside plant had to come from David," she remembered. "It was like pulling teeth to even get him to read a meter on the gas tanks or whatever they had down there so I could come up with some kind of a usage number. It would take several requests to get that information. It was like it was nobody's business, they didn't have to account to anybody."

Wayne Langton joined the construction crew in early 1953. He said working for David Hanisch was very difficult because of his moodiness. "I was fired or quit several times under Hanisch," he recalled. "One day my brother-in-law (construction foreman Bob Heintz) went to work and I didn't because the previous day David and I had a blowup and he had canned me. The next day, Hanisch

*Aerial view of Roseville in November 1954. Roseville Telephone served only Roseville proper with farmer lines serving the remainder of the mostly agrarian population in southwest Placer County and northeast Sacramento County.*

asked Heintz, 'Where's Wayne?' and my brother-in-law replied, 'Don't you remember yesterday you fired him?' David would then call my wife and say, 'Tell Wayne to come back to work.' Well, this happened about five times. They were hard people to work for. His moods changed almost every day, it seemed."

David Hanisch would explode if any of the regular crew attempted to drive the old Army construction rig. Ed Gardetto remembers an incident when Carl Weiss, another crew member in the early years, got in to drive the rig.

"One time Weiss was going to back that old rig out and Dave jumped on him good. 'You get out of that truck or I'll fire you. You don't belong in that Army truck.' Nobody was allowed to drive, nobody. Dave would come out on the job where you were and either he or Pappy Hubbard would drive it."

Paychecks didn't necessarily come regularly back then either. Employees recall sometimes waiting for days to get their checks. According to Janie Opich, "It was to the point where they didn't care when our paychecks came out. If they got them within the range of four or five days, that was OK. And I think that's one of the things that brought Mr. Doyle into the office, because some of the employees called him because they weren't getting their paychecks. We always had the payroll checks prepared on time, but it was a matter of calling Mr. Doyle to come and sign them, but sometimes Walter or David wouldn't bother to call Mr. Doyle to tell him to come in and sign the checks. They needed two signatures."

David Hanisch's view was altogether different. "Mr. Doyle would almost never come into town to sign the checks, so I had to go out there on the farm in the middle of the vineyard to find him so the employees could get paid on time. And if he did come into town, he'd want to get it out of the way fast so he could go play 'pan.'"

Langton also remembers not always getting paid on time. Other employees corroborated Langton's recollection.

One day in the late summer of 1953, the crew, including Langton, Gardetto and Apostolos, had had enough. Langton recalled what happened. "One day in the summertime, we just all sat down there in the construction barn and Dave came down there and said, 'OK, come on, let's roll.' And all of us just sat there, Tommy, Ed, me and a couple others, and we said, 'We're not moving.' We weren't union or anything but we had decided enough is enough.

"So Dave goes back up to the office and pretty soon here comes Walter. His head's down and he walks toward us. 'What's going on?' he asks, and everybody says, 'We need a raise. Whether it's a nickel or a dime or whatever.' And Walter says, 'You're not going to move? You're not going to go to work?' And we said, 'No, by god, we've had enough.' So Dave and Walter went back up to the office and pretty soon they came back. I think we got 10 or 15 cents an hour more."

Janie Opich held a similar view:

"When we were going to dial, David hired this one fellow to be the wire chief before Doc Harrington came. The problem was that at that time David really didn't know much about how dial equipment operated yet probably he couldn't admit it. Accepting that someone else knew something that he didn't was difficult for David. He always had to have his own way. No one ever talked back to him. David didn't think he was accountable to anyone, including his father."

Opich remembers getting her first phone. "I had applied for a telephone while building our new house in early 1953. For some reason, my order came up rather rapidly and Tommy Apostolos, who I had known since school, came to the house we were at then and told me he was ready to put the phone in. I said, 'Tom, I don't want it now, it's for when we move into our new house,' and Tom said, 'Janie, you better take it, because if you say no, you may never get a phone.' So I took the phone then."

According to the retirees, neither Walter nor David Hanisch felt Citrus Heights would ever be much more than farms and a rural area. Langton remembers David Hanisch saying, "There's never going to be anything in Citrus Heights, but teepees and Indians." And it was said that Walter Hanisch, when criticized for not putting in fixed plant to serve Citrus Heights, would answer, "Let them communicate with smoke signals. That's good enough for them in Citrus Heights."

Of course, Citrus Heights would soon become the fastest-growing area in Roseville Telephone's service territory and one of the prime reasons the company has become so large today. But the Hanisches had no use for Citrus Heights then. They cared only about Roseville.

## RATE HEARINGS IN 1953
## EXPOSE COMPANY DEFICIENCIES

The challenges faced by Roseville Telephone in the early 1950s were enormous. Independent companies throughout America had been for decades upgrading their plant and equipment to utilize "dial" phones, which enabled customers to reach their desired party without going through an operator. Moreover, Pacific Telephone had already converted Sacramento to dial, which meant that Roseville Telephone must keep up or be classified as a second-class operation.

The company contracted with Automatic Electric of Chicago to install Strowger Automatic dial equipment. Automatic Electric was a major supplier to independent telephone companies in those years. Until 1984, when the Bell System monopoly was broken up, independents such as Roseville Telephone couldn't buy any equipment from Western Electric, the giant manufacturing arm of AT&T, unless there was no alternative place to buy the necessary equipment.

In 1953, when the company had filed with the CPUC for a sizable rate increase to help pay for the investment in dial equipment, the elder Doyle finally had to face up to the dire situation the telephone company was in. It was crisis time. The company needed more than just new equipment. It needed a new management direction, too.

"He knew there was a problem," recalled Tom Doyle, "but he just really didn't want to face up to it, I think. He was getting old."

And Walter Hanisch, who had always been old-fashioned, was getting old, too. This was evident when the 69-year-old Hanisch represented the company during the public hearings conducted by the CPUC in June 1953 in Roseville. His testimony showed a lack of awareness and knowledge of the depth of the company's problems.

Janie Opich remembered the hearings. She had just come to work at the company.

"He was so old at that time and would be easily flustered," she recalled. "At that PUC hearing, they had Mr. Hanisch on the stand, and he got very confused and rattled with the questions being asked. David was particularly upset when the PUC commissioners questioned Mr. Hanisch about who would take over as manager after he retired. He just said, 'My son will take over,' but he didn't elaborate about what David's training was, in engineering and all that. Walter was so rattled he forgot to mention anything about David's qualifications. It didn't go well at all and things were tense around the office after that. I don't think David ever forgave his dad for not bringing forward what his background was at those hearings."

The CPUC hearings in 1953 signaled the beginning of the end of the Hanisch management reign of the Roseville Telephone Company.

The pressure from the CPUC on Roseville Telephone to improve its service was direct. In its 11-page rate request opinion written in October 1953, commission staffers J.T. Phelps and J.F. Donovan castigated Roseville Telephone for its poor service and threatened repeal of the rate increase if no action were taken to alleviate service problems plaguing the territory. After describing and agreeing in general to the company's justification for rate increases, the opinion listed some of the complaints subscribers had made about Roseville Telephone (referred to as "applicant" in this setting).

*"In the main, the participation of interested parties and other subscribers of applicant had to do with two phases of service matters. The first concerns past and present inadequacies and deficiencies of telephone plant and service. The second concerns applicant's held order situation and the establishing of service in areas not presently served.*

*"A number of witnesses complained about their inability to obtain an operator, delays in completing both local and toll calls and the general inattention of*

*applicant's personnel to the daily and routine service needs of subscribers. In most instances, applicant's manager claimed he had no knowledge of such deficiencies. In others, conditions of poor services were admitted. Applicant alleges that all such service deficiencies will be overcome upon completion of the dial cutover.*

*"As previously indicated, applicant recorded 536 held orders for primary service as of March 31, 1953. By June 12, 1953, its records indicated that the number of held orders had been reduced to 414. Of this latter number, 51 are recorded as having been awaiting service since 1950. None are recorded as having been received prior to that year. However, one witness testified to having repeatedly applied for service since July 1946. He still remains unserved. Such a situation is neither normal or reasonable.*

*"Applicant's latest available commercial survey is now more than two years old. Applicant has taken no later view of population growth nor has it made any more recent estimate of its potential market.*

*Dial the Roseville Press-Tribune at "2145."*

Roseville Press-Tribune, October 30, 1953

*"The needs and desires of the public, except for the desire of present subscribers for dial service, seem to be unknown to it. As an example, applicant's manager was under the impression that telephone facilities were some two miles distant from certain applicants for foreign exchange service, where the actual distance may be as short as 50 feet. Repeated requests for such service have been ignored. We see no reason why these people were not served as soon as the needed foreign facilities were available.*

*"In our opinion, applicant's lack of awareness indicates palpable inefficiency of management and clearly indicates failure fully to meet applicant's utility obligations."*

It was clear from this opinion that the CPUC considered Roseville Telephone's management at the time to be inept and unable to properly serve its existing population, not to mention the projected population growth of the territory. Moreover, the CPUC opinion suggested that expense projections from company management were too low "… predicated on the need for additional management, supervisory and maintenance personnel if present unsatisfactory operations are to be corrected and a more reasonable and adequate service rendered to the public." In conclusion, the CPUC opinion warned Roseville Telephone that it must quickly address its problems or possibly face a repeal of its rate increases.

*Local businesses congratulated Roseville Telephone in newspaper ads on October 30, 1953.*

Roseville Press-Tribune

The following are excerpts from the "Conclusions" portion of the CPUC opinion:

*"The results of the operations for the test year ... are predicated on the future faithful performance of applicant's utility obligations in providing and maintaining adequate service to the public throughout the exchange area. Applicant will be required to provide primary service to all waiting applicants and complete its now known construction program ... within a one-year period.*

*"We place applicant on notice that no less than satisfactory service is acceptable and that this proceeding may be reopened for the purpose of rescinding all or a part of the rate increase authorized herein if reasonably adequate performance is not obtained."*

With the CPUC hearings concluded, Bill Doyle had to face the fact that Walter Hanisch must soon give up his management role. While the CPUC opinion officially threatened to roll back rate increases if its directives were not satisfied within a reasonable time, Doyle and the Board of Directors knew the CPUC could and would force a change of ownership if the numerous problems were not corrected quickly. It was an implied threat. The CPUC was not going to let the service remain horrible forever, particularly since all signs pointed to rapid population growth in the telephone company's service area. The CPUC could have ordered Pacific Telephone to take over the Roseville franchise because it was the CPUC's top priority that California's residents have adequate service. It didn't matter who provided that service.

The management issue was not an easy one to deal with, however. Walter Hanisch had been the manager (he was never called general manager) since 1914, and an employee since the company's founding. Although Doyle had always been the majority owner, in many ways Roseville Telephone was even more Walter Hanisch's company, since he had run it day in and day out for 40 years. Moreover, the elder Doyle had to deal with the fact that David Hanisch was the assistant manager and considered by most observers to be the heir apparent to his dad.

Janie Opich remembered that in 1953 David Hanisch had taken command of the company in fact if not in title. "David never really felt that he had to report to anybody, I don't think. He literally ran his father. I don't think David ever grew up with the feeling that he was accountable to anybody. I think he just went into the company with the theory that, 'This is mine and when my dad goes, it will be mine.' He'd always been led to believe that someday Roseville Telephone would be his to run."

Walter was set in his ways and David shared his father's reticence and reluctance to take risks. According to employees who were there when the Hanisches ran it,

Walter and David managed Roseville Telephone as if it was their private enterprise. The most common complaint about the Hanisches was that they were satisfied with the status quo. They were not seen as progressive. They wanted to keep the company as it always had been. And they thrived on control.

## ROBERT L. DOYLE JOINS ROSEVILLE TELEPHONE

Although Bill Doyle concluded Roseville Telephone had outgrown Walter Hanisch's ability to manage it, he didn't have the solution to the problem either. Appointing David Hanisch manager would mean more of the same style of management that was no longer effective. Faced with the certainty that the CPUC would force the owners to sell to another telephone company if no action were forthcoming, the elder Doyle asked his second son Bob if he would be interested in coming into the company.

"My father came to me and said, 'We have to find somebody to straighten out the telephone company. Would you like to try to do it? Walter Hanisch and present management really would like to find their own person, but if you would like to do it, I'd like you to do it.' That's how I got to work at the phone company."

Bob Doyle was farming with his brothers Jack and Tom at the time — they called themselves the "Doyle Brothers" — but earlier in the summer Bob had hurt his leg playing softball. According to Tom Doyle, his brother's broken leg may have been a factor in their father asking Bob to get involved with the phone company. Bob remembers the time slightly differently, although both brothers agree that perhaps Bob wasn't cut out to be the farmer of the family. "I think it was clear that Tom was too young at that time and certainly Jack was the best farmer in the family. So my dad chose me," said Bob Doyle.

"I told my dad that I don't know anything about running a telephone company. Hell, all I know is what a telephone was and what a directory was. That's about as much as I knew." Bob Doyle also remembers reminding his father that learning in general, at least book learning, was not Bob's forte.

" 'You know I wasn't a good student,' " Bob recalls telling his father at the time. 'They damn near had to burn the high school down to get rid of me.' But I did tell him, 'I think I'm capable of finding somebody to run the company. Then I'll come back and go to work with Jack and Tom.' I told my brothers, 'Look, you guys take care of the farm. I'll go to work and protect the interests in the telephone company and when I find somebody, I'll come back to work.' "

On Aug. 15, 1953, Bob Doyle, then 34 years old, went to work at the Roseville Telephone Company. It was his brother Tom's 24th birthday. At that time the company owned about 2,800 "main station" phones and in total served more than 3,000 phones. Its subscribers were packed mostly in an area proximate to

downtown Roseville. The rest of the territory, which included much of Citrus Heights and other rural areas surrounding Roseville, was primarily serviced by different "farmer lines." These lines provided multi-party service to the scores of ranches that stretched out for many miles around Roseville and the northeastern Sacramento County area.

When Bob Doyle joined Roseville Telephone Company, the 40-year-old utility was at a major crossroads in its history. Both Bob and Tom Doyle will admit that in the early 1950s the Roseville Telephone Company was probably "the most hated telephone company in the United States." There was every reason to believe this statement.

Families in the 1930s and 1940s who moved into the company's service territory, but not close to downtown Roseville, would sometimes be required to wait 10-to-12 years to receive telephone service! Although it was not uncommon in the '50s for there to be "held orders" for a period of weeks and sometimes months, particularly among smaller independent telephone companies, Roseville Telephone's held order situation was horrible. Again, this lack of servicing the territory was directly linked to the owners' and management's refusal over the years to invest in necessary capital improvements as the population in their service territory grew. It was accurate to say Roseville Telephone Company was on the precipice of disaster when Bob Doyle joined the company.

*Howard Greenhalgh, left, talks with Wayne Langton in mid-'50s.*

Roseville Press-Tribune, 1955

## BOB DOYLE'S EXERCISE IN FRUSTRATION

Bob Doyle's first few months on the job were tense. He called himself "the janitor," but in fact he went to work in the business office. His pay was $200 a month — $1.25 an hour — not bad for the time, but certainly no gilded contract that might have been expected for the son of the president and majority shareholder in the company. And although Bob Doyle came in with his father's blessing, the Hanisches were not ready or willing to give up their management control to a young man who knew nothing about the telephone company and one who they felt was an intruder.

Bob Doyle recalled how uncomfortable he was in his first few months as an employee of the Roseville Telephone Company.

"I remember that first day. I came in through the screen door and just looked at the girls, the operators and the business staff. I was standing there while Dave Hanisch and Walter were in back, just kind of looking at me. They didn't even come up and introduce me," Doyle recalled.

"The girls didn't know what was going on. They didn't know why I was there. I felt about this small," he said putting his forefinger and thumb about an inch apart. "Then the Hanisches finally came up and showed me to this little cubicle in the business office with a tiny, odd-looking desk. That was my desk."

The next morning Doyle found his desk locked. "I had to wait for Walter Hanisch to unlock it for me — even though the desk was empty!" That continued for a number of weeks. Doyle attributed this unusual practice to a general distrust by the Hanisches of the company's employees at that time. It was management by fear, or at least it seemed so to the new kid on the block, Bob Doyle.

"And David left this manual on my desk about PBXs and technical stuff like that," he added. "I had no idea what that stuff was all about and I had no intention of learning about it. It was terrible. They didn't want me there."

Roseville was still a small town in 1953 and the news spread fast that Bob Doyle had joined the telephone company.

"Immediately a lot of people knew who I was and they figured, 'Oh, maybe we will get something done about our telephone service. We got some new blood in there.' But they didn't realize that I couldn't change this around just because I had joined the company. I had to face them and tell them the truth."

"People would come in and ask me when they could get their telephone. I would say, 'Well, Mr. Customer, when did you apply for a phone?' So I would get the card box out and look through it. Remember, this was in 1953. I'd often find that the customer might have first applied for service in 1946 or 1947! And I knew there were no plans to do anything soon to get that customer service because there was no money! I would have to tell the customer, 'I'm sorry, we

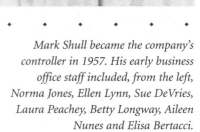

*Mark Shull became the company's controller in 1957. His early business office staff included, from the left, Norma Jones, Ellen Lynn, Sue DeVries, Laura Peachey, Betty Longway, Aileen Nunes and Elisa Bertacci.*

do not have any facilities in your area at the present time, but we are going to…' And that is about as far as I would get, and the customer would go through the roof because he was hearing the same old story he had been listening to year after year after year! You could see why we were so hated. We weren't providing service."

Doyle's first months as a "commercial representative" were filled with apologies to customers about why the company couldn't provide them service, even though the company was soon to complete its conversion to dial service. But dial service only benefited those customers who already had their phones. It didn't help those customers moving into the many areas within the company's service territory who were not getting their phones installed. After a few months, a frustrated Bob Doyle went to his father and asked for help.

"I finally went to my dad and said, 'Look, management isn't doing a damn thing about trying to get this mess straightened out and I don't have any ability to go out and do anything to help straighten it out because I don't have any authority. Walter Hanisch is the manager and his son is the assistant manager and I'm the guy in the business office that don't know doodedly doo about anything. And I am not going to learn anything from them because they don't want me around in the first place. So, if you just give me some authority, I'll try to do something. Otherwise, my suggestion is to sell.

"So we talked about the problems I was facing and then he said, 'When it comes time for the stockholders meeting, I'll step down and make you the president and manager.' "

In the meantime, Walter Hanisch's final year as manager marked a continuation of the financial trends that had been in place for several years. Revenue climbed, but profitability was again modest. The company had an operating profit of $21,169 on revenue of $210,391. The installation of the new dial equipment plus a more-than-25 percent increase in wire mileage during the year ramped up the total investment in plant to more than $700,000 compared to $435,779 at the end of 1952. As the Bob Doyle era was to begin, the company was finally prepared, albeit belatedly, to invest in fixed plant and equipment. But, as had been the case for the previous five years, the company again needed to raise capital or borrow. The first step was the decision to declare another stock dividend and sell more shares than had ever been contemplated prior to that time.

## BILL DOYLE DIVIDES HOLDINGS
## AMONG FIVE CHILDREN

When Bill Doyle decided that son Bob would replace him as president and come on the Board of Directors, there was one small technicality he had over-looked — Bob was not a shareholder yet. "So my dad gave me one share of stock so I could be a member of the board," Doyle recalled.

As it turned out, however, by the time the younger Doyle did formally succeed his father in early 1954, he had already become a major stockholder. This was accomplished through a series of events that occurred in the summer and fall of 1953.

At its August meeting, the Board of Directors declared a one-for-six stock dividend that would be payable on Nov. 1, 1953, the same day the telephone company planned to go on-line with its new dial equipment. It's presumed that this generous dividend was declared in part to make up for the previous year when no dividend was paid. In any event, the stock dividend increased the number of shares outstanding from 30,180 by 5,022 to a total of 35,202 shares.

In addition, between the declaration date of the dividend in August and the end of the year, the company sold another 4,383 shares, both to existing shareholders

*The Doyle family gets together for rare family photo in 1952. It was the last time Bob Doyle, left, would be photographed with long hair. He changed to a crew cut in 1953 and has sported one ever since. In the front, from the left are, Betty (Doyle) Radford, Marjorie (Doyle) Strauch, and Hazel and Bill Doyle. Tom Doyle is in the middle and the late Jack Doyle is on the right.*

Courtesy of Betty Radford

and 20 new shareholders. Among this first wave of new shareholders were chief operator Gladys Ellis, prominent banker M.J. "Joe" Royer, Pacific Fruit Express executive C. Mason Gerhart, auto dealer John Macario and some of the company's employees, including operator Pat Conley Ruggles. A few of the old Italian families of Roseville showed up on this early list of shareholders, too, including Pugliese, Paolucci, Mazzucchi, Bello and Presti. They were the first of thousands of shareholders who would over the years buy stock in Roseville Telephone.

Immediately after the stock dividend was paid, Bill Doyle owned an additional 2,444 shares, bringing his total to 17,107 shares. It was then the elder Doyle, now 78 years old, divided 17,000 shares into five equal blocks of 3,400 shares and distributed them to each of his five children, sons Jack, Bob and Tom, and daughters Marjorie and Betty. Bob Doyle had already been given the single share his dad had promised him earlier. In November 1953, the elder Doyle became a small shareholder in the enterprise he had controlled for 40 years. Bill Doyle now owned 107 shares.

It was Bob Doyle's idea to sell stock to the general public. He convinced a skeptical board and his father that the company needed to raise a lot more money than the board was at that time contemplating, to replace outmoded plant and meet future service needs. Moreover, he requested that the board allow him to try to sell the stock himself rather than sell it through stockbrokers in a customary public offering. If he failed to find buyers for the 10,150 shares the company hoped to sell in 1954, Bob Doyle told the directors he'd agree to bring in brokers to market the shares. Bob Doyle had a grand plan to keep control of Roseville Telephone in local hands even if it meant the Doyle family's ownership position would be diluted in the process.

Roseville Press-Tribune, October 30, 1953

## ROSEVILLE GOES DIAL

It was big news when the Roseville Telephone Company converted to dial service. Finally, this much-maligned local company was modernizing. Customers could now reach the parties they desired by calling them directly rather than going through an operator. There was definitely a sense of nostalgia as well ... an era had passed.

Officially, it was at 12:01 a.m. on Sunday, Nov. 1, 1953, that William J. Doyle made the first dial call to his daughter, Marjorie Strauch. The *Roseville Press-Tribune* gave extensive coverage to the dial conversion with photos and feature stories about what going dial meant to users. In the Friday, Oct. 30, 1953, edition of the *Press-Tribune*, Roseville Telephone ran what was probably its first full-page advertisement. The large, bold type said:

*1. Get the correct number from the current telephone directory.*

*2. Lift the receiver and listen for the "hum" of the dial tone.*

*3. Dial the numbers listed for the party you are calling.*

*4. Let the dial return freely after each letter or figure is dialed.*

*5. If a mistake has been made, hang up for a moment. After hearing the "hum" again — redial.*

*6. For long distance, dial operator.*

The newspaper carried the obligatory article about the mayor throwing the switch to initiate service. The headline read:

## *MAYOR WILL THROW SWITCH TO MARK MILESTONE IN ROSEVILLE'S PROGRESS*

"This Sunday, Nov. 1, is D-Day — dial day" is how the article began. The story called it "… the culmination of the Roseville Telephone Company's $200,000 project for improved phone service … the 'hummm' telephone users will hear on the phone after 12:01 a.m. Sunday will be the dial phone's way of saving: 'Number Please.' "

Roseville mayor Hal Wentworth did the honors at the appointed time and Roseville caught up with the much of the civilized world that had already converted to dial.

The newspaper carried an editorial that welcomed the new service and alluded to the poor service of the past. It is reprinted in its entirety to give a reader a sense for this momentous occasion:

## *ANOTHER STEP FORWARD*

*CONGRATULATIONS CERTAINLY are in order today for the Roseville Telephone company. The switch on Sunday to dials marks another step in Roseville's advancement, and will be a truly welcome thing to the phone subscribers.*

*Yet, as for most anything old that gives way to the new, there's bound to be a touch of sadness in the change. We're probably one of the last cities of this size in the west to install a dial system, and to do away with the switchboard and the operators. The old system has been a trial, many and many a time, and has caused untold numbers*

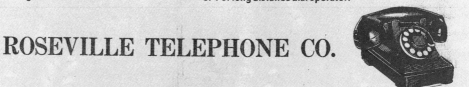

# ROSEVILLE GOES--------DIAL

## On Sunday NOVEMBER 1st
## At 12:01 A. M.

We are proud to have a part in the progress and development of Roseville. The new dial system will enable our patrons to obtain the utmost of service-efficiently and rapidly. To be sure of the best results, however, we have outlined the following steps, which, if followed, will assure you of the service you expect and deserve.

1. Get the correct number from the current telephone directory.

2. Lift the receiver and listen for the "hum" of the dial tone.

3. Dial the numbers listed for the party you are calling.

4. Let the dial return freely after each letter or figure is dialed.

5. If a mistake in dialing has been made, hang up fo a moment. After hearing the "hum" again--redial.

6. For long distance dial operator.

## ROSEVILLE TELEPHONE CO.

October 30, 1953, Roseville Press-Tribune

*of profane words, but still there was something personal about it that now has to give away to the mechanized impersonal.*

*Walter Hanisch, the veteran telephone company manager, likes to recall the times lives have been saved, and aid rushed to the injured or ill, through the alertness of the operators. Many a phone user, lost in the confusion of trying to reach a number, has received help from the girls that will be more difficult to get under the new system. When fires have broken out, the operators went into action to rally the firemen. And then there was the informal, pleasant chit chat that often developed between the caller and the operator, even though the company frowned on such.*

*But mechanization is the need in these modern times, and the old must yield. The advantage — time saving, the easing of wear and tear on the nerves, the feeling of greater privacy — far outweigh the personal touch of the old system. Something badly needed is being added to give Roseville another touch of the modern.*

*Recollections of the early days of Roseville Telephone are discussed by two of the company's operators with longest service. Pictured above at left is Sybil Moore, night operator, who has been with the company for more than 28 years. With her is Mrs. Gladys Ellis, right, head operator with service dating back to 1925.*

Roseville Press-Tribune, October 30, 1953

*The Press-Tribune also carried a story about what would happen to the operators and a feature on the history of dial service in telephony. Throughout the pages of the newspaper were brief tips on how to use the new-fangled equipment. One such "tip" for callers was the following: "ATTENTION: Listen attentively. This eliminates the annoyance of repetition. If the other party is speaking at length, indicate your attentiveness by an occasional word."*

Not everybody was happy because the conversion to dial was accompanied by a stiff increase in telephone rates. As the *Press-Tribune* reported, "Roseville residents will get the good with the bad this Sunday, Nov. 1 … While the long-awaited dial system will be put into operation by the Roseville Telephone Company, new rates will go into effect starting the same day to finance the cost of the $200,000 project …"

Basic residential service went from $2.60 a month for a one-party desk phone to $4; two-party desk phones went from $2.35 to $3.50, and four-party service climbed from $2.10 per month to $3. Business rates were slightly higher. "Coin box stations," as pay phones were called then, went from a nickel to a dime.

The conversion to dial was greeted with a substantial boost in calls made that first day and for the succeeding weeks as residents got the hang of using dial. About 30,000 calls were made that first Sunday, according to written reports.

Although Roseville residents and businesses were elated to go dial, some of the farmer-line customers were in no such rush. They refused to be converted, which meant they had to be accommodated through the old manual switchboard. This continued until the telephone company acquired the farmer lines and converted those on the lines to dial service.

## BOB DOYLE INVESTS IN 'EXECUTIVE TRAINING'

As the heir apparent to be president and manager of the Roseville Telephone Company, Bob Doyle decided he'd better invest in "executive education." He enrolled in a Dale Carnegie course being given in Sacramento.

"I figured, Christ, if there was one thing that I could not stand to do, that was to get up in front of people and speak ... talk. For example, if there was a book report in high school to give and it was supposed to be oral, I would miss school that day and either write it or not do it at all. I suffered from stage fright," Doyle recalled. "But I figured, if I am going to be the president and try to do something with this company, I'd have to learn to get up in front of people. So I took the Dale Carnegie course and paid for it myself."

When Bill Doyle informed the Board of Directors in 1953 that after nearly 40 years he was stepping down as president and nominating his son to fill the vacancy and also become the manager, the members were not unanimous in their support of Bob Doyle being elected to the positions.

"So it was really a split decision," Bob Doyle remembered. "But there were enough of them who wanted to see a change that I did become the president."

Bob Doyle believes the older members of the board didn't have confidence a 34-year-old fellow with less than six months experience in telephony had enough knowledge to run the company, even as small as it was then.

"These guys were all old-timers and they had lived back when you earned a dollar a day. My dad was born in 1875 and those guys were all virtually back to that era. I was 34 years old and they thought that I was just a fat ass kid ... they thought I was too young to know anything. In truth, I didn't know anything, but it wasn't because I was too young ... I just didn't know anything."

After agreeing to elect Bob Doyle president and manager of the Roseville Telephone Company, the next decision was what to pay him. The senior Doyle was earning a fee of $100 a month at that time, but he didn't work at the company in any operational capacity. Bob Doyle recounted the discussion about his pay.

"They asked me, 'What do you earn now?' and I replied '$200 a month.' That's when old L.C. Anderson asked, 'Walter, what the hell do you make?' Walter didn't respond because he really didn't know. 'You mean to tell me you don't know what you're making?' And one of them said, 'Well, how about giving him $350?' But L.C. piped in, 'I think he ought to get $400 a month for being president.' So they doubled my wages. But I couldn't blame those old guys, they were used to a dollar a day. You get a bunch of old guys like that that have been raised on the farm and out here in the area where nothing was really going on, and they thought $400 was crazy. You don't pay people that much money. Who the hell's worth $400?"

Bob Doyle had to earn the respect of the older directors, particularly Etzel and Baker. The Hanisch, Etzel and Baker families had been close through the years, often vacationing together and spending holidays at each other's houses.

"Etzel was a good Mason and so was old Walter Hanisch and David Hanisch. My dad wasn't in the Masons. But on my mother's side, there was a lot of them in the Masons. So anyway, Etzel didn't like me at first," Doyle explained. "But somebody got to him because not long after he came to me and said, 'Can I talk to you for a minute?' That's when he told me that he really didn't know what was going on at the company. He apologized because before he didn't believe me. I'll never forget that, it made me feel pretty good, because he was a smart man. He was the head of the whole Pacific Fruit Express. His office was in San Francisco and he lived in Oakland, but he ran this whole deal up here, the ice plant and the whole thing. He would come up on the train for the board meeting and then he'd go back on the train. Etzel never missed a board meeting. But the poor guy, the only way he'd know what was going on, he'd come up here and get together with the Hanisches and they'd probably talk about the Masonic lodge. But when I first came in here, he was dead on my ass. Having turned Etzel around, I then had Baker to convert."

Bob Doyle went to Baker's house to talk to him and the old director wouldn't let him in. Shortly thereafter, Baker got ahold of him and asked him to come back. "It was his wife," Doyle recalled. "I think she gave him a real chewin'. She knew what was happening at the company. Well, when I got there he let me in and we had a good talk. I convinced him we needed to do something because people weren't getting the service."

*Charles A. Baker was a long-time director and secretary/treasurer. He stepped down in late 1953 and was replaced by L. C. Anderson.*

The elder Doyle didn't help his son in dealing with the old-timers. "I had to convince him, too," Bob Doyle remembered. "F.A. Lewis was the best one of the bunch. Everybody in town knew about how bad things were, but they weren't on the board. When Baker figured out what was happening, he resigned from the board and let L.C. Anderson take over. Baker knew L.C. would do something about the mess. Then I had things starting to go my way."

"I think my father had expected that David Hanisch would take over and probably wanted that since our families were close growing up," remembered Marguerite Smart, Roy Etzel's older daughter. "The telephone company was Walter's whole life, but when Mr. Doyle told them Bob would be taking over as president, I think Walter kind of withdrew from the thing. It was about that same time my dad finally realized that the Hanisches couldn't do what was necessary to make the company grow and that they wouldn't hire anybody else to do it either. That was one thing about the Hanisches, they thought if they couldn't do something, it couldn't be done. Bob Doyle, of course, said he'd hire people that knew something about the business."

"I remember my father telling my sister and me to stick with Bob Doyle because he was a planner and had good vision," added Etzel's younger daughter, Betty Benedetti. "My father told us he thought the telephone company would do well under Bob Doyle even though Bob did have to prove himself at first."

## ROBERT L. DOYLE BECOMES PRESIDENT AND MANAGER

On Jan. 23, 1954, Bob Doyle took over the reins of president from his father. He also took over the title of "manager" from Walter Hanisch, who was appointed a vice president. It didn't take long for Bob Doyle to begin his drive to "make this the best goddamn telephone company there is." That was his goal then and it remains his goal today.

While it's true Bob Doyle didn't know much about the mechanical aspects of the business, he recognized immediately that Roseville Telephone did not possess the expertise to solve the numerous problems it faced and build for the future. Relying upon his intuitive management abilities — because certainly none was learned in schools — Doyle set about to solve the problems that had plagued the company for decades and to build a forward, progressive and modern telephone company. Doyle understood that to reach his objectives, he had to bring in experienced telephone people, raise enough funds to replace the antiquated plant and equipment and continue to modernize in an effort to keep up with a fast-growing population.

Doyle still laughs about how helpful the Dale Carnegie course was to him. "The full course took about seven months because I can remember getting up in front of the class and telling others in the room that as far as I was concerned, there was nothing like the Dale Carnegie course. I said, 'When I started this Dale Carnegie program, I was a janitor at the Roseville Telephone Company ... I haven't even completed the course yet and now I am the goddamned president!' So I said, 'You've got to say that the Dale Carnegie course has done a lot for Bob Doyle.'"

*Bob Doyle as new president in 1954.*

# Doyle's Commitment To Growth

INTERSTATE 80, FOLSOM DAM BRING THE PEOPLE

*"I always felt that my job was to find people smarter than I am, leave them alone and get out of their way. Put them in the right place, encourage them, make sure they work together."*
— Bob Doyle

Two significant developments in the mid-1950s were to transform Roseville from a one-horse, bawdy railroad town into a fast-growing, medium-sized city in the northeast sector of the booming Sacramento metropolitan area. One was the extension of U.S. Highway 40 (later re-named Interstate 80) from Sacramento to Roseville. When the freeway — which bisected the old Doyle ranch — opened, it meant workers in Sacramento could enjoy an easy 20-minute commute to the bedroom communities of Roseville, Citrus Heights, Antelope and Orangevale in the telephone company's service area. With the suburbanites came commercial, retail and industrial expansion to serve their needs.

The second major development was the construction of Folsom Dam in 1948-1956, which created Folsom Lake on Roseville Telephone's southeastern border. The dam not only protected Sacramento from winter storms and summer thirst, but it became a major recreational attraction. It made all the land around Folsom Lake much more attractive for development. This led to almost continuous growth near the lake. Much of this population growth would occur within Roseville Telephone's service territory.

And, of course, the state government kept expanding. Those state workers who enjoyed a more rural or suburban life found that in the northeast suburbs of Sacramento. No doubt about it, growth was going to occur in the company's territory; it was just a question of how fast it would happen.

Since joining the company in 1953, Bob Doyle always believed the area's growth would exceed most people's expectations. His management decisions reflected this. In exact opposite fashion to his predecessors, Doyle instructed his managers to build more fixed plant than they thought they'd need in the foreseeable future. He had a rule of thumb.

"The outside plant engineering people would tell me what they thought we needed, and I'd almost always say, 'Yeah, we need that, but add about 50 percent more capacity than you think, because we'll need it.' I must have been lucky

*Construction of Folsom Dam began on
Oct. 12, 1948, and was completed on
March 14, 1956. It began generating
electric power on May 20, 1955.*

Courtesy of U.S. Bureau of Reclamation

because I was usually right. Doing it right the first time meant we didn't have to go back and put in more cable in areas we had just been in. I did that all the time. Add 50 percent to what you come up with, I'd tell them."

Doyle's job when he took over the presidency was more than just learning the ropes of running a telephone company. First on a long list of priorities was to begin replacing the shoddy outside fixed plant the company had built over the years. Most of the Roseville Telephone outside plant consisted of "open wire" and miles and miles of "drop wire." Telephone companies at that time were installing cable, usually sheathed in lead. The benefits were obvious. You could get a lot of wire pairs inside a cable, and being inside a closed sheathing protected the wires from the elements, particularly moisture.

"They had what was called ringed-cut wires back then and every time it would rain, the service would go out because the water would get in there. It was terrible," Doyle remembered.

So Doyle had on his plate the need to replace substandard existing plant, plan for and add new fixed outside plant, add more switching capacity to the central office to keep up with growth, develop a management team of experienced telephone people, and raise money to pay for it all. This was the situation that faced the 34-year-old farmer whose only management experience had been toiling with his brothers to develop a prosperous farming business. He'd never taken any management classes and through the years never did. He was too busy being successful in implementing the management techniques that business school professors try to teach. Bob Doyle's skills were obviously intuitive, because he did most things correctly from the very beginning. A student of common sense and an observer of his father's business affairs, Doyle put into practice what he now calls his "Baseball Management" philosophy.

## DOYLE MANAGES COMPANY LIKE A BASEBALL TEAM

In the late 1930s and early 1940s, Bob Doyle was regarded as one of the better baseball players in the Roseville/Auburn area. He even had a tryout with the Cincinnati Reds. His timing, however, was poor. Just as he was at his baseball peak, Uncle Sam called him to play on a military field. But Doyle's love for baseball paid off in his business life. From the the beginning of his career at the telephone company, it occurred to Doyle that running a company isn't a lot different than managing a baseball team. And although he knew nothing about the telephone business, he did know a lot about baseball.

"I tried to think of my job as manager as if I was managing a baseball team," Doyle said. "I learned more on a baseball diamond than I ever learned in

*Folsom Dam with five of its gates lowered to release runoff after a heavy storm. In 1955, although not completed, Folsom Dam saved the Sacramento area from potentially disastrous flooding. It has saved the area from flooding several times since.*

Courtesy of U.S. Bureau of Reclamation

school. I learned how to win, I learned how to lose and how to work together. And it's the same in business, it seemed to me. Put the people in the right place and leave them alone.

"I've always said that my job is to hire people smarter than I am. Maybe people think I'm joking about that, but I'm not. I always felt that my job was to find people smarter than I am and then leave them alone. Get out of their way. Put them in the right place, encourage them, make sure they work together.

"You put the second baseman on second base, the catcher behind the plate and the pitcher on the mound. If you put the pitcher in right field and the catcher on second base and the shortstop behind the plate, you're not going to win very many ball games. So you put the people where they want to work or where they like to work, encourage 'em and make sure that they have the same attitude. That's real important.

*Folsom Lake attracted new residents into Roseville Telephone's service territory. In addition to recreation, Folsom Lake provides water supplies for irrigation, domestic, municipal, industrial, and power production purposes. The dam controls the American River east of Sacramento.*

Courtesy of U.S. Bureau of Reclamation

"I told my supervisors the same thing. 'Hire people smarter than you are because your responsibility as a supervisor is to see that the job gets done. And the only way it's going to get done is to get some people to do it. Unless you want to do it yourself. And you can't go too far doing it all yourself.' So from the beginning, that approach is what I believed to be the secret of successful managing. And I told my people that.

"Hell, if I went out there to install a pay telephone, I'd probably put the damned thing in upside down ... the money wouldn't stay in it. But I've made sure that the guy that goes out there knows how to install that pay telephone so the money stays in it."

In early 1954, when Doyle became president, he may have had his baseball theory of management, but he didn't have a team. He had no players who knew a lot about the telephone business, other than perhaps David Hanisch, who was not a team player. And although Hanisch knew a lot about the old manual switchboards, he was no expert in dial systems. Doyle had no other trustworthy managers in place other than Gladys Ellis, the reliable veteran chief operator who had toiled nearly 30 years under the Hanisches.

As much as Bob Doyle might have wanted to replace David Hanisch at the very start of 1954, he didn't feel it was the right thing to do.

"There was no reason he couldn't have made a good employee, if he'd wanted to," Doyle explained. "But I learned he didn't want to. He was just one of those bullheaded guys and you weren't going to change him."

On the other hand, Walter Hanisch was helpful and supportive of Bob Doyle after Doyle became president and manager. "It turned out Walter was really a nice old guy. Whenever I wanted to do something after that, at the board meetings Walter would be the first one to say, 'Yes, I think we should do that.' He was behind me all the way."

If one of Bob Doyle's first agendas was to "clean house," there wasn't much of a house to clean. "Just about all we had then were operators," he recalled. "There may have been a few men around, but the company was mostly made up of operators." Doyle was correct in his recollection. Of the company's 47 employees, there were only eight men, including both Hanisches.

## A FARMER WOOS THE FARMERS

One of Doyle's first objectives was to figure out how to acquire the farmer lines that served most of the areas outside Roseville. Getting these lines was important. The farmer lines represented what could have been long-term competition to Roseville Telephone because they were in effect telephone cooperatives owned

*When Roseville Telephone acquired several "farmer lines" in its territory in 1957, the company had to put new wire, cable and poles throughout much of its service territory.*

Photos by Merle Ruggles

by the families on the lines. These users owned their own telephones and all their own wires and poles, as bad as they were. They only paid a minimal rate to tie into the telephone company. Of course, they paid for their toll calls. But Doyle saw that if the farmers got together and invested in better outside plant and equipment, they would never need Roseville Telephone for anything other than a connection to the outside world. For that they would pay low connection rates for all time. That scenario did play out in other large farming areas served by independent telephone companies throughout the Central Valley of California and in other states with large farming communities.

Although the farmer lines served fewer than 400 customers in the early 1950s, had the farmers improved their system, they could have added new residents to their lines rather than having them become direct Roseville Telephone subscribers. If Roseville Telephone didn't succeed in merging the farmer lines into its network, the potential to lose enormous future revenue was there.

To minimize that possibility, Doyle knew he had two courses of action to take. The first was to get new wires and cables to these outlying areas as fast as possible so he could offer newly-arrived residents service superior to farmer lines. Simultaneously, it was critical to purchase these lines and bring them into the expanding Roseville Telephone grid.

"I went out to meet with the farmers to explain that with our switching to dial their 12-and 14-party farmer lines wouldn't work anymore — the maximum we could get on them was eight parties," Doyle explained. "I told them that we couldn't use their outside plant, that we'd have to tear it all out and replace it with new cable and poles and such. The only thing we could use was the telephone instrument itself. I think we offered them about $35. That's all the telephone was worth."

Doyle's early efforts to acquire farmer lines went nowhere, which made it imperative that the company immediately begin investing in plant and equipment to be able to serve Citrus Heights and after that the Folsom Lake areas. It was a race that Roseville Telephone must win or forever be doomed to be a small company.

The effort to buy the lines began even before Doyle became president. "That wasn't an easy thing, because you went out there and as far as the farmers were concerned, with their own telephones and wires and stuff, they had a bigger investment than the $35 we were offering," Doyle said.

"All they had to do is to say, 'The hell with ya' and put up their own plant, which they could have done. They could've continued to pay us just one dollar a month. And maintain their own plant ... and there are some places down the valley where that happened. They had some guys that knew something, probably worked at telephone companies or something. They went out and put up some good plant. That's what I was up against. I was sweating bullets. I didn't know if I'd get them ... But I was always hoping ... I guess it's the luck of the Irish, but I was just lucky. It just seemed that about the time I would be ready to give up, it would happen. We finally got them."

It would be three years after he became president before Doyle finally was able to purchase the farmer lines. It turned out that Doyle's consummate skill as a stock salesman was what finally turned the balance in the company's favor.

## DOYLE'S REAL ESTATE ACUMEN SPEEDS EXPANSION

In 40 years, the Roseville Telephone Company owned only its small main office and the maintenance/construction shop down the street. It owned no other land or buildings. Immediately upon becoming president, Doyle set out to acquire real estate to use for future growth. At first, he acquired properties adjacent or near the headquarters office. Within a few years, he also acquired parcels that would hold future telephone buildings to fulfill Doyle's determination to serve the entire 83-square-mile territory, not just a fraction of it. And as might be expected, Doyle negotiated the real estate purchases himself and didn't use a broker.

"When we bought property around here, hell we never really used real estate outfits until just the last three or four purchases," Doyle said. "Always before then, I just contacted the owner or owners myself. We'd make a deal, go to the title company and get it done. Some of the parcels we purchased way ahead of time. As I've probably told people a hundred times, I bought all the properties that I'll ever need and no one is going to hold up old Bob Doyle."

The first property Doyle picked up in 1954 was the adjacent building north of the company's offices on Lincoln Street. It housed the old Welcome Club and a hotel on the second story. The next one was on the other side of the office, south on Lincoln Street, which was owned by long-time director Charlie Baker. The purchase was for $20,000, $5,000 down and $5,000 each year for three years at 5 percent interest. Baker's property housed the Pall Mall club, a bar, and offices upstairs, including that of director L.C. Anderson, an attorney and Doyle's key adviser the first year of his presidency. After that, Doyle bought

*The old Welcome Club was one of the many bars for Roseville patrons to visit. The building to its right was Roseville Telephone's main office in the early 1950s.*

**FROM BAR TO BELLS** *July 1956*

**Former Hotel Taken Over By Telephone Co.**

*"New Face — As part of its expansion program, the Roseville Telephone Company is putting a new face on this building at Lincoln and Atlantic. The company, now doing business in the one-story building at the right, found its quarters too cramped for its growing operation, and will move a portion of its equipment into the larger building when remodeling is completed in October. The site was formerly used as a bar and a hotel."*

Roseville Press-Tribune, July 1956

property across the street on the northwest corner of Atlantic and Lincoln streets.

While these purchases prepared the company for future growth of the Roseville central office and headquarters offices, one of Doyle's first priorities was to find a suitable piece of property in Citrus Heights for a new central office. The company needed a central office there to be able to give that area "baseline service" with one-, two- and four-party service rather than eight-party "suburban" service. The longer the distance from a central office, the less service the company could give. Central offices are strategically placed through its service area to put switching capabilities within a few miles of any user. This improves service.

In Citrus Heights, Doyle knew of a parcel of land that would be ideal, on Old Auburn Road near Mariposa Avenue. The real estate broker, Tom Pugh of Pugh and Barbieri, was having a difficult time selling the parcel, however, because an elderly woman, Lizzie Blake, lived in a house in the middle of the property. Pugh had made a deal in 1941, allowing Blake to live out her life in the house. Obviously, this made the parcel hard to sell. The broker figured the woman would die soon enough and then he could sell the property.

"Well, she had no intention of dying and seemed determined to outlast the broker," Doyle said. "So I went to the woman and told her we wanted to build on the back portion of the property. She could stay in her house as long as she wanted. In fact, I told her it would be good for her to be there to kind of watch over our central office."

So Doyle acquired a little more than an acre there and later added to it by buying connected parcels. The cost of his initial purchase was only $3,600.

Another example of Doyle's real estate creativity is his purchase of two acres on Barton Road in Granite Bay that now holds the Folsom Lake central office and warehouse. He bought the property in 1958, but it wasn't until 1962 that the central office was constructed.

The property was owned by an electrical contractor, Tom Owen, and his wife Eleanor. Doyle explained, "I had known his wife … Eleanor Keehner was her name. She was born and raised in Roseville down the street from us and I knew her all her life. So I asked Tom if he wanted to sell two acres of their piece of property. He said no, but it wasn't really him saying no. It turned out his wife didn't want to sell. He said, 'I wouldn't mind, Bob, but Eleanor, she won't sell anything.' And, I said, 'Well, we got to get a location around here some place and that would be a good place.' We talked some more and agreed that if it could happen, that $8,000 would be the price."

Then Doyle added a wrinkle to his offer. "I said, 'you know something, I'm selling stock right now. Why don't you tell Eleanor that I'll trade you $8,000 worth of stock for your property.' Hell, she could have got the $8,000 and turned around and bought stock, same difference. But, anyway, for some reason that approach rang her bell. He came back and said, 'She said OK.' So that's how I bought that piece of property."

Eleanor explained why she opted for the land/stock trade rather than taking cash or buying stock outright with the money. "I knew if we got cash, it would go into our business, and I didn't think we should put more money into the business at that time. I thought it would be better to get stock," she recalled. "Although I figured the stock was going to be good over the long haul, I didn't think at the time we could afford to pay cash for it. But if we could buy it like that ... trade land for stock, that was great. It was also a factor that Bob said he'd take the two acres on the back end, that made it easier, too."

After remodeling in late 1956, the old Welcome Club became an office building, housing several Roseville Telephone departments.

The eventual deal was struck on Oct. 31, 1958. The Owens received 667 shares valued at $12 apiece, or $8,004.

"Through the years, Eleanor has been a happy stockholder. They purchased more through the years ... Her husband has passed away, but it all started with the sale of that piece of property," Doyle said.

Bob Doyle remains a student of the land. Every morning before coming to work he drives around the territory scouting for evidence of dirt being turned or chalk marks drawn on the ground to indicate imminent construction. After lunch, he often does another brief tour. He knows the stage of all developments in the region. Bob Parsons, the company's director of customer services, has been along on many of Doyle's real estate scouting missions.

"He'll see a truck go by and if it's empty, he wants to know where it came from," Parsons said. "If it's full, he wants to know where it's going. If they're blacktop or cement trucks and if there are more than one or two, we're going to follow that and find out, if they're empty, where they came from, and where they're going if they're full. He'll stay with it, if it takes an hour we're going to find out. It doesn't usually take that long. Once he gets there, he can see they're either digging out a basement area for a big building and hauling that dirt away or they're filling in a road. He's taught me to keep my eyes open for those trucks coming and going. Then you know what's going on.

"Also, I think he's got some kind of a extrasensory perception when it comes to chalk marks for footings and foundations. We can go to a very remote area and he'll start weaving in and around what's going to be the road for that subdivision," Parsons continued. "We'll get out there and he'll say, 'Hell, look, they have been out here today. There are three foundations today on this street and two over there.' But how does he know? When they chalk for a foundation, it's within a few days of actually doing the work. And for him to be right on time … he hasn't told me that secret. I accuse of him smelling chalk."

Doyle is also willing to share his real estate expertise, when asked.

"I remember not too many years ago a fellow asked Bob Doyle what he thought about putting a warehouse out on Douglas Boulevard," said Parsons. "Well, Bob is the wrong guy to ask about a warehouse because he's in the telephone business, and how many phones do you have in a warehouse? So he's going to think of something else. 'How about putting up a commercial building,' Doyle suggested, 'and then lease out the spots?' Then all the tenants have to have a phone system for their own business.

"So part of Doyle's thinking was related to the number of phones that would be needed, but at the same time he didn't give the guy bad advice," Parsons added. "Douglas Boulevard is prime property and that guy's land was suited to a much higher use than a warehouse. So Bob gave the guy the right advice, but it sure didn't hurt the telephone company any either."

Doyle's understanding of the development process enabled him to complement his engineering department in arriving at plans for future growth. His knowledge of the area allowed him to intelligently question his engineers' assumptions about growth. Clearly, Bob Doyle didn't sit at his desk all day. He knew his territory better than anybody else. And he still does.

# Selling Stock On The Phone

## DOYLE DECIDES TO SELL STOCK WITHOUT BROKER

*"This is Bob Doyle. I'm working for the Roseville Telephone Company now and we're trying to straighten this goddamn company out. I'm selling some stock and it's $10 a share. I'd like to have you as a new stockholder."*
— Bob Doyle (1953-54)

Bob Doyle's name came to be virtually synonymous with Roseville Telephone. But before he became president in 1954, he had no experience of any kind in managing people, corporate planning, engineering or corporate finance. He did know something about debt — he was in it over his rather large ears during the "Doyle Brothers" years of farming.

Although the Doyle name meant something in Roseville, no one could have guessed that Bob Doyle would become a master stock salesman who over the years has sold millions of dollars worth of stock. Few standard-issue stockbrokers probably have ever sold as much stock as Bob Doyle. The big difference, of course, is that for all these years Doyle has sold only one stock — Roseville Telephone.

"The first time I sold stock actually was before I became president," recalled Bob Doyle. "I told the board that we had to do something for the people out there. We had automobile dealers on four-party lines. We had people that couldn't even get a phone although they lived in Roseville. I said we're giving them terrible service and that we'd need money to do the job. They asked me what to do and I suggested we sell stock. They talked about using brokers, and I said, 'Hell with the brokers. Damn it, I'll try to sell it myself, and if I can't, then we'll use brokers.'

"So the board gave me the green light and let me go ahead and do it. Even though I wasn't the president, I figured I knew everybody in Roseville. And I would call the automobile dealers, guys who owned the retail stores, service station guys ... everybody in town that I knew. I'd say, 'This is Bob Doyle. I'm working for the Roseville Telephone Company now and we're trying to straighten this goddamn company out. And we're trying to raise some money, so I'm selling some stock and it's $10 a share. I'd like to have you as a new stockholder.' Well, they'd say, 'Hell yeah, I'll take 100 shares or 200.' Some would say, 'Well, let me think about it.' I don't think out of all the people I called ... I don't

---

## Phone Firm Is Authorized To Sell Stock

The Roseville Telephone Co. has been authorized by the state Public Utilities Commission to issue 55,000 shares of common stock at a par value of $10 each.

The issuance, authorized at the request of the telephone company, will be for "plant additions, improvements and betterments to meet the increased demand for telephone service."

Five thousand of the new shares will be issued to present shareholders as a dividend, on the basis of one new share for each 10 outstanding shares. In making this distribution, the telephone company will transfer $50,000 from its surplus account to the capital stock account.

These shares will be issued before Dec. 31, according to the PUC ruling. The remaining 50,000 new shares will be sold before Dec. 31, 1958.

In applying for authority to issue new stock, the local telephone company stated it has invested approximately $1,400,000 in the plant, as of April 30. The common stock equity capital is listed at $598,833 and outstanding long-term debt is calculated at $813,000.

Capital expenditures by the Roseville company during 1957 were estimated at $325,500, according to the application. The 1958 estimate is $292,000, and the company plans to invest $403,000 in 1959.

*Roseville Press-Tribune, June 1957*

*Stock certificate used in the years 1914-1953.*

think really anybody turned me down because, hell, they wanted better service, too. They'd do anything to see it get better. It ended up ... I sold the whole issue, over $100,000, just about all of it on the telephone."

One new shareholder was Doulton Burner, who was to become a good friend of Bob and Tom Doyle and a director in the company. He owned the retail credit bureau in Roseville and Auburn at that time. Bob Doyle did not know Burner then.

"My office was right down the street from the phone company office, up over what is the Riolo Club now," Burner recalled. "And I just had myself and two women employees. So one day, Bob Doyle came walking up the steps there, and let me know he was selling stock in the telephone company," Burner remembered. "It was $10 a share and I had $1,100 in the bank, which at that time was plenty. But I bought $500 worth and my wife has chewed me out ever since that I didn't buy the whole $1,100. You know what that's worth today — many, many times what we paid for it."

Doyle's decision to try and sell the stock himself was naive at best, nervy at the least. He didn't know a thing about selling stock, and at that point he knew as little about the company. And certainly he knew nothing about the telephone business. Doyle simply had faith in his own ability to sell and the company's ability to eventually perform for its new shareholders.

From the outset, however, he was selective about his stockholders. He was determined that as long as the Doyle family's stake was going to be diluted over time, he would do his best to keep ownership in local hands. Also, he believed it would be an excellent incentive if employees owned a good share of the company as well. To him this approach was good common sense, that people in the community and employees be the ones to benefit from a growing telephone company that served the region. It wasn't as if the headquarters office was in San Francisco, Chicago, or New York City. The top people at Roseville Telephone would remain in Roseville and keep the benefits of ownership local. That became Doyle's grand plan, although he probably didn't have it well formulated at the time.

"I purposely didn't look to sell the shares outside of town," Doyle recalled. "Mostly I sold 100 or 200 shares at a time, but sometimes 25 and even 10. If somebody local came in here, someone I knew real well, I might sell more, say $5,000-$10,000 worth. But if it was somebody who came in here and I didn't even know the person, I might not even sell one share.

"I actually had people come in who would ask me a bunch of questions," he added. "That might make me real suspicious. Then just as they started to ask more questions, I'd say, 'You know, come to think of it, I don't think I want to sell you any shares.'"

According to Tom Doyle, the Doyle family name helped the stock sales in the beginning. "Nobody else could have sold the stock then but a Doyle, because the Doyles had been here forever. People in Roseville believed in the Doyles, so even though Bob didn't know that much about the telephone business, people figured Hanisch wouldn't do anything, but a Doyle would. So the business people all would buy a little bit of stock on the expectation that Bob was going to do something to improve service. And it happened. But it wasn't easy."

In retrospect, the fact that Bob Doyle knew nothing about selling stock was an advantage. "By not knowing anything, it was an advantage to me," Bob Doyle said, "because everything was a challenge. I just thought, hell I could sell it, and that's what I did."

In 1953 and 1954, Doyle sold 10,415 shares netting the company $104,150 in new capital. At the end of 1954, there were 105 shareholders who together owned 50,000 shares. Of them, 89 listed their primary residence as Roseville, eight lived in Sacramento, three in Citrus Heights and one each in Loomis, San Francisco, Tracy, Vallejo and Oakland. The out-of-towners had strong links to Roseville, primarily family.

Those early shareholders represented a "who's who" of the Roseville community in the early 1950s, including prominent business owners and engineers at the railroad. Names of some of the new shareholders included Pulse, Macario, Dunn, Boston, Erskine, Epling, Hunzeker, Lauppe, Gigax, Paolini, Arnold, Braden, Erickson, Lonergan, Lasick, Peer, Mahan, Minard, Peck, Pugliese, Royer, Gerhart, Brady, Gordon, Palmer, Hubbard, Garbolino and Palmer. Of course, the Doyle family remained the largest shareholder group, but the first public stock sales cut their ownership from more than 50 percent to about 35 percent.

INCORPORATED UNDER THE LAWS OF
The State of California, June 20, 1914

No. 13200

Shares

# ROSEVILLE TELEPHONE CO.

CAPITAL STOCK $5,000,000    500,000 SHARES

Principal Place of Business, Roseville, California

THIS CERTIFIES THAT

is the owner of

Shares of the Capital Stock of

ROSEVILLE TELEPHONE CO.

transferable only on the books of the Corporation by the holder hereof in person or by Attorney upon surrender of this certificate properly endorsed

In Witness Whereof, the said Corporation has caused this certificate to be signed by its duly authorized officers and to be sealed with the seal of the Corporation this _____ day of _____ A.D. 19__

Secretary

President

SHARES $10.00 EACH

© GOES 53

*Stock certificate used in the years 1953-1970.*

One of the happiest members of the earliest shareholders was Gladys Ellis, the long-time chief operator. "I asked Mr. Hanisch for a long, long time to sell me stock. I wanted it for years. Finally, I bought some." Gladys and her late husband, Homer, purchased 600 shares in 1953.

Other than Gladys, there were only a few employees who bought stock in that first public issue, including Art Williams and Pat (Ruggles) Conley. While a few other employees purchased stock from other stockholders after 1955, it wasn't until the second public stock sale in 1957 that the payroll deduction plan started with most employees participating.

## DOYLE SHUNS REA FINANCING

In the early 1950s, Roseville Telephone was not alone in its need to raise capital. Smaller "rural" telephone companies throughout the United States were in similar straits — their service territories were experiencing rapid growth and they needed capital to satisfy that growth. The federal government helped such companies in these years by expanding the lending authority of the Rural Electrification Administration (REA) to include telephone companies. REA was originally set up to help bring electricity to rural areas by making low-cost loans to power providers serving those areas.

The availability of "REA money," as it was called at the time, was a boon to small independents because the interest rate was only 2 percent in the mid-'50s. Many telephone companies, including large independents, took advantage of REA money at that time. Had Bob Doyle agreed to take REA money, the Doyle family today likely would own an appreciably larger percentage of the company. But borrowing money from the government was against the principles of the fiercely independent Bob Doyle.

Soon after becoming president, a few members on the Board of Directors learned from a Roseville banker that the independent telephone exchange in Colfax had borrowed REA money. The directors pressured Doyle to meet with an REA representative to discuss the feasibility of Roseville Telephone lining up some of this low-cost financing. Doyle didn't relish the idea, but agreed to follow through.

"I was just named president about that time so when the board says, 'Why don't we look into this,' I couldn't very well say, 'Go dip your right eye in shit,'" Doyle remembered. "Anyway, this guy from the REA comes and gives me his pitch. He's talkin' and talkin' and I can't get rid of him.

"'In the first place,' I told him, 'I can get my own money. The REA is for companies that can't borrow money, the rural companies that are out in the boondocks. And that's what REA is for...' He interrupts me and says, 'Oh, yes, you qualify.' I said, 'Hell, we're 15 miles from Sacramento ... you call that rural?' Then he says, 'But look, there's nothing here. It's all farms.' So now I'm getting mad and said, 'That doesn't make any goddamned difference. I know that I can go and borrow money, so therefore the government shouldn't be giving me money at 2 percent because somebody else is helping pay out of their pocket to run the Roseville Telephone Company. It's coming out of their taxes and I don't believe in that. It's not right.'

"Everybody else was grabbing it because it was easy, and they spent more money than they needed because they got it cheap and there wasn't anybody to watch them," Doyle said. "So I told the guy we didn't want any government money."

At the next Board of Directors meeting, Doyle reported on his meeting with the REA official and convinced the directors that REA was not the way to go for Roseville Telephone.

"I said, 'Why should we get involved with the damned government? I can raise the money and we'll be free and clear of the government.' So I convinced them that we didn't have to. But this REA guy came back again, if you could believe it! And I told him, 'You know something, we don't qualify ... I've told you we don't qualify. I don't want any REA money, and I'll tell you something else ... I don't want to see you back in this office again. If you come back, I'm going to throw you through that door next time. I don't want your goddamned government money!'

## Phone Firm Notes Are Authorized

Roseville Telephone Company was granted permission by the State Public Utilities Commission yesterday to issue $300,000 in notes in order to keep up with the growth of the Roseville area.

The notes, which will be purchased by the Pacific Mutual Life Insurance Company, bring the phone company's obligation to the insurance company to $920,000. They are in the form of a second supplemental mortgage and loan agreement.

In granting the application, the commission pointed to the growth of the company since 1951. Telephones in service increased from 2,851 to 4,921 in 1955. Value of the telephone plant skyrocketed from $278,358 in 1951 to $1,072,818 as a result of the company's modernization drive.

Explaining its approval, the commission states "it appears that the applicant has need for additional funds, that the insurance company is willing to make such funds available on reasonable terms and that the earnings of the applicant appear sufficient to meet the fixed charges the additional debt financing will impose."

The new notes would be payable in 1982 at 4¾ per cent interest.

**IMPROVEMENTS LISTED**

Some of the proposed additions to the plant are a new line truck, $14,700; 2,000 new telephones, $56,000; 10 public pay booths and phones, $59,490; Dial equipment for the Roseville office, $9,380; two-position test board for Roseville office, $7,555; balance due on new business office, $20,000; office equipment and furniture for business office, $10,000; new central dial office in Citrus Heights, $50,000; cables for central dial of-

Sacramento Bee, June 1957

**ROSEVILLE TELEPHONE COMPANY**

INCORPORATED UNDER THE LAWS OF THE STATE OF CALIFORNIA JUNE 20, 1914

NUMBER 151500

COMMON

This certifies that ___ is the record holder of

fully paid and non-assessable shares, of the common stock of ROSEVILLE TELEPHONE COMPANY transferable on the books of the Company by the holder hereof in person or by duly authorized attorney upon surrender of this certificate properly endorsed.

WITNESS the seal of the Corporation and the signatures of its duly authorized officers.

Dated:

*Thomas E. Doyle* SECRETARY

*Robert L. Doyle* PRESIDENT

*Stock certificate used in the years 1970-present.*

"So we stayed away from government money. We did it the hard way. Anytime you do something easy, it's because it's usually the wrong way. Hell, I could have borrowed government money at 2 percent, all the money I wanted. Why have the government own your company? I can't understand it," Doyle continued. "Companies that borrow from the government don't have stockholders that can kick them out ... They own all the stock and the government owns the rest of it, but half the time the government owns over 50 percent of the company because it has a bigger investment than the poor guy that owns it! And that's bad. That's been going on ever since I came to work here because REA hit me right as soon as I got here trying to loan me money, and I said no."

Doyle's passion against REA was directed against those telephone companies that abused this government program. For those small companies that struggled to serve rural areas of their service territories, REA was a valuable source of financing that enabled those companies to survive and resulted in far superior service and rates for those rural subscribers. It was a good program for those for whom it was intended. The problem was, as is common in government funding programs, there were many abuses.

"For the small telephone company in the Midwest that has to go out two miles to give a farmer a phone, that's what you need REA for and it's good," Doyle said. "It's like welfare. There are families that need help to get on their feet, but those who are taking it and don't really need it ... that makes me mad, damn mad. It isn't right."

# 1954-1960: Doyle Builds His Team

## GUNNING TAKES A CHANCE ON ROSEVILLE

*"Gunning, if I can find the right group of people here, we are going to put together a hell of a telephone company."*
— Bob Doyle, 1954

One of Bob Doyle's first objectives as president was to find an experienced telephone man who knew how to operate, maintain and repair the company's new dial equipment that had gone on-line on Nov. 1, 1953, three months before the younger Doyle became president.

"One of the first things I did when I became president was to approach Al Johnson about helping me find someone who might know something about the equipment," Doyle remembered. "Johnson was a sales engineer for Automatic Electric then and was the sales engineer on the job for the first addition to the dial equipment. I told Johnson we had no one who knew anything about dial equipment. We had no records ... we had absolutely nothing. I said, 'Al, we don't have anybody that knows anything about the equipment. What in the hell are we going to do?'"

Johnson, who knew his way around the nation's independent telephone companies, had someone in mind. He told Doyle about T. Emerson Gunning, whom Johnson had worked with many years earlier at Mare Island Naval Base in Vallejo, Calif.

"I was out there at that time in the Installation Department and Gunning was a telephone equipment technician," Johnson recalled. "After the war, I visited Mare Island as a staff engineer, assisting them in engineering additions, laying out their equipment, and while I was there, Gunning asked me if I knew of any place that was looking for a telephone technician. Gunning had come from a small Illinois town where they had a small telephone company and he had always said he really would like to work for a small telephone company instead of the government. So I told Bob Doyle about Gunning and gave him a telephone number."

It didn't take long for Doyle and Gunning to talk, and soon thereafter, in mid-1954, Gunning agreed to come to Roseville to take a look at the company and meet with Bob Doyle.

*T. Emerson Gunning was the first of the experienced telephone people hired by Bob Doyle to build Roseville Telephone. Gunning came aboard in November 1954 and served in a variety of capacities in his 20-year career.*

"I remember Al Johnson telling me that Bob had always been a farmer, and that he had been in the service, but never worked much with tools," Gunning recalled. "Johnson said Bob was going to handle the management end of the company and was looking for somebody to handle the equipment. So we talked and Doyle invited me and my wife to Roseville to visit."

Emerson and Clarice Gunning came to Roseville for a "tour" and immediately hit it off with Bob and his first wife, Rose.

"Bob and I got into his car and circled the whole area," Gunning recalled. "I remember going around by Rocky Ridge Road (now Douglas Boulevard). At that time, there was nothing there except a graveyard across the street. The vineyards belonged to the Doyles and all the rest was farming out there. It was barren.

"But Bob had a sight for the future. He took me out and said, 'Gunning, it won't be long before this will look like Fulton Avenue down here.' At that time the area around Fulton Avenue in Sacramento was growing real fast. And even then — in 1954 — he said that Roseville Telephone's territory had room for over 250,000 telephone stations. The company served only about 3,000 then. Who'd ever have thought we'd have this many people right now? But Bob knew … he always had a knack for knowing where the growth was going to be."

Doyle worked hard to get Gunning to say yes to his offer to join Roseville Telephone, but there were complications. The first involved pay. Gunning had a civil service job with the federal government and was earning a good wage for the times, nearly $600 a month. He was 45 years old and he and Clarice were settled with a nice new home and had two children in school. They enjoyed a comfortable life in post-war Vallejo. But Gunning had always harbored an ambition to own a small telephone exchange one day. Perhaps working with tiny Roseville Telephone would help satisfy that life-long desire. Nonetheless, Doyle's offer wasn't very appealing at first.

"Gunning," Doyle remembers saying, "if I can find the right group of people here, we are going to put together a hell of a telephone company. But I got one problem. I'm the president of the company and my wages are $400 a month, and I'll be damned if I'm going to pay anybody more than I'm making. If you are willing to come to work for $350, you've got yourself a job. But I want you to know that after we get things going here, I'll take care of myself in the future, and when I do, I'll take care of you, too. You will just have to trust me on that part."

"That's what Doyle said," Gunning confirmed. "He said we had to crawl before we could walk, and looking back I can honestly say we crawled a long time. We were driving used cars, never had a brand new car at all. We got them from the state. The old ones they'd turn in, we'd get them. And the trucks, they were ancient."

Clarice Gunning had no reason to want to move. She liked life in Vallejo, working at a school and bringing up their two children. "I didn't know anything about Roseville, and the only thing I heard about the town was from a store clerk in Vallejo who had grown up in Roseville and still had relatives there. She certainly didn't think much of the telephone company. 'Shittiest telephone company in the world,' she called it. So it didn't sound good. The company wasn't going to pay anything either.

"But what Emerson wanted at one time more than anything was to have a small telephone company of his own," Clarice added. "And because of that longtime desire of his, we decided to make the move."

Gunning joined the company as wire chief, in charge of the central office. His broad experience in telephony enabled him to be of assistance in a number of other departments, too, as it was needed.

So it was T. Emerson Gunning — who would thereafter be known simply as "Gunning" — who became the first of a number of experienced hands recruited to help Bob Doyle start to build "a hell of a telephone company."

Tom Doyle remembered that his older brother's strategy to hire experienced people to build Roseville Telephone made a lot of sense. Despite the company's rotten reputation, the deplorable situation appealed to experienced telephone people who enjoyed a challenge. The retired Pacific Telephone guys had telephones in their blood and the opportunity to build a company virtually from scratch while working for a boss who gave them free rein — that was appealing.

"Bob got input from all of us and from businessmen around town," Tom Doyle said. "So we succeeded by getting some retired PT&T guys — they weren't ready to completely lie down and die — and they didn't need a big salary. They loved coming here to a little company and helping us build it. They really took an interest. So it was good for them and good for us, because they helped train the people that we've got working here right now. Getting those retirees was the key to the whole thing. Those guys were good and they knew they were good, because back in those days, our company wasn't sophisticated like it is now. Things had never changed at Roseville Telephone, so what these experienced guys knew worked perfectly here. And it started with the hiring of Gunning."

## OTHER EXPERIENCED TELEPHONE PEOPLE COME ABOARD

The next experienced telephone man Doyle hired was Page Ellis (no relation to Gladys) who came in early 1955. Ellis had worked originally for Pacific Telephone, but left there to start his own business. But his venture did not work out, and when Pacific didn't take him back, he went to work at McClellan AFB Doyle first heard about Ellis from Keith "Doc" Harrington who had worked with Ellis at Pacific. Doyle talked to Ellis and made the identical offer of $350 with the promise of better pay in the future if operations improved as Doyle

Page Ellis was the first outside plant engineer for Roseville Telephone under Bob Doyle. He planned the company's drive to replace outmoded "junk" with modern cables and equipment.

*Keith "Doc" Harrington worked with Page Ellis at Pacific Telephone before coming to Roseville Telephone in 1952 to work for Walter and David Hanisch who managed the company before Bob Doyle. Harrington was Doyle's "wire chief" and a key member of Doyle's early management team.*

*Fred Spring joined the company in 1955 as construction foreman. Retired from Pacific Telephone, Spring was known as "Mr. Construction" at Pacific.*

was determined they would. Ellis joined Roseville Telephone as outside plant engineer. David Hanisch was still plant superintendent.

Ellis' job was a big one — to develop an engineering plan to replace the company's outmoded outside plant and to plan for growth. Ellis brought a professionalism and experience in engineering that had never been part of Roseville Telephone. When Doyle hired Ellis, Gunning shifted to installation and made Harrington the wire chief. "Gunning's experience in all aspects of the business made him invaluable," Doyle said.

"For Gunning, Ellis and the others I hired in those first few years, a main priority of mine was that they train the young people I was going to hire and those who were already here," Doyle recalled.

Ironically, one of the first experienced ex-Pacific Telephone veterans was hired by Walter Hanisch, who was still at the company for a more than a year after Doyle became president. That was "Doc" Harrington. He had worked at Pacific, but left on medical leave. When Pacific declined to take him back, Harrington went to work at the U.S. Army Signal Depot in Sacramento and "was a real central office man," according to Doyle. "He not only knew the central office, but he was a stickler on details, on keeping records and really setting the thing up. Our records were a shambles when he got here."

But Harrington couldn't be effective under Dave Hanisch's critical eye. It took Doyle's ascendancy as president, a few more experienced Pacific veterans to come into the fold and, eventually, Hanisch's departure for Harrington's expertise to be fully utilized and recognized. He became an integral part of Doyle's "new" team of ex-Pacific Telephone veterans that laid the groundwork for the future growth of the company.

Doyle's next hire after Ellis was a real coup — that was Fred Spring, a legendary veteran with the Pacific company. Spring had been with Pacific for more than 40 years and was expert at outside plant construction.

Doyle remembers Spring well. "In the Pacific company, they called him 'Mr. Construction' because he put the lines over the Sierra and had been out in the boondocks of Nevada. He had done just about everything … any kind of dynamiting, whatever it was he had done it," Doyle recalled. "I got ahold of him — he was living in Auburn at the time — I told him I'd heard about him and explained I wanted to get somebody to come and teach our people how to do construction because we knew nothing really ... We were lucky that the company was in such terrible shape. It was just like starting over. I think he saw this as a real challenge, so when I approached him, he was tickled to death to come to work for the Roseville Telephone Company. And of course I offered him $350 a month."

Soon after Fred Spring came aboard in the summer of 1955, Doyle inquired of his newly-recruited team of telephone veterans if they knew any cable splicers. The company would need them as plans to build new plant and facilities started to come on stream. Spring suggested a man who had worked with him at Pacific.

"His name is Tom Trimble and he's an old-timer," Doyle recalled Spring telling him. "And he is a hell of a splicer. I think I can get him to come to work." So Trimble was the next link in the team. The crew was shaping up nicely and they also began teaching younger employees their skills.

Beginning with a handful of experienced former Pacific Telephone employees, Roseville Telephone and Bob Doyle began the decades-long strategy of hiring local area youths — often fresh out of Roseville High — and teaching them how to run a modern telephone company. And what these veterans instilled in their young apprentices was more than basic skills. They also inculcated the discipline of doing the job right the first time and every time.

There were no shortcuts for Roseville Telephone in the era after the mid-1950s. What evolved over only a few short years beginning in 1954-1955 was the development of an outstanding corps of loyal employees who not only had the skills to run a telephone company, but a "can do" attitude as well. That attitude would in later years become evident in a number of ways as Roseville Telephone sought to become as independent a telephone company as possible. And it all started with Bob Doyle's vow that this telephone company could become the "best goddamned telephone company anywhere."

The formation of Doyle's "management team" came just in time because growth in the area served by the company was on the verge of exploding. Folsom Lake was filled in 1955 and Highway 40, which was later christened Interstate 80, stretched to Roseville from Sacramento at about the same time.

Doyle said, "When those big projects were completed, instead of being just a sleepy little railroad town, Roseville began to change. People that worked for the state and at other businesses in Sacramento started to move to Citrus Heights and Roseville. It was an easy 20-minute commute. Other growth started to happen out here, too, as industry and commercial moved in. First thing you know, Roseville was no longer strictly a railroad town."

Doyle's prediction of Roseville's growth had started to happen, and those early employees watched it. Events were unfolding as their boss said they would.

"The amazing part of it is, I sold them on the whole deal," Doyle said about his early hires. "I sold them on it, because *I was sold on it*. And if you're sold on something, by god, you can sell somebody else. They knew I was sincere."

Gladys (Ellis) Ross had been an operator since 1925 and chief operator for three decades before retiring in 1970. She exhibited fierce loyalty to the company and was loved by "her girls."

1950s company business card.

Doyle's pep talk to his recruits was identical. "I know our wages are the shits and that we don't have any benefits or anything. But I'll guarantee you that's not what it's going to be. I'm going to take care of Bob Doyle and when I do, I'm going to take care of you, too. Because if I don't take care of you, this thing is not going to do what I want it to do. We've got to work together as a team. I have to have satisfied employees to get the job done. If I don't, I'm not going to get to first base."

## DAVID HANISCH LEAVES ROSEVILLE TELEPHONE

*Dave Hanisch was assistant manager before Bob Doyle assumed leadership of Roseville Telephone in 1954. He left the company in June 1955.*

When Bob Doyle became president of Roseville Telephone in early 1954, he had been on the job less than six months. He knew there were big problems and he had formulated his basic plan to hire experienced people and let them train younger employees in the necessary skills. He also knew that raising money, by both selling stock and borrowing, was imperative. He also knew that eventually he'd have to deal with David Hanisch, because it was clear that the younger Hanisch was not about to be on Bob Doyle's team. Although Hanisch's father and Doyle's father worked together for 40 years, it wasn't likely the two sons could truly work together for 40 minutes. Nonetheless, David Hanisch stayed at Roseville Telephone until June 1955 before the final clash occurred.

As Doyle was assembling his team of former Pacific Telephone veterans, Hanisch stayed out of the office in his role as plant superintendent, overseeing the accelerating investment in outside fixed plant. In effect, Hanisch was "Mr. Outside" and Doyle "Mr. Inside." Employees at the time say Hanisch never accepted the fact that Doyle was his boss. He carried on as he had before, except that he kept out of Doyle's way most of the time.

Doyle and Hanisch saw their roles very differently. Doyle felt that with some time and nurturing, he could swing Hanisch to his side and make him realize that the company needed to grow, spend money to build plant, and to grow some more. Doyle probably never explained his strategy in those words, but his actions certainly told the story.

Hanisch clearly wasn't happy that Bob Doyle was coming into the company. "I remember old man Doyle came to see my father and me and just announced to us that he was going to step down as president and put Bob in there," Hanisch recalled. "No explanation or anything. We were furious. What the hell did a guy from the farm know about the telephone business?

"But seeing as he was coming, I figured I would try to teach Bob about the telephone business from the ground up. But he didn't want to learn. He was above that ... he was president, you know, the guy at the top ... He didn't want to know anything about how the business worked."

Doyle's promotion helped Harrington deal with the moody Hanisch, because now Harrington had someone to appeal to when conflicts arose.

"It was still like they were walking on eggshells," remembered Janie Opich, who worked in the business office in 1953-54. "I don't remember Bob as being real assertive. He wasn't coming in and saying, 'OK, you guys, shape up,' and that sort of thing. But in subtler ways, he was trying to because he helped Doc Harrington when he and Hanisch clashed.

"Yes, there were a lot of vocal arguments that we would overhear," Opich continued, "but I never felt that Bob was being pushy at all. If anything, he was giving David plenty of rope to hang himself with. David never really felt that he had to report to anybody."

After Emerson Gunning came aboard in late 1954, this further tilted the scales against Hanisch. Now Harrington and Gunning together could offset Hanisch's tirades, aided by a president who was gaining confidence. Soon after Page Ellis joined the company in early 1955, Doyle's new team was taking hold, to the exclusion of Hanisch. But Hanisch could still make life difficult for the new employees. It came to a point where Doyle's hires were threatening to leave if something wasn't done.

"I told them that Hanisch had been here a long time and that maybe we could turn him around," Doyle recalled. "I also told them that if I just up and fired Hanisch, what the hell are people in the community going to think? I said I owed it to him to try to see if maybe we could make it work. I asked them to have a little patience. I also said, 'If you think I'm having fun, you've got another think coming.' I tried with Hanisch, but finally I had had enough. My crew was going to walk if I didn't do something."

The break came in June 1955 when Doyle sent the younger Hanisch to an industry convention to represent Roseville Telephone. Doyle remembers the time:

"I figured when he comes back from the convention, maybe he'll think about this thing and come back different … but it didn't change him a damned bit. When he came back and didn't even report to me what happened at the convention, I figured there was no use. What kind of a damned fool am I? Everybody could see it but me? No way I was going to lose these guys I hired. The day before I was going to fire Hanisch, I told Gunning and all the supervisors. I said, 'OK, you guys, get ready. Tomorrow morning at 8 a.m. I'm going to fire Dave Hanisch. I don't know what the hell he's going to do, but stick around, because I don't want him tearin' anything up.'"

The next morning Doyle summoned Hanisch to his office. "'Dave, you know something, you've done everything you can to make everything miserable for me, and I'm at the end of my goddamned rope. The reason I called you in here is to tell you that I'm firing your ass. It's 8 o'clock now. You've got till 11 to get your ass out of here. I want you to go around and pick up anything that belongs

to you in the company and be out of here by 11. If you're not, I'm going to throw you out. I'll mail your check to you and your severance pay and the whole works, but you're out of here by 11.'"

Vern Roberson, a lineman hired by Hanisch in 1953, remembered that day.

"Dave came out and told us he'd been fired. Mario Giovonni and I were working together out in Citrus Heights. Dave came out and told us, 'I was just fired by that blankety-blank so-and-so. I won't be seeing you no more.' He told us he already had a job with some phone company. Then he came back a while later and asked if I wanted to quit Roseville and go with him to Garberville. I let on like I was real sorry, but I wouldn't want to get into a dog fight with that man."

As the plant superintendent, David Hanisch had all the keys to the offices, warehouse and vehicles. When he left, he took the identifying tapes off the keys and left the 20 or so keys in a cigar box. Doyle had no idea what keys opened what.

"Nobody knew where anything was anyway. It didn't make any difference," Doyle said. "They didn't have any records. All they had was drop wire out in all these alleys, just a bunch of wires, and no records. There were no terminals, there wasn't anything. One of the first things we had to do was get a guy out there measuring to find out how much wire we had. We didn't know. Doc Harrington did that and later we hired a consultant, J.F. Brennan from San Francisco, to help us create records. Brennan took Page Ellis and Jack Poulsen and they went around the whole area and counted the poles. And then we started having some records."

As might be expected, Doyle has never had regrets about firing David Hanisch. "I had to do it. It was either do that or lose the people that were here. Doc Harrington and all the rest of them were going to quit. David Hanisch didn't want to see this thing work. And when I told the other guys, you never saw a happier bunch of people in all your life, because I think they thought I'd never do it. I probably did wait too long, but in my heart, I felt that I gave him every chance I could give him."

Heart problems resulted in the 71-year-old Walter Hanisch retiring from the company in May 1955, a month before his son left. But the senior Hanisch remained on the Board of Directors until he died at age 88 on New Year's Day, 1972.

"Walter was a nice old guy," Doyle said. "He'd come to the board meetings and no matter what the hell I wanted to do, he was the first one to back me up. I thought that was pretty good, damn good. I believe he knew what I was doing was right. But he just couldn't do it himself. And he never said a word to me about firing his son. Never a word. He knew why I did it."

With David Hanisch gone, Roseville Telephone was now ready to move fast along its growth track. But it was like building from the ground up, starting over. Doyle and his crew relished the challenge.

## INVESTING IN NEW PLANT AND EQUIPMENT

Roseville Telephone's equipment in the early 1950s was old. Furnishings were antique, office equipment was ancient and the vehicles were barely running.

"When I first came to work here, the installation rig, if that's what you want to call it, was this old 1929 pickup that had the ladder on the driver's side so you had to get out the other side of the truck," remembered Doyle. "I thought, 'How the hell are we going to do all the installation we need to do with this truck? We're going to have to get some kind of equipment.'

"So I went to Johnny Macario, who was the GM dealer down here then. 'Johnny,' I said, 'I'll tell you what. I want to deal local and I'd like to buy a chassis from you. And I'm going to go down to Oakland and have Utility Body put it on to make it an installation rig.' He said, 'That's good.' I said, 'By the way, you know, that pickup we got up there ... the one that Walter Hanisch drives around? How much would you give me on that for a trade-in?' He said, 'Well, I'll give you $50 if you'd keep that son of the bitch. I don't want it.' That's how bad it was.

"Then, of course, we had this old Army rig for construction. Well, you can imagine, the crew would take that thing and they would put some cable and stuff on it and head out to the job. And the first thing, you know, they break an axle. Well, the only place you could get an axle was to go to a damn army surplus place. That's the way it was. We didn't really have any equipment."

Carl Andree described the company "fleet" back then. "We had an old GI line truck, the Army rig. We also had a '35 Ford with mechanical brakes on it and an old '40 Chevy pickup," he said. "We also had this ladder truck which was mounted on a 3/4-ton truck with a 30-foot wooden ladder that you cranked. It would tip over if you didn't watch what you were doing. That happened a couple of times."

Shortly after Fred Spring arrived, he asked Bob Doyle if he could "engineer" his own construction rig, using a novel idea that to Spring's knowledge had not been tried before. Doyle remembered the conversation.

"'Bob,' Spring said to me, 'I've got an idea. It's a bucket that you get in. Guide it yourself. Go up, you know. It's something I've always wanted to do, but,' he added, 'the Pacific company ... they didn't think anybody like me would have a good idea. I never got a chance to do anything, but I really think that this thing would work.' So I said to him, 'Well, let's give it a whirl.'

"Well, he put this damn thing together and we went to Utility Body down in Oakland. And they studied it, and so they put the thing together, the basket, and the whole thing, with the controls on it ... It's like everybody has today. Spring's idea worked. I don't know if that was the first boom construction truck ever made, but it had to be one of the first because I didn't start seeing them around until years after that. Old Fred Spring, he was quite a telephone man."

When the rig was outfitted to Spring's specifications, Doyle and Spring drove to Oakland to pick up the truck. "When he saw it, he got this big smile on his face … after all, it was his idea," Doyle recalled. "So when we came home, Fred suggested we celebrate. The guys at Utility Body had given each of us a quart of whiskey. My wife and I were supposed to go someplace that night, a celebration or party. But Fred said, 'You know, Bob, we ought to taste some of that snake bite that those guys gave us and …' I said, 'That's a damn good idea.' We sat at our kitchen table and we drank a bottle of that booze. Of course, my wife's face went down and we never did go out that night."

As soon as Bob Doyle took over the company, he was intent on giving his employees the proper tools and best equipment available. But it took awhile.

"We never had any good tools until Bob came there," said Ed Gardetto. "We used to dig pole holes by hand and shovel. The old Army rig had an auger there to dig holes. That was just as bad, you'd have to hold the auger and it would just vibrate."

"Fred was always yelling for bigger trucks and more equipment," added Bobby Oldham, a recent retiree who started in November 1954. "He was quite a guy. Before Fred came, we'd usually dig pole holes by hand, with a spoon (a narrow, spoon-shaped shovel) and shovel. You had to go one foot down for every five foot of pole. We generally went down about four feet, but if you had a 25-foot pole, you had to go down five feet.

"I wasn't too unhappy to get out of that construction crew, I'll tell you," Oldham added. "That was tough work. The first morning I came to work in splicing, I was handed a pair of hooks and a belt. I didn't even know how to put the damned hooks on. When I came in that evening, though, I knew how to use those hooks and how to put them on. That's how we learned back then."

Gunning remembered that there was no money for tools when he came in November 1954, the same month as Oldham.

"We were poor. This company didn't have the money to go and do a lot. We had to just go along to get things moving and get the telephones installed for people so we could start getting some revenue in," Gunning said. "I took my own tools and let my crew use them until we were able to buy the different tools and supplies we needed. You can't just go out and buy a whole carload of stuff. You had to know what you had to get. And the same way with parts. The company didn't even have parts for the equipment they had just installed. It took a long time, it seemed."

The office equipment wasn't any better. "We had really primitive equipment, old typewriters, old adding machines, and they had some sort of billing machine, where it came from, I don't know," said Janie Opich who joined the company in June 1953. Virginia (Neel) Amick agreed. She worked at the company for a year from May 1954 until May 1955. "Everything was so old fashioned. It was just antiquated, the typewriters … just everything."

But this changed in the years after Doyle assumed the presidency of the company. By 1958, according to a report commissioned by the company and conducted by the engineering firm, William M. McKay of Ripon, Calif., the fixed plant had improved considerably. The study's objective was to arrive at an appraised value of the plant and equipment from which appropriate depreciation assumptions could be derived. This was important for the company's rate increase filing with the Public Utilities Commission in 1958-1959.

*Construction crew in late 1955, with Fred Spring (middle with hat), displaying new independent company logo on their truck.*

In the section discussing pole lines, McKay's study said "… field inspection disclosed practically no damage to poles from insect and bird attack, although evidence of such damage on foreign poles in this area was noted … On the whole, the poles on this property are in better condition than those of the average telephone system. This may be attributable to the recent growth of the system and the consequent newness of the plant …"

In the section on aerial cable, McKay's study made references to "the extraordinarily high retirement (of old cable) experience in 1956-57" and the "heavy re-building program of 1956 and 1957." The average age of the underground conduit was 3.9 years in 1958 compared to a 50-year average service life for this type of cable at that time. For office equipment and furniture, McKay's study assessed the value of the company's property in this category at nearly $55,000 in 1958, "about three-fourths of which was expended in 1956, 1957 and 1958

*The old Army construction rig truck used by the company for many years. It was unbalanced and unsafe, but it was all the company could afford in its early years.*

for modern office furniture, calculating and other equipment. Field inspection showed these to be of good quality."

And finally, McKay's report showed that the quality of Roseville Telephone's "fleet," which was so decrepit and dangerous when Doyle joined the company in 1953, had come a long way in five short years. "This group is composed of 20 vehicles (including trailers) at an appraised cost of $49,853, and tools and miscellaneous equipment with a cost of $15,593, making the total for the account $65,466. The motor vehicles and trailers range from 1/2 year to 10 1/2 years. Tools and miscellaneous were estimated at 2 1/2 years old as of Dec. 31, 1958."

Clearly, Doyle's promises that his employees would be well equipped were beginning to come true. As Gunning said, "Bob told me when I first joined the company in 1954 that we had to walk first ... then we could run. And he said it would take some time. He was right."

The period of 1954-1960 was so important to Roseville Telephone because in those years the new team Doyle assembled not only corrected the wrongs of the past, but set the foundation for a bright future, too. The formula — "Give the customer good service and the revenue will rise" — proved itself during the 1950s. As Doyle predicted when he joined the company, "The money is out there." He was referring to the vast square mileage then served by the farmer lines. "We just need to build the plant so we can go get it."

## 1954-1960: BIRTH OF MODERN
## ROSEVILLE TELEPHONE COMPANY

With the dial system cut over at the end of the previous year, Bob Doyle set out to follow through on improving and expanding service, particularly to Citrus Heights. Since the company was already adding more capacity to its new dial system, Doyle knew the company would soon need more space for the downtown Roseville operations. In 1954, the company acquired what had been the old G.M. Hanisch building on the corner of Atlantic and Lincoln streets, and in late 1955 it acquired former director Charles Baker's property, which housed the Pall Mall tavern, on the other side of the telephone company building.

The company mounted its first true public relations effort in May 1955 when it ran a full-page advertisement in the *Roseville Press-Tribune*. In large bold type, the ad read:

*MEET YOUR HOME-OWNED...*
*ROSEVILLE TELEPHONE CO.*

Under the headline were photos of the key executives as well as the different departments ... "Operators, Office Staff, Construction, Installation and Repair." Under the photos were statements about the company's progress — *"Now serving 4,000 subscribers in the Roseville area. New equipment being installed at present to accommodate another 1,400. New equipment will be installed to accommodate the growing population of Roseville. It is our desire to serve you in the most efficient and courteous manner possible."*

This statement of purpose and commitment was unprecedented in the history of Roseville Telephone. It was the first in a series of Doyle's public pronouncements through the years that the company was now a viable, growing concern with the interests of its customers and and the community a top priority. This advertisement in the *Press-Tribune* was also the first public display of Doyle's career-long loyalty to his employees. The ad didn't just contain his photo, it contained the photo of every employee in the company at that time. This was Doyle's way of telling the community that Roseville Telephone is not a one-man operation, but a team of dedicated employees.

*In 1955, Bob Doyle was enjoying his second year as president and manager of Roseville Telephone.*

Six months later, an article in the *Press-Tribune's* Dec. 6, 1955, edition read "…Expansion Plans Afoot … TELEPHONE FIRM BUYS PROPERTY NEAR OFFICE…" Excerpts from the story read "… Doyle announced that it was decided to purchase the property to be assured of room for anticipated future expansion. He said that it 'may be three, four or five years before we need it,' but the directors decided to make the acquisition while the property was available because of the 'certainty' of future expansion."

In the same article, Doyle announced that the company offices would be moving to the corner building at Lincoln and Atlantic early in 1956, in the building that housed the former Welcome Club. After those early real estate acquisitions, Roseville Telephone owned more than half the east side of the Lincoln Street block between Vernon and Atlantic. Doyle would continue this pattern of buying property before it was needed throughout the next 40 years.

Since David Hanisch was still at the company through mid-1955 and in charge of the outside plant activities, Doyle's position as president in the first year was still more in name than in practice. He was not heavy-handed as chief executive. His early inquisitiveness became a trademark of his management style in later years. Doyle spent a lot of time in his first year observing how the company operated, thinking all the while about how operations could improve. He asked questions and wanted to learn.

"It was entirely different when Bob took over," said Bernice Moser, the long-time operator. "Bob would walk in and want to know what everything was. He was very curious. Since he didn't know a thing about what we all did, he just set himself busy getting all the information he could from everybody."

The outside crew that worked out of the maintenance shop down the street saw an immediate benefit when Doyle hired Gunning as their boss. "At 100 Lincoln, our old tin building there didn't have a bathroom," said Wayne Langton. "When you had to go to the head, you went outside near the creek or to the service station down the street.

"When Gunning came on board, he couldn't believe it. He demanded we have a bathroom, so they dug a septic hole out there, took one partition and put an old faucet in there for washing your hands. I took a bunch of old blueprints and wallpapered the inside of the bathroom to make it look half way decent. Gunning thought it was great."

## DOYLE'S RECIPE FOR NON-STOP GROWTH

Although Doyle's career is a legacy of near non-stop progress and change, he was not a rash decision-maker. He was a thinker first and a doer second. And, his initial day-to-day activities as president were not all that "executive."

"One of the duties I had at first was to collect the coins from our pay phones," said Doyle. "I'd go around to the four or five pay phones we had at the time and empty the coins. Then I'd bring the coins back to the office and separate the nickels, dimes and quarters by running them through the old wooden coin rack. And, of course, I had the job of public relations, trying to keep the public off our ass. It wasn't fun."

The company's progress, however, could be delineated by the growth in the fixed plant and telephone instruments and systems over Doyle's first years as president.

In 1953, for example, the company's dial step-by-step switching equipment had 1,200 exchange circuits serving 3,381 company-owned telephones, as reported to the CPUC. By the end of 1954, the number of company telephones served rose to 3,745, an increase of 364 phones, or nearly 11 percent. By 1955, another 600 exchange circuits were added to the central office and total company telephones served jumped nearly 1,000 to 4,712, an increase of more than 25 percent. This reflected the addition of 600 new subscribers in Citrus Heights who were finally able to get service from Roseville Telephone. It was the installation of more telephone cable to Citrus Heights in concert with the addition to the central office capacity that enabled the company to bring aboard these new customers.

Ironically, it was common in those years to install the telephones well in advance of the service being activated, sometimes months ahead of time.

"Back when we had all of these held orders, you had hundreds of people that had been waiting for phones, sometimes for many years," Doyle said. "Most of them were in Citrus Heights, but we had them all over. Our installers would go to these people's homes and say, 'We've noticed you have had your application in for a phone. Well, we're going to come in … now you're not going to be able to use your phone yet … but we want to install your phone ahead of time. When the equipment is ready, your phone is going to ring and you're going to be in service.

"The guy on the test desk then was Carl Andree. He'd call the numbers as they were put into service and inform customers that their phones were now working. He'd say something like 'Hello, Mr. Customer. This is the telephone company …' Naturally, of course, when the customer's phone rang, he or she just about fell over backwards … scared the hell out of them. Then Andree would say, 'We just wanted to call and tell you that your phone is now in service.' One woman told Andree, 'My god, you know, when we applied for the phone, I was pregnant. Now my daughter's in the eighth grade …' They were thrilled."

New service meant placing cable from the central office to the home. In Citrus Heights, the distance from the homes to Roseville's central office was up to seven miles. To string cable this far took time and a lot of money. That's why the pre-Doyle management and ownership didn't do it. It cost too much. By the end of 1955, however, Roseville Telephone had installed new cable to Citrus Heights to supplement the existing farmer lines. The new cable meant that anybody who wanted service in Citrus Heights could receive it, although at first it was eight-party suburban service. This changed in 1957-1958 when Citrus Heights got its own central office. Then customers could be upgraded to the standard one-, two- and four-party service common in the years before 1960.

Cable mileage over Doyle's first years increased tremendously, but even the dramatic increases in mileage didn't reflect the total work being accomplished. Not only did the company expand its cable network, it also replaced most of the wiring and cabling already in. It truly was like starting over.

In 1953, total wire mileage in cable was 2,265 with 363 miles of aerial wire, which represents wire to the individual homes or offices. In 1954, miles of inside wire cable more than doubled to 5,062. This was paced by a near three-fold jump in wire mileage inside aerial cables plus about a 30-percent increase in wire mileage contained in underground cables. Aerial wire not in cable grew by about 30 percent, too. Total cable mileage jumped about 25 percent in 1955 and by more than 30 percent in 1956.

In 1957, in preparation for serving Citrus Heights with its own central switching office, the company's cable mileage nearly tripled, from 8,549 miles in 1956 to 24,104 miles. Aerial wire itself neared 700 miles by the end of 1957. By 1958, the wire cable mileage was 27,908 miles with nearly 1,100 miles of aerial wire.

The dramatic growth in infrastructure brought Roseville Telephone current with its demands for service in the territory. The 12-fold increase in wire cabling mileage from 1953 to 1958 showed how much progress the company had made in those few short years.

Other statistics were equally telling. In 1953, the company's switching capabilities numbered one central office with 1,200 circuits. By the end of 1958, the Citrus Heights central office was built and operational, which gave the company two central offices with a combined capacity of 4,800 circuits, a fourfold increase.

The total number of telephones served by the company jumped to 7,173 at year-end 1958 from 3,777 at the end of 1953. Pay phones in operation increased from only five in 1953 to 45 by 1958. The increase in pay stations came in concert with the increase in small businesses that attended the corresponding growth in population. More people meant more restaurants, grocery stores, barbershops, gas stations, etc. — and more pay phones.

Of course, as Roseville Telephone invested more in its service territory, revenue grew. But for the first five years after Doyle took over, revenue grew faster than profits. In 1954, Bob Doyle's first year at the helm, the new chief executive was proving a prophet as revenue jumped nearly $74,000 to $283,996 and net income more than doubled to $46,890 from $21,169 the previous year. The sizable rate increase that took effect Nov. 1, 1953, upon conversion to dial played a big role in this improved financial performance. The new public shareholders were rewarded with two $.15 per share dividends in 1954.

In 1955 and 1956, revenue rose to $335,433 and $427,734, respectively, producing profits of $39,987 and $50,435 in those years. New investment in fixed plant was staggering in that two-year period, totaling more than $685,000. It was clear that Roseville Telephone under Doyle was not afraid to spend money. It was doing only what was necessary, according to Doyle. But the shareholders were taken care of, receiving $.45 per share in dividends in both 1955 and 1956.

"You have to remember, Roseville Telephone hadn't spent anything for 40 years!" Doyle explained. "We had so much to do, the only question was where do we start?"

By 1957 and 1958, the strain of the heavy investments in fixed plant weighed on the company's profitability. Earnings were only $29,810 on $469,505 in revenue in 1957 and $50,617 — less than $4,000 higher than in 1954 — on revenue of nearly $600,000 in 1958.

New borrowings and the sale of more shares of stock in 1957 financed the capital investment in those first years, but by 1958 Doyle and his newly-hired accounting manager, Mark Shull, were working on the third piece to the financing solution — another rate increase.

Over his career, the fiscal recipe that Bob Doyle developed to grow in his first five years as president was repeated time after time. The formula was simple enough in theory, but what makes Doyle's stewardship so remarkable was that his recipe for profitable growth worked as well in practice as it did in theory.

The first step in Doyle's formula was to ensure that enough funds were available to keep investing in fixed plant, not only to increase the company's service capabilities, but to improve service all along the way. And as a regulated utility that is authorized by the CPUC to earn a pre-determined rate of return (profit percentage) on its fixed plant investment, the more invested in fixed plant, the more the potential profit.

The company has raised funds for capital investment primarily in four ways. Foremost has been Doyle's ability to sell stock, which Roseville Telephone did virtually non-stop from 1953-to-1983. The second was by tapping traditional borrowing sources, insurance companies and banks. The third was through the issuance of numerous stock dividends to shareholders, typically five percent dividends. This financing technique in effect reinvested shareholders' dividends to purchase more shares. It has provided a reliable and inexpensive source of capital to Roseville Telephone for nearly 40 years since the first 10 percent stock dividend was paid in 1957. The fourth piece is reinvestment of profits.

The second step in Doyle's recipe for building a successful company was to continually invest in new facilities, equipment and people. As the population grew, the company expanded to meet demand and continued investing to keep ahead of the growth curve. This strategy has kept Roseville Telephone among the most modern and technologically-advanced independent telephone companies in the nation, even though most observers, including Doyle, admit it wasn't until the mid-1970s that Roseville Telephone was the equal of its Bell counterpart, Pacific Telephone, in service capability and satisfaction.

Roseville Telephone has benefited from other favorable characteristics which have contributed to its success over 40 years. The company's service territory, as mentioned earlier, lacks geographic barriers to growth, such as mountains, large rivers, canyons, heavy-forested areas, etc. So not only was it relatively easy to build the infrastructure that is the backbone of Roseville Telephone's grid, but it was less expensive, too. Most of the company's growth occurred on former ranch acreage, virgin land that was easily developed.

The small territory also was a boon for Doyle because employees have not faced the unsettling necessity of having to uproot their families in order to advance up the corporate ladder. This feature has helped attract and keep exceptional talent at Roseville Telephone.

The decades after the first five years from 1953-1958 have seen Doyle and his team at Roseville Telephone expand and refine the recipe for success that was established early on in his term.

## 'FRIDAY NIGHT MEETINGS' BUILD CAMARADERIE

As president and manager, Bob Doyle was both conventional and unconventional. Like most managers of small companies, he held weekly departmental meetings to assess what those departments intended to accomplish in that week and the immediate future. In those meetings, he would share what future plans the company had in mind, too. In this regard, he was completely different from the Hanisches, who never informed employees about future plans, mostly because there weren't any.

Of Doyle's meetings, one in particular — the "Friday Night Meeting" — became important in the early years of his presidency. To use a modern term, it was at these meetings that the management team "bonded."

Doyle explained how these worked. "On Friday evenings after a long work week, the department managers would come to my office. There would be Page Ellis, Gunning, Mark Shull, Fred Spring, Doc Harrington … whoever was available. We'd review what we did over the week and talk about what was coming up. All of us would talk about the company, then we would go to dinner, have a few drinks and raise hell. We didn't have to go to work the next day so it was OK."

Gunning remembered the meetings. "Yeah, we'd have a meeting in his office and talk about what was going on. He'd take each department and then we'd talk about what they needed in cable, what they needed in splicing, what they needed in installation and in the central office. Central office … Doyle was with that more because it was right here, and many, many times, we had to make studies way ahead of time. We had to place our order for equipment up to two years before we needed it, because at that time, they had to manufacture the equipment for that particular job. So we talked a lot about the future in those meetings, what our needs would be. Once we had our meeting, we'd go out and have pizza and beer or some other dinner. But even afterward, we spent most of the time talking telephone. Bob always wanted to know how many stations we added that day. He'd say, 'Hey Gunning, how many did you get today?' He was always interested in growth."

Doyle and his crew would go to a different restaurant every week. "We'd go down to the Coral Reef, then the next week we'd drive down to the original Shakey's Pizza parlor on J Street near Sacramento State College. Then we'd go to the Valencia Club or Grouchy's Log Cabin … just a different place every time," Doyle recalled. "We use to have a hell of a time. And as we added new guys to the company, the crew got bigger. It was really something. When you have people that are just dying to have a meeting … then you have a good meeting. But they were all interested in what we were doing back then, buying up farmer lines, putting up new plants, buying property, building buildings … it was something constantly. Yeah, we raised hell, but all the time we were talking about things happening at the company."

On one Friday night excursion returning from the Coral Reef, Keith "Doc" Harrington got sick. "He asked me to pull off to the side of the road — it was when there was only the Coral Reef and Town and Country Village on Fulton Avenue, that was about all. The rest of it was open farm lands," Bob Doyle remembered. "So he asked me to pull over … you know, so he could heave … Then he gets back in the car and we're halfway back to Roseville when he says, 'Hey, we have to go back. I lost my teeth!' So we go back to where he got sick and looked through the bushes. Finally, one of us found old Doc's teeth."

Occasionally, there would be stretches when the "Friday Night Meeting" was postponed for one week, two weeks or even longer. "Then somebody would mention to me, 'Hey Bob, when the hell are we going have a meeting?' They really missed those meetings because although it was on their own time, the guys enjoyed what happened after the meeting more than anything else. It pulled us close together."

The "Friday Night Meeting" in those early years reflected the times. It was not uncommon in Roseville or across the nation for employees, particularly men, to convene at the nearest bar after work to lift a few glasses and discuss the events of the day, including work. It was a form of employee communication that has dwindled in importance over the decades.

"On pay day we always went to the Owl Club or the Pall Mall, which was right next to the telephone company," remembered Wayne Langton. "Everybody wound up in there, including Bob Doyle. He'd buy us the first round of drinks. It was hard work and a hard life, but those were the times. Nobody had any money, really."

It was Bob Doyle's personality that facilitated communication among employees at Roseville Telephone. Bob could drink with the boys, but he also enjoyed excellent working relationships with the women in the company.

Gladys (Ellis) Ross remembered it was easy to work with Bob from the very outset. "With Bob's personality, it was like we were working with him. We were not afraid of him ever. He made us all feel like we were an important part of the company."

Gladys recalled an incident when the company used a pneumatic tube system to send documents between departments. "Here I was with an artificial snake, sticking it down the pneumatic tube, you know, trying to send it to another department and Bob came up. 'Hello Gladys,' he said, and all the while I'm thinking he's wondering what I'm doing wasting his time. Then he looks at me, smiles, and said, 'Let me help you send this snake.' That's the kind of guy he is. He just joined in."

In those early years Doyle got to calling Gladys by a nickname that wouldn't be appropriate today. "Bob always called me 'Happy Bottom,' " said Gladys.

"You know, Glad-ass … Happy Bottom," laughed Doyle.

## DEBT TAKES ON MORE IMPORTANCE

Perhaps the most noteworthy difference between Doyle and his predecessors at Roseville Telephone was his attitude toward debt. Doyle understood that growth required capital and that borrowing was a legitimate and useful mechanism to get money. The Hanisches and the old entrenched Board of Directors viewed debt as the last option, period.

Doyle had already experienced the leverage that appropriate debt could provide a growing company. The Doyle Brothers farming partnership borrowed $28,000 in 1947 to finance the start-up of their operations, and that loan, sizable for the time, enabled the brothers to purchase the heavy farm equipment needed to conduct a large-scale farming operation. This successful use of debt taught Doyle the virtue of wise borrowing.

Since the company's first public stock offering raised a little over $100,000, it wasn't long before Doyle knew he'd have to arrange for more debt because the company's growth requirements would absorb a lot of money. Since the company already had a $200,000 loan with Pacific Mutual Life Insurance Company arranged in 1951-52 to finance the conversion to dial, it was appropriate to seek new debt again from the same company.

In 1955, Pacific Mutual loaned the company $250,000 at 4.25 percent over 20 years. In early 1956, a third loan was granted for $200,000 at 4.25 percent and in late 1956, a fourth loan was negotiated for $300,000 at 4.75 percent. By early 1957, Roseville Telephone owed Pacific Mutual nearly $1 million.

Back then, the company didn't borrow for "general corporate purposes," as the popular phrase goes today. The specific needs were listed in newspaper articles reporting on the loans.

For example, in the Dec. 19, 1956, *Sacramento Bee*, an article entitled "Roseville Phone Firm Gets Okeh To Issue Notes" reported that the telephone company was borrowing $300,000 from Pacific Mutual with the funds used to partially finance "… $151,000 for dial equipment for a central office, $150,000 for dial office cables. Other planned expenditures included 2,000 new telephones, $56,000; a new central office in Citrus Heights, $50,000, and a new business office, $20,000. As of September 30th of this year, the company had a net investment of $1,165,139."

The magnitude of the company's borrowings must have shocked Walter Hanisch and the older board members. "Old Walter shook his head, but he always supported me," Doyle recalled. "It must have scared the hell out of him."

Bernice Moser remembered the general sense of the employees at that time when the loans were disclosed. "Everybody near had a fit," she said. "Nobody could borrow that much money to do anything with … But Bob was willing to take the chance."

Every time the company wanted to borrow or raise capital from the sale of stock, the CPUC had to approve the request. It was the encouragement, and perhaps even gentle tutoring by the CPUC staff, that helped Doyle muster the courage to borrow as much as he did. Doyle and Mark Shull, who joined the company in 1957, spent a lot of time at the CPUC's offices in San Francisco in those early years.

"We used to go down to the PUC every chance we got, because we knew they were watching every move we made," Doyle remembered. "And they should have been watching, because unless we were making progress, there was sure as hell going to be something done. So we'd go down and tell them what we were doing and what plans we had. We made it a point to ask for their opinions and guidance. That's always a good idea, you know, because they wanted us to succeed, too. We also wanted them to know that we were working our tails off to try to get something done, and for Chrissakes, leave us alone for a while.

"We'd meet with a whole bunch of them and tell them our problems, trying to buy the farmer lines and stuff like that," Doyle continued. "They could see we were making a hell of a lot of progress. I had already sold stock and borrowed money, and we were putting up plant and buying property for future use. I think they saw we were doing what we needed to do."

Mark Shull remembered all the activity at the CPUC. "It would seem we used to spend two days a week running back and forth to San Francisco to meet with the PUC or the attorneys or somebody all the time. We had a lot to learn and they helped us."

Nonetheless, Doyle's use of debt scared the old-timers. "The Hanisches had thought I'd lost my goddamned head," Doyle added. "We were spending money and they said, 'What are you trying to do?' I said, 'Damn it, we're trying to take care of business. Not only do we have to take care of the people that haven't been taken care of, but we got to think about the future.' And they said, 'This bubble's going to break.' And I said, 'Well, if it breaks, that's all right, but these people expect us to give them service and that's what we're going to do.'

"And, of course, the challenge was to sell all our people on the same idea, that this maybe was the worst telephone company now, but some day it was going to be the best. And there was a lot of satisfaction that we were accomplishing something, buying property ... putting up buildings. They could see it happen.

"It was way back then I decided if we were going to do something, either do it right, or don't do it at all," Doyle said. "That was my motto. If you start cutting corners, you're going to pay for it later on, so let's do it right the first time. That's the way we've done it, and I've seen it pay off in spades."

Pacific Mutual apparently was happy with its role as chief lender to the company. In 1956, it ran a large advertisement in an industry magazine under the heading:

*ENTERPRISE TO MATCH THE VISION OF THE WEST*

*"...In 1956 today's Pacific Mutual — in behalf of its policyholders — has more than $500,000 invested in Roseville Telephone Company, an investment that enabled this enterprising firm virtually to double its facilities to meet the needs of fast-growing Roseville..."*

## SECOND STOCK OFFERING IN 1957 GOES WELL

By 1957, Bob Doyle and Roseville Telephone were well into the growth phase and transformation of the company. After four loans totaling nearly $1 million, Doyle and the Board of Directors determined the company needed to raise equity.

Ever the optimist, Doyle was confident that the recent progress of the company would enable him to sell new stock. As an inducement to existing stockholders, the stock price was raised 20 percent from $10 a share to $12 a share. In addition, each of the existing shareholders would benefit from a one-for-10 stock dividend paid prior to the sale of the new shares. Certainly, existing shareholders were getting a good deal and most of them bought more stock. But this offering wasn't a $100,000 deal that could be sold over the phone. Along with the growth of the company came a bigger appetite for capital — the second offering would be for $600,000. Instead of selling a little over 10,000 shares, Doyle's second offering totaled 50,000 shares at $12.

"So here's a guy that bought the original stock and earned a cash dividend on it. He'd bought 100 and got 10 shares and the price went from $10 to $12. Well, that was pretty good. In the meantime, he could see some progress. We had done what I said we were going to do," Doyle said. "So the second time, we had $600,000 out, which was a hell of a lot of money. By then we were doing business, not with the local banks because they couldn't handle it, but with Bank of America in San Francisco. They said, 'You can't sell that issue up there in that little old railroad community,' and I replied, 'Well, that's what they told me on the first issue, but I did it. What makes you think I can't do it? If I run out of gas, then I'll get a broker.' I told them, first of all, I'd like to keep the stock local. Everybody agreed, go ahead."

Doyle had honed his sales pitch by the time he started selling the second issue in 1957. He'd approach an existing shareholder and the conversation usually went something like the following, according to Doyle. "I'd tell them 'You remember when you bought 100 shares? Now we're going to give you one new

*The new business offices inside the remodeled Welcome Club building in 1956 were very modern compared to the previous quarters.*

share for every 10 you already own and in addition your stock is now all worth $12. Your cash dividend will go up because you have more shares.'

"Well, this was a hell of a deal and the shareholders knew it," Doyle explained. "Then I told them what we planned to do with the money. Most of the stockholders that originally bought said, 'That's good' and bought some more. They could see I had hired people, bought a little bit of property, and they were getting better telephone service. They saw we were improving things. I didn't sell it all by telephone, but the $600,000 was sold and it wasn't too hard to do."

It was during the second stock sale that employees first were able to buy stock by payroll deduction. The company set aside shares for employees to buy over a six-month period. Many employees began building their nest egg in this second sale, because the stock was available to them and they were themselves living the progress that was being made.

Bernice Moser bought shares in 1957 when they were made available to employees. "I didn't think too much about it at the time. It was just something to do," she explained. "Bob gave us all the idea that it was money that was going to make money, and in the long run, it would supplement retirement. When Bob started, there was absolutely no retirement set up. You don't miss money you don't have and they took it right out of our pay check. If you don't have it, you don't spend it."

Another employee then, Bobby Oldham, bought in early, too. "I bought some as soon as it became available. Bob wanted employees to buy the stock, but not enough that it would interfere with your family. I got my mother buying stock, and my aunts and my brothers, too. Anybody I could talk into buying stock. I believed in it."

For young, single Ed Gardetto, it took his father Jim's wisdom to set up his son for an investment that has been sensational over the years.

"My dad always worked for the railroad and he used to buy stock, and he said to me, 'You need some stock in your telephone company, it's an investment.' I said, 'Dad, I'm young, I don't want to fool around with that.' But my dad noticed an ad in the newspaper that 200 shares were available for $2,400, so he bought them for me. After he bought those, I never bought one more share on the outside. I just bought them out of payroll deduction. Now, I have quite a few shares, but if my dad hadn't seen it in the paper, I wouldn't have gotten any."

Most other employees at the time bought shares, too, because they could see the progress and they had faith in Bob Doyle. Their faith was rewarded many times over.

## $2.26 MILLION STOCK SALE
## STARTING IN 1960 GOES SLOWLY

After several years under Bob Doyle, the progress of the telephone company was visible to everybody. But the growth needs of the company continued to be enormous as Roseville and Citrus Heights continued to boom. Roseville's population climbed from 8,723 in 1950 to 13,421 in 1960. Meanwhile, the unincorporated areas of Sacramento County, including Citrus Heights, Rancho Cordova, Fair Oaks and other growing communities in the county, more than doubled to 291,357 from only 128,919 in 1950. For the third public stock sale, Doyle and the Board of Directors decided to sell $2,260,000, a staggering increase over the earlier stock sales.

"We were really getting into heavy construction then and had a lot of things we needed to do, buying additional property for future use, putting up buildings and everything. So we decided the third stock issue was going to be $2,260,000," Doyle said. "To induce our current shareholders, we received permission to raise the price of the stock from $12 to $15 and again gave them one new share for every 10 that they had. So the shareholder who bought 100 shares

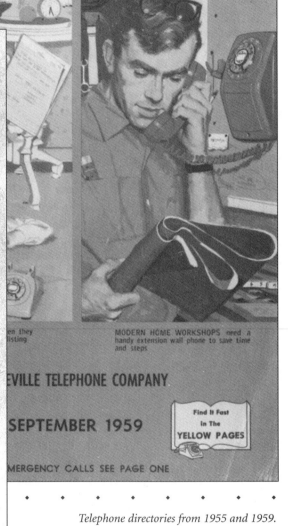

# ROSEVILLE CITRUS HEIGHTS

MODERN HOME WORKSHOPS need a handy extension wall phone to save time and steps

...EVILLE TELEPHONE COMPANY

SEPTEMBER 1959

Find It Fast In The
YELLOW PAGES

...MERGENCY CALLS SEE PAGE ONE

# ROSEVILLE, CALIFORNIA

## Telephone Directory

### NOVEMBER 1955

RAILROAD CENTER
OF THE WEST

ROSEVILLE TELEPHONE COMPANY

SEE PAGE 1 AND INSIDE BACK COVER FOR EMERGENCY CALLS
AND OTHER IMPORTANT INFORMATION

REFER TO THE
YELLOW PAGES

THE *Yellow Pages* TELL
WHERE TO BUY

YOUR CONVENIENT
SHOPPING GUIDE

*Telephone directories from 1955 and 1959.*

at $10 for $1,000 when the shares first sold in 1953 now had 121 shares at $15 worth $1,815. That was a good selling point for me, at least for the initial investors. I also said we're going to raise our cash dividend to $.15 per quarter, which is 4 percent. Back then, most small companies paid their cash dividend on an annual or semi-annual basis. I said we were going to pay ours every three months, quarterly.

"The reason I did that was so the investors got a check every three months. It was a little more hassle for me and cost a little more money to do it that way, but it was good public relations. These guys would go out and buy stock in the bank or some other company and get one check a year, or two maybe. But with Roseville Telephone Company, they were getting that check every three months. Well, it seemed like they were getting a lot more than they were getting. The women would run around and say, 'That telephone company, I just keep getting checks from them.' People thought they were getting more than from other companies, although as a percentage they probably weren't. So the first dividend check would be received on March 15th, just before income tax. And then June and September and then the last one was just before Christmas. The investors thought they were getting a bonus! Smart timing, I thought. The investors thought it was great. My critics, however, said mailing four dividend checks a year cost more money and I said, 'Sure it's going to cost more money, but we're going to be here a long time. We're going to be selling the stock. We're not using a broker, so we saved a lot of money there.'"

The sale of $2.26 million of stock in a small company like Roseville Telephone was an enormous task in 1960. The company's annual revenue didn't exceed $1 million until 1960 and at the end of 1959 the total plant investment was only $2.7 million. The equivalent stock offering today, factoring in Roseville Telephone's current revenue and fixed plant investment, would be about $200 million. Even Bob Doyle underestimated the immensity of the undertaking.

But in 1959, thanks in part to a rate increase authorized by the CPUC, revenue soared to $916,461 from $597,785 the previous year. And net income jumped to $163,304, more than triple the $50,617 in earnings in 1958. The numbers gave Doyle a good story to tell. And after Roseville Telephone became a full toll center in November 1959, the company's profitability promised to be even better.

"Well, there weren't a lot of people who thought it could be done," Doyle said about selling the third stock issue. "The bankers in San Francisco and everybody else, too, said it was absolutely impossible to sell that much stock locally without a broker. It just couldn't be done. There were times that I thought they sure were right because we just about ran out of gas a few times. But after 2 1/2 years, we finally finished that sale. You never forget a sale like that one."

Doyle used what developed into his standard formula, selling shares first to existing shareholders and to employees by payroll deduction. He would also send out a letter in the billings to telephone subscribers and companies doing business with the company to make them aware of the stock sale. After giving those people a chance to buy shares, he would then try to sell them to anybody who would listen. And that third stock sale took a lot of sales effort on Doyle's part.

As might be expected, there were humorous episodes during Doyle's selling of stock.

"One old Italian had a grocery store, was always working and got home late. So I went to his house, and he said, 'Would you like a glass of wine?' and I said, 'Sure.' You know you got to have a glass of wine with those guys. So he gets a glass of wine and then brings out this old box of money. He lays that old box down and starts counting out money … I think he bought a couple of thousand worth of stock! And there was still money in that box!

"I'm sitting there, and he says, 'Do you want another glass of wine?' and I said OK so he gets up, leaves. Here's all this money. I could have reached in there and grabbed money … he wouldn't have known. But that's the way these guys dealt … cash.

"So we sat there and had another glass of wine and I finally pick up the money and give him a receipt and after I left, I got to thinking to myself, 'What if he didn't have that money counted right, and when I left, he counted it and it wasn't exactly right? He'll think I took it,' because I sure could have. But he bought stock and I was happy."

Mark Shull remembered that third stock offering.

"We had a lot of people come into the office with cash. In fact, most did," Shull said. "The money actually smelled of moth balls. This money would come in plain old cash, dug up out of the backyard, I guess. It would smell so strong of mothballs Doyle couldn't wait to get it to the bank and out of his office. It smelled so bad."

In 1960, George Minasian joined Roseville Telephone after nearly 14 years with Pacific Telephone. He was in charge of the business office and one of his first duties was to help sell the stock.

"In the old days, people would come in here with money belts and pay me cash for stock. Once a week or once a month, people would come in here and buy two shares of stock," Minasian remembered. "Some of these old-timers around Roseville didn't trust the banks. This one old guy came in with $100 bills. He had a ton of money and bought about $1,200 worth of stock. People had been keeping their cash in bags and sacks at home. They were the old-time people in Roseville, the old Italians here, and a lot of those people bought stock."

Bob Doyle recalled another early stockholder, a Greek named Sam Meekas, who owned the Rainbow Club in Roseville.

"We'd go in after work and he'd come over and say, 'Mr. Doyle, can I buy some stock?' And he'd give me an envelope and I'd say, 'Just a minute, let me give you...' and he'd say 'no, no, no receipt. If I don't trust you, I won't buy the stock.' That's what the old guy did," Doyle said. "And once in a while when we'd go in there he'd give me an envelope full of cash. Sometimes it would be $400-$500 in $20 bills. That happened all the time! I had guys come into my office and lay the money down there and they would not take the receipt. I'd say, 'Why don't you want...' They'd say, 'Because I trust you. That's the reason I'm buying the stock.' And 90 percent of the people that bought this stock didn't know the first thing about stock. But they knew the Roseville Telephone Company and they figured we were honest people, and by god, they were local people and it was the best thing for them to do, own telephone company stock."

It wasn't only old-timers and ethnic businessmen in Roseville who became early stockholders. "We had quite a few Japanese stockholders from Newcastle, Loomis, Penryn, Rocklin, all around here," added Doyle. "And they don't sell it, they hang on."

Some of the original stock certificates have come into the office in recent years as families convert ownership to trusts or when heirs receive shares left to them. Virginia Amick, Doyle's current secretary, describes these old certificates.

"I just can't believe how they would come in. You'd have to put the certificates in the file cabinet and then you'd open it up and, oh, that odor. You'd have that odor in there for two or three days," Amick said. "You couldn't get rid of the odor because the certificates had been buried for so many years."

But $2.26 million worth at $15 a share is a pile of shares to sell, more than 150,000. And in spite Doyle's salesmanship, the merits of a quarterly dividend, and the excellent progress of the company, selling the third issue was the most difficult task Doyle had undertaken.

"We were so hard up I told Minasian to sell even one share at a time," recalled Doyle. "I told him, 'I don't care if they want one share, sell it to them. Make a stockholder out of them, get their money. We're not going to say they have to buy so much. One share, that's enough.' If some guy came in with 14 bucks, I'd probably loan him a buck to buy a damn share. It got to the desperate stage where we weren't selling anything. So I got hold of my brother, Tom. He knew a guy named Jack Neugebauer who lived in Truckee and was a railroad yard master there. Neugebauer also had the theater at Brockway on the lake ... so I said let's go up and see if Neugebauer knows anybody who wants to buy some telephone stock.

"So Tom and I went up there and I thought maybe we can get this thing rolling again. Of course, Neugebauer knew everybody around there so he got a few shares," Doyle remembered. "Then we met some people who owned a golf course in Tahoe City. They bought some stock. Two or three other people in there bought some stock, too.

"Then Neugebauer suggested we go see John Rayburn, who owned the Crystal Bay Club. We cruised down there and this old guy's got a ball cap on and he's chewing tobacco. Just a hell of a guy, John Rayburn. So we went in. He got behind the bar and poured us a couple drinks. All the while I'm telling him about the stock. After about an hour or so just talking about hunting and this and that, Rayburn says, 'How much is the stock?' I said $15 a share. He said, 'I'll take 1,000 shares.' I just about shit my pants. He said, 'I want you to go around to Brockway. The real estate guy there, his name is Sutton. He's my brother-in-law. Go tell him I told you to have him buy some stock.' So we went over there and he bought 300 shares.

"Anyway, while up there at Tahoe I called old George Minasian to ask him how he had been doing," Doyle continued. 'Jesus, I sold one share,' George said. He wasn't doing anything. That trip to Tahoe got us going again and after 2 1/2 years, we finished that sale.

"I can remember that stock sale as well as I can remember my own name. When you start selling something, and 2 1/2 years later, you're still struggling with it, you know you've been some place."

## MORE GOOD PUBLIC RELATIONS

In 1956, Roseville Telephone celebrated what would be the first of several open houses through the years. The open house has served several purposes, the first of which was to show off the newly-remodeled business office in the old Welcome Club building. The company showed the public, including share-holders, subscribers and vendors, that the company was making progress. New buildings, equipment and offices greeted the public. The open houses also helped the company develop a positive image in the community. In those years Roseville Telephone needed to do almost anything it could to improve a reputation that had been so poor for so many years.

In the *Press-Tribune* of Wednesday, Nov. 14, 1956, a "double-truck" (two full facing pages) advertisement invited the community to the company's first open house on Nov. 15.

This first open house ad contained much of Bob Doyle's philosophy on running a company. There were photos of every employee. The managers had individual photos while the other employees were pictured in their work groups. Doyle's picture was not prominent, as he prefers to be viewed as one of the employees and not just the "boss." The advertising text reflected the core beliefs that to this day Doyle finds most meaningful.

" ... *We want everyone in this area to come in ... to meet our personnel and go through our modern business office ... we feel sure that everyone who visits us will understand more about their dial telephone service and we are certain that all will* have a new appreciation for the many problems a telephone company faces in order to render service."

Doyle was quoted in the ad: "*Telephone plants ... are like an iceberg of which only a fraction is visible above water. The telephone is the only item of the plant equipment with which our subscribers are acquainted. But for every dollar invested in his telephone, many more are required for the equipment which will connect his telephone with another.*"

In an effort to position the company's key role in the community, the advertisement emphasized that the employees were like family.

"Big Family in Telephone Group" read the headline on the second page of the advertisement. "*...The list of people associated with the local telephone service covers a wide range of skills and talents. As a group, they make up a large working force in this community and generate an annual payroll of approximately $180,000...*"

Furthermore, the ad said, "*... Many of the employees own their own homes, or are from established families in the community. In keeping with the telephone tradition, they are solid citizens interested in the community and proud of the company for which they work.*

Eugene Garbolino joined the board of directors in April 1957, replacing F.A. Lewis who died. Lewis had been on the board since the company's founding.

"*Most of our telephone family consists of people with long experience and service in the telephone business. Newcomers who enter the business are quickly trained by the veterans, not only in the 'know how' of telephone technology, but also in giving prompt and courteous attention to all telephone subscriber needs.*"

Cynics might call this standard business hyperbole. But make no mistake, Bob Doyle believed every word in his 1956 advertisement. Imagine the change in public posture in less than three years under Doyle. A company that for decades was despised by the community now trumpets its progress, solid citizen/ employees and hefty payroll. Quite a turnaround, indeed.

A little box within the advertisement showed two cartoon characters stretching a dollar bill. "HOW YOUR TELEPHONE S-T-R-E-T-C-H-E-S YOUR DOLLAR" the headline read. "Your telephone grows more valuable with each new installation ... you can call more people, more people can call you. And, even in the face of rising prices for everything from apricots to zippers, telephone service remains a low cost bargain ... the biggest in your budget."

Through the years Roseville Telephone's basic advertising theme has remained virtually the same — that Roseville Telephone is a progressive, successful company composed of talented, loyal employees, and also a company that invests in its future and the community for the betterment of both.

## ARTHUR YOUNG & CO. HIRED AS ACCOUNTING FIRM

In early 1957, Doyle added another key member to his management team when Mark Shull moved from Kansas to become chief accountant for Roseville Telephone. Shull heard about the job through family. His mother-in-law, who lived in Sacramento, noticed in a *Sacramento Bee* classified ad that Roseville Telephone was looking for a person experienced in telephone accounting.

Shull's previous employment had an ironic twist. He was working for a small-town exchange in Junction City, Kansas — Roseville's original name was Junction. Also, the company Shull worked at in Kansas was owned by two brothers — coincidentally, named Bob and Tom — who didn't get along. Although Shull wanted to change jobs, he didn't find Doyle's initial offer attractive enough.

"I came out to California in early 1957 and interviewed with Bob," Shull recalled. "At that time we didn't get together because what I wanted and what he was willing to pay were two different things. A month or so passed, then Bob called me back in Kansas and said that if I still wanted the job, I could have it with the salary he and I had discussed. It was about the same pay I had been getting, but he didn't offer to pay moving expenses. I said OK.

"I came to work for the phone company in March of 1957 and was kind of the auditor, office manager, general flunky of all duties working for Bob. Merle Ruggles had just come aboard in 1956 and he dumped our pay stations and did other odd jobs. We were a very small company by California standards, with a gross plant investment of less than a million dollars."

With the company's second stock sale looming in mid-1957, Doyle knew it was time to raise the caliber of the company's financial expertise. Shull's hiring was the first step in strengthening the company's fiscal posture, an important issue to the lenders and regulators. Financial accounting was not a strong suit of Doyle's.

Another important step was made in 1959 when the company retained the accounting firm of Arthur Young & Company in San Francisco. As the company grew, Doyle and Shull decided the company needed more outside accounting help.

"It was part of my plan to strengthen the financial area," Doyle said. "First of all, we recruited Mark to come to work here. At that time we had L.F. Martin out of Fresno auditing our books. I had inherited that firm from the

# MY, HOW WE HAVE GROWN

During the past decade, the Roseville Telephone Company's growth has been truly representative of the progress made in this area. Back in 1950, the Company's total assets amounted to only $356,437, while today they amount to a whopping $3,516,594. In the past ten years, the number of stockholders has increased from 11 to 468, and their holdings have jumped from $62,500 to $1,049,850. These factors are indicative of the faith local people have in this local business. The Roseville Telephone Company has sold stock locally, and will again sell stock to local residents in 1960.

*San Juan Record, 1959*

Hanisches. But Mark and I agreed that since we planned to sell more stock in the years ahead that we should have a stronger accounting firm signing off on our annual report.

"I found out from the California Independent Telephone Association that Arthur Young audited several telephone companies, so we decided to contact them. At that time Arthur Young had an office in San Francisco, but not in Sacramento. I got in touch with them, we got our heads together and they took us on."

Doyle had also learned about Arthur Young from the Western California Telephone Company, an independent based in Los Gatos near San Jose and an Arthur Young client. Doyle was elected to Western Cal's Board of Directors in the summer of 1958. The announcement of Doyle's election appeared in Western Cal's July 1958 newsletter. It said, "Mr. Doyle will bring a wealth of experience to his new role here..." It noted that managers at each company had visited the other and that at the time of his election, "The Roseville Company serves about 6,600 subscribers in a fast-growing area just north of Sacramento ... Mr. Doyle, who is manager as well as president, heads a staff of 67."

The decision to hire Arthur Young was important to Roseville Telephone for a number of reasons. Arthur Young was one the nation's leading accounting firms and, as a client, Roseville Telephone gained credibility. Also, "A-Y," as the company was called, was a large, international firm with significant expertise in a broad range of utility management issues. For example, a comprehensive

## ...AND WE'RE NOT THROUGH GROWING YET!

study A-Y did for Roseville Telephone in 1961 laid the groundwork for how the company would manage its fast growth. Finally, A-Y had numerous contacts in the banking and legal community that Roseville relied upon over the years. One such contact was Cooper, White & Cooper, a San Francisco legal firm that became Roseville Telephone's counsel in 1965. Ernst & Young, the merger successor to Arthur Young, remains the company's CPA firm, and Cooper, White & Cooper still advises the company on legal issues.

As has been the case in the growth and development of the company's physical infrastructure, Doyle consistently seeks the most expert advice available, even if the fees are generally higher. "As I always say, if you cut corners, 99 percent of the time, you'll end up paying more in the long run," he said. "We try to get the best, but we're careful we get our money's worth, too. That's just the way we do things."

Roseville Telephone's investment in expert advice indeed has paid enormous dividends through the decades.

## COMPANY NEWSLETTER, 'LINE CHATTER,' BEGINS PUBLICATION

At about the same time that Doyle became a board member of Western California Telephone, Roseville Telephone inaugurated its newsletter, *Line Chatter*, which was first published in July 1958. Doyle doesn't recall exactly how or why *Line Chatter* got started, but it's likely Doyle fashioned *Line Chatter* after Western Cal's monthly newsletter, *Crosstalk*.

Company newsletters were not as common in the late 1950s as they are today. Their purpose is clear — to disseminate information to employees about company affairs and to provide a forum for ideas, functions, musings and just about anything else. Certainly, *Line Chatter* has served those purposes and more since 1958.

The format of *Line Chatter* hasn't changed dramatically over the years. Certain staples are present in every issue. One is the station count — access line count in later years — which shows the monthly increase or decrease in telephones in service. Amazingly, there have been only two months out of more than 400 months since 1958 that Roseville Telephone showed a decrease in telephones in service. This fact more than any other reflects the company's growth since Doyle took over.

Another mainstay is the letters section. Each month the company receives dozens of unsolicited letters from customers complimenting employees. In some companies, these never see the light of day, but at Roseville Telephone, complimentary letters get top priority. It's one reason for the outstanding employee morale enjoyed at the company over the years.

The step-by-step switching equipment "frames" kept employees busy ensuring all circuits were operating properly.

Each edition includes reports from various company departments — executive, business office, central office, outside plant engineering, installation, splicing, construction, etc. *Line Chatter* enables each department to keep the rest of the company abreast of developments in its area. Doyle has skillfully used the newsletter time and again to remind employees about the value of being a stockholder. Any news item regarding the company's stock is usually on the front page.

Budding employee writers have used *Line Chatter* as a forum to exhibit their talent. Cartoons and other items of humor make the publication readable, even to non-employees. Functions such as retirement parties get plenty of space in *Line Chatter* as do company picnics, Christmas parties, Telephone Pioneer Association activities, the Roseville Telephone Foundation, Tommy Apostolos Fund, United Way and assorted charitable activities.

Birth announcements, deaths, marriages, engagements, new hires, company anniversaries, vacations, horoscopes, bowling results, softball statistics, "corporate challenge" news, "Dillon's Dash" and the best places to hunt and fish are among the ingredients in the successful communications recipe that is *Line Chatter*.

The Employee Relations Committee (ERC) uses the publication to keep employees abreast of issues being discussed by management and labor. It also keeps employees informed about changes in company benefits and the frequent changes in taxation affecting employees. One could sense the writer's distaste when near-annual tax rate increases are explained to employees through *Line Chatter*.

Of course, the early *Line Chatters* were more free-wheeling than current ones. For example, it seems the installation crew in the late 1950s was the beneficiary of a bet between Bob Doyle and Page Ellis, the company's long-time plant engineer, over the number of telephone installations the crew could do in a month. Doyle bet Ellis that the crew could do 150 new installations a month. To give the crew added incentive, Doyle promised the installation crew "a fifth" if this goal was reached. A fifth of booze, that is … incentive programs were different back then.

"I was always doing something like that in those years," Doyle admitted, "to stimulate the crew to do a little more, you know."

With about 500 employees at the company today, *Line Chatter* remains an important communications vehicle. *Line Chatter* is a must read for anybody who wants to stay on top of events at the company as well as developments in the telecommunications industry.

One of *Line Chatter's* most devoted readers is Bob Doyle.

"He amazes you sometimes. I'll ask him how he knows something and he'll say

*Renovation of the old "Pall Mall" bar creates room for Roseville Telephone's expanding central switching office.*

he read it in the *Line Chatter*," said Bob Parsons, director of customer services. "I'm pretty sure he always reads them closely to make sure he isn't missing anything."

"That's true," agreed Doyle. "*Line Chatter* has always been important reading for me and it should be for all employees. There's a lot of good stuff in it."

## DOYLE FINALLY GETS THE FARMER LINES

As indicated earlier, an important step in the growth of Roseville Telephone was the acquisition of the several farmer lines that served those rural areas that in the first 40 years the company didn't directly serve. Their acquisition was instrumental in the company's ability to maintain explosive growth throughout its territory.

Of all Doyle's earliest accomplishments, including hiring new people, raising funds and borrowing money, perhaps none was as difficult as buying the farmer lines. It required determination and selling skills that are vintage Bob Doyle. His attempts to secure these lines began in 1953 even before he became president.

"There were about five separate farmer lines we wanted to buy," recalled Doyle. "When I was trying to get them interested, I'd invite the farmer-line customers to a meeting, usually at a school or a grange hall in the area.

"I told the farmers that we were about ready to go dial and that their service, which had 12 and 14 people on a line, wasn't going to work any more. 'You are going to have to eliminate a lot of these people on the lines and, in fact, this plant you have out here is not going to work,' I told them. 'Your plant isn't worth anything to us and we're going to have to replace it. It is going to cost us a bunch of money. We will purchase the phone from you. We'll pay you $35 …' I'd get about that far and one of them would yell, 'We want $100, at least $100.' And I would say, 'Can't do it. We can't afford to pay that much … ' That's how those early meetings went."

At one meeting at the Eureka School, Doyle gave his pitch and the angry farmer-line customers asked him to wait outside a few minutes while they discussed his proposal.

"It was in the winter … colder than hell," Doyle remembered. "I went out and got in my car and sat there for a long time. Finally the door opened and one of them waved for me to come in. I went in there and they said, 'Go to hell! We don't want any part of you, we're not going to sell … ' They treated me like a damn stepchild."

After the conversion to dial on Nov. 1, 1953, the farmer-line customers who didn't have dial telephones — some of them did — continued to go through the old manual common battery switchboard. The old board stayed in use because the CPUC issued an order allowing the Sylvan-Antelope farmer-line to delay switching to dial. It wasn't until 1957 that Doyle was finally able to secure the farmer lines for Roseville Telephone. He paid $40 per farmer-line customer. There were approximately 300 customers at the time.

It should come as no surprise that Doyle's exceptional stock-selling skills played a role in winning over the farmers. Many farmer-line families became shareholders during the stock sale of 1957. As new shareholders, they could see the long-term benefit of incorporating the farmer lines into the Roseville Telephone system. Finally, Doyle's sales pitch succeeded.

"My efforts to buy the farmer lines began to pay off when I started selling some of these people stock," Doyle explained. "As stockholders, it made the cheese more binding, you know. The farmers would say to themselves, 'Hell, I'm a stockholder now,' and that made a difference. They got the benefits of buying the lines, including better service, and they didn't have to worry about repairing the plant and putting up new stuff. They finally came around to seeing that it was the right thing to do."

Although Doyle's efforts were finally working, it didn't happen quickly. He needed help from some of the farmer-line customers themselves.

"I kept getting a few more people on my side all the time. I sold stock to Jim Denio and a few others who were on farmer lines. Where Denio's Auction is, that was on the Dry Creek farmer line. It was like a domino effect. Once I got the first farmer line, I could go to stockholders who were connected with the other farmer lines to help me sell the others on the idea. I figured they trusted one another even if they didn't trust me.

"The first outfit I bought was the Antelope farmer line. They met out at the Grange Hall. I told them, 'We will take down all the poles. You tell us where to stack them. And all that open wire, we'll roll it up and put it any place you want. You can string it up and raise berries and do all kinds of things with the wire.' For some reason, that approach rang somebody's bell because they agreed to sell. I was so proud …

"Once I got the first one, then at least I could say, 'Well you know Antelope sold and we're starting to replace their lines and put up new plant.' I got one at a time until we bought all of them," Doyle continued. "It was no small job getting those farmer lines. All they had to do is to say, 'The hell with you' and put up their own plant. That's what I was up against. I just kept plugging and plugging. I think it helped that I had been a farmer myself before joining the company. Hell, I was one of them and they knew it. I wasn't some slick sales guy out of Sacramento or San Francisco trying to put something over on them."

Another factor in the farmers' decision to sell was prompted by the changing telephone technology of the '50s. The cooperatives' owners knew they would eventually face a major investment in new equipment if they chose to remain separate from Roseville Telephone. Also, by 1957 Doyle had built credibility in the community because everyone familiar with the company witnessed the tremendous strides that Doyle and his management team had made in a few short years.

There were three small farmer lines Doyle didn't buy in the 1950s because they had so few families on them. "I didn't really care to buy the small ones because it didn't make economic sense," Doyle said. "For example, the Fiddyments lived out west of town where Del Webb's Sun City is going in now. In the 1950s, there were only three different Fiddyment guys on that line. If we had bought that line, we would have had to put a line all the way out there, probably about five miles in all. It was the same with Cliff Johnson at Johnson Ranch. It didn't make sense for us to buy those lines."

Al Johnson worked for Automatic Electric during the years Doyle was trying to buy the farmer lines. As a sales engineer, Johnson was familiar with smaller telephone companies throughout the West and their difficulties in acquiring local farmer lines.

"It was a tremendous feat to convince these hard-headed farmers to give up their stuff and sell to Roseville Telephone," Johnson said. "Not just anybody could have convinced them. Quite a few farmer lines in the Central Valley of California stayed independent. It sure made a difference to Roseville that Bob was successful in acquiring the ones here."

"Getting those farmer lines picked up was one of the first things we had to do," recalled Tom Doyle, who joined the board in January 1952. "Bob did a magnificent job of convincing these farmers that they should sell their lines to us. They never really had anything, but they thought they did."

## DEATH TAKES TWO FARMERS

By 1957, Bob Doyle's vision of Roseville Telephone was taking shape. He had come a long way since 1953 and the company was readying for another burst of growth. No doubt his father was proud of his second son's accomplishments at the telephone company, but old Bill Doyle never complimented Bob directly.

"Oh sure, I think he was happy about how things were going at the telephone company, but he never mentioned it to me," Bob Doyle said. "It just wasn't his way to pass out compliments. He probably told his buddies that he was proud of what we were doing at the company, but he'd never tell me himself. It didn't bother me because I knew he was feeling good about it — he didn't need to say it. I understood how he thought. He was from the old school."

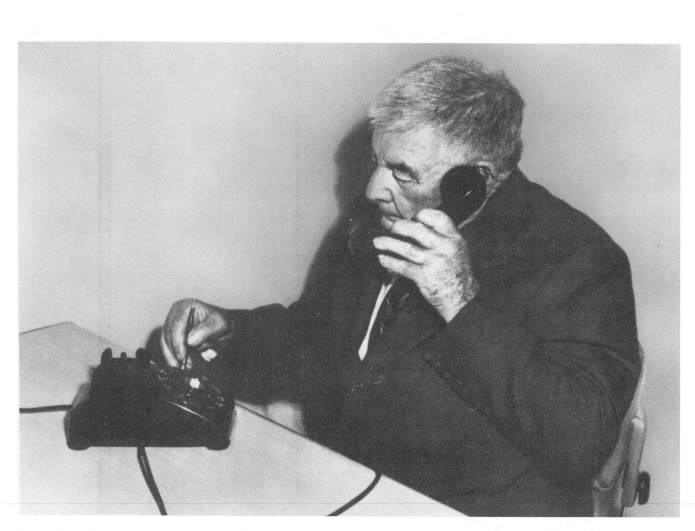

*William J. "Bill" Doyle died in May 1957 at the age of 81.*

The long-time company president and life-long farmer died in late May 1957 after spending his final months in an Orangevale nursing home. At 81, W.J. Doyle had lived a full, successful life.

A little more than a year later, in August 1958, death visited the Doyle family again, this time unexpectedly and tragically. William J. Doyle's oldest son Jack drowned while vacationing in Ft. Bragg, Calif. with his young family. His death was a great loss to the family, especially to his brother Bob. Born 13 months apart, Jack and Bob Doyle were close.

"He had never been on vacation before with his family," Bob Doyle remembered. "They were fishing at Ft. Bragg and on the evening before they were to leave, some local fishermen asked Jack how he had done fishing. He said he hadn't caught anything. So they convinced him to stick around one more night when they'd take him fishing. Well, they got on this little boat to go out to the big boat, but the little one capsized and he drowned.

"I got the call about 4 o'clock in the morning or whatever the hell the time it was, telling me that my brother had drowned up at Fort Bragg. I said, 'You've got to be kidding me.' 'No.' I thought, 'What am I going to do now? I've got to call my sisters, and my brother. And I have to make sure my mother knows about it.'"

After calling his brother and sisters, Bob Doyle went to see the family doctor, Dr. Kelly, who lived across the street from Hazel Doyle. "I told him what happened and asked if he could go with me when I broke the news to my mother, to give her medication if she needed it. My sisters and Tom — we were all shocked. It was a sad, sad situation."

Jack Doyle's untimely death at age 40 cut short what probably would have been a substantial career. Not only was Jack an outstanding farmer, but he had already kicked off a promising political career as well.

"I don't know why Jack did it, but he decided he wanted to be a county supervisor, so he went out there, worked real hard and did it," Bob Doyle remembered. "After he died, Tom ran in his place during the next election and won."

Nobody knows how events would have unfolded had Jack Doyle been alive through the years, but it's clear to Bob that his older brother would have been a prominent member of the community. "There's no doubt in my mind Jack would have been pretty influential around here. The whole thing was just so sad."

## CITRUS HEIGHTS CENTRAL OFFICE BUILT

The first big addition to the Roseville Telephone system, the first expansion that proved that the company was now truly interested in serving all its customers, was the Citrus Heights central office. The land was purchased in 1956 and construction started in 1957 to build a central office that would house a 1,000-line, step-by-step switch. The new central office enabled all Citrus Heights customers to convert their eight-party "suburban service" to the standard "base rate service" of four-, two- and one-party service.

The new central office didn't come too soon. From the late 1950s to the present day, ongoing development has changed Citrus Heights from a land of pastoral ranches and farms into a tightly-woven mesh of housing subdivisions and commercial developments, large and small. In addition to the creation of Folsom Lake and Interstate 80 (U.S. 40 at that time) through Roseville, Aerojet's operations in Rancho Cordova grew almost exponentially from 1951 through 1964. Many Aerojet employees settled in Citrus Heights. At its peak in 1964, the company had about 20,000 employees. Aerojet was by far the largest single employer the Sacramento region has ever had, other than the giant state government complex, which was also growing fast in the 1950s. These factors contributed to the rapid growth of Citrus Heights, and to a lesser extent, Roseville.

On Sept. 8, 1957, the $305,000 Citrus Heights central office went on-line and, for the first time, Roseville Telephone customers began using descriptive prefixes on their telephones. Citrus Heights began to use PArkview prefixes and Roseville subscribers began to use SUnset prefixes.

Not all Citrus Heights customers received their desired service immediately, Doyle told customers at the time in an interview with the *Roseville Press-Tribune*. He said service upgrading was a lengthy process because of the difficulty at that time in getting the necessary dial equipment and cabling.

"The lack of more rapid progress is not the fault of your telephone company," said an advertisement in the Aug. 30, 1957, *Citrus Heights Bulletin*. "Equipment must be ordered months and even years in advance. Because of the tremendous growth over the nation, equipment manufacturing concerns have been unable to keep up with the demand. Our orders, for instance, have only partially filled up to this time."

## RATE HIKE SOUGHT IN 1958, APPROVED IN 1959

The heavy capital investment during the years after Doyle became president eroded the company's margin of profitability. Given the prospects of even greater capital investments in the next few years, Doyle and the Board of Directors decided it was time to request a general rate increase. Preparation for the rate filing was one impetus for hiring Mark Shull in early 1957.

"I think I was some help to Bob in putting all the information together for that rate filing," said Shull. "We also had help from Neil Hasbrook, who was the secretary of the California Independent Telephone Association at that time. Tom Srednik, a practicing attorney in Roseville, was our legal counsel. He was also a board member.

"Bob and I did the work, I put it in draft form, and Srednik finished it up, as I recall. It was a lot of work because you had to make studies of the various rates of return and project what your needs would be. It took a long time."

The formal application went to the PUC in June 1958. The company sought to increase its rates by 53 percent, which would generate a 7 percent profit on revenue. (By the PUC's calculations, it was 8.1 percent.) Hearings were held in November 1958. Doyle, Shull and Page Ellis, the company's plant superintendent, stated the company's case.

"The telephone company is asking the commission for authority to increase its rates so that the company will get a fair return on its investment to guarantee its stockholders fair rates of returns on their investments," Doyle said. A new rate schedule was necessary to offset "the declining net revenues and rates of return on present rates."

Doyle said the company had already invested $1.5 million in plant and equipment since the previous rate increase in 1953. Moreover, the company was planning another $1 million in capital spending in 1959 and 1960. Shull testified that the rate structure existing at that time would generate a return of only 3.5 percent on revenue in 1958.

Less than two months later, the PUC announced that it had granted Roseville Telephone increases that would allow it to earn a projected 6.5 percent return on investment. The new rates went into effect Feb. 1, 1959. Doyle proclaimed himself "completely satisfied" with the decision.

One-party basic monthly service fees went to $6.25 from $4 and $5 in Roseville and Citrus Heights, respectively; two-party went to $5.15 from $3.50 and $4.25, and four-party service went to $4.35 from $3 and $3.50. Business line charges nearly doubled.

"So we got through the rate increase and received essentially what we wanted," Shull recollected. "From that point on, the company enjoyed a pretty good rate of return."

## OPERATORS MOVE "UPSTAIRS"

A major sign of progress to the company's operators occurred June 1959 when they moved "upstairs" from their cramped, street-floor quarters on Lincoln Street into much larger, newly-renovated space on the second floor of the old Welcome Club building at the corner of Lincoln and Atlantic streets. Welcoming the operators when they moved upstairs was a new 12-position operator board. The move came just in time, according to Bernice Moser.

"Through the 1950s, they had added to that board downstairs, both lengthwise and going up. There was no more room. Because our chairs downstairs were real high like a stool, and there was a ring around the bottom where you put your feet, our shortest operator, Eleanor Nichols, would have to almost stand straight up to hit some of the top ones. I swear she could take the cord and fling it into the hole like a dart.

"After we moved upstairs, everything just seemed to fall into line to where it was grow, grow, grow. It was exciting, we had our new lounge, we had our new board, our new information positions. When we first moved up there though, we still had the round information files, which were kind of like a large Rolodex.

"But we didn't have a rug on the floor, so one day they just gave me some money to go and buy a rug for the floor," Moser said. "We just marveled at having a rug because the room was so stark and bare and all closed in. There weren't any windows except for the one or two we had in our lounge. Later,

*The operators enjoyed moving to a more spacious, newly-remodeled area upstairs in the old Welcome Club building.*

they put a mural on the wall that went from floor to ceiling and wall to wall. That mural really helped. It gave us the feeling we were outside."

It wasn't until the following year that the operators had automatic toll-ticketing equipment. Prior to this, the operators had to keep time themselves and keep track of the toll tickets. As one can imagine, it was a paper nightmare.

The space downstairs from the operators had been occupied in late 1956 when the business office and administrative offices moved in from next door. It would be only a few more years until Doyle and the business office would move across Lincoln Street to a new administration building as the company spread out in downtown Roseville, gradually acquiring contiguous properties to fuel its non-stop growth.

## ROSEVILLE BECOMES A FULL TOLL CENTER

One of the most important steps along the way to building a modern telephone company occurred in November 1959 when Roseville Telephone became a full toll center. This meant the company no longer relied upon Pacific Telephone operators to place toll calls to locations outside the Sacramento region.

Prior to 1959, the company did not have the switching capabilities to be a full toll center. For calls going outside the Sacramento/Auburn area, Roseville operators would switch the calls to Pacific operators in Sacramento who would complete them. Roseville Telephone had to compensate Pacific Telephone for this service. The two companies would reach "settlements" which split toll revenue between the two companies according to specified formulas and usage.

In becoming a full toll center, Roseville Telephone operators completed outgoing calls (other than international calls, which came later). This enabled Roseville to retain a larger percentage of the toll revenue, since it handled the entire call, not just a portion of it. Al Johnson explained the financial significance:

"As a toll center, Roseville Telephone would share the full revenue, the total revenue. It was very financially advantageous to a telephone company to become a full toll center. Pacific Telephone had told Bob and his people that they weren't capable of being a full toll center, that they were too small and did not

*Chief operator Gladys Ellis enjoyed the city-scape mural in her new office upstairs in the remodeled Welcome Club.*

have the expertise to undertake such a program. Bob insisted they could, and he finally showed Pacific, because they did it."

Bob Doyle was confident all along, of course.

"I told Pacific, 'Listen, if you can do it, we can do it. The only difference is, we can do it better.'"

The conversion to full toll was a key building block in the long-term growth of the company. Not only was the toll business lucrative, but the formulas for settlement of revenue encouraged Roseville Telephone to invest in the latest technologies, because part of the settlement was a function of investment in the related plant and equipment.

"A lot of money was made from toll," said Mark Shull. "The toll rate of return was high, so the company made money in spite of itself. We had all the growth, plus we had an excellent rate of return."

The modernization of the 1950s prepared Roseville Telephone for the century's pivotal decade, the 1960s. This decade was a time for social upheaval across America, but at Roseville Telephone, the '60s were nothing short of fantastic.

A full-page spread in the Nov. 2, 1959, *San Juan Record*, recounted the 1950s at Roseville Telephone.

"MY HOW WE HAVE GROWN" bellowed the large, bold headline at the top of the page. A photo spread below offered ample evidence of progress — new buildings, offices and equipment — and an accompanying narrative summed it up:

"During the past decade, the Roseville Telephone Company's growth has been truly representative of the progress made in this area. Back in 1950, the company's total assets amounted to only $356,437, while today they amount to a whopping $3,516,594. In the past 10 years the number of shareholders has increased from 11 to 468, and their holdings have jumped from $62,500 to $1,049,850. The factors are indicative of the faith local people have in this local business. The Roseville Telephone Company has sold stock locally, and will again sell stock to local residents in 1960."

On the bottom of the page, in large, bold headline type, it read: "… AND WE'RE NOT THROUGH GROWING YET."

# 1960-1977: Ongoing Modernization And Expansion

## DOYLE'S 'SECOND TERM' KICKS OFF 1960s

*"1960 was another year of dynamic growth for our company. Revenues reached an all-time high, as this was the first year to bill in excess of one million dollars ... with the continued growth of California, our future looks very bright indeed."*
— 1960 Annual Report

If the years 1954 through 1959 were Bob Doyle's first term in office as Roseville Telephone's president and chief executive officer, 1960 to mid-1977 was his second term. During this stretch, Roseville Telephone grew from a small, provincial utility company into a sophisticated, medium-sized telephone company that attracted attention for being progressive and far-sighted. During this period, a new wave of experienced people joined the company to succeed the core group of telephone industry veterans Doyle hired in his "first term."

The rate increase granted Roseville Telephone in 1959, the huge stock sale of $2.26 million from 1960 through 1962, and another $1 million in debt gave Doyle the resources to accelerate the building of the telephone company.

"After hiring the first group of managers, many of whom were retired from Pacific Telephone, I knew that I'd need to add new experienced people to head up the departments in 1960s," Doyle said. "The old guys got us started, but we continued to require outside expertise to help us grow."

By all measures, 1960 was a banner year for the company. For the first time ever, revenue exceeded $1 million, rising to $1,271,178 from $967,900 in 1959. Local service revenue increased by $103,763, up more than 20 percent, and toll revenue by $193,026, an increase of 46 percent. The benefits of Roseville Telephone becoming a full toll center in 1959 were paying off in dramatically increased revenue as the company got to keep more of the income generated by toll calls outside the area. After August, the company also got a revenue boost from the introduction of direct distance dialing.

In addition, the service territory was the beneficiary of significant growth in the Sacramento area's military bases, state government and rocket-maker Aerojet General.

· · · · · · ·

*Aerojet came to suburban Sacramento in the early 1950s and grew rapidly. The rocket maker had nearly 20,000 employees in the early 1960s, as the United States and the Soviet Union battled for supremacy in space.*

Courtesy of McClellan Air Force Base History Office

Aerojet outgrew its facilities in Southern California and expanded in 1951 to the Sacramento suburb of Rancho Cordova. The company's impact on the region was immense.

A subsidiary of General Tire and Rubber Co., Aerojet made a name for itself in the 1940s with its first small rocket engines, called JATOs, which stood for "Jet-Assisted Take Offs." These engines boosted the initial acceleration of airplanes to enable them to take off from short runways and aircraft carriers. Then Aerojet, which began operations in Pasadena, Calif., moved its headquarters to El Monte and its rocket engine manufacturing to Azusa, both in Southern California. In those days, Aerojet was called the "General Motors of rocketry" and the company's growth curve was almost identical to its products — an unbelievable acceleration followed by a flameout.

As the space race with the Soviet Union heated up, Aerojet's employment at Rancho Cordova mushroomed from 253 in 1952 to 4,400 in 1956. In 1957 — the year the Soviets launched the world's first man-made satellite, Sputnik — Aerojet added another 2,500 employees in Rancho Cordova and finished the year with 6,970 employees.

As rapid a build-up as this was, the Sacramento region hadn't seen anything yet. Hundreds of millions of dollars flowed from the Defense Department to rocket makers and Aerojet expanded its line, engineering and assembling rocket motors for the Titan, Polaris and Minuteman series of missiles.

By 1960, Aerojet's complex in Rancho Cordova was virtually a small city with more than 17,000 employees. From 1960 to 1964, local employment at Aerojet approached 20,000, making it by far the largest private employer to ever operate in the Sacramento region. During these years the company owned or controlled about 26,000 acres. It seemed like most people in the Sacramento area worked at Aerojet or in businesses supplying the huge company.

Aerojet's explosive growth fueled a tremendous housing spurt that included the communities north of Aerojet's Rancho Cordova complex, including Citrus Heights, Orangevale, Fair Oaks and to a smaller extent, Roseville. Roseville Telephone benefited directly from the huge Aerojet presence since some Aerojet employees lived in the telephone company's service territory. The company also benefited from Aerojet's dramatic downsizing in the late 1960s because a large pool of technically-talented employees was set adrift. These were highly-skilled individuals who found themselves suddenly out of work at Aerojet, but who had put their roots down in the Sacramento area. It was the same then as it is today; once one has lived in the area, it's hard to leave. Several former Aerojet employees joined Roseville Telephone, including Robert Parsons, director of customer service.

Roseville Telephone's growth didn't follow the boom/bust nature of Aerojet; steady growth continued. Investment in plant and equipment totaled $1.5 million in 1960 as the company renovated the old Baker building adjacent to the original company premises on Lincoln Street, erecting a new central office on the site. Automatic toll ticketing was installed at a cost of $425,000. Although expensive, the cost of manually timing and ticketing toll calls was also steep given the labor-intensive nature of the work. Aerial cable additions alone in 1960 amounted to over $400,000. Heavy capital requirements forced the company to borrow another $1 million in 1960. This brought long-term debt to $1,830,500 at the end of 1960. The stock sale announced in 1959 kicked off in September 1960.

DDD, or "Direct Distance Dialing," debuted on Aug. 1, 1960, for Roseville Telephone. Customers could now directly dial nearly every telephone in the country through long distance connections via the Bell System. It was a major advance for customers, of course, and for the telephone company, too, because DDD made it easy to call long-distance. At the outset, callers had to dial "1-1-2" followed by the area code, and the local number. The automatic toll-ticket-

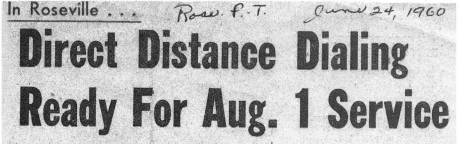

# Direct Distance Dialing Ready For Aug. 1 Service

August 1 the patrons served by the Roseville Telephone Company can start a complex switching equipment reaction with a mere flick of their finger.

That is the date that Direct Distance Dialing goes into effect in the Roseville Telephone Company service area.

Nationwide distance dialing has received the enthusiastic support of every area in which it was inagurated. With service extended to all 50 of the states, as well as Canada and parts of Mexico, Direct Dialing is another step forward for the Roseville Telephone Company.

Robert Doyle, president of the company, said that direct distance dialing means only a few extra spins of the dial as far as the caller is concerned. The magic of toll ticketing does the rest.

### Three Steps

To dial long distance the caller follows these three steps.

Dial the numerals 1-1-2 . . . that connects the call to the toll ticketing equipment.

Then dial an area code number, also consisting of three digets, depending on which part of the country you are calling. A complete list of area codes will appear in the new directory to be published shortly.

Dial the prefix and number that you are calling. An operator will then ask for the caller's own telephone number and the toll ticketing equipment does the rest.

The ticketer is the most important of the units involved in the DDD system, Doyle explained.

### Toll Call

It is composed of relays and rotary switches. The ticketer is seized at the beginning of a toll call and is held during the duration of the call. Hence, the number of ticketers primarily indicates and determines the traffic capacity of the system.

The basic function of a ticketer is to record and store the most essential ticketing data pertaining to a toll call; to time the call when answer supervision is received, and to store the conversation time.

When the conversation is completed, the calling line and the toll circuit are immediately released, but the ticketer is automatically connected to a tabulator and transfers to it, in high speed code, all stored data pertaining to the completed call.

As soon as this transfer is completed, it requires about six seconds, the ticker is restored to its normal condition and is available for another call.

If an attempted toll call does not result in a completed chargeable connection, due to a busy signal, does not answer or abandonment, the ticketer is released instantly when the calling party hangs up. No tape record is produced in this case.

The ticketers are equipped to record a maximum of 11 digits in the called number, which would include an area code, and seven digits for the calling number.

Doyle said, "Direct Dialing Service for Roseville is another step forward in our effort to provide subscribers with the most modern and efficient service in telephone communications."

The company is planning an open house July 22 and 23 to introduce the new service to the public.

Roseville Press-Tribune

ing equipment tracked and recorded the toll information. This was far more efficient than having operators assist and log each long-distance call.

Direct dial was lucrative for Roseville Telephone and other independents. "Long Lines," AT&T's long-distance subsidiary, was enormously profitable and it was in the Bell System's best interests that all telephones in the country be easily accessible, independents included. The more toll traffic, the more profit for both AT&T and local telephone companies, who shared in the revenue. Ron Amick was a liaison between Pacific Telephone and California's independent companies in the late 1950s and early 1960s.

"My orders were to get the independents attached to the network because, for the system to be valuable, it had to reach every telephone in the country. In order to be part of the network, however, independents had to meet certain criteria. They had to meet transmission criteria, dialing criteria and all this sort of thing. So that's when the independents really started to get interested in upgrading their equipment because they didn't want to be left out of this magical nationwide long-distance network that was being built by the Bell System," Amick explained.

AT&T published manuals and aided the independents as much as it could to facilitate their going to direct dial. Toll settlement arrangements took into account the local company's expenses related to providing direct dial service, including the associated equipment and operators. A generous division of toll revenue from AT&T encouraged independents such as Roseville Telephone to invest in the necessary equipment and facilities. It was a partnership of interests that served all parties well, the telephone companies and the customers.

At the end of 1960, the company served 9,740 telephones vs. 8,476 at the end of 1959, a 15-percent increase. Reflecting the rapid growth, employee totals jumped to 108, an increase of 22 over the 86 employees on staff at the close of 1959. Even more telling was the 43 percent jump in employee payroll in 1960 compared with 1959. The payroll was now $554,196. The 22 new employees had experience totaling 80 years in engineering, construction, splicing and the business office. Key department managers that came aboard in 1960 included George Minasian in the business office and Warren Tinker in engineering. Both were Pacific Telephone veterans. Leon Bower joined in December 1960. He later succeeded Tinker as director of outside plant engineering.

The significant growth of 1960 apparently didn't faze the confident Bob Doyle who after six years as president seemed to be growing accustomed to success. In the 1960 annual report, Doyle commented on operations: "This year we added experienced people to our staff, whose previous experience will aid us immeasurably in the years ahead. With the continued growth of California, our future looks very bright indeed."

Moreover, with the accelerated expansion that 1960 brought, some employees hired in the late 1950s assumed a higher profile in the 1960s and later. Included in this group were Bob Sharples and Ned Kindelt, both hired in 1957, and Walter Gordon, hired in 1958. These would be key people for the next 20-to-30 years.

Mark Shull remembered those early years:

"By 1960 we were now getting pretty good size and getting to the point where we were going to have to split off the company's finance operations from the business office. We looked for hiring somebody from Sacramento (Pacific Telephone) and interviewed several people," Shull said. "The guy we first tried to hire didn't take the job but he sent up George Minasian and he worked out, so we hired him as commercial office manager.

"At about the same time, Page Ellis was having some health problems, so Bob hired a plant superintendent from Pacific, Warren Tinker. George and Warren started on the same day in January 1960."

While at Pacific, Minasian had worked with Roseville Telephone in connecting foreign exchange lines between the two companies. But he had no particular desire to work at Roseville Telephone.

"It was just a small company and I really had no great interest in it. My conception of them was that they were backward and not very modern. That was also the thinking of most of us down in Sacramento (at Pacific Telephone)," Minasian recollected. "We thought Roseville was really a hick company, and although we wanted to help Roseville out a little bit, our heart wasn't really into it.

"Roseville's outside plant was not up to standard in many areas, and in some places they were unable to give service to people. But in December of 1959, I

*George Minasian joined the fast-growing Roseville Telephone Company in January 1960. A veteran of Pacific Telephone, Minasian headed up Roseville Telephone's business office for 30 years.*

*Information operators used large Rolodex-like revolving files to access names and files for callers. Keeping the directory up-to-date was an ongoing challenge before computers came on the scene.*

had heard that Bob was looking for someone to manage the business office. So I came up, looked around and still was not very interested. And my wife ... she definitely was not interested. I was living in South Sacramento out by Executive Airport, so it was a long commute."

At the same time, however, Minasian perceived that Pacific Telephone's management culture was changing, that there were greater opportunities in management for college graduates than for long-time company employees who hadn't attended college. Minasian believed his management path was blocked at Pacific.

"I had been at Pacific for almost 14 years in 1959 and was an outside customer representative," Minasian said. "I was up for a promotion at that time. But one day a new guy came to work there, and my boss told me, 'George, would you take this guy and show him what you do. He's going to be here a few weeks and then will be gone.' In talking with this fellow, I starting thinking, 'How come you get to go around like this, what's the deal?' I asked him what classification he was in and he said, 'I really don't know.' I said, 'Are you hourly or salaried?'

He said salaried, and I said, 'How long have you been with the company?' He said three weeks.

"I went to my boss and asked what was going on. 'This guy is already a manager while I've been here for 14 years trying to get my promotion.' I didn't get a satisfactory answer so I took it to higher management. I was told there was a new policy going into effect where Pacific Telephone was hiring college graduates (for management positions). They said my opportunity would come, but they didn't know when. I had nothing against these young guys, but the fact was I had been working at the company for years and felt I deserved a chance even if I wasn't a college graduate. The practice at Pacific used to be to bring their management people from the ground up, but obviously that was changing. So after thinking it over and talking to my wife again, I came back to Bob Doyle and agreed to take the job at Roseville Telephone."

Although Minasian came to Roseville Telephone as a manager, he earned the same pay he had made at Pacific. "But there was a title and responsibility and Bob's promises that things would improve as the company grew. And, of course, he had great expectations," Minasian remembered. "When Bob starts talking to you about what he believes is going to happen, he's very convincing. But in 1960 there were open fields everywhere. We had problems with customer requests and were not always able to provide the service. It still was a small outfit. I guess it was a bit of a chance on my part."

Although Minasian may have joined Roseville Telephone for self-serving reasons, it didn't take long for him to become a devoted employee and one of Doyle's closest cronies. For not only did Minasian bring much-needed expertise in business office management, he also helped Doyle sell that difficult third stock issue. Moreover, Minasian always bought telephone stock through the years and proved a ready and willing participant in the after-work "gatherings" conducted by Doyle in local taverns in the '60s. Within a year, Minasian moved from Sacramento to Roseville and never regretted it.

Stories abound of employees leaving larger companies to join Roseville Telephone. Bigger companies, replete with bureaucracy and impersonal employee interaction, frequently wear out the truly motivated because change and progress don't happen quickly enough to satisfy the ambitious employee. In these respects, Roseville Telephone was a welcome change, a place where talented people could blossom and grow.

The constant growth that was the norm at Roseville Telephone created challenges that kept ambitious employees fulfilled. One prime example was Walter Gordon, for many years the head of the Roseville central office and later director of the network and property management departments. He joined the company in 1958 and retired in 1994. During his long career, Gordon was presented with an ongoing mix of challenges and opportunities that kept him motivated through 36 years.

In the mid-1950s, Gordon took a leave of absence from Western Electric to go into the Air Force Reserve. When he came out in 1958, Western Electric was laying off employees. "So my supervisor suggested I come here to Roseville because it was growing," Gordon explained. "I can tell you how prominent Roseville was … I had lived in North Sacramento for a year and a half and didn't even know where Roseville was!"

In truth, Gordon was more interested in two other job opportunities, one with the Federal Aviation Administration in radio navigational aids, and the other for Shell Oil in Australia ... opportunities with considerably more allure than working for a small telephone company. Nonetheless, Gordon applied at Roseville Telephone. One reason was that his wife liked her job at California Western States Life Insurance Company in Sacramento.

"I still remember very distinctly that I met my wife for lunch after interviewing here, and she asked me how it went," Gordon said. "I told her it appeared I have a job here if I wanted it. She asked if I was going to take it, and I said, 'I don't really know because I want to tell you, that's a rinky-dink outfit.' And I understood from talking to Doc Harrington and Page Ellis, the two who interviewed me, that the company had made a quantum leap from 1953. It must have been really terrible back then, I remember thinking to myself."

At Western Electric, Gordon had installed switching equipment. "When I came to Roseville," Gordon recounted, "I did a little of everything, but basically I was central office switchman and did maintenance of central office equipment. I like telephone work, but, candidly, at the time I just felt Roseville was a place to work until I could get a better position somewhere else."

One of his earliest assignments was to work with Ned Kindelt to regrade farmer lines and eight-party lines to four-party lines upon the opening of the Citrus Heights central office. That work was different from anything Gordon had done before, so he found it interesting.

"Originally, I didn't feel there were a whole lot of challenges here, but as the company started growing, we had more changes and it became more of a challenge to me. I became satisfied with the work. There was always something new happening."

Later, Gordon helped replace an old 1930s Western Electric toll board with a new one. "The old toll board was in fact a couple of older ones that had been amalgamated together. I was very instrumental in writing up the procedure to put that into service which for that time was quite a challenge," Gordon remembered. "Later on in 1959-60, we put automatic toll ticketing on, and that became more of a challenge. There was a lot to it, especially since it was electro-mechanical. It was a lot more than just lubricating switches."

In 1960, Gordon and Kindelt helped with the installation of additional step equipment in the Citrus Heights office. That effort led Gordon to suggest that the company could do its own installation work rather than paying the manufacturer to do it.

"I worked a lot of overtime in 1960," remembered Kindelt. "That's when we started installing our own equipment. That allowed me, in I think 1964, to start engineering our own equipment additions, so we wouldn't pay GTE (parent company of Automatic Electric) for the engineering. All we did at the time was to buy the equipment from GTE."

Kindelt credited Walter Gordon with the idea for the company to do its own equipment installations. "I believe Walter did it through (Emerson) Gunning to Doyle," Kindelt recollected. "I think Walter made the suggestion to Gunning who passed it to Doyle because Gunning was in charge of the central office group at that time."

As is Doyle's style, he agreed to let his employees try it on their own.

## FOLSOM LAKE OFFICE OPENS

In 1962, Gordon spearheaded the internal effort to install step-by-step switching equipment in the company's new $510,000 (land, building and equipment) Folsom Lake central office. This project was important to Roseville Telephone and also instrumental in retaining skilled people like Gordon and Kindelt, two of the employees involved in this successful installation.

*Roseville Telephone took another giant step in 1962 when the Folsom Lake central office came on line, enabling subscribers in the fast-growing Granite Bay area to receive upgraded service.*

"It was a big challenge when we decided to install our own switching equipment in Folsom Lake," said Gordon. "A lot of people thought we couldn't do it, but I had already done installation work at Western Electric. We wanted to do our own installation for two reasons. First of all, it was a matter of quality. We felt we could provide better quality of installation than the manufacturer did. The second factor was cost. We could do it for less money."

The Folsom Lake central office installation marked a huge step in Roseville Telephone's road to independence. That installation showed that the company had enough technical expertise on staff to assemble state-of-the-art systems. Subsequent jobs of this type were done by the company. The savings were considerable.

Roseville Telephone Co.

CAPITAL STOCK

OFFERS WANTED

WRITE OR TELEPHONE

DAVIS, SKAGGS & CO.

ESTABLISHED 1927

MEMBERS PACIFIC COAST STOCK EXCHANGE

111 SUTTER STREET ☆ SAN FRANCISCO 4

Telephone: DOuglas 2-2484

*Occasionally, brokerage firms such as Davis, Skaggs & Co. had Roseville Telephone shares to sell.*

Roseville Press-Tribune, 1962

Gordon estimated that doing the work enabled the company to spend about a third of what it would have cost with outside vendors. This "can do" attitude spread through Roseville Telephone and has been a hallmark of the company over the decades. To this day, as much work as is possible and feasible — including complex engineering, installation and mainte-nance work — is performed in-house, saving millions of dollars through the years.

Although Gordon, Kindelt and the others involved in that first major installation prided themselves on a job well done, it couldn't have happened without oversight and guidance from Automatic Electric, the manufacturer of the switching equip-ment. Again on the scene to help Roseville Telephone was A.A. "Al" Johnson, the AE sales engineer who 15 years later would become Walter Gordon's boss.

"Al was instrumental in that operation. Not only was he our sales engineer who took care of problems, but he gave us guidelines to help with the installation," Gordon said.

The Folsom Lake central office went into service in August 1962, much to the satisfaction of the employees and Bob Doyle. It was an important step, because the Folsom Lake central office was the third of the four central offices the company would eventually need to adequately serve its 83-square-mile territory. A few years earlier, Folsom Lake telephone users, although technically in Roseville Telephone territory, had no choice but to use Pacific Telephone because Roseville didn't yet have the capability of serving customers that far away from Roseville's central office.

The company's fourth central office would not be constructed for nearly another 20 years, in 1980 at Crowder Lane and Base Line Road west of Roseville. In typical Bob Doyle fashion, however, the two-acre parcel for that fourth office was acquired in 1961.

The early 1960s also brought into the company other young employees who later developed into high-level managers. Hazel Snider, currently manager of operator services, came to work in 1960 as an operator trainee. She had been a waitress in a local coffee shop. The current director of network and property management, Rulon Blackburn, joined the company in late 1961. John Jones came aboard in 1961 and is now a supervisor in the splicing department. Another new employ-ee in 1962 was Jay Kinder, who worked summers for the company before joining full-time in January 1963. Kinder has never worked anywhere else and is now the director of marketing and planning administration.

The value of long-time employees who developed into managers is significant. These managers became extremely knowledgeable about their work, experts in their industry. Also, younger employees have seen that the company generally promotes from within. This helps overall company morale.

## BATTLES OVER "EAS" AND "FEX"

Much of the company's dealings with the California Public Utilities Commission in the late 1950s through 1964 focused on two related issues — EAS (extended area service) and FEX (foreign exchange service). These deep-seated, emotionally-charged issues pitted customers against the telephone companies and the companies against one another.

Extended area service (EAS) enables callers from one service area to call toll-free to another service area operated by a different telephone company. In other words, the caller's basic service area is extended to another service area, primarily for reasons of proximity. Prior to EAS, customers who lived along the border between the two companies' exchange territories would pay a toll to reach a phone in the other company's service territory. Since the Roseville/Pacific Telephone boundary cuts through populated areas, there were many instances when neighbors were subject to tolls for calling across the street or next door. In the late 1950s and early 1960s, as Citrus Heights grew rapidly, residents with Roseville Telephone service demanded free calls to nearby Sacramento exchanges operated by Pacific Telephone and vice versa.

Obviously, from the telephone companies' point of view, EAS was justified as long as the lost toll call revenue was recovered by higher rates in another category, usually base rates. Obviously, customers clamoring for free extended area service called those exchanges frequently, paying the prevailing toll rates. EAS would save them money. On the other hand, customers who infrequently dialed outside their own exchange areas would be penalized by EAS because they would end up subsidizing the others by paying higher base rates.

Further, EAS would require Roseville and Pacific to incur significant expenses. They would have to make studies of what needed to be done and what the costs would be. Once that was done, there would be expense in re-configuring their trunking and switching connections to allow for the EAS service. The telephone companies wanted to be sure any rate revisions were adequate to pay for conversion costs and produce an adequate return on investment, too.

*Roseville Telephone issued regular financial reports to its shareholders.*

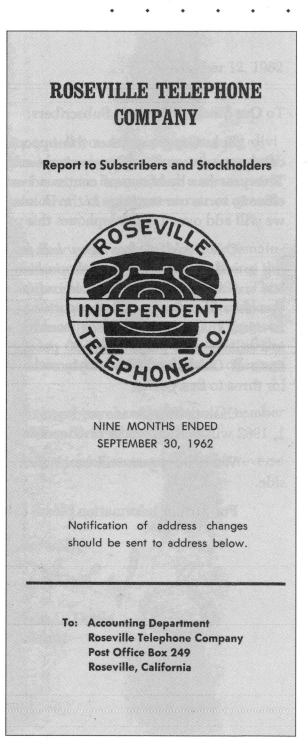

**ROSEVILLE TELEPHONE COMPANY**

**Report to Subscribers and Stockholders**

NINE MONTHS ENDED
SEPTEMBER 30, 1962

Notification of address changes should be sent to address below.

To:  Accounting Department
Roseville Telephone Company
Post Office Box 249
Roseville, California

## FOREIGN EXCHANGE MAY RISE

# Roseville Co. To Seek Phone Rate Increase

The Roseville Telephone Company will seek to obtain an immediate raise in rates for its foreign exchange service in a hearing before the California State Public Utilities Commission scheduled for March 7-8 in Sacramento.

According to Bob Doyle, manager of the company, the company now has approximately 500 subscribers on foreign exchange service plus a sizeable number of held orders.

The foreign exchange service is available to persons who live in the Roseville Exchange area but who use a Sacramento phone listing. By this means they pay only the regular rate plus mileage, but do not have to pay long distance tolls in calling Sacramento numbers.

"To be perfectly frank," said Doyle, "the foreign exchange subscribers have not been paying their way."

According to Doyle, when extended service goes into effect in 1963, the foreign exchange rates will be raised automatically. Most such users will then probably prefer to go on extended service.

"Our problem is right now," said Doyle. "We would like to raise the foreign exchange rates prior to the time extended service goes into operation so that users will become familiar with what it will cost."

If applications for foreign exchange service continue, Doyle maintains that they will necessitate substantial investment in additional equipment which would not be used once extended service is available.

A rate raise right away would discourage further applications at the present time.

"This is in the long-range interest of the users," said Doyle. "Any outlays for extra equipment must inevitably be born by the phone users. If these can be avoided, they will naturally benefit."

The extended service, which has already been approved by the Public Utilities Commission, will permit toll-free service between Roseville's Parkview exchange and all Yukon, Yorktown, Ivanhoe, Wabash, Edgewood and Wyandotte numbers.

Roseville Press-Tribune, February 1962

Complicating EAS was the related issue of foreign exchange service (FEX). This applied to customers who lived in the exchange of one company, but who desired the service of the other telephone company. In the 1950s and 1960s, Roseville Telephone had numerous FEX customers located in its exchange area, but who paid extra to have Pacific Telephone service. FEX users paid what was called "mileage," which meant they paid extra for each quarter mile they were located from the telephone exchange boundary. Their reasoning was logical. If they were in Roseville's territory, but made frequent calls to Pacific's Sacramento exchanges, it was cost effective to pay the extra "mileage" rather than to pay a toll for each call to the "foreign" exchange. Obviously, FEX worked both ways and there were callers in Pacific's territory who paid extra to get Roseville service. However, many more Roseville customers paid extra for Pacific Telephone service because of the distribution of population in those years.

Considerable revenue and profit potential were at stake on the eventual resolution of these EAS and FEX issues and neither telephone company was willing to accept any PUC decision they felt was in error. The big stakes resulted in these issues being dragged out for several years before finally being resolved in 1964.

Along the way there were numerous public hearings and these typically received newspaper coverage. Roseville Telephone, led by Bob Doyle, was on the hot seat several times. At one noteworthy public meeting in Citrus Heights in April 1963, a new assemblyman, Leroy F. Greene, skewered Doyle and the company. Not only did he stir up the crowd of about 250 residents at the meeting, but he made several inane remarks that only served to exacerbate the tense atmosphere existing between the company and its FEX customers. The following was reported in the April 1963 *Line Chatter*:

"Mr. Doyle, perhaps you should consider raising pineapples," said Greene in a sarcastic reference to the famous Dole pineapples of Hawaii. He added, "If I had any of their telephone stock, I would sell it tomorrow," and "They're a pygmy trying to compete with a giant, and I for one cannot see how a pygmy requires more money than a giant."

The *Line Chatter* then editorialized: "If this man is representative of our elected representatives, then the citizens of California are indeed in trouble."

In a subsequent article in *The Sacramento Union*, Greene tempered his criticism of Roseville Telephone. "Although the Roseville company had reasons which justify the rate increase, it is hard to convince a man with a phone that looks like everyone else's that he should pay more than others in surrounding communities."

As a result of rate hearings, the FEX rate increases were postponed twice before being implemented later in 1963. The availability of EAS service within six months to these same protesters would eliminate the FEX problem. At the time, however, residents were angry.

Hearings on EAS and FEX were sprinkled through the years until finally being resolved in 1963 and 1964. The bottom line was that residents paid more for basic services — not as much as the telephone companies sought, of course — but customers also won significant EAS coverage to many Sacramento area prefixes. EAS skirmishes were also waged over service to Auburn and more distant locations in Sacramento County. Eventually, the furor over EAS died down. An effort later in the decade to introduce EAS throughout Sacramento County failed when it was determined it would be too costly to provide the service.

Industry observers believed the EAS and FEX decisions of the early 1960s ended up being favorable to Roseville Telephone. Certainly, Pacific Telephone arduously protested the CPUC's EAS ruling and worked assiduously, albeit unsuccessfully, to have it overturned. Although attorney Bob Raymer was not Roseville Telephone's legal counsel during the EAS hearings, he was familiar with the controversy.

"In effect, the PUC imposed this extended service traffic agreement between Pacific Company and Roseville and told

## Hearing Set Monday On Phone Rates

California Public Utilities Commission will hold a public hearing in Roseville Monday on the request of Roseville Telephone Company, which is asking to increase its rates by about 53.2 per cent.

The hearing will be at 2 p.m. in the council chambers of City Hall.

"The telephone company is asking the commission for authority to increase its rates so that the company will get a fair rate of return on its investment to guarantee its stockholders fair rates of return on their investments," Rober L. Doyle, president and manager of the company, states.

The company asked the PUC for the increases in June due to "declining net revenues and rates of return under present rates."

The independent company also has asked that Roseville and Citrus Heights rate areas be consolidated in a Roseville base rate area.

Doyle pointed out that since 1953—when the company's property and equipment holdings were valued at $500,000, now grown to the present investment of more than two million dollars—no major rate increases have been asked.

If approved, the proposed new rates may become effective by Jan. 1, 1959.

*Record May 31 '56*

## Extended Phone Service Forecast For A Year Hence

It's going to be about a year before telephone calls between Sacramento and Fair Oaks turn from long distance to local, says Pacific Telephone. So hopes that extended service might arrive months ahead of the July 1 deadline went a-glimmering this week.

Pacific Telephone is now in the midst of the project which will wipe out long distance charges on calls from Fair Oaks to Folsom and Rio Linda to Sacramento, and calls from Sacramento to any of the three communities. Losses in long distance revenue will be madeup by increased monthly basic rates and operating economies.

But Hugh Weber. the company's new north area manager, said it propably will be June of next year before the project is completed and the "extended" telephone service can be inaugurated.

**MANY STEPS TAKEN**

On paper, the change to such service sounds simple, but here's what it takes to bring it about.

To begin with, new multi-message cables must be placed between Fair Oaks, Folsom and Rio Linda and Sacramento. And in Sacramento itself, new cables must be placed between the central offices there.

By next summer, there will be eight central offices in Sacramento. The new cables are necessary to handle the expected extra-flow of telephone traffic once the long distance rates are discontinued.

**EXPENSIVE PROJECT**

These cable jobs alone add up to more than $1,200,000, although some of the cables would have to be constructed even if there were to be extended service at all.

Besides the cable jobs, extra equipment must be added in the Fair Oaks, Folsom, and Rio Linda offices and in all the Sacramento offices too. All are time consuming projects.

In approving the extended service arrangement, the California Public Utilities Commission ordered it into effect by July of next year.

Weber said that date would be met, but probably with not very much time to spare.

*San Juan Record, May 1956*

them to settle the issue of revenue division, considering the lines of both companies are used on some of the calls," explained Raymer. "The real thing behind this was that it was the commission's staff that in effect got the commission to adopt this arrangement, which was ever so favorable to Roseville and really did all kinds of good things for them.

"What was going on in a regulatory sense during this period was that the commission staffers were practically, for regulatory purposes, the sponsors of Roseville Telephone Company," Raymer said. "Roseville Telephone was sort of the protege, the poor little fellow that needed somebody to help him. Bob Doyle and Mark Shull played this very humble role very well, in effect saying, 'Oh, please, Mr. Commission, please, Mr. Staff, help us. What do you think we ought to do now? Is there some way you can figure out how we can get some assistance in this regard?' I think they played the role so well that they got a very good settlement arrangement. Pacific was screaming to high heaven that the decision was unlawful, while Roseville was sitting there saying this is great. But the ruling stuck and it was a matter of great importance to Roseville Telephone because it got the company going and also established a way of doing things for a long time."

The favorable toll settlement formula was instrumental in powering strong earnings for Roseville Telephone through the years. It enabled the company to post a healthy fiscal performance and also helped provide the cash flow to grow quickly. In fact, Ron Amick, the retired Pacific Telephone executive, said he occasionally expedited settlement payments to relieve a cash flow crunch at Roseville Telephone.

"Arranging for toll settlement arrangements was one of my jobs with all the Northern California independents. Many times I was the banker for Roseville Telephone Company. I advanced them thousands of dollars ahead of time so they could meet certain commitments and pay some bills. It was their money, of course, but I was giving it to them ahead of time."

Had the EAS and FEX settlements to Roseville Telephone been lower, the fiscal crunch of keeping up with the growth likely might have forced Roseville Telephone to seek general rate increases or perhaps even a sale of the company. At the least, Roseville probably wouldn't have had the ability to grow and modernize at the pace it did.

## HATED 'POST PAY' PHONES CONVERTED TO 'PRE-PAY'

Although the Roseville Telephone Company had made significant strides in repairing its formerly horrendous reputation, one aspect of the company's operation still generated almost universal hatred — its pay phones. The price of a call was still only a dime — if the caller was careful. The problem was that Roseville's pay stations operated on a "post-pay" basis instead of the customary "pre-pay" mode of operation utilized by Pacific Telephone and just about every other telephone company at that time.

Doyle explained how post-pay, coin-operated telephone stations worked.

"With our post-pay phones, the caller was supposed to dial the number of the party he was trying to reach first before putting in the coin," Doyle explained. "If the other party answered the call, then you put the dime in the phone so he could hear you.

"We had an instruction panel plain as day on each phone telling the caller how to use the phone, but people didn't read it. They would put the dime in the phone right away, then make the call. The problem was that you could hear the party on the other end, but they couldn't hear you. You lost your dime. Then people would do it again, thinking there was something wrong with the phone. They'd just lift it up, put the dime in and lose another dime. People hated us for that, but if they'd only have read the panel, they would have understood how to do it."

Long-time operator Bernice Moser remembered how upset customers would get losing their money.

"When I started, our pay phones were post-pay where the person would just walk up to a phone, call the operator and we would connect them to a number. They didn't put in their money until that party came on the line. When the party came on the line, the money itself would open the connection," she said. "But you had absolutely no way of returning it, so those people who put the money in first lost it. A lot of people got mighty upset putting money in before they were supposed to."

In the 1958 rate increase hearings with the Public Utilities Commission, Doyle tried for approval to convert the pay phones from post-pay to pre-pay, but the request was denied. The commission felt it would cost too much to do it at that time.

"I told the commission I wanted pre-pay phone services. One of the commissioners said it would cost about $100,000 to change our dial equipment to be able to accommodate this service, and he asked me if it was worth $100,000 to do it. I said it was a big public relations problem for us, but our request was turned down nonetheless. So the public was giving us a lot of grief over these pay phones, but it really wasn't our fault. We wanted to change them, but couldn't," Doyle said. "I'll tell you one thing, I didn't go out there in the public with identification on my car … the less some of them knew about me the better. It was a mess, they hated us."

It wasn't until 1962 that Roseville Telephone finally received approval to rid itself of the post-pay coin-operated service. It cost about $35,000 to do the conversion, a lot less than the original estimate. Why? Because the initial estimates assumed an outside vendor would be called in for the conversion, but by 1962 the company's own personnel were able to do the work themselves.

*Emerson Gunning spent many hours on the ladder fixing and maintaining the labor-intensive step-by-step switches in use at Roseville Telephone for many years.*

## 1960: THE FIRST PROFESSIONAL ANNUAL REPORT

Another step toward professionalism and credibility was taken in 1960 when Roseville Telephone published its first annual report designed for all shareholders. Prior annual reports were done for management and the regulatory bodies by the company's outside accounting firm, which was L.F. Martin of Fresno through 1958. Arthur Young & Co. came aboard in 1959 and indicated that a more inclusive, standard-style annual report was appropriate for the company since it was adding many more shareholders.

The 1960 annual report was a not an easy one, according to Mark Shull, the company's financial manager at the time. "Bob and I published the first report ourselves. I wrote the thing up basically with his approval. I came up with the front cover of the sheet for the annual report and we printed it ourselves," Shull remembered. "We were ignorant about how we should do it exactly and didn't realize all that was involved. I remember Arthur Young in San Francisco blew up at us about our report because, 'You don't do it that way,' they said. We were supposed to go through all this rigmarole with the SEC, but we did it our way, and it worked.

"Every year from there on, I was probably as much of the architect of writing the thing as anybody was and always worked with Bob on designing the cover," Shull said. "I also worked with the lawyers getting the text approved, the proxies done, etc. It was a fun project, but it took a lot of time. Those sessions were among the most interesting in my 34-year career with the company."

In 1965, when Cooper, White & Cooper became Roseville Telephone's legal counsel, the annual report publishing process got even more involved. Bob Raymer remembered those meetings:

"During those early annual reports, we had a group that worked on it together," Raymer recalled. "Doug Page, the Arthur Young audit partner, was an

ROSEVILLE TELEPHONE COMPANY 1966 ANNUAL REPORT

*1966 Annual Report Cover*

Englishman. He was also a very meticulous dresser, very formal and very English. Nice clothes and a beautifully well-spoken guy. Doug fancied himself as having a pretty good command of the English language.

"When it was time to begin writing the annual report, we'd all get together, Bob and Mark, sometimes Tom Doyle, I would be there and Doug, and we would try to write the annual report by committee, not an easy thing to do. A committee really can't write anything," Raymer continued. "But Doug would end up writing it, and the rest of us would be sniping at him and making suggestions, most of which he would reject on the basis of awkward or imprecise language. They got to be all-day sessions with a lot of hilarity and a lot of stopping and starting. It was an annual event and it would be pretty funny. Of course, Bob did not consider that he was a particularly strong writer, but he always had some down-to-earth things to say. He'd tell Page, 'You're writing the president's letter, but you forget what I have to say.' Then in very explicit language — you can imagine — Bob would tell Doug what he wanted to say. There were some great sessions, that's for sure."

Jim Porter, now retired from Arthur Young, became part of the annual report writing team in the late 1960s. It was a fun experience for Porter, too.

"We'd meet at Raymer's office to hash out the wording for the report and always go to the Bohemian Club for lunch," Porter recalled. "There, Gordie Soltau, a former San Francisco 49er end and place kicker, would join us for lunch. We thought that might impress Bob Doyle. But I don't think Bob was ever impressed ..."

After a number of years Doug Page was transferred to New York to head up Arthur Young's international division and the annual report got written with other people involved.

"But it was always a time of great frivolity," Raymer added. "Bob always wanted the more direct approach. He couldn't stand bullshit, still can't, so he was always wondering why we had to pussyfoot around, why the long notes to the financial statements had to be all so precise and boring, which they were. But all that was done in a different world."

Aside from the president's letter, which recounted the prior year's business, the annual reports included sections on construction, financing activities, telephone service items, the number of employees and payroll for the year and tax figures. The message to the reader was clear — Roseville Telephone was a growing concern, hiring more employees every year and paying more taxes each year. This was a company carrying its own weight in the community. Moreover, in every annual report since 1960, photos of *all* employees are included, grouped by departments. Very few, if any, other companies with about 500 employees put all their photos in the annual report. But Roseville Telephone does. It's another way the company demonstrates its genuine regard for employees.

## COOPER, WHITE & COOPER
## BECOME COMPANY ATTORNEYS

In 1965, a disagreement between Bob Doyle and the company's legal counsel, Tom Srednik, came to a head. Srednik had been the company's attorney and a board member since early 1955 when he replaced L.C. Anderson, who had died. A Roseville lawyer, Srednik settled into the Roseville Telephone inner circle in the late 1950s when he married Jack Doyle's widow, Catherine.

From 1955 to 1965 the company grew rapidly and Doyle's confidence grew as well. The company he took over in 1954 had progressed nicely. It had solid earnings, happy shareholders and the prospects for continued growth appeared excellent. Doyle clearly was bullish. During the same period, however, Srednik grew more cautious. While Doyle's outlook was positive — he typically sees the cup half full — Srednik worked to temper the optimism. For example, in the board minutes written by Srednik to describe Doyle's presentations at annual meetings, Srednik generally diluted Doyle's enthusiasm about the company's prospects, typically referring to the "challenges" presented by the growth ahead, implying that failure and difficulty were possibilities. Naturally, it was Srednik's objective to protect the company and himself from liability if in fact any major financial adversity unexpectedly struck the company. It's an attorney's job to err on the side of caution in order to minimize potential liability.

Thomas E. Srednik became a director in February 1955, replacing L.C. Anderson who died in January 1955. Srednik was Roseville Telephone's legal counsel and a director until early 1965 when he resigned following a dispute with Bob Doyle.

Also, in 1964, the company received shareholder approval for three amendments to its Articles of Incorporation. The purpose of the amendments was to protect the company from unwanted suitors. In the late 1950s and early 1960s, many smaller independent telephone companies were acquired in a major consolidation phase of the telephone industry. Although Roseville Telephone was determined to stay independent, many similar-size telephone companies succumbed. The attraction to be acquired was powerful. Not only could the owners make handsome profits, but they wouldn't have to face up to the rigorous capital commitments necessary to keep their telephone plant modern. The easy thing was to sell out, but Doyle had no intention then — and still has no intention — of ever selling the company.

The three amendments stated: 1) the company's assets could not be sold unless approved by 80 percent of the voting shares; 2) that the corporation could not

*Bob Doyle was already a confident and successful chief executive in the mid-1960s.*

merge or consolidate without 80 percent voter approval; and 3) that changes to the first two amendments could not be made without approval by 80 percent of the voting shares. The amendments were approved by the stockholders at the June 26, 1964, annual meeting.

By 1965 there were just over 2,000 shareholders, a stockholder base large enough, Srednik argued, that the sale and re-sale of shares should be handled through traditional stockbroker channels rather than through the company itself. Doyle, of course, disagreed. He believed the only way to maintain local ownership of the company was to keep the shares in local, friendly hands. Doyle contended that if the company did go the traditional stock brokerage route, its shares would inevitably wind up in the hands of a potential acquirer. Doyle remained adamant that local ownership was necessary for the good of the company and the community and the only way to ensure local ownership was to handle all stock transactions in-house.

In 1965, Roseville Telephone's capitalization and number of shareholders had reached a size that required it to register with the Securities and Exchange Commission (SEC). Srednik, ever the cautious attorney, felt strongly that Roseville Telephone should abandon all involvement regarding its own shares. Doyle refused to go the brokerage route, although at the time he wasn't certain his position was legally correct. In early 1965, when Srednik threatened to resign over this disagreement, Doyle responded as one might expect.

"I said, 'I think that's a damn good idea,' " Doyle recalled, "and then I said to him, 'I'll have your check next week.' Of course, the board was sitting there and didn't know what the hell to do."

In the minutes of a special board meeting on March 3, 1965, it was stated that on a motion by Eugene Garbolino, seconded by Walter Hanisch, that the board accepted "the resignation of Thomas E. Srednik, secretary and legal council (sic) for the Roseville Telephone Company. All members voting I." The succeeding motion that Tom Doyle be named secretary to replace Srednik also carried. "All members voting I," the minutes said. It wouldn't be until the February 1967 board meeting before "aye" was used in the minutes by the new secretary instead of "I" to report votes of board members.

After Srednik resigned, Bob Doyle immediately asked Arthur Young to recommend another law firm to represent Roseville Telephone. A San Francisco firm, Cooper, White & Cooper, was Arthur Young's suggestion. Cooper, White & Cooper had significant experience in regulatory and SEC-related matters. Doyle went to San Francisco to meet with senior partner Sheldon Cooper and his young, Harvard-educated associate, Bob Raymer.

"The first thing I wanted to know was whether the way we handled the sale, re-sale and transfer of our shares was legal," Doyle remembered. "I explained that we did it ourselves because if we didn't, I felt we'd lose the company. I told them other small telephone companies were going down the tubes … the larger companies were grabbing them up. I didn't want that to happen to Roseville Telephone.

"I told Cooper and Raymer every move that we had made and they told me we weren't doing anything wrong, that we could continue doing what we were doing. I said, 'OK. That's all I wanted to know. You're hired.' They've been our attorneys ever since."

Since that first meeting, Bob Raymer and Doyle have enjoyed a close relationship, albeit an unlikely one. Raymer and Doyle are opposites, Raymer being an understated, smooth, intellectual Ivy League type, while Doyle is boisterous, bull-headed, self-educated, profane, but equally bright. Despite their differing styles and backgrounds, mutual respect fostered an exceptional relationship.

Doyle runs anything important to the company past Raymer for his opinion. Raymer has always understood — and admired — Doyle's fervent desire for the company to remain independent. Many Doyle associates through the years credit Raymer for keeping Doyle "within bounds" when others sometimes couldn't. Doyle could certainly be bull-headed, but Raymer was his equal, in a more subdued way.

"I give Raymer a hell of a lot of credit," Doyle said. "I'm sure that over the years I worried the hell out of him with some of the things I wanted to do. Sometimes he'd nearly go crazy when I'd tell him things I wanted to do. But he always heard me out even if he didn't always agree with me."

*Tom Doyle became secretary-treasurer of the corporation after Tom Srednik's resignation in early 1965, a position Doyle still holds.*

"Although we have had a very good relationship, it naturally has had its rocky moments," Bob Raymer recalled. "Bob has the abilities of vision, leadership, shrewdness … all of these things … but at the same time he can be very impatient. Regulatory actions can be very stifling when you have to conform to mandates not only from the PUC, but also the FCC and SEC. And when you also have agreements with lenders, whether they're insurance companies or banks, you're constantly struggling to comply. With Bob's impatience, he'd want to do things that might very well make good business sense, but conflict with some requirements.

"Moreover, Bob has always been in a position to override people who work for him; he's the boss and they don't want to cross him, but by being on the outside, we lawyers can be more forthright with Bob, and although we can risk getting fired, too, by and large Bob has been understanding of some of the occasions when we've vetoed some of his plans because they simply couldn't work, given all the restrictions," Raymer added. "But Bob has very high intelligence and when complications are called to his attention, he's really quite amenable to doing sensible things. Someone not as directly under his control can say to him, 'Hey, Bob, that's not going to work and I'll tell you why.' Sometimes it went pleasantly, but there were occasions when it didn't.

"So, it's been both a pleasure to deal with him and to be with him, but it's also been a challenge," Raymer said. "On the whole, it's been a very good relationship. I think part of it has been our willingness to be up front with Bob and tell him what we think is in the best interests of the company. Then he'll listen."

Doyle admires Raymer's broad expertise in his craft. "Raymer is sort of like an Al Johnson," Doyle explained. "Raymer's got knowledge of the whole workings of how we fit into the regulatory process, plus he's got good old common horse sense. And that's what you've got to have to be a good businessman. You don't have to be too smart, you just have to have good common horse sense."

Over the years Raymer has overseen his firm's extensive activities with Roseville Telephone, but as both companies grew, Raymer — like Doyle — delegated some of the work to others in his office. The two who work most closely with the company today are Garth Black and Jed Solomon. Their relationship with the company is as close as Doyle's is to Raymer.

## DECADE OF STEADY GROWTH

Blessed with a growing population and guided by experienced hands, the 1960s were excellent years for the Roseville Telephone Company.

In 1960, the beneficial effects of being a full toll center came through in revenue. Toll revenue jumped to $608,000 in 1960, up from only $415,000 in 1959.

By the following year toll revenue climbed to $683,000 and slightly exceeded local exchange revenue. Toll revenue would continue to exceed local revenue until 1964 when extended area service agreements reduced toll revenue temporarily. A few years later, toll revenue would again exceed local service revenue.

In 1961, properties across the street from the headquarters offices on Lincoln Street were acquired from the Chilton family for $125,000. Once again, Doyle's strategy was to buy property before it was needed. By 1964, the buildings across the street were knocked down to make way for a new administration office building that housed the commercial, purchasing, accounting and executive offices. The new building was occupied in October 1964.

Arthur Young, the company's outside accounting firm, completed an exhaustive study in 1961 to analyze and review the telephone company's budgeting techniques and administrative systems. The study was commissioned to prepare management for the anticipated rapid growth ahead. Over 10 weeks, Arthur Young personnel reviewed all work routines done at the company.

The conclusions were important, if not unexpected. Determining manpower expense was crucial to the success of the company, the study determined, because it was such a large component of total costs. It was recommended the company develop detailed operating forecasts and budgets, delegate the authority to bring plans to fruition, and compare actual results to the plan, with formal explanation required for all significant variances.

*Walter Hanisch contributed his reservoir of knowledge about telephony as a board member for nearly 20 years after retiring as the manager of Roseville Telephone.*

Arthur Young's consultants advised the company to "manage by exception." This meant that "top management's time should be directed toward the exceptions and directed immediately at trouble spots" rather than be expended searching for problems. The review found that the company's management systems at the time were "functioning well and not in serious difficulty."

The management study gave a boost to formalized, structured planning that Roseville Telephone had not instituted up to that point. The effects of the study were illustrated in September 1962 when *Line Chatter* carried this brief item:

"Mr. Doyle has been busily holding meetings with each supervisor and the word is 'hold expenditures to what we have to have, not what we would like to have.'"

05/29/64

*Roseville Telephone's new administration building takes shape in 1964 as the growing company changes the face of downtown Roseville.*

*Roseville Telephone's first computer, an RCA 301, is moved into the new administration building in 1964.*

More importantly, the company's employee growth was moderate in the succeeding years. The increasing workload on employees did not go unnoticed. *Line Chatter* correspondent Paula Surry noted in August 1962: "The rush and overload of work and orders in the business office is enough to turn us all gray. This reflects all departments, we know, but it keeps our paychecks coming. Happy Day!" The burgeoning workload also may have been behind the "Thought for the Day" that appeared in the November 1963 *Line Chatter*: "Every horse thinks his own pack heaviest."

One of the highlights of 1962 was the installation of the company's first automatic time announcer equipment in May. Prior to then, callers wanting the correct time called the operator. The $8,000 equipment was a major time-saver. Studies showed that prior to the automatic service, operators handled up to 2,500 requests in a 24-hour day for the correct time. The new equipment paid for itself in a few months.

Prices for ordinary expenses were going up in 1962. Late in the year, a *Line Chatter* item bemoaned the rising cost of postal service — air mail was going up to 8 cents from 7 cents; first class was rising to 5 cents from 4 cents and the "penny postcard" went up to 4 cents from 3 cents.

Also from 1963 *Line Chatters*:

In February 1963, a retired operator, Sybil Moore, died. She was a night operator for 36 years. She was also the first and only employee to have received a pension from the company. In April, land adjacent to the company's existing warehouse on Yosemite Street was acquired from Horrell & Son. In mid-summer Doyle acquired the Haman property adjacent to the Chilton properties across Lincoln Street.

Male bonding came into fashion in August 1963 when the Roseville Telephone Men's Club was formed with 21 charter members. Aside from facilitating socializing among male employees, the club also held fund-raising events for charities.

Technical re-engineering and equipment conversions resulting from new foreign exchange (FEX) and extended area service (EAS) agreements that went into effect in 1963 kept all departments humming. The engineering department, in particular, was loaded with work to accommodate FEX and EAS conversion work. An unidentified, but creative writer from the engineering department adopted a theme popular in those years to explain how the department was progressing in the April 1963 *Line Chatter*:

"We are happy to announce the successful launching of the anxiously-awaited FEX Conversion Space Mission. Following the completion of intensive preliminary probes of the area by various members of the team, the target for the mission was established and the necessary preparation began. As with all missions of this kind, extensive information was gathered from all special groups within the company and fed to computers scattered around the base. We knew the margin for error was small if this was to be a successful launching. When all was in readiness, the countdown began … This is a manned flight and our crews report all systems are go at this time… "

It was this kind of light-hearted approach to the difficult, highly-technical conversions of those years that kept the company's crew fresh and in good humor.

There was plenty of growth in 1963, as reported by Page Ellis, the company's chief engineer then.

"Building construction is not down in our area," he wrote in the July 1963, *Line Chatter*. "Residential construction is climbing at a rate we haven't seen for a few years … A recent count shows there are twice as many units under construction now than at any time in the previous year. Did you know that since 1954 there have been 117 new subdivisions in Roseville Telephone Company's serving area containing 14,878 lots?"

Progress was not without its hazards, though. Jack Poulsen lamented some of the realities accompanying growth. "The widening of Auburn Boulevard is moving right along. I caution anyone who wants to inspect this road work, to drive there in something you don't value too much. Chances are you might drive off into one of the many monstrous chuck-holes, and lose your car completely.

"Incidentally, for those of you who drive in the Citrus Heights area, there is a new game being played by the contractors installing the sewer system. It's called close the roads. The basic rules are: tear up a different road every day, never tell anyone, and never post any road closed signs. It is rather nerve shaking, to say the least, to come sailing over a hill and suddenly come face-to-face with a ditching machine. It makes for real interesting motoring, though."

Revenue went over $2 million for the first time in 1963 with toll revenue providing more than $1.1 million. In the same year, the company drew down $850,000 on a $2 million 4.75 percent loan from its long-standing lender, Pacific Mutual Life Insurance Co.

Back then, loan proceeds were not wired directly into the company account the same day. Instead, the insurance company issued a check to the company for the amount borrowed. Depending on when the check cleared and the amount involved, the daily interest on the "float" could be considerable. This fact did not escape Bob Doyle, as was noted in the November 1963, *Line Chatter*.

*Jack Morris remembered November 22, 1963 – the day President Kennedy was assassinated – as the busiest day in the company's history to that point.*

ROSEVILLE
TELEPHONE
COMPANY
1974
ANNUAL
REPORT

*1974 Annual Report Cover*

"When Mr. Doyle realized that a check mailed from San Francisco would not be available in Roseville for three days, and with the interest at the bank amounting to more than $100 a day, Mr. (Merle) Ruggles was immediately dispatched to the city (to bring back the check the same day)."

The remainder of the loan proceeds were borrowed in 1964 as the company continued apace with its rapid expansion program.

Of course, the biggest news event of 1963 was the assassination of President John F. Kennedy on Nov. 22, 1963. At the very instant the terrible news was reported, Jack Morris was working in the Citrus Heights central office. He immediately knew something major had occurred.

"The one thing about the old step-by-step equipment, you could hear all the noises because it was so mechanical. All of a sudden, the noise took off, it just became a roar. We knew something big had happened," Morris recollected. "That's when we found out that President Kennedy had died. It was chaos. Callers would try to dial through, but they couldn't get out because the whole office was locked up. For example, if you're serving a thousand people on a switch, all those people cannot make a call at the same time. Maybe 35 percent could make a call, but that was it. The other 65 percent trying to make a call couldn't even get a dial tone because all the switches were busy. People would pick the phones up, nothing. Just locked up. It was incredible. That was the first time anything like that ever happened."

Walter Gordon was working in the Roseville central office on that fateful day.

"I was talking to Emerson Gunning and all of a sudden I knew something had happened because that switchroom just lit up. I said to Gunning, 'Something's happened. What are all these people talking about?' They were talking about the president being shot. That was the biggest day and the most traffic that we had ever carried up until that time. Everybody was calling everybody.

*Sheriff Bob "Deadeye" Doyle and his two trusty deputies, Merle Ruggles, left, and Emerson Gunning, right, take a break from their law-and-order duties during Roseville's Centennial Days in 1964. Whiskers were in fashion during this weeks-long celebration.*

*Page Ellis, left, marketing manager of Roseville Telephone, looks on as Walter Hanisch, vice president of the company, examines several artifacts unearthed at the site of the phone company's new building at Tahoe and Yosemite streets.*

Roseville Press-Tribune, 1968

"When you worked with the step equipment for a long time, you could stand in an aisle with 640 switches around you, and if one of them was not adjusted right, you could point to it and know there's a problem," Gordon added. "That used to impress new employees. You really got to know sounds from those old steppers."

The electromechanical era's demise at Roseville Telephone started in the business office when in 1964 the company acquired its first "electronic computer," as it was referred to then, an RCA 301. Its job was to compute customer billing, toll rating and process stockholder dividend checks. It was also in 1964 that total telephones serviced by the company surpassed 15,000 for the first time, ending the year at 15,879. In May 1964, Roseville, with plenty of help from employees at the telephone company, celebrated the city's centennial. On the last page of the 1964 annual report, a photo of bearded "Sheriff" Bob Doyle gave shareholders insight into the frivolity. The type along side read:

"Coincidentally, 1964 was the semi-centennial of the beginning of the Roseville Telephone Company. It was altogether fitting, therefore, that we in the telephone company make a substantial contribution to the gaiety of the occasion — which we did — in the person of our president, Bob Doyle. With cowboy hat, fearsome beard and sheriff's star, he whooped things along while 'patrolling the boundaries and maintaining order at all times.'"

In January 1965, the company once again welcomed the community to an open house, this time at its new administration building. It was another opportunity for the company to show off the progress it had been making. By 1965, Citrus Heights' population had mushroomed to 36,000 from only 3,000 in 1950. Although the economy slowed slightly in the mid-1960s, the telephone company used the breather to catch up.

Also, in 1965 long-time director Leroy "Roy" Etzel died. It ended the 51-year involvement of the Etzel family in the company. His mother, Lena Etzel, was one of the company's original directors and his father, Chris, was on the board for nearly 15 years. The Board of Directors closed the year with five members, as neither Etzel nor Tom Srednik, who resigned early in the year, was replaced.

It was in 1965, more than 15 years before cable TV came to Roseville, that the board authorized Doyle to investigate the merits of entering the cable television business. In January 1966, the company made a proposal to the city of Roseville for a cable TV license. In February, Doyle reported to the Board of Directors that cable TV reception at a test site in Penryn was "very good."

As Roseville Telephone grows and prospers, more space is needed. In 1966, the company put up a new building at 99 Yosemite St. The first photo (below) shows the building under construction. After moving day (above), members of the Board of Directors pose in front of the new facility.

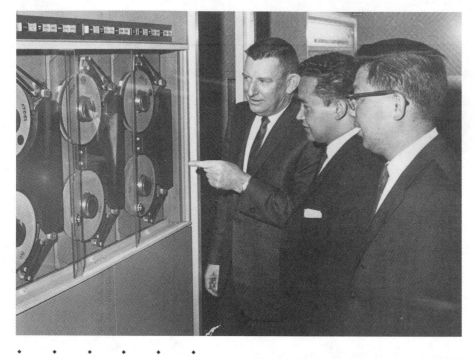

*Bob Doyle shows Roseville Telephone's first computer, the RCA 301, to visiting officials from Costa Rica's telephone company in 1966.*

Unfortunately, soon thereafter the Federal Communications Commission (FCC) issued a ruling prohibiting local telephone exchanges from owning and operating cable TV systems. This forced Roseville Telephone to drop its ambitious plans to be in this business.

Total plant in service surpassed $10 million for the first time in 1966, climbing to $11,161,857 from $9,628,485 in 1965. The company had 144 employees at the end of 1966 and payroll exceeded $1 million for the first time. The maintenance, engineering, splicing, supply, installation and purchasing departments moved into new $500,000 offices at 99 Yosemite St. in May 1966. Ironically, although the company earned nearly $500,000 in 1966, cash on hand at the end of the year amounted to only $28,485, down from nearly $600,000 at the end of 1965. This reflected unusual year-end cash planning and was nothing to worry about. By the end of the following year, cash in the till was up to nearly $300,000.

Toll revenue in 1967 once again accounted for more revenue than local service business as total revenue topped $3 million for the first time. Profitability, however, remained stagnant. Net income hovered in the $400,000-$500,000 range from 1963-1967, slipping slightly in both 1966 and 1967. The company tapped Pacific Mutual Life Insurance Co. for an additional $1.5 million of long-term debt at 6.5 percent interest in 1967, and used the proceeds to pay down short-term, higher-interest bank debt and to finance additional plant investment.

Improvements and technological refinements were not limited to central office equipment alone. One of the company's major investments through the years was in transmission — the wires, cables, conduits coursing through the extensive network of overhead and underground facilities to connect customers with the central offices and through them to the outside world. By 1967, the company reported in its annual report that most of the outside plant was 100 percent pressurized. Pressurization technology was an important advance in cabling because of its ability to keep moisture out of the system, which caused most service interruptions.

One of the most important actions taken in 1967, although it became effective on Jan. 1, 1968, was the adoption of the employee savings plan. This plan enabled employees to purchase shares in the company with the company matching their contributions 50 cents on the dollar. The plan also served to attract and retain quality people. Another reason, according to the board minutes of October 1967, was "to provide a source of funds to purchase RTC stock as it becomes available to help present management keep control of the company."

A. Stanley "Stan" Anderson, a Rio Linda chicken rancher and a company director since 1952, died in September 1967. Bill P. Sheppard, the owner of the Roseville Feed Store and a prominent turkey farmer, was elected to fill Anderson's position.

In every annual report, the company is required to publish the amount of firm dollar commitments it had made to acquire major capital assets in the following year. In 1967's annual report, the reported commitments at Dec. 31, 1967, "for additions to its telephone plant and equipment" amounted to only $96,000. This was by far the lowest commitment of the decade. It reflected the relatively slow economic conditions of the mid-1960s.

The following year, however, the economy began to bounce back. The company's results in 1968 exceeded projections for the first time in four years. Total telephones in use reached more than 20,000 for the first time and revenue rose 16 percent over the previous year to $3,725,721.

In 1969, the final year of the tumultuous 1960s, Roseville Telephone's revenue was not quite $4 million and net income was still under $600,000. Growth, while steady, was not fabulous in the final five years of the 1960s. The gross plant investment had climbed to just over $14 million with telephones in service at 21,639 at year-end. Over the decade, however, revenue had climbed nearly four-fold and the number of telephones served more than doubled.

The sophistication of the company had made great strides in the 1960s, but party lines still accounted for nearly 30 percent of the service provided by the company. The goal set earlier in the decade was to convert 85 percent of telephone subscribers to single-party service by 1970. It was one of the few targets through the years the company failed to reach on time.

Another landmark of the decade's end was the retirement of Gladys (Ellis) Ross. Her tenure of 45 years at the company was the longest ever. She had been an important and much beloved manager during a career that spanned radical change at her local telephone company.

## SUNRISE MALL SPURS BOOM IN HOUSING

In the 1969 annual report, there was mention of a new shopping mall that was being planned for the Sacramento region. The annual report read:

"Plans have been announced for the start in 1970 of the Sacramento Metropolitan Area's largest shopping center, anchored by four major department stores and many smaller ones. A major portion of the complex will be located

*Opening weekend at Sunrise Mall,
March 1971.*

Photo by Bill McNabb, Jr.
Courtesy of James J. Cordano Co.

within the area we serve and this development, when completed, will add greatly to our number of telephones in service."

That was the first mention of what was to become Sunrise Mall, a joint effort of prominent San Diego mall developer Ernest Hahn and Sacramento developer James J. Cordano. Located just south of Greenback Lane on the east side of Fair Oaks Boulevard, the mall straddled the boundary dividing Roseville and Pacific Telephone service territories. Since both telephone companies wanted to serve the mall, the only solution was to split the mall's service. On the north half of the mall, the service was Roseville Telephone and on the south half, Pacific Telephone.

"There was nothing in Citrus Heights. It was like in the late 1940s when Town and Country was built on Fulton Avenue. There was nothing there at the time," Doyle remembered. "You went down Fulton Avenue from Auburn Boulevard to the H Street Bridge into Sacramento. There was nothing but farms out there. Then one day I went by and saw all these big timbers, tiles for the roofs, and soon enough, I learned there was going to be a shopping center called Town and Country out in the middle of nowhere.

"The same thing happened out there in Citrus Heights. In the old days, you went out Sunrise to Greenback Lane, a two-lane road. Sunrise dead-ended at Greenback. It didn't go through," Doyle said. "There was nobody out there. Lots of people, including me, wondered what Hahn and Cordano were thinking about. The freeways were not close, Orangevale was a ways away, as was Folsom, and there was nothing in between. But those guys really had a vision. They built that mall and you see what happened. They did the exact right thing."

Obviously, the site occupied by Sunrise Mall was not chosen by chance. Its location was in fact determined by the long-range growth plan for the Weinstocks department store chain. James J. Cordano, Jr. explained how Sunrise Mall came about.

"The land was originally owned by Hale Brothers Associates," Cordano said. "These were the Hales of Carter Hawley Hale of Los Angeles, which owned Weinstocks. They owned about 90-plus acres at the present site of the mall with the intention to eventually open their northeast Sacramento area store there. It was all part of a strategic plan to locate Weinstocks stores in the anticipated path of growth for the Sacramento area. They already had positioned themselves in the south area at the Florin Mall.

"Hale Brothers selected us along with the Ernest Hahn company from San Diego to develop the mall," Cordano added. "As it turned out, we bought the land from HBA. There was a reciprocal agreement worked out where we own the small stores in the mall and outbuildings, but the four anchor tenants — Weinstocks, Macys, Penneys and Sears — each own their land and building."

Cordano said the Sunrise Mall site, while seemingly desolate in 1970, was ideal. "It was far enough from our Country Club development in Sacramento, which was one consideration. We could have put the mall in the Roseville area along Interstate 80 — that was another option — but it turned out the site chosen worked well."

Doyle Phelan, manager of Sunrise Mall, came to the area in 1971 to help open the J.C. Penney store.

"I was skeptical when I first saw the site and the area around the proposed Sunrise Mall in March 1971," Phelan recalled. "It was all cow pastures — there weren't any homes around. I remember thinking that someone had made a tremendous mistake. But I guess they took the strategy of 'build it and people will come' because it was successful from the very beginning."

Construction began at the mall in 1971 and by March 1972, the first phase — including Weinstocks — opened to the public. In all, there were 1.1 million square feet of retail space in the mall when it opened. Currently, there are 110 small stores in addition to the four anchor stores and the square footage has

*Bill P. Sheppard became a member of the Board of Directors in September 1967, replacing Stan Anderson, who died. In 1967, Sheppard owned and operated the Roseville Feed Store and was a prominent turkey farmer as well.*

expanded to 1.24 million. It has been the largest mall in the area since opening more than 20 years ago.

Jay Kinder remembered Sunrise Mall as by far the most complicated installation attempted by Roseville Telephone to that date. "Of the four major anchor stores, two were in our service territory and two in Pacific's," explained Kinder. "Pacific Telephone called us wanting to know if there was any possibility of moving the boundary lines so that the mall could be served by a single utility."

The typical procedure for determining service was straight forward, but had to that time applied primarily to residential service in housing developments that straddled the boundary between the two companies. If for some reason the boundary line went through a unit, that customer had the option of choosing either company's service.

"So when we got this call from Pacific on the shopping mall, the first question was what's the possibility of moving the boundary line so that one company would provide service to the entire mall," Kinder recalled. "I remember Bob Doyle saying, 'Hell, I think that's a great idea. Let's move the boundary all the way down to Madison Avenue and we'll take care of the whole damned thing.' Well, that wasn't quite what Pacific had in mind."

It ended up with Roseville Telephone taking the business customers on the north end of the mall, including Weinstocks and Penneys, and Pacific Telephone serving those stores on the south end of the mall. The telephone companies shared an equipment room in the middle of the mall where their lines trunked together.

"The first challenge for us was Weinstocks on the north end. Weinstocks' main store at the time was in downtown Sacramento, and the company originally wanted to serve the new location as a satellite of the downtown store, meaning customers would have to dial a downtown Sacramento number and then be extended back to Citrus Heights.

"Our objective was to persuade Weinstocks that this wouldn't be a wise arrangement, since it was a long distance call into downtown," Kinder said. "The solution was to convince them that a new solid-state electronics ITT PBX (private branch exchange) was the right move for them. They agreed to let us install it and we were one of the first companies, and we think the first company, to install a solid-state private branch exchange on the customer's premises. And it was for Weinstocks at Sunrise Mall. Penneys came after that."

Phelan, who was then operations manager at the Penneys store, remembered being leery of Roseville Telephone's ability to adequately service the store's needs.

"Yes, I was a little concerned. In those years, you still heard a lot of negative things about Roseville Telephone, that it was little hick telephone company," Phelan said. "And I had never dealt with an independent before, so I didn't know what to think. But it turned out fine and to this day I have the utmost respect for the people at Roseville Telephone. They've always been very service-minded."

The new mall made 1972 a banner year for the company, with the station gain the highest to that time, an increase of 3,306, or 13 percent over 1971. Sunrise Mall was a boon to Roseville Telephone, and spurred the growth of Citrus Heights, too. Although Aerojet's fortunes had already waned and the region struggled for years absorbing the enormous layoffs from the rocket maker, new residents kept flocking to the area. Sacramento County grew from 291,357 in 1960 to 367,349 in 1970. Roseville grew from 13,421 in 1960 to 18,221 in 1970. Citrus Heights had grown to 42,661 in 1970, an increase of 40,000 in only 20 years.

## GROWTH ACCELERATES IN EARLY '70s

The new decade brought accelerated growth to Roseville Telephone's service area. The housing surge was again paced by Citrus Heights, which was home to more than 56,000 residents by 1975, a 31.5 percent increase since 1970. Roseville's growth was more modest, rising about 10 percent to 20,000 in 1975.

Roseville Telephone's financial performance strengthened throughout the 1970s, although a non-recurring toll revenue adjustment in 1971 penalized revenue and earnings in that year. Revenue surpassed $4 million for the first time in 1970 and net income that year reached a record $744,899. By 1976, revenue climbed to $9,729,000 with net income reaching nearly $1.5 million. It was the fourth consecutive year that net income had exceeded $1 million. Telephone station growth doubled in that time frame, rising to 47,341 instruments in service at the

*Frances Kelly, center, took over as chief operator in 1970 when Gladys (Ellis) Ross retired.*

*An important part of the Roseville Hospital's major expansion in 1966 was its telephone system. Here a Roseville Telephone employee is making final adjustments before the system goes on line.*

Roseville Press-Tribune, 1966

end of 1976 compared to 23,567 at year-end 1970. Gross plant investment in those years more than doubled to $34.3 million after 1976 from $15 million at the end of 1970.

The formula Doyle developed early in his stewardship was a successful one for the company — invest in the future and the revenue will come. The rate of growth in the early '70s was enough that additional borrowing was necessary for the first time since 1967. In 1973, the company borrowed $3 million, paying 7.75 percent for 25-year money, and in 1976, the company borrowed $5 million more at 10 percent. It was the highest interest rate the company ever paid for long-term money.

Supplementing the debt and internally-generated funds from earnings and depreciation, the company sold $2 million in shares in 1973-1974 and a similar amount in 1976. The company also filed for a rate increase in 1974, but later withdrew the request as conditions improved.

The subject of electronic switching came up at the shareholders meeting in June 1971. Bob Doyle told his shareholders that it was clear to him that electronic switching represented the future of the industry and, while it would be expensive to replace the existing step equipment, long-range economies from the new technology would benefit the company. The following month the directors approved the purchase of electronic switching equipment to serve fast-growing Citrus Heights. However, it wouldn't be until 1974 that the new equipment could be delivered and installed.

Also in 1971, Doyle resurrected his successful strategy of hiring experienced retirees from other companies to help him guide Roseville Telephone. One important consultant was Rene Baker, who for 43 years worked for Pacific Telephone. Baker was an expert in toll separations and dealing with the Public Utilities Commission. Baker's expertise benefited the company directly, of course, but he also passed along his knowledge to Roseville employees. In a *Line Chatter* five years later, Baker's role with the company was discussed.

"Mr. Rene L. Baker, who has been retained by our company on a consulting basis since his retirement from Pacific Telephone in 1971, is probably busier than ever. His case is a perfect example that retirement plans that carry a mandatory retirement age force many people with productive years still ahead of them into a new mode of life. However, Pacific's loss is truly our gain. And we keep 'Bake' very busy. During the past five years, RTC's people have relied on his invaluable assistance in many areas; e.g., separation studies, rates of return, filings with the California Public Utilities Commission, depreciation studies, ad infinitum. While some might find the commute between Roseville and Sacramento disheartening, Bob Parsons, of our traffic engineering department, makes the commute to Los Altos almost on a monthly basis to confer with our man Baker. And from time-to-time Mark Shull has made the same journey to Los Altos to cover CPUC matters. Recently, our marketing manager, Jay Kinder, went down to get advice on a study for non-recurring charges. In the not too distant future, Ned Kindelt's name may be added to Mr. Baker's list of conferees to discuss 'Economic Engineering.' Baker says he is available to talk with anyone at RTC on anything telephone related."

While one telephone industry veteran joined the Roseville Telephone brain trust, its elder statesman departed. Walter Hanisch died on New Year's Day, 1972, at age 88. His association with the company stretched to 1912 when he joined the original Roseville Home Telephone Co. as a lineman. For 60 years, Walter Hanisch's primary interest was the Roseville Telephone Company. The company's progress was very satisfying to him because he had seen it grow from 160 telephones into a respected, fast-growing utility serving thousands and thousands of customers.

Local businessman George Campbell was elected to replace Hanisch at the next meeting in late January 1972. Campbell was to serve the company with distinction for 15 years.

*Hunting was a favorite activity of the Doyles in their earlier years. In the mid-1960s, Tom Doyle, left, and Bob Doyle, second from the right, enjoyed hunting trips with Mert Diener, second from left, Doulton Burner, and Frank Galli, far right.*

Doyle's real estate acquisition talents were in much use during 1972 as he acquired property at Vernon and Jefferson streets from the Haman family in April and the dentist Dr. Berry Boston's property on Vernon Street a month later. Boston's buildings would be remodeled later to house the engineering department, and currently the Roseville Telephone Museum.

Financing continued to command much of Doyle's attention in 1972-1973. In discussing the company's heavy capital requirements with the CPUC, Doyle floated a few trial balloons past the commissioners, including the prospects of an $8 million loan and a rate increase that would raise the company's return on investment to nearly 10 percent. Both ideas were rejected. An $8 million loan was too big for the company, the commissioners said, and the return sought was too high. Reluctant to request another restrictive loan from Pacific Mutual, Doyle decided on another tack. Through industry contacts, he had heard about Harry Sheldon, who was known to have arranged financing for other telephone companies. Sheldon, who lived in the Boston area, had extensive contacts with insurance companies throughout the country. Doyle commissioned Sheldon to place $3 million in long-term debentures. He came back with a Philadelphia-based insurance company, Provident Mutual Life, that was willing to loan Roseville Telephone $3 million at 7.75 percent. The deal was done.

The PUC staff was impressed with the rate Doyle was able to get because the prevailing long-term money at the end of 1972 was going at about 8.25 percent. Sheldon's contacts had saved the company a half-percent, which over the years would amount to thousands of dollars of interest savings.

"I think we paid him something like a $10,000 commission to get us that loan," recalled Doyle, "but he saved us a lot more than that over the years. He was a good one, Harry Sheldon."

In 1975, Sheldon put together a consortium of four insurance companies who lent $5 million to the company. The entry of Sheldon to help the company also served to break the long-time hold Pacific Mutual had on Roseville Telephone. The company's long-term debt arrangements from the early '70s on were not as restrictive as the earlier loan deals with Pacific Mutual. Through the years, the relationship between the company and Pacific Mutual had become strained as Doyle tried unsuccessfully to have the insurance company ease up on its loan covenants.

In April 1973, Doyle's showed his disdain for the lender in a letter mailed immediately after Roseville was rocked by bomb blasts when cars in a naval ordnance train exploded in Southern Pacific's rail yards in Antelope, west of Roseville. Bob Raymer recalled the times:

"The damned Navy train blew up right in Antelope! And it was tremendous. But at that very moment, we were being asked to write our lender — insurance companies are terribly careful — to certify that everything at the company is OK, that the company was not in violation of any agreements, the plant and equipment was insured and in good condition, etc. So this explosion occurs and one of our young lawyers had an idea that Doyle liked, too. We got a piece of bond paper, scrunched it up, put a lot of dirt on it, oil, blood, all kinds of things. And then we wrote in scraggly longhand:

> Gentlemen:
>
> We have had a few problems here, but we want you to know that we're still in business, almost. Our entire plant and equipment will certainly be operative before many years pass. If you want to know whether any of our equipment is still running, we would have telephoned you, but for the moment this letter must suffice.
>
> Robert L. Doyle, President

"We got a big kick out of that," Raymer said. "I think Doyle even kept the letter, a dirty blood-soaked, oil-soaked letter, saying that we had weathered this tremendous explosion and were OK."

The company did weather the crisis, but the explosions created an emergency atmosphere during that weekend. Vern Roberson was at work on that Saturday morning at the Roseville central office. The huge blasts caught Roberson … well, with his pants down.

"There was me and one other man working that Saturday. I was the test board-man, working inside. I used to come in early and get the stuff tested so when the outside guy came to work, I'd have something for him to start on," Roberson said. "I'm working and I had to go to the pot. We had a little bathroom back there and I'm sitting back there contemplating the world when all of a sudden, boom! That little swinging door went ka-bam, ka-bam! I thought, 'Good God, some drunk's run into the building!' So I jumped up and ran out the back door with my pants down. I looked out and said to myself, 'It ain't nothing.' I went back in and did my necessaries and got my clothes put on straight. I went back to the test board, then ka-boom! I looked out the front door and I could see smoke. I thought a gas station had blown up. I thought the smoke was coming from the west. Immediately, things started happening. I got calls from the police department, from the state. They wanted to get people out to start picking up telephone lines, doing this and doing that, and I'm trying to call people. They wanted some emergency lines run to the Grand Oaks Shopping Center, but I couldn't get find anybody. Lord, it was fun. I finally got Walter (Gordon) at home and he started asking questions. I told him, 'Don't ask stupid questions, Walter, get your ass down here.' So anyhow, we got through it, but I put in about an 18-hour shift that day."

Bernice Moser, the retired operator, remembered that long weekend.

"I was home when I heard it, about two miles away, so the first thing I did was find out what it was and beat it into work. The town was sealed off and people were evacuated. Some of those bombs aboard were large and if they had all gone off, it was bye-bye birdie! There was a guard on every street corner and the police kept anybody from coming in. They told everybody else to get out. They didn't realize that the operators were still there. We had so many calls coming in that we finally had to start monitoring them and only let a few calls go through, just the priority ones," Moser remembered. "The Army, the Navy, the Marines, I think everybody got into the act. But we had calls coming in from everywhere so we had to keep the lines open for emergency calls coming in and going out.

"Our biggest problem as far as the operators was concerned was getting some food. I remember we finally got some Kentucky Fried Chicken and then we would call the girls that were coming in and tell them to bring things to eat and drink. It got cleaned up within about 36-48 hours, but during that time, it was a real emergency."

## ELECTRONIC AGE ARRIVES

On Feb. 9, 1974, Roseville Telephone entered into the electronic age when it installed its #1 EAX electronic switching equipment in the Citrus Heights central office, serving 6,000 lines of the 726 prefix. The installation of #1 EAX was the first giant step in a 20-year modernization wave that would catapult the company to the forefront of the telecommunications industry.

EAX stands for Electronic Automatic Exchange switch. It was manufactured by Roseville's long-time equipment supplier, Automatic Electric, a subsidiary of General Telephone (GTE). The cost was $2.5 million. The new switching equipment replaced the electromechanical step-by-step equipment that was first installed at Roseville Telephone in 1953. From 1974 to 1985, section by section, step equipment would make room — and plenty of it, by the way — for increasingly sophisticated electronic switches. In fact, the square footage freed up in converting from step equipment to electronic switches was significant. It enabled the company to expand office space. The timing was good, too, because the fast-growing company was voracious in its appetite for office space in those years.

The efficiency of the #1 EAX was remarkable. A call could be connected in thousandths of a second vs. 6-7 seconds on the step equipment. One of the employees involved in the installation of the #1 EAX was a new hire, Russ Kelley. He had worked with Western Electric for nearly nine years and had experience installing electronic switches. He was also a very confident young man.

"When I first came here, I told Walter Gordon I could install anything he could buy," Kelley remembered. "He began testing me from the very beginning."

The first electronic switch was a challenge to Kelley because the equipment differed at Western Electric and its big customer, Pacific Telephone. "But when you do telephone equipment installation, the difference in technology is not a real factor. All wires connect together somehow. I always said if the engineer does his job, I can do my job."

The installation was a two-part process. One part was readying the existing switching equipment to be cut over to the new equipment. This was the part of the total installation done by Roseville personnel with Kelley in charge. The new equipment was installed by Automatic Electric personnel. It was a combined effort.

Kelley was taken aback at first, however, because he had no experience with the step-by-step equipment. "Walter asked me how I could install equipment if I knew nothing about the step equipment. I again said if the engineer does his job, I can do my job. I'd never worked one of the old toll switchboards before. So it was all quite a challenge."

*      *      *      *      *      *

*Walter Gordon minds the controls of Roseville Telephone's first electronic switching machine, #1 EAX, which went into service in 1974.*

But the "can do" attitude of Kelley and his crew prevailed and the installation was a success. The dollar savings to the company for assisting AE with the first electronic switch installation were substantial. More important was the pride it instilled in the participating employees.

A few years later, Kelley and his crew installed a 1,000-line addition to the #1 EAX, the first one ever done by an independent company. In 1977, when growth in Citrus Heights was exploding, they did another 7,000-line addition. That huge effort was completed in 24-hour days by 24 employees under the direction of Kelley and Tim Fritts. Kelley later calculated that by doing the installation of the $2.2 million line addition in-house, the company had saved at least $200,000.

That first EAX installation touched off a continuous flow of installation, upgrade and replacement of switching equipment at the company's three central offices, Roseville, Citrus Heights and Folsom Lake. The fourth office west of Roseville came on line in 1980.

Although the step switching equipment was being replaced as quickly as the company could afford, it still worked well and often was re-installed to increase capacity at one of the other central offices. For instance, the step equipment that was replaced by the #1 EAX in Citrus Heights ended up increasing the capacity at Roseville's central office where it was re-installed. In later years, step equipment was sold to smaller independent companies that still used it. In other words, although the step equipment was becoming out-moded, it still worked well. Less progressive companies with telephone service territories that weren't growing fast like Roseville could have retained the step equipment a lot longer.

It was symbolic that soon after electronic switching came to Roseville Telephone, Doyle's first management hire, Emerson Gunning, retired after 20 years with the company. Gunning was an expert in the electromechanical machinery that served Roseville Telephone so well through Doyle's first two decades.

The new electronic age offered so many dazzling possibilities for service — and enhanced revenue — that it was correct for Roseville Telephone to replace the old steppers as fast as possible. And there was nobody better prepared to help guide the company into the new era than Al Johnson, the former sales engineer for Automatic Electric who had become a top executive with General Telephone's equipment manufacturing subsidiary.

## AL JOHNSON JOINS THE COMPANY

*Al Johnson, joined the company in 1977 and is now Executive Vice President.*

Roseville Telephone had made great technical strides since 1954, but by the mid-1970s Bob Doyle knew that the growth prospects of the company, plus the rapidly-changing technology landscape required that he get more expert help to run the company. The electronic age was in full swing and the digital era was coming up fast. These trends meant dramatic efficiencies and many more capabilities would accrue to those telephone companies that had the courage to acquire the latest technologies.

True to the tradition he established in his first year as president, Doyle decided to hire an experienced hand to help him navigate these techni-cal waters and also take a huge management load off his shoulders. In May 1977, 55-year-old A.A. (Al) Johnson joined Roseville Telephone as operations manager. He retired from a 30-year career with General Telephone's Automatic Electric subsidiary to join Roseville.

Doyle wasn't hiring an unknown quantity. Al Johnson was very familiar with Roseville Telephone and had first met Doyle just before he became president in 1954.

"I was in the engineering department at Automatic Electric from 1950 to 1953, when I was transferred to the sales department as a staff engineer in our San Francisco office," Johnson recalled. "My function was to assist our sales representative to sell central office equipment, and once it was sold, to ensure that the equipment was the right type, capacity, configured properly, and so forth. I first met Bob in very early 1954 when our salesman at the time introduced me to him as Roseville Telephone Company's 'assistant janitor.'

"I don't know if Bob had a title at that point, so it was just like him to refer to himself as 'the janitor,'" Johnson remembered. "At that time, Walter Hanisch was still the manager and David Hanisch was still plant superintendent. I worked with David and Walter in engineering a major addition to their dial service, which had only gone in a few months earlier. That was my first project with the company. I believe it was in February 1954 that we sent our proposal to them. The addition was 50 percent of the size of the initial installation, so you can see that they needed a lot more equipment than they had."

In the process of engineering that addition in 1954, Johnson became acquainted with Doyle and was the person who brought Emerson Gunning's name to his attention. In fact, had history gone a slightly different direction, Johnson might have been Bob Doyle's second hire.

"Actually, Bob offered me a job shortly after he had hired Gunning. I gave it very serious consideration, then I said no. I decided to keep doing what I was doing, for the time being. Nearly 25 years later, I changed my mind."

As a sales engineer for Automatic Electric, Johnson was involved in equipment sales and engineering for installations at independent telephone companies throughout the West, including Alaska and Hawaii. He was very well versed in small independents such as Roseville. In 1968 he was transferred from San Francisco back to Northlake, Ill., where Automatic Electric had just built a large manufacturing facility. It was also corporate headquarters for AE. He became a manager and then a director and handled the sales and support liaison between AE and General Telephone's operating equipment needs.

"I would always attend the USITA (United States Independent Telephone Association) annual convention, and see Bob and Tom Doyle there. We would always have a night out together and he'd bring me up to date with what was going on at the company and so forth," Johnson recalled. "That happened from late 1968 until 1976, and it was in late 1976 that I called Bob and asked if he was going to be hiring anybody to help him run the company. I told him I wanted to be considered, if he had that in mind."

Johnson's call came at exactly the right time.

"I had been thinking for some time that I needed help because it was getting too much for me, but I didn't know who the hell I would get," remembered Doyle. "When Al called and asked about working here, I thought, hell, he's perfect. Here's a hard-working, honest guy who knows the company backwards and forwards. How could I go wrong? But if he hadn't called, I wouldn't have known he was going to retire from AE and be available."

A week later, Doyle called Johnson and asked him when he could come to California to talk.

"I just happened to have a trip going to California that week," Johnson recollected. "It was between Christmas and New Year's. We met, talked about it and I was offered the job. We shook hands and agreed I'd come aboard."

It was a hard decision for Johnson, but after three decades with the same company in an industry that was rapidly changing and consolidating, he felt it was time to do what he had always wanted to do — be involved with a small, independent telephone company.

Bernice (Harris) Moser, standing, monitors the company operators in the early 1970s.

"I was 55 years old, but I felt that I had graduated and now I was getting ready to enter into what I had been trained for over the last thirty-some years," Johnson recalled. "In my activities at Automatic Electric before I went back to Illinois, I handled nine western states, plus Hawaii and Alaska, and had dealt with just about every independent in that area at one time or another. For the real small ones, I designed just about everything, laid out the floor plans for them, conduit systems, participated in their coordination meetings, and generally advised them as to what they could and couldn't do equipment-wise, switching-wise. I got involved in all operations as a supplier. With all this experience, I really felt by this time I was qualified to run a small telephone company."

Johnson was in charge of all the departments except the fiscal and regulatory organization. That was Mark Shull's domain. After hiring Johnson, Doyle had only two people directly reporting to him rather than everybody in the company. It took a major load off of him.

The timing was fortuitous, because in just a few short years economic conditions would be such that Doyle would need to concentrate on stock sales.

Although Johnson admits there probably was resentment among a few managers that an outsider was hired for the No. 2 job, the feeling today is nearly unanimous that Johnson's hiring represented another masterful move by Doyle.

Bob Raymer, the company's long-time attorney, remembered that Johnson's arrival gave a significant boost to the overall management of the company. "At the time the only two people in general management were Bob Doyle and Mark

Shull, but Mark was never an operations man. The department heads and Bob took care of that, and when Al came in I thought it was a very significant improvement because then a big segment of the company could report to Al, which they did," Raymer recalled.

"When Al came in the late '70s, there were still people in the Roseville area that remembered how Roseville Telephone had been when it was in bad trouble and gave bad service," Raymer continued. "But I think that reputation carried over far beyond the period of time it should have. By the time Al was here a few years, it was apparent that this reputation would soon go away. When Al came in, the company entered into significant contracts to upgrade the facilities, to acquire really the latest central office equipment and to do those things that made Roseville a cutting-edge company."

Long-time director Bill Sheppard was a Johnson fan from the start.

"That guy is down there at 5 or 6 every morning working. There isn't anybody in this telephone business that knows as much as that man, but he doesn't let on like he knows everything. He's a very low-key guy, he appreciates a compliment, a handshake and stuff. He's a hell of a guy."

Another long-time director, Doulton Burner, remembered when Johnson was hired. "Bob always looked around to get experienced people who knew about specific areas of the business. Guys like Gunning and Fred Spring. It was the same with Al. Here was a guy who had national if not international knowledge of many aspects in the telephone business. And Bob looked to hire somebody who would be able to cover an area, the equipment side, that he perhaps was a little leery about. Al had knowledge of the whole thing."

Another life-long telephone man, company director Ralph Hoeper, also believes one of Bob Doyle's best personnel moves was hiring Johnson.

"I'd see Bob regularly at meetings back in the 1970s and he told me he was getting to the point where it was more than he could handle, that he needed somebody to take that day-to-day load off his shoulders," Hoeper remembered. "He picked a very good one. Al has done a terrific job for Bob and the company. He's got a strong technical background and is also a good administrator."

Chuck Spooner, manager of data processing at the company, remembered when Johnson came aboard.

"It made a lot of real good sense to me at the time. Bringing Al in and putting him in charge of large sections of the company, outside plant engineering, splicing, construction, the warehouse, marketing, the business office, and the central office especially, was the right thing at the time," said Spooner. "I think Al provided Bob with a buffer, a good strong manager to look after operations and take some of that load off of his shoulders. Then Bob had the operations manager and the chief financial officer reporting to him, two people he could listen to and have confidence in what they brought to him. That was the big value of bringing Al into the company, in my opinion."

Outside plant director Leon Bower appreciated the manner in which Johnson took over. "He spent a great deal of time learning the company, what everybody did and how they integrated and tied together," Bower explained. "He didn't come in with a big hammer and whip. He spent a good deal of time getting to know the company organization and what each section did and how they interrelated. I've been very pleased. I know that Bob needed the relief."

"Al brought a lot of expertise with him," said Mark Shull. "He knew the business from the mechanical end so Al has been a real asset to Bob. He really does know the telephone business."

Johnson's arrival coincided with another milestone at the company. In the week prior to Johnson coming aboard, Roseville Telephone hit 50,000 telephones in service. It was on May 20, 1977, that the Jackson family of Roseville became the 50,000th customer. The Jacksons received a commemorative extension phone and a check for $100. Naturally, Doyle talked them into buying four shares of stock.

With 50,000 telephones in service and an experienced Al Johnson on board, Roseville Telephone was ready to evolve from a small telephone exchange into a modern telecommunications corporation.

# 1977-1989: Electronics, Digital, Cellular Eras Dawn

JOHNSON'S EQUIPMENT EXPERTISE SHOWS IMMEDIATE IMPACT

*"My strong suit was definitely network switching, central office equipment and network facilities. I knew, in detail, what it took for each of these operations to work properly, and how they fit together."*
— A.A. "Al" Johnson

When Al Johnson joined Roseville Telephone in May 1977, he brought with him state-of-the art knowledge about the latest technology available to independent telephone companies. As a top executive with the equipment manufacturing subsidiary of General Telephone, GTE Automatic Electric, Johnson had more overall knowledge of the hardware and network system side of telephony than anybody at Roseville Telephone. He also was well-versed in whatever new technologies were on the horizon. His arrival came at an ideal time as Roseville Telephone was ready to dramatically expand its commitment and investment in high technology.

"When I came to Roseville, I felt my strong suit was definitely network switching, central office equipment and network facilities," said Al Johnson. "I knew, in detail, what it took for each of these operations to work properly, and how they fit together. My weak spots were outside plant and the financial side, accounting procedures, etc.

"When I was transferred from San Francisco to Northlake, Ill., in 1968, the electronic era of telephone switching was just starting. At corporate headquarters, I saw first-hand the first generation electronic switching systems that were going into General's exchanges. I was totally involved in that system and other later-generation electronic switching systems.

"Roseville Telephone had already begun to get into electronic switching a few years before I came, so it would be a mistake to attribute the modernization solely to my arrival," Johnson added. "Roseville was growing so fast in the late '60s and early '70s, instead of perpetuating the old equipment, they went with the latest equipment on the market. In fact, Roseville Telephone was the first non-General Telephone company to buy and place into service electronic automatic switching exchange (EAX) equipment in 1974. After that, any time the company needed major office switching equipment, they would buy the next generation of equipment."

With Johnson aboard, the policy of buying the latest equipment accelerated. Johnson's technical knowledge augmented the considerable expertise and "can do" attitude of Walter Gordon's network engineering group. With their technical know-how and the company's pressing growth requirements, Roseville Telephone has remained at the leading edge of technology for nearly two decades.

## COMPANY PREPARES FOR GROWTH SURGE

In 1977, the company's growth was sizzling. By May, when Johnson arrived, 2,670 new telephones had already been installed for the year. Development was creating new customers by the thousands as builders cleared the farm lands to make way for new residents. Russ Kelley and his crew were pulling 24-hour shifts to complete the installation of a $2.2 million, 7,000-line addition to the Citrus Heights central office. Outside plant manager Warren Tinker talked about the dramatic growth in the April 1977 edition of *Line Chatter*.

"Perhaps many of our employees read about our newest subdivision in Roseville. It is called Cirby Ranch and is located on the south side of Cirby Way opposite Oakridge Drive. It is a $26 million development and ultimately will contain 376 homes for Roseville residents. Judging from the large clouds of dust that have been rolling up at this location, it looks like they mean business. I think this typifies a trend that has been developing for some time and, that is, Roseville will soon come into its own as a major growth area. It should be noted that along with this development, there are three other large subdivisions in Roseville: Huntington Oaks, Lexington Greens, and Cirby Woods. Construction will soon begin in each of these. Many more are in the planning stage and construction is scheduled to start soon. In fact, it looks like Roseville and Folsom Lake will be giving Citrus Heights a run for its money in the not-too-distant future.

"I think it is interesting to note that in our overall area, we presently have 182 projects either in the planning stage or under construction. Of these, Roseville and Folsom have a combined total of 80 projects that will ultimately contain 9,605 homes. Forty-eight of these are in the planning stage and 12 are presently under construction. Citrus Heights has 102 projects that will contain 7,058 lots, 51 (projects) of which are presently in the planning stage and 28 are under construction. If you have not had an occasion to drive through our area recently, I suggest that it would be a good way to get acquainted with it and get a sampling of the growth to come."

This strong residential growth demanded significant capital investment by the company. Bob Doyle talked about the growth in the 1977 annual report.

"1977 was another year of progress and achievement. We continued to enjoy the benefits of serving what must be one of the fastest growing areas in California. In the course of the year we added 7,614 phones, the largest gain we ever recorded. We continue to build capacity for the future growth that lies within our service area. This is best evidenced by the fact that gross plant investment increased by more than $10 million. Additionally, plant investments for 1978 and 1979 are projected to be $4 million and $7 million, respectively."

In 1978, Roseville Telephone added another 8,070 new phones to its system. In fact, more telephones were added in each of those years, 1977 and 1978, than the company had placed in service after its first 44 years through 1958! In that year, the company had a total of only 7,173 telephones in service. In March 1978 alone, 927 new phones were installed, the best month for growth during the '70s. In the March 1978 *Line Chatter*, Norm Pilliard of outside plant engineering warned employees to expect even bigger workloads in the months ahead.

"If you think 1977 was a demanding year for Ma Roseville, outside plant-wise, brace yourself for the spring of 1978," Pilliard wrote. "Many new subdivision maps are coming in and it looks like the Roseville area is going to catch up with Citrus Heights in the near future. We have many other projects going at this time that are just too numerous to mention, and I think it's time for an end to this article and time to get back to work."

The capital construction program continued unabated. In 1978, a new $1.2 million electronic switching system was installed in the Folsom Lake office to replace its step-by-step equipment. Rulon Blackburn described in the June 1978 *Line Chatter* the difference between this new second generation electronic switching system (No. 2 EAX) and the older step gear.

"I believe that it has improved the service to our subscribers in the Lake area by 100 percent at least. For example, a toll call from the old step equipment took from 25 to 30 seconds to complete. Have you ever sat and listened to a seemingly dead phone for a half a minute? Try it — it seems like a lifetime," Blackburn wrote. "With the No. 2, a toll call is completed in about seven seconds or less; quite an improvement!"

MORE CALLS can be handled over single telephone wire with use of new channel decoder examined by Bob Parsons of Roseville Telephone. One wire per six calls will now be needed, while old mechanical equipment required use of four wires for each call.

Roseville Press-Tribune, December 31, 1980

*114 Vernon Street*

Also, in late September 1978, the new $3.6 million equipment building at 114 Vernon St. in Roseville was completed. The 42,000-square-foot facility was the new home for the latest digital switching equipment, the test center, equipment engineering, traffic engineering, line assigners, operators and central office personnel. Employees liked this new building because all office areas were carpeted and their lunch room was equipped with a range, oven, microwave oven, refrigerator (dispensing ice and ice water from the door) and dishwasher. They could also enjoy lunch or breaks on the landscaped patio and deck. The building also contained a 560,000-watt emergency back-up generator.

These investments in the future came none too early, because in the succeeding few years Roseville Telephone would welcome several new, large corporate neighbors to the region, companies with world-class names such as Kaiser-Permanente, Shugart Associates, Hewlett-Packard and NEC. Their arrival would fuel a new wave of growth for Roseville Telephone and, in the process, reshape the utility's business from one that served primarily residential customers to one that now serviced a comparatively large business community. The industrialization of Roseville Telephone's service area benefited the company. Business service is generally more profitable than residential. Furthermore, the high quality of the companies was sure to attract more suppliers and vendors as well as the professionals who staff and service large corporations.

## TEAM APPROACH WINS
## KAISER-PERMANENTE'S BUSINESS

In the spring of 1978, a marketing representative at the time, Ann Herman, fielded what she expected would be a routine service inquiry. But the question asked by the pleasant-sounding caller on the other end "made her gulp hard to keep her cool," she reported later. This was because the call came from Oakland-based Kaiser-Permanente, the state's largest HMO (health maintenance organization). Kaiser was considering Roseville as a site for a new outpatient clinic. "Could Roseville Telephone Company meet their needs?" the caller asked.

As the story was told in the May 1980 *Line Chatter*, the Kaiser contract launched Roseville Telephone into the big time. It was the biggest job won by the company since the Weinstocks' job eight years earlier when Sunrise Mall opened. But Kaiser needed to be shown Roseville Telephone could perform.

The unidentified author of the *Line Chatter* article explained how the entire company pulled together to land this contract. Excerpts of the article are reproduced here because it explains in some detail how the company's large contracts required coordinated efforts from all departments.

"If these were not words heard round the world, they certainly were heard throughout RTC," the *Line Chatter* article said of Kaiser's telephone inquiry. "In a short period of time, a flurry of activity was begun. Marketing manager Jay Kinder quickly responded to the request and there followed many planning meetings by representatives from all departments — including the president, Bob Doyle. The decision was made — 'RTC COULD AND WOULD!'

"Communications consultant John Costa was appointed to the account and has worked almost full time since with the Kaiser representatives, interpreting their needs, listening, writing orders, suffering through changes of plans and telephone numbers, coordinating what at one time RTC would have considered impossible. And in the marketing department, Larry Lasick was busy trying to devise tariffs to cover these new innovations — not the least of which was something called two-tier pricing!

"Many questions had to be answered — how would such a large account be billed and how could our computer keep records on such an account? After much head scratching, pencil sharpening, and plain hard work, the data processing team designed the single line record card. Everyone, everywhere, had to keep tabs on their calendars to make sure one planning meeting didn't conflict with another planning meeting.

Aerial view of Roseville in 1978 shows continuing importance of the railroad.

"But answers began to formulate as a result of these many meetings and careful planning. A big question was what switch should RTC order for Kaiser? A PBX (private branch exchange) survey committee with representatives from outside plant engineering, central office, plant installation and marketing was formed, and after careful study, the Rolm CBX (computerized branch exchange) switch was chosen. Now the traffic department became involved, since Hazel Snider and the service advisers, Debbie Uribe, Cindy Bosco, and Darla Weber, had to travel to Santa Clara to be thoroughly trained on this new sophisticated Rolm equipment.

"Training for many was to follow. Bob Schmidgall from installation spent a month learning the installation and maintenance of the switch. Dick Davis will be attending this same course in June. John Naylor, John Costa, and Larry Lasick went for a week orientation. Soon the freeway between Rolm and RTC saw a steady stream of RTC vehicles going for conferences and learning.

"Behind all of this was a growing mountain of paperwork. Typists could type KAISER in their sleep. The change and innovation one new customer had generated seemed amazing. But these were all healthy changes and the team progressed. Designs, drawings, reports, and outlines all began to take shape.

"In the meantime, the heavy equipment arrived at the construction site and ground was broken. The job was really under way. Engineer Norm Pilliard even felt short some days when faced with the stacks of blue prints and awesome responsibilities. Finally the day came when RTC personnel started to work on the Kaiser site. A T-carrier facility was actually to be installed on the customer's premises. Another first. Experienced though the construction and splicing crews were, they were challenged by a gigantic job and much overtime followed. By December 1979, the outside plant facilities were installed and the Rolm CBX was delivered.

"Even though the Kaiser switch was originally designed to work on step-by-step central office equipment, in the midst of all of this, the DSS (digital switching system) was installed and cut over in February 1980. So the switch had to be modified to work with the new electronic equipment and the Kaiser trunks installed in the DSS," the article continued. "By this time, many of the RTC personnel were speaking their own vocabulary which included such buzz words as RLT, CRT, and ACD. The team became more polished all the time.

"A complex phase of coordination came when meetings were held with Pacific Telephone to verify the compatibility of Rolm's CBX with PT&T's ESS (electronic switching system) central office. This was successfully resolved by the end of 1979. Early in 1980 the site was ready for the complex installation crew. Bob Schmidgall took up residence there and installed the switch and Ron Keenan is still hard at work in the sets. Now the testing began! Would the trunks between Sacramento and Roseville Telephone work? Where are the bugs? John Costa's hair thinned and he chewed his nails … Was all this hard work going to pay off?"

Of course, the team effort paid off in spades for Roseville Telephone. The smooth cutover of the new communications system to Kaiser on May 30, 1980, proved that Roseville Telephone could handle huge, complex installations. It set the stage for bigger challenges to come.

Moreover, Rick Bawden reported in a subsequent employee newsletter, "The Kaiser communications people said that this was the smoothest cut they have ever had; a thanks to all involved." Then Bawden added, "Oh, by the way, Kaiser is already talking about and preparing for a new building that will require their present switch to triple in capacity."

In addition to gaining valuable experience in the Kaiser installation of the Rolm computerized exchange, the telephone company installed Rolm switches in its own offices. This not only improved the company's internal communications system, but it gave all the department personnel even more experience with this new, sophisticated equipment. In 1980, computers were not yet commonplace, and computerized telephone switching systems designed for office use were in their infancy. Having in-house the system they were selling gave the marketing people an edge against competitors.

## SHUGART ASSOCIATES OPENS PLANT

The first large high-technology company to have manufacturing operations in Roseville was computer disk-drive maker Shugart Associates. Based then in Sunnyvale, Calif., in the heart of the Silicon Valley, this subsidiary of Xerox had plans to build 320,000 square feet of manufacturing space in two phases at its site on Sunrise Avenue east of Douglas Boulevard and south of Interstate 80 in Roseville. Fittingly, Shugart built on acreage formerly in the middle of the old Doyle ranch. Shugart's first two buildings were completed in January 1981.

In the bidding to win Shugart's communications system business, the major competitor was Rolm, the interconnect company (a company that manufactures branch exchange equipment) that already served Shugart at its home office and manufacturing facilities in Sunnyvale. But Roseville Telephone prevailed in winning this important contract. As events unfolded, Shugart played an important, albeit brief, role in vaulting Roseville into the high-technology big leagues. In a September 1980 edition of the *San Francisco Chronicle*, reporter Bill Soiffer wrote a piece headlined, "Roseville — A Chip Off Old Silicon Valley." Soiffer described the heady plans in Roseville for Shugart and Hewlett-Packard, two of Silicon Valley's premier companies at the time.

Shugart, he wrote, intended to have 2,000 employees in its Roseville complex by 1983. The company's site alone would attract engineers.

"Shugart is so job-conscious that it is building on a highly visible hill overlooking Interstate 80 so that engineers who ski in the Sierra will drive by and think, 'If I worked here, I'd be home by now,'" Soiffer wrote.

Shugart's grand plans never came to pass, however, as the weakening national economy of the early 1980s collaborated with brutal competition in the disk drive industry to eventually doom Shugart. The company had a little more than 400 employees in Roseville when it closed its doors in mid-1984.

Despite its short-lived stay in Roseville, Shugart helped put Roseville on the map as a place for high-tech manufacturing. Also, its complex communications needs gave Roseville Telephone employees valuable experience that helped in attracting business from high-tech firms that were to come into the area later.

Sandy Frazer, Al Johnson's secretary, put the Shugart sale into perspective in a 1981 *Line Chatter*.

"As a result of Shugart settling in our community, it means more revenue for our company and, of course, more people which in turn means more telephones, possible stockholders and employees. It is very evident that it takes a great deal of teamwork before the actual project of putting telephones into service is completed. A BIG THANKS goes to each and every one of the employees involved with a big project of this nature."

## HEWLETT-PACKARD OPENS; NEC FOLLOWS

Although Shugart's arrival in Roseville generated plenty of excitement among those eager to attract high-technology companies to the area, the prize was unquestionably Hewlett-Packard. From the very beginning, its plans for Roseville were considerable. The *San Francisco Chronicle's* Soiffer said in his September 1980 article that H-P projected it would have 22,000 employees working in 34 buildings at Roseville by the year 2000.

Roseville's attractions were many, Soiffer said. In 1980 Silicon Valley had 10,000 jobs looking for people to fill them. The jobs went begging because the South Bay Area's housing prices were out of line with wage scales in the area, even

*In 1980, Hewlett-Packard constructs its first buildings for Roseville operations. H-P's decision to choose Roseville was a major factor in the region's growth.*

Roseville Press-Tribune, December 31, 1980

Wednesday, December 31, 1980    THE PRESS-TRIBUNE

Above is a picture of our new facility. Completion date is forecast for June 1981. The first phase of the project will house seven additional structures over the next five years.

The Hewlett-Packard Company wishes the residents of South Placer County a Happy Holiday Season.

HEWLETT **hp** PACKARD

though high-tech wages were climbing rapidly. On the other hand, Roseville's housing prices were modest. To employees who were tired of paying the ever-escalating rents in the Bay Area, the opportunity to own a house at an affordable price was very appealing. Soiffer quoted Marta Belisle, the executive director of the Roseville Chamber of Commerce at the time, who described the area's allure with a racy frame of reference:

"We don't need to solicit firms," she said. "Roseville is like a gorgeous hooker. She doesn't have to walk far. She just has to stand on the corner."

Of course, attracting industrial companies to an area depended on many factors, not the least being the capability of the local telephone provider to service the companies' needs. It was in this flourishing period that the Roseville and Placer County investments in infrastructure paid off. One of the important investments was a large waste water treatment plant. Bob Doyle was a strong supporter of expanded sewage treatment facilities for the region and he thanked employees for their support in a July 1979 letter.

"Our company has become so large that it is impossible to talk to each of you personally. It is my hope that each of you will take this letter as a personal note," Doyle wrote in *Line Chatter*. "I want to thank every employee who gave time in the recent campaign to pass the sewer bond proposal. We all know that its passage meant a great deal to our company and to our area."

Another important improvement was the long-sought-after Highway 65 bypass. It connected the huge Placer County Industrial Tract north of Roseville directly with Interstate 80. The bypass was needed because the existing Highway 65 went through downtown Roseville and was not suitable for the heavy auto and truck traffic that would be generated by more industry.

The bypass finally received state approval in 1980 after 15 years of lobbying by Roseville and Placer County interests. It wasn't until November 1985, however, that construction began on the bypass. The five-year delay no doubt cost the region some industrial companies. The poor economic climate of the early 1980s was also a factor. The $50-million-plus bypass was dedicated in August 1987 to much fanfare.

Hewlett-Packard's expansion in Roseville presented the telephone company with a challenge unlike any in its history. Al Johnson recounted in the July 1981 *Line Chatter* the effort required to get the Silicon Valley giant's new facilities up and running:

"On June 15, 1981, service was established to the Roseville site of Hewlett-Packard. On that date, a 288-line, 48-trunk Rolm CBX, fully-tested and ready for service, was turned over to our customer. This will enable them to schedule the movement of personnel from their Cincinnati Avenue site to the Roseville site in an orderly manner. It is anticipated this will require a two-to-three-month period to complete.

"This concludes the first part of a project which started in October 1978 with a visit of Gene Doucette and Ed Smith from H-P to our company. Since that time, a tremendous effort has been expended by all departments within the company. Some of the major projects that were required to establish this service were as follows:

- Conduit system — Sections on Main Street to extend conduit system to Foothill Boulevard.

- Conduit system — On Foothill Boulevard from Main Street to the H-P site.

- Conduit system — From H-P site to Industrial Road to north boundary.

- Outside cable — From Roseville main central office to H-P site.

- Outside cable — From H-P site to north boundary on Industrial Road for OPX's (off-premise extensions).

- Carrier repeater project to arrange cable from the Roseville main central office to the H-P site for T-1 carrier systems.

- Engineer requirements for PABX system.

- Installation and testing of PABX system.

- Cabling and wiring of the H-P building for communication services.

- Develop new tariffs and pricing techniques.

- Establish new procedures to handle the maintenance and operation of the system on a joint basis with our customer.

- Establish new billing and accounting procedures.

"This is by far the largest undertaking by our company to meet one customer's service requirements.

"You are all to be congratulated on a job well done. This effort demonstrates that we are a very professional company and capable of filling any type of requirement for communication needs of our customers, no matter the size, types of services, method of operation or other requirements our customers might impose on us."

Through the early 1980s, Hewlett-Packard maintained its steady growth and by 1984 employed approximately 1,500 in Roseville. H-P's commitment to

# NEWSMAKERS

## Doyle in hall of fame

Doyle

ROSEVILLE — Bob Doyle, president of Roseville Telephone Co., has been inducted into the California Independent Hall of Fame for his contributions to the independent telephone industry.

Doyle, a lifelong resident of Roseville, was honored Saturday during a convention of the Independent Telephone Pioneer Association at the Disneyland Hotel in Anaheim.

Doyle has served as president of Roseville Telephone since 1953. When he took over, the utility served less than 3,000 telephones and had assests of $400,000.

Nearly 30 years later, Roseville Telephone serves 78,000 telephones and has assests of more than $100 million.

The firm is the 20th largest independent telephone company in the U.S. There are about 1,500 independent telephone companies nationwide.

Roseville Press-Tribune, October 15, 1981

Roseville has grown through the years with employment topping 3,500 employees in early 1995.

The next large electronics manufacturer to choose Roseville for expansion was NEC Electronics USA Inc., the U.S. subsidiary of the Japanese industrial giant. NEC decided to build just down the street from H-P on Foothills Boulevard. Its plans called for an initial investment of $100 million to build a 120,000-square-foot plant in mid-1984 employing 150. Later plans called for NEC to invest another $300 million with the objective of having 1,500 employees by 1990. NEC built computer memory products at its Roseville operation. Roseville was NEC's first major semiconductor manufacturing facility plant in the United States.

Having NEC in the service territory was appropriate for Roseville Telephone, because through the years NEC telephone systems have been leading products among those sold by the company's sales force. In true Bob Doyle fashion, since NEC was doing business with Roseville Telephone, it was fitting that the telephone company sell NEC products. In fact, even before NEC opened its South Placer plant, Roseville Telephone's Tom Massie was cited in 1983 for being the second highest salesperson in the United States for NEC's 16/48 electronic key telephone system.

Through the 1980s, other substantial companies opened major operations in or near Roseville Telephone's service area. They included Western Electric, Formica, American Olean Tile, H.B. Fuller, Ace Hardware, Reynolds Aluminum and Herman Miller. Each contributed to the rapid growth of Roseville Telephone during the 1980s.

## DOYLE OVERCOMES "THE SLUMP"

The growth spurt of the late 1970s demanded that Bob Doyle sell a ton of stock during the years 1977 through 1983. In that time period, the company had four separate stock sales to keep up with the heavy capital needs and to maintain a prudent debt-to-equity ratio. In all, not reflecting any stock splits in that time frame, the company sold approximately 950,000 new shares, raising more than $17 million.

During the same period, five times the company paid 5 percent stock dividends that resulted in about 570,000 shares being issued to existing shareholders. These stock dividends transferred more than $11.5 million from retained earnings to stock equity. The combination of selling new shares and issuing stock dividends gave the company a strong equity base to support its borrowings. A strong equity foundation was especially important during these years that witnessed the highest interest rates in memory.

While the first three of the four equity offerings went well, the fourth offering turned out to be by far the most difficult stock sale in the company's history. This $6 million, 300,000-share offering began in June 1981, but wasn't completed until Aug. 31, 1983. The sheer size of the offering — it was the company's largest ever — plus the economic climate of those years made selling shares very difficult. Bob Doyle's long-time secretary Ellen Lynn labeled the years 1982-1983 "the slump."

Doyle remembered that period as the most challenging of his career. The big 1981 offering came on the heels of a most successful offering in 1980 when the company sold 300,000 shares at $15 to raise $4.5 million in only four months. But a lot had changed by the time the next offering was ready to go. Late in 1980 the bank's prime lending rate — the rate for the highest-quality borrowers — soared to 21 1/2 percent. Certificate of deposit rates, bond yields and other interest-sensitive investments climbed accordingly. The 4 percent cash dividend historically paid by Roseville Telephone — even adding the near-annual 5 percent stock dividend on top of it — looked puny in comparison.

The wacky economic conditions of the time forced even long-time holders of Roseville Telephone stock to reconsider their investment. Why hold stodgy telephone company shares earning only 4 percent when one could get 20 percent at the bank? And for those needing money to finance a new home, car or vacation, why borrow at exorbitant interest rates when a better option might be to sell telephone stock to fund those major purchases? Ironically, the stability of Roseville Telephone's stock price exacerbated the situation, because unlike the shares of companies traded on the exchanges, Roseville Telephone shares had not gone down in value.

In this kind of environment, Doyle was swimming against both the current and the tide. Not only did he have what he would call "a potful" of new shares to sell, but suddenly he was also getting hit with thousands and thousands of shares from existing stockholders. In the backdrop of widespread economic uncertainty, Doyle's sales burden became enormous. He explained:

"If a shareholder wanted to put a roof on his house or do something else that required a lot of capital, the only thing he could sell that would pay whole dollars was Roseville Telephone stock. So he'd come into me and say, 'Bob, I hate like hell to do this, this is the best investment I've ever made in my life, but I'm not going over to that Citizens Bank and give those guys 22 percent so I can put a roof on my house or buy a car. This is the only thing I can sell that's worth anything. All my other stock investments are way down.' People would come and dump shares on me and, of course, I'd have to sell the existing shares before I could sell the new ones. The stock piled up and I thought, where am I going to get rid of these shares? Maybe I would have to go to a broker."

The 1981-83 stock sale started reasonably well. In 1981, more than half of the issue, $3.6 million worth — 180,288 shares at $20 each — was sold in seven months. In 1982, however, stock sales fell way off. As Doyle labored to place existing shares on top of selling new shares, he managed to sell only 26,446 new shares in 1982, generating only $529,000 in new equity. It was his worst year selling stock of all the six stock issues during the 1973-1983 span. In 1974, only $578,600 worth of stock was sold. But that was all that remained from the previous year's stock issue. In 1982-1983, there wasn't anybody Doyle leaned on more than Bill Baxter. A Dean Witter broker at the time, Baxter was by far the most active stockbroker in re-selling Roseville Telephone stock. Baxter remembered those years:

"I was very involved because it was not a situation where you had people clamoring for the stock. Bob had what seemed to be an infinite amount of stock on the street and he was beating the bushes to find buyers. There wasn't anybody Bob knew he didn't talk to about buying the stock."

In addition to the horrendous economic climate, unrelated events turned this particular stock sale into a bear for Doyle. One involved a very large estate sale that dumped several thousand shares on Doyle at the very worst time. The sellers were sympathetic to Doyle's plight, but Uncle Sam had to be paid. Doyle wasn't sure if he could find enough buyers. It was his most difficult year in 30 years at the company.

"Bob was sweating it out that he was going to have to make the bid and buy all that stock back from the estate," Baxter recalled. "And, of course, he had all that stock to sell on top of it. This was when he called to ask for my help. I'd been sitting on a warm bench, and he expected me to step to the table and play my position. That's just the way it was."

At the same time, many of Baxter's clients wanted to sell Roseville Telephone stock to switch to higher-yielding investments. In more normal times, Baxter would call Doyle to see if he knew of any buyers. During "the slump," however, that avenue was not available.

"I knew I had better call my clients or my prospects and move that stock without bothering Bob because he had his own problems up in Roseville. I mean people were bitching and moaning. They'd say to me, 'Why the hell should I buy a stock that only pays 4 percent that never moves?' They considered the 5 percent stock dividend at that time just an Irish dividend. Since the stock price didn't go up, the stock dividend really didn't represent a lot of value to them. They figured it's 5 percent plus 4 percent, that's only 9 percent. At that time, they could get 14 percent in money market accounts.

"I remember going to one of the substantial medical groups in Roseville and telling them I had a golden opportunity for them. I had a big chunk of telephone stock to sell — about 5,000 shares and they could buy it below the market. It was one of the rare times I had gotten stock below the market price. The price was $20 then and I could sell it to them for $18.50. They laughed at me."

Compounding the dilemma in 1982-1983 was Doyle's maxim that Roseville Telephone shares stay in friendly, local hands. If a sizable number of shares got

*Ellen Lynn was Bob Doyle's secretary for more than 25 years. She took great pride in encouraging shareholders to retain their stock rather than selling it.*

into the wrong hands, the independence of the company's ownership could be in jeopardy. In hindsight, if there was ever a time that an unfriendly takeover attempt of Roseville Telephone might have had a chance to succeed, it was during 1982-1983. This stricture put even more pressure on Baxter.

"Although I scrambled to place shares that came in, I also knew I was not going to sell stock to an outsider Bob might have to worry about. I understood where he was coming from. Selling stock to just anybody was not in the cards."

Dick Wise, the insurance broker, was another who remembered those tense years.

"There were big blocks of stock coming in, some with 2,000 and 3,000 shares, and I didn't know where the money was going to come from to soak up those shares. Bob didn't either. I was scared for him. I thought he was going to lose the company. I don't know how the hell he did it, but somehow he finally got all the stock sold."

The hardship in maintaining a stable market in the shares took its toll on Doyle in 1982-1983. For 30 years his outlook was fast forward, aggressive and progressive. After each new building was built or each new stock issue was successfully sold, he was on to the next challenge in his never-ending quest to build "the best goddamn telephone company in the country." In 1982-1983, for the first time, he was gloomy. He was in a tough fight and it wore on him. His secretary at the time, Ellen Lynn, remembered Doyle's frustration.

"He was at the point he'd say, 'What do I do next?' He wasn't concerned about company operations; it was the stock that concerned him. What we were going to do ... who was going to help us out of it. He would drive me crazy walking up and down the hallway figuring what we were going to do."

At home, Doyle was quieter than usual, his wife recollected.

"I remember that he was stressed out — you could see it," Carmen Doyle said. "His blood pressure was very high. He keeps things inside so he didn't talk a lot about his problems, but you could see things were hard on him. His way of relaxing was to get in the car and ride around until he cooled down."

George Minasian estimated Doyle "spent about 99 percent of his time" in the early '80s selling stock.

"Bob would have people come in who would drop 2,000, sometimes 3,000 shares. It would take Bob weeks to find buyers. He dreaded people coming in here asking him to sell stock. He'd do anything in the world to talk them out of it."

Virginia Amick remembered that Doyle was ready to put Ellen Lynn out on the street selling shares. Although it was done in jest, the idea was for Ellen to walk up and down Vernon Street peddling stock like the cigarette girls did in fancy nightclubs.

"They even had a sign made for me, 'Stocks For Sale, Stocks for Sale,'" Lynn remembered. "But I was most proud that I was able to convince people to hang on to their stock. I said it might be a bad time then as far as the cash yield, but in the long run, our stock would be good as gold."

It took great faith not to at least consider selling shares, particularly in 1982. Growth had slowed in 1981 and continued slow into 1982. In 1981, the company decided not to replace 10 retired employees with full-time employees, relying instead on temporary employees. Also, net income in 1981 dropped nearly $1 million from 1980, although this was due to a non-recurring adjustment related to how the company treated investment tax credits. Had there been no such adjustment, net income would have been higher in 1981 than in 1980. To the unsophisticated shareholder, however, the decline in earnings in 1981 could have given cause for concern.

Conditions slowed to such a crawl that in July 1982 the company added only seven new access lines. In more normal times, new access lines and phones ran into the hundreds each month. Access line growth in 1982 was the slowest in many years.

Business was so sluggish that in June 1982 Roseville Telephone had the only significant layoff in its history. Thirty employees received their pink slips — about 10 percent of the work force. Given Doyle's loyalty to his employees, a layoff was a last resort, but in his view, a necessary action to protect the long-term interests of shareholders. Still, Doyle believed the business downturn would be short-lived. He even predicted the future would hold unheard-of-growth for the region and the company. At the June 1982 stockholders meeting, Doyle reaffirmed his long-term confidence in Roseville's growth prospects. The following are excerpts from David Watt's report on the annual meeting that appeared in the *Roseville Press-Tribune:*

" 'We have not seen anything yet,' Doyle told more than 160 stockholders gathered at an annual Roseville Telephone meeting. The phone company president said large investments in buildings, electronic equipment and field equipment will put the firm in 'a healthy position' to handle expected growth. Doyle assured stockholders the firm's lay-off of 30 employees was the result of only a temporary lull in the economy. 'We've got a boom ahead of us that is going to be hard to believe,' Doyle added."

Doyle then outlined major projects under way and on the drawing board for the region, noting that in addition to the major construction, at least a half-dozen financial institutions were building in Roseville.

" 'On top of this, there is virtually no home building going on,' Doyle said. 'You can imagine what is going to happen when interest rates go down.' Doyle blamed the drop off in home building for forcing the company's first layoffs. He assured stockholders the 30 workers will be hired back as soon as 'things pick up,' " the *Press-Tribune* reported.

"Company officials told stockholders equipment buildings in Roseville, Citrus Heights, Folsom Lake area and the Dry Creek area west of Roseville are large enough to accommodate growth through at least the year 2000. Doyle added that the company will be converted to full electronic switching by 1985. 'I can't think of any other phone company large or small that can make that claim,' Doyle said of the shift from electromechanical to electronic switching."

As Doyle had predicted, within a few months after the annual meeting, the government's anti-inflation medicine began to take effect and interest rates began coming down. By late 1982, the prime rate had plummeted several percentage points and business began to improve throughout the nation. As Doyle had predicted, the Roseville region was on the verge of major growth.

In the tradition of his grandfather, "Lucky Jack" Doyle, when Bob Doyle's luck changed for the better, it became a lot better. Chuck Spooner, the company's manager of data processing, described how events had changed in the November 1982 *Line Chatter*.

"As of today (Oct. 20), the rate case is settled and implemented, the wage freeze has been lifted, the prime rate is down to the 12-13 percent level, the stock market has been booming, another electronic firm has announced plans for a plant in Roseville and we had our largest service gain of the year in September. Do you get the feeling that things are looking up?"

Indeed, the outlook was improving for Roseville Telephone for several reasons. Although Doyle had been struggling for more than a year to sell $6 million in new shares, the unexpectedly slow growth of 1981-1982 meant the company didn't need as much capital to satisfy its growth requirements. In other words, the company's capital needs turned out to be significantly lower than $6 million. It wasn't mandatory to sell the entire stock issue. The pressure was off.

"Everybody was saying, why worry about selling the whole thing, but I said I was going to sell it, and we did. That surplus money was an ace in the hole, because we floated for a long while on the proceeds from that stock sale," Doyle said. "It also meant we didn't have to borrow money at 15 percent. Instead, we were paying shareholders a 4 percent dividend. You can't beat that."

The 1981-1983 stock issue was finally completed on Aug. 31, 1983, more than two years after it started. The final wave of stock sales came relatively easily, mostly because Doyle decided to employ a time-tested, stock-selling catalyst — the two-for-one stock split.

"Even in 1983 we had quite a few shares to sell, but it finally hit me what we needed to do to get the rest of the stock sold — a stock split," Doyle remembered. "People love a split. I always have people coming in here asking me, 'When are you going to split again?' In a split, the shareholder ends up with twice as many shares as he had before, but the value is the same. For instance, if the shareholder has 100 shares and they go for $20 a share, you split the stock and now he has 200 shares, but at $10 apiece. The dividend per share is cut in half, too, so the total value of the shares remains the same, but the shareholder feels like he has more.

"So the board decided to declare a two-for-one stock split and we sent a letter out to people saying that anybody who is a stockholder as of Aug. 1, 1983, and purchases more stock prior to Aug. 31, 1983, will be entitled to a two-for-one split. Hell, that did it. The people started beating the doors down because they wanted that split. It was the shot in the arm that we needed to sell the remainder of the issue. We just beat the wire, but we sold every share."

"The slump" was over. Through force of personality — helped a little by improving economic conditions — Doyle and Roseville Telephone had sold the entire $6 million issue. Those who bought shares in that stock sale — the last one Roseville Telephone has had — have enjoyed an exceptional return on their investment. The shareholder who bought 100 shares at $20 a share, or $2,000, during that stock sale would own 370 shares at $24 per share worth $8,880 as of Dec. 31, 1994.

Of course, shareholders who didn't sell out during "the slump" earned equally high returns.

"I never lost any friends who sold shares during this time — we were able to get rid of the stock," Doyle added. "I wasn't happy about it, though, but what could I do? I knew each one of them and they needed the money."

## RATE INCREASE IN 1982
## PAVES WAY FOR GROWTH SPURT

Ironically, the historically high interest rate environment of the early '80s was an important factor in the company's ability to produce exceptional profits in subsequent years. Economic pressure helped the company when in 1981 it filed for its first general rate increase since 1959. This laborious process involved many months of work from all departments in the company. Brian Strom, who was a consultant at the time, recalled how the rate filing proceeded.

"Our job was to go in there to the Public Utilities Commission and give it our best shot to say we need more money. And it's their job to try to minimize the money they give to you. It's a grueling experience," Strom said. "We probably

*Roseville Telephone was the first telephone company in the United States to use TRS-D (Traffic Room System-Digital). This enabled the company to computerize operator services as operators converted from the old cordboards to video display terminals. Phil Germond, above, is now manager of the company's products and services department.*

Roseville Press-Tribune, December 31, 1981

worked for six-to-nine months at putting the application together. Then the PUC beats it up for another six-to-nine months. After that, the application is officially filed with the commission and you spend several months waiting for a decision as you argue it in front of the commission. We had some very important issues in those years, mostly regarding investment tax credits, that made it very difficult for us to reach what we call a quick conclusion."

Making projections in the early 1980s was a lengthy process. "Everything was done by hand pretty much with your little calculators. There was no such thing as Lotus 1-2-3 or electronic spreadsheets," Strom explained. "Every time you changed your assumptions, you had to do it over again. It would take at least a day, and in terms of trying to put it in presentable form, somebody had to sit at a typewriter and type it up, lining up columns, etc. Today, the personal computer can handle all that for you, the word processing aspects of the proposal as well as the computational. But back then, we used up a lot of erasers."

The prodigious effort paid off. Bob Doyle explained to employees in the November 1982 *Line Chatter* how the rate increase would help the company:

"We have now received the formal decision #82-9-030 from the California Public Utilities Commission granting us a $3,836,000 annual increase in local revenue on our rate application. This, as you know, was our first rate application since 1959, and many of us had very little experience in the activity involved in rate cases. Thanks to an exceptional effort by all employees, we were very successful. To review, we filed our application on Aug. 14, 1981, requesting a $6,693,000 increase. As the result of technical hearings with the PUC staff and the administration law judge in San Francisco during mid-February, we reduced our request to about $4,200,000. This reduction was the result of improved settlements from the Pacific company, a slowdown of inflation since we prepared our application, and other matters. The granting of over $3.8 million represents more than 90 percent of our revised request, which is very good indeed.

"Some of the reasons for this excellent decision are due to the type of service we are rendering our customers, the professional manner in which our budget for test year 1982 was presented and the excellent way the complex tax issues were handled by our accounting department. The decision quotes the PUC staff as stating, 'Roseville Telephone Company's overall service performance level is good.' To achieve this has taken the total dedication of all employees to provide the best service possible.

"I would like to thank all employees for the superb job that was done in preparing this rate application and following it through to a successful conclusion. I know there were long hours spent in this preparation and many frustrations, but in the end we achieved our objective."

The increase enabled the company to earn a historically high rate of return, about 13.5 percent in the first few years, because the PUC's allowable rate of return was heavily influenced by interest rates. And since the cost of money at the time was high, the company's rate of return was high as well. As interest rates came down over the succeeding years, the company benefited with lower payments on its adjustable-rate bank debt.

In hindsight, the rate case couldn't have come at a better time to aid the prosperity of Roseville Telephone.

"Some might say it was good timing, but I prefer to think it was good management," Bob Doyle remarked, at the same time flashing a sly smile.

## SHREWD STRATEGY GARNERS BIG PIECE OF CELLULAR PIE

If 1982 was the most difficult year financially for Bob Doyle and Roseville Telephone, it was perhaps its finest year when viewed from a long-term perspective. It was on Nov. 8, 1982, that Roseville Telephone formally applied to win one of two cellular telephone licenses that would be available for the Sacramento MSA (Metropolitan Statistical Area) consisting of Sacramento, Yolo and Placer counties. It was an expensive foray into the unknown for Doyle and his managers — the application alone cost about $250,000 to develop. Looking back, however, it may be the company's best investment ever.

The early 1980s were heady days in telecommunications. Deregulation began to take hold following the landmark anti-trust settlement announced on Jan. 8, 1982, that broke up the giant Bell System to allow more competition. For the first time, traditional wire-line companies such as Roseville Telephone and the newly-labeled "Baby Bells" would face competition in the sale and leasing of telephones and communications systems for business and residential customers.

In addition to the changing competitive landscape, mass market wireless telephone service — cellular — was on the horizon. This technology enabled customers to conduct their business on mobile phones that required no wires. Radio waves carried the telephone conversations. Cellular carried with it enormous potential as well as great risk and expense. Looking to the future, Roseville Telephone believed it had to be a player in the industry.

Al Johnson was an early booster of cellular. He watched with great interest the technology developing at AT&T and lobbied Bob Doyle to get involved in

*Attorney Robert "Bob" Raymer and his firm, Cooper, White & Cooper of San Francisco, have represented Roseville Telephone since 1965.*

cellular. After listening to Johnson and discussing the issue with directors at several meetings, the decision was made to go into cellular. Questions abounded. How should it be done, in what form? Should the company go it alone or should it seek to be part of a consortium of wire-line companies? These were crucial decisions that would affect the company's future. Johnson explains the background:

"Advanced Mobile Phone Service, or AMPS, was invented by Bell Labs. AT&T was in the process of implementing AMPS in the early '80s, but then divestiture came and everything was up for grabs. At the same time, AT&T changed the name, calling it cellular. But it was the same system. The FCC issued an order saying it would grant two licenses in every area in the United States. One license would be held by any wire-line carrier ... any telephone company. The second license would be held by the winning bidder among non-wire-line carriers."

Prior to divestiture, the Bell companies started working on a plan, trying to allocate those licenses on the wire-line end of it. In those areas where independent telephone companies were involved, the licenses were based on MSAs. The idea was that the independents would receive the same percentage interest in the local cellular license as their percentage of access lines in that area.

Had Roseville Telephone decided to follow this approach — and many independent telephone companies did — it could have looked forward to owning a small percentage, probably no more than 5 percent, of the wire-line company cellular license granted for the Sacramento MSA. The company wouldn't have needed to file a separate application; it merely needed to agree to be part of a consortium led by Pacific Telephone. That would have been the easy alternative ... but for Roseville Telephone uncharacteristic.

After analyzing the potential risks and rewards of going it alone, Roseville Telephone decided to file an application to acquire the Sacramento area license for itself. It was a case of David taking on Goliath, but the rules of the game gave Roseville Telephone at least a chance at winning the much-coveted license.

"Any telephone company that had a presence in a certain MSA could develop an application and have the same chance of getting that license as the Bell company serving that area," Johnson said. "Each company could file only one application. The application had to be complete, which meant you had to prove you were financially able to do the job. Also, you had to design a system and show you could do the engineering and build the network. You had to show locations of your cell sites. You also had to have leases, show that you could get a lease on a particular location for a cell site — on top of a building, on top of a mountain, or wherever you were going to put your cell site. And, of course, the marketing plan was important.

"This was a very costly process to develop the facts and figures needed for a good application. In talking to Bob about it, I said, 'Should we do this? It will

OLD FALLS to make way for new as workmen clear away buildings on site of Roseville Telephone Co. administration building at Vernon and Lincoln streets. Building, which will contain 17,300 square feet, is expected to be completed in mid-1981. Contractor for $1.7 million project is Harbison-Mahony-Higgons of Sacramento.

*Aug. 14, 1980*

*Work was under way in downtown Roseville as the telephone company prepared the site for its new administration building.*

Roseville Press-Tribune, August 14, 1980
top and right photos

**Telephone building rises in downtown Roseville**

cost a lot of money.' He said, 'Let's try it.' And he gave me the go-ahead on it and we spent over a quarter of a million dollars on the application alone."

The expertise involved in filing this application required the company to use outside consultants in addition to the company's resources. Since cellular was a new technology and the license derby also had no precedent, there were no true "experts" in filing for this license. Even Pacific Telephone's superior resources didn't automatically mean its application would be any better than Roseville Telephone's. All were in uncharted territory.

In 1982, Brian Strom, then with the accounting firm Arthur Young, was one of the consultants brought in to help assemble the application. He recounts the reasoning behind Doyle's decision to file for the license:

"I remember Bob said, 'Let's go ahead and file our own application so that when Pacific comes back to us and talks about splitting the area up, we'll be in a position to talk about alternatives as opposed to just being in a position of weakness and taking what they offer us.' Bob told Pacific he wasn't prepared to accept 5 percent. He said, 'That's because I have as good a chance of getting 100 percent as you do. You've only got one application in there and I only have one application in there. It sounds to me like I've got a 50-50 chance of getting 100 percent.' That got Pacific's attention."

Johnson said the jockeying for position started long before the application was filed in November 1982. The big companies, the Bells, General Telephone and Continental, were making deals, swapping territories and angling for the best areas they could. Roseville Telephone only served one area so it had no other territories to swap. Its only choice was to go it alone with a comprehensive application with the objective of pressuring Pacific Telephone and the other telephone companies operating in the Sacramento MSA — Citizens Utilities in Elk Grove and Continental in Colfax — into making a deal favorable to Roseville. That's exactly what happened.

Although the application was filed in late 1982, negotiations among the prospective licensees didn't conclude until early 1984. Roseville's extremely thorough application put Pacific and the others on notice that it was serious in its bid to win the whole thing.

"Roseville Telephone's application had to be taken seriously because on the face of it — this is prior to any hearings on cellular — it was a serious application that you simply could not ignore," recollected Bob Raymer, the company's counsel. "There was no indication that we couldn't have done the whole damned thing. Bank of America was very accommodating; they gave us a letter of intention that would have permitted a tremendous amount of financing. Our exceedingly strong balance sheet was very important, too."

In those areas where multiple companies were qualified to operate the cellular franchise, the victor would be chosen by what amounted to virtually a lottery. There would be one winner; the rest of the applicants would lose. This route was too risky for the Bell companies, according to Raymer.

"The wire-line companies were saying, 'We ought to form a joint venture. Why let it all go to chance? Here's a marvelous opportunity. Let's share it.' Well, their initial idea of sharing was rather limited. But Doyle is a very good negotiator, and he never has any self doubts about the correctness of his position," Raymer said.

"Citizens sent out its president to negotiate and Pacific's negotiators happened to be younger guys at that time, who later went on to be the top executives at the company. They included Sam Ginn and Phil Quigley.

"During these two days at a San Francisco hotel, we were all together for a long time. We had lunch and dinner together. It took two days of bumping heads with these guys to eventually make a deal," Raymer recalled. "By that time, Roseville had experienced some real success and Bob had gotten recognition. He'd also been a director of the Independent Telephone Association, and was a president of that organization. His name was well known in the industry.

"Also, early on, even though Bob wasn't present at the meetings, the other parties could see from the quality of Roseville's application and the amount of money that had been spent that the company was determined. And even though these particular Pacific people may not have known Bob, other Pacific Bell people did, because we have a lot of relationships with them, we always have.

"When the first meetings occurred many months prior to those final meetings, I'm pretty sure that Pacific thought that if Roseville ended up with 5 percent, that would be max. But Doyle cannot be bluffed, and I think what they and the others learned over this period of time, and particularly in the final meetings, was that they weren't going to be able to push him around," Raymer said. "I think they got an understanding of Bob Doyle that was partly new and partly a reconfirmation. He had some reputation before.

"After all kinds of compromises and problems, Roseville Telephone ended up with nearly 25 percent of a venture called Sacramento Valley Limited Partnership. The partnership not only was awarded the franchise for Sacramento, but it picked up other franchises, too. One of Doyle's stipulations was that if Pacific got the license for Reno, it would have to add it to our system," Raymer continued. "So by good bargaining — really shrewd bargaining — Roseville became a major player in a cellular franchise which now encompasses about 3 million people. It was Doyle's persistence and his ability and willingness to take a risk — investing a hell of a lot of money and effort into an application that might have been worthless — that won Roseville Telephone a big piece of a very valuable franchise."

Al Johnson and Mark Shull attended the meetings as negotiations evolved. Johnson remembered the discussions:

"Originally, Pacific Telephone was talking about giving us just a few percentage points of the Sacramento MSA. After all these negotiations, Bob got involved and we ended up with not 2 percent, 3 percent or 4 percent, but 24 percent, and not of three counties, but of 17 counties from California and four counties in Nevada. That was Bob's doing."

Retired Pacific Telephone executive Ron Amick credited Doyle with knowing how to take advantage of giant Bell companies to win concessions for Roseville Telephone.

"Bob always went all the way and wanted all he could get, which is the only way to go. Bob knew how to take advantage of dealing with a big company, particularly when the federal government says, 'Don't play like you're Mister Big and push yourself around, Bell System.' Bob was smart and aggressive. His attitude

was, 'I'm as good as you are and I want my fair share and I'm going to fight for
it.' And he did, whether it was extended area service (EAS) agreements, toll
settlements or whatever. By god, Bob wanted all he could get and he got it, generally. I remember he threw one of our vice presidents out of his office one day
because he said something like, 'Oh, hell, I think we'll take you over and then
we won't have to put up with you.' Doyle threw him out. He didn't take any
crap from anybody. That's what I always admired about him. But he always
backed up his bragging."

The cellular partnership came on line in August 1985 when the first ceremonial
call was made. By that date 108 customers had already signed up for the new
service. Tim Sproul, a splicer at that time, received kudos in the November
1985 *Line Chatter* for being "the first RTC employee with his own personal
cellular telephone."

Roseville Telephone's involvement in the Sacramento Valley Limited
Partnership has grown beyond a passive ownership stake. Al Johnson explains:

"Everything kind of fell into place on cellular. We were able to lease to the
partnership space in our Citrus Heights central office for the MTSO (mobile
telephone switching office). Switching calls between cell sites is controlled by

equipment in the Citrus Heights central office. We were able to lease that space because in 1985 we were replacing our last step-by-step equipment there and ended up with excess space for our own needs," Johnson said. "In addition, the partnership leases microwave dish space on our 295-foot tower at the West office. There microwave signals connect with our fiber optic routes. So we're not only a partner, but we also provide services and space to the partnership."

Clearly, the cellular partnership — the operating unit was originally PacTel Cellular, now called Air Touch Cellular — is an important asset of Roseville Telephone. The partnership broke even in 1986 and has been solidly profitable since 1987 when Roseville Telephone's share of pre-tax earnings exceeded $600,000.

In subsequent years the partnership expanded to encompass a vast territory. Brian Strom said, "It may be the biggest cellular footprint in all the United States. Footprint being like LA is a footprint. Ours goes from Modesto up to Redding, Davis over to Reno. The potential is huge because the area is fast-growing. Also, major highways cut through the territory which generates significant roamer traffic. This is profitable business for us."

In 1993, after several years of significant capital investments, Roseville Telephone's share of cellular profits increased dramatically to almost $1.6 million before taxes. The future looks equally bright.

"I think in the longer scheme, our cellular investment will be golden," Strom predicts. "As we feel pressure on our basic telephone earnings in the next few years, I look for the cellular company to pick up some of that. Cellular will be a much bigger portion of our bottom line."

Through 1994, Roseville Telephone has about $20 million invested in its share of the cellular partnership. What is that stake worth? Nobody knows for certain, but based upon valuation methodology used in appraising large cellular properties, Roseville Telephone's 23.4 percent of the Sacramento Valley Limited Partnership is estimated to be worth well in excess of $100 million.

Had Bob Doyle and Al Johnson concluded in 1982 that filing a cellular license application was too much work and too expensive, Roseville Telephone's likely share of this partnership would not have exceeded 5 percent. That decision would have cost shareholders millions of dollars over the years. Not a bad return on a $250,000 investment!

When asked to name his most important contribution to the growth and prosperity of Roseville Telephone, Johnson is quick to answer.

"I feel best about urging Bob Doyle to go ahead with the cellular application," Johnson said. "Over time we believe our cellular stake will be worth even more than our traditional telephone company. I feel very good about that."

## PROGRESS EVERYWHERE

In the late 1970s and mid-'80s, the progress at Roseville Telephone was remarkable. Computerization was introduced into all levels of the workplace, greatly aiding productivity. Telecommunications capabilities expanded exponentially as generation-after-generation of ever-more powerful systems came on line, to the benefit of both the telephone company and its users. Sophisticated switching equipment, along with better transmission capabilities, enabled users to take advantage of enhanced services at reasonable cost. Miniaturization paved the way for decentralized switching schemes. Buildings were going up and revenue and profits were accelerating. By any measurement, Roseville Telephone was exploding.

At the start of this tremendous growth phase, the company was in transition from a small company into a medium size one. Revenue surpassed $10 million for the first time in 1977, reaching $11,682,000, a 20 percent increase over 1976. Revenue was generated almost equally from local service and toll calls plus an additional $688,000 from the company's share of directory advertising sales. Profit soared 75 percent over the prior year to $2,612,000, a healthy 22 percent return on sales. Telephones served exceeded 50,000 for the first time, ending the year at 54,955, 16 percent higher than the previous year. Gross plant investment neared $45 million, an increase of more than $10 million from 1976. The company had 288 employees and 4,153 shareholders at year-end 1977.

Financing activities were bustling as well. In 1977, the company kicked off a 120,000-share offering at $25. It was sold out the following year, raising $3 million. In addition, $6 million in debt was placed with insurance companies in two $3 million debentures closing in 1977 and early 1978 at 8.75 percent and 8.5 percent interest, respectively. In 1979, the company would raise another $3 million in long-term debt, paying 9.125 percent. Long-term debt at the end of 1979 was $20.1 million, the company's biggest debt load to that time. The following year, 1980, would be the last year Roseville Telephone's long-term debt would increase until 1991. The timing of the long-term borrowings turned out to be exceptional because the early 1980s saw long-term rates soar to historic levels as inflation ravaged the American economy. Short-term, renewable credit lines, the company's strong earnings, and $17 million raised in new stock sales helped to fuel the company's growth through the 1980s.

In the midst of all the changes occurring in the industry, technology, and its service territory, Roseville Telephone boomed during 1977-1980. Revenue in 1980 was $21,305,000 and net income climbed to $3.5 million. Telephones in service jumped nearly 50 percent to 74,588 by the end of 1980 and employee ranks had grown to 372. The number of shareholders climbed to 6,775 from 4,153 at the end of 1977, and gross plant investment jumped to more than $72 million in 1980.

Bob Doyle said in the 1980 annual report:

"Technology, market place demands, regulation and evolving competition are creating a swiftly changing environment for the telecommunications industry of the '80s. Technology is exploding about us. Satellite radio, fiber optics, computer-based systems of all sorts and high-tech digital applications are only the beginning. Your company is busy planning how to best utilize the new technology to guarantee its future marketing strength."

The signs were everywhere that Roseville Telephone was stepping into the big time. In the July 1978 *Line Chatter*, only a little more than a year after he came aboard, operations manager Al Johnson gave employees a preview of the modernization plans just ahead:

"Our plans have been finalized for expanding the central office equipment in our switching centers at Roseville and Citrus Heights. In Roseville, we will use a DSS-1 (Digital Switching System), designed and manufactured by ITT North Electric Company. A combination Class 4 and Class 5 (toll and local) office will be placed in service during the second half of 1979. This equipment will replace in its entirety the existing electromechanical step-by-step equipment used for our 786-prefixed customers, handle growth requirements, and prepare us for automating our operator-assisted type toll traffic.

*Bob Doyle, right, and Tom Doyle, left, listen as Don Dye of ITT North explains how Roseville Telephone's new digital switch operates. It was installed in 1980.*

Photo by Sirlin Studios

"In the first half of 1980, we will place in service a TRS-D (Traffic Room System-Digital). This will give our customers the capabilities of dialing their person-to-person, collect, credit-card, third-party, and calls originating from pay stations. The operator will come in on the call only to provide the assistance required, based on the instructions received from the customer. This would include ensuring the desired party is on the line on person-to-person calls, recording the calling party's credit-card number on credit-card calls, requesting the deposit of the correct coins on pay station calls, etc. It will no longer be required for our operators to make manual toll tickets or to time the call as this will be accomplished automatically and all billing information will be recorded on a magnetic tape.

"Also in late 1979 or early 1980, we will be placing into service line units which will be located in our future West office area (the southwest corner of Base Line Road and Crowder Lane) and will be controlled by the DSS-1 machine in our Roseville switching center. This is what is referred to as an RLU (Remote Line Unit) and will permit the outside plant in the West area to be engineered for a wire center to be located at Base Line Road and Crowder Lane.

"In Citrus Heights we will use a No. 5 EAX designed and manufactured by GTE Automatic Electric to fortify the existing No. 1 EAX. This is a PCM digital switching machine capable of handling up to 100,000 lines or more. Our plans call for this system to be placed into service during the second half of 1980. It will replace our 725-prefix electromechanical step-by-step equipment and provide equipment to handle our growth requirements in this area."

Clearly, Johnson had dug into his work after only one year at Roseville Telephone. Amazingly, most announced projects were actually completed on time, although the weak economy of 1981-1982 delayed a few installations. All this progress did not come without angst and effort by employees, however. Chuck Spooner described in a November 1978 *Line Chatter* how computer conversions could get under one's skin. " 'Con-ver-version, kon-ver-shan. The act or state of converting; a physical transformation from one state or form to another.'

"Conversion — that's what we have been doing for the past several months in data processing. We 'converted' from our old NCR Century-200 to a new Burroughs B-1860. On Oct. 10, they hauled the NCR computer away and left the new Burroughs machine standing there, naked and alone! Looking back on the past few months, I would like to propose a new definition for the word conversion: 'A frustrating, exhausting, humbling, infuriating experience to which data processing people subject themselves every five or six years; a form of masochism.'

"Anyway, it is finished — almost. Now we can get on with what we should have been doing: station gain reporting, continuing property records, accounts payable, general ledger, and so on. Compared to the old computer, the new one has four times the memory capacity, twice the disk storage, faster magnetic tape drives, and the ability to execute more than one program at a time. What all that means to RTC is greater throughput — more work completed in a given period of time."

In those years, everybody at the company experienced rising "throughput," whether they were familiar with the term or not, because the workload was growing inexorably. Edie Olver described what the outside plant workers were doing at that time.

"Looking back on the figures compiled in 1978 for additions to our outside plant, it was a very productive year," Olver wrote in the March 1979 *Line Chatter*. "We placed 40.8 miles of buried cable in 30.9 miles of trench. That's a lot of work for our construction and splicing crews, but just a portion of what they did."

Operators closed the decade of the 1970s by moving. After 20 years "upstairs" on Lincoln Street, the operators — now called operator services — once again moved downstairs, this time into new quarters in the beautiful new equipment building on Vernon Street opened in late 1978. For operators, the new age of computerization was just around the corner. It would mark the end of the plug-in cordboard, the operators' standard equipment over the first 100 years of telephony.

Chuck Spooner is manager of Roseville Telephone's data processing department. His department helps the rest of the company make the best use of computer systems and technology.

The construction and splicing departments moved, too, occupying renovated quarters at 98 Yosemite St. in downtown Roseville in 1979. Few employees were spared the moving blues as management juggled and reconfigured their departments' space needs to satisfy demands created by rapid growth.

In early 1980, employees were in a congratulatory mood as new equipment came on stream. Once again, *Line Chatter* articles reflect the enthusiasm of the times. The following came from the March 1980 edition:

"With the successful completion of the DSS, congratulations are in order to Ned Kindelt as the coordinator of the project, to Rulon Blackburn as supervisor, to Craig Mosca and Bill DeMuth as maintenance technicians, and to everyone in all the offices that put forth the extra hours, hard work, and sweat to bring the project to a successful completion."

It was quite a project. The $1.5 million Digital Switching System (DSS) was placed in service on Feb. 3, 1980, in the new telephone equipment building at 114 Vernon St. It marked the first phase in a conversion program to provide full electronic switching for telephone calls in the Roseville area. Digital systems offered greatly-improved transmission characteristics compared to analog counterparts, enhancing the qualities of both voice and data signals.

"Additionally," read an explanatory article on DSS in *Line Chatter*, "DSS provides telephone central offices with significant cost-saving reductions in the areas of floor space required, installation times, outside plant costs, and maintenance and administration requirements. These benefits will enable Roseville Telephone to better control operating costs in the face of inflation, while continuing to provide customers with superior telephone service at traditionally low rates.

"Since the DSS is fully electronic, this system can more accurately be described as a data transfer or processor system rather than a conventional 'switching' system. This electronic base gives significantly more reliable performance than its mechanical predecessors, and offers energy-saving features with the elimination of moving parts. A unique aspect of the DSS is its remote-line switch capability, which can extend full customer services from a host office to remote clusters of subscribers in areas where a complete central office set-up would not be feasible.

"Perhaps most important of all, the technology inherent in DSS lays the foundation for future developments and advances in the communications area along the lines of fiber optics transmission, digital telephone instruments, and in-home data communications."

*Bob Doyle makes a phone call from his car in August 1980 using IMTS, or Improved Mobile Telephone Service, a precursor to the cellular phone technology that followed about five years later.*

In early 1980, well before cellular telephone service became part of telecommunications nomenclature, Roseville Telephone received approval to offer what was called "Improved Mobile Telephone Service." The approval culminated three years of work on the project. IMTS was an entirely different technology than cellular, but its usage was similar, i.e., to allow customers to call from cars, trucks, boats, etc. The base unit for the radio telephone service was housed in the new West central office at Base Line Road and Crowder Lane. In order to provide coverage for the entire Roseville, Citrus Heights and Folsom Lake areas, a 200-foot tower was erected adjacent to the new building. Its construction went quickly, according to an article in the June 1980 *Line Chatter*.

"After putting the first 20-foot section on footings, the next nine 20-foot sections were put together on the ground with the antenna affixed on the top. A giant crane hoisted up the 180-foot tower and placed it on top of the 20-foot base section. In no time at all, it was a 200-foot, self-supporting tower, complete with antenna."

*Tom Massie of RCC Cellular demonstrates the portable Transpak phone.*
Roseville Press-Tribune, August 29, 1985

"Each mobile unit will have its own distinctive 7-digit-telephone number," the company said in a press release issued in early 1980. "All mobile telephone services will be on a dial basis with local and long distance calls completed automatically without the aid of an operator."

Although IMTS did not receive widespread acceptance because it was soon replaced by superior cellular technology, it did serve Roseville Telephone in these respects: The tower was used for cellular transmission and customers were introduced to the concept of mobile service, which would help sell the cellular service later in the 1980s.

## STRUCTURAL CHANGES IMPACT INDUSTRY

Structural changes swept the industry in the late 1970s and early 1980s as deregulation of communications was phased in. One of the earliest challenges for Roseville Telephone was how to contend with the "unbundling" of services.

Historically, the local telephone exchange provided all products and services that enabled calls to be transmitted and completed within its service territory. It also contracted with other telephone companies to ensure that calls could be made anywhere in the world, sharing toll revenue with these providers. Included in its comprehensive service, the company leased telephone equipment to customers and included maintenance and repair in its basic services.

With the mandate for competition in the industry came the bundling concept, which segmented the communications process into parts, including the basic dial tone, local service, toll service, custom features, telephone equipment, etc. The idea was to allow competition in providing some of the pieces of the process. One of the first to be "unbundled" was telephone equipment itself. This meant customers no longer had to get their phones from the telephone company. The telephones could be bought elsewhere.

The "phone store" was Roseville Telephone's and other companies' answer to competition. Customers could buy a telephone at any electronics store, but to ensure the highest quality and fullest compatibility, telephone companies suggested that customers buy this equipment from them. In 1980, Roseville Telephone opened its first "phone store" adjacent to its Citrus Heights business office. A second store opened in 1981 to serve Roseville customers.

In the same year, the company formed a wholly-owned subsidiary, RTC Communications Corp., to focus on marketing communications systems, services and consulting. Thereafter, personnel in the company had to think in terms of the "regulated side of the house" and the "unregulated side of the house." The subsidiary's employees were authorized to sell products and services to anyone. Their sales turf was not limited to the company's service territory.

The company learned a lot about competing in an open environment. This early experience was helpful as AT&T's divestiture, which officially took place on Jan. 1, 1984, and continuing efforts by regulatory bodies to foster a more open communications industry, brought more competition — and opportunities.

Deregulation caused some confusion among telephone companies and customers, too. The following are excerpts from an anonymous item called "Divestiture Blues" that appeared in the January 1984 *Line Chatter*, years before "rap" came into the modern lexicon:

*"Got them divestiture blues;*

*"Lord, have mercy on me;*
*I fear we been divested right into bankruptcy.*

*"Now Charlie's got Western 'Lectric; he got the Bell Labs, too;*
*He even got the Long Lines and all that revenue.*

*"The FCC say the access charge will make you whole, no fear;*
*But Congress say 'ain't no way in an election year.'*

*"The customer, he all confused; don't know what to do;*
*He reads it in the papers; he hears it on the news.*

*"It's gonna cost him money; ain't that a bitter pill;*
*The judge say it'll do him good, to pay a bigger bill.*

*"All Ma's children changed their names, changed their business, too;*
*If THEY sell phones at the grocery store, WE'LL sell bologna, too.*

*"And a voice is out there, cryin' in the wilderness alone:*
*'If it ain't broken, don't fix it, just let me keep my phone.'"*

## RAPID GROWTH CONTINUES THROUGH 1980s

Intelligent, aggressive implementation of technology played a crucial role in Roseville Telephone's successful growth spurt in the 1980s. Walter Gordon outlined in a *Telephony* magazine article in February 1982 how the company used technology cost-effectively to meet the rapid growth of those years. Excerpts from his article follow:

"A visit to Roseville Telephone and its new digital traffic room brings to mind adjectives that any telco would be pleased to fit — modern, progressive, advanced, state of the art. Roseville Tel thinks of itself in these terms, operating with a philosophy based on matching significant growth with the latest industry innovations and technology."

After giving readers a brief historical sketch of the company, Gordon recounted how the company had decided in the late 1950s and early 1960s that "the only way to ensure good service to its customers was to have total control over as many telephone services as possible." He reviewed the early installations of electronic switching equipment and explained how they later enabled the company to fully utilize inter-connected equipment technologies to obtain significant cost efficiencies, at the same time providing improved and more extensive services.

One of the most important developments at Roseville Telephone during this period of sweeping technological change was the computerization of operator services. The old cordboard stations, a variation of the original manual switchboard, were replaced by computer video terminals. It was the end of an era.

As Gordon explained, in the late 1970s the company made two studies of its future needs in the operator services area. One study compared future operator staffing requirements using the cordboard arrangement in use at the time. The other study assumed this department would be computerized. The projected savings from converting to a digital, computerized system were impossible to ignore.

At that time, the company employed roughly 80 operators. Had the company stayed with the cordboard system, it was projected another 26 operators would be needed within five years to accommodate the anticipated growth in toll traffic. Conversely, if the computerized operator traffic room had been in existence at the

*Roseville Telephone prepares to face competition.*

The Sacramento Union, July 7, 1983

# BUSINESS

The Sacramento Union

E2—Thursday, July 7, 19

# Roseville Telephone: no fear of deregulation

**By STEVE CHANECKA**
ASSOCIATE EDITOR/FINANCIAL

Much has been made of the potential effects of deregulation on Ma Bell and its "Baby Bell" offspring. But how are independents such as Roseville Telephone going to fare?

Just fine, reports Bob Doyle, president of Roseville Telephone, the 19th largest of this country's near-1,500 independents phone companies.

"Telephone service would have been more economical the way it was," said Doyle in an interview, "but if the FCC (Federal Communcations Commission) wants it changed, that's the way it will be."

Roseville Telephone's initial corporate answer was to form a new subsidiary, RTC Communications, which will pursue all potential business opened up by deregulation. One such new line is the sale of business telephone systems to clients outside Roseville Telephone's traditional 83-square-mile service area.

"We've already sold a few systems in downtown Sacramento," said E. Duane Reeves, the company's marketing staff supervisor. "Our approach is one of the total communications company. We are

> "Telephone service would have been more economical the way it was but if the FCC wants it changed, that's the way it will be."
>
> **Bob Doyle, president, Roseville Telephone**

not only able to provide a selection of quality telephone equipment and systems, but as a company that's been in business since 1914, we have the backup to provide the service."

Doyle said the difference between what Roseville Telephone offers and that of newly formed interconnect firms is stability and, again, service.

"We have a reputation to uphold," Doyle said. "Some of these companies have been around for a year or two. We've been around for 69 years. What it gets down to is service. We are going to be offering service."

Roseville Telephone selects its line of business telephone systems from a number of manufacturers including International Telephone & Telegraph (ITT), Rolm, Nippon Electric Company (NEC), Toshiba and GTE.

While Roseville Telephone can now sell its equipment and expertise anywhere, the reverse is also true. Other companies such as Pacific Telephone and American Bell can now invade the Roseville area. That potential competition doesn't concern Doyle.

"A lot of businesses owners here and in Sacramento are stockholders in Roseville Telephone," Doyle reasons. "I think many of them would rather do business with Roseville Telephone."

Since the number of telephone equipment suppliers has proliferated in the past few years, how is one to know what's the right system for his or her business?

"We've set up another service to answer that question," Reeves said. "It's an objective consulting service for businesses that don't know how to determine their telephone needs.

"If we originate the relationship as a consultant, we remove ourselves from consideration as a vendor," Reeves

explained. "At this point we're selling expert advice. This service we can offer anywhere whether it be in Sacramento, San Francisco or Chicago, for that matter."

Fees for such consulting vary depending on the size of the job and the extent of the services, Reeves said.

"Some businesses just want us to analyze their needs and leave it at that," Reeves said. "Others want us to follow up on it and do it all — in essence provide a turnkey system."

Doyle expects the new marketing arm of Roseville Telephone to grow to one third to a half of the company's overall business after a period of years.

"As everything become deregulated, RCC will become a bigger part of the company," Doyle said. "Of course, our shareholders will benefit from any growth in RCC, too, because it is wholly owned."

The company is coming off its best year ever in 1982 when it racked up revenues of more than $30 million and earned profits of $4.3 million, or $1.25 a share. The company plans to split its stock 2-for-1 in September, Doyle added.

time of the study, the company would have needed only 60 operators. Moreover, after five years only another six operators would be required to handle the expected growth in toll traffic. Assuming conversion, the savings over five years were projected at $4 million.

"Beyond the cost savings," Gordon wrote, "the new traffic room gives Roseville Tel needed features for its increasingly sophisticated customer base."

Naturally, change causes stress and company officials knew the operators were understandably leery about the radical change in the way they did their jobs. So the new TRS-D (traffic room system-digital) was phased in over several months. Simultaneously, comprehensive training brought the operators into the computer age. Once they were familiar with the new system, Gordon wrote, "they were reluctant to go back to the cordboards; the initial apprehension had turned into enthusiasm."

*Roseville Telephone advertised its strengths as deregulation entered the telecommunications industry.*

Bernice Moser was nearing retirement when TRS-D was installed. Befitting her many years training operators, Bob Doyle asked her to learn the new system and train the others. She relished the challenge. After extensive training in Florida, she came back and made up a training manual using materials from the manufacturer, ITT-North, and other information she had collected.

"There's an awful lot of information in that little training book I manufactured from all I had gathered," Moser remembered. "Everybody in training got one of those and I think it helped a lot."

Larry Jenkins wrote in the April 1981 *Line Chatter:*

"The world is going to bits. In a way we've joined the ranks of a digital revolution where parts of our analog world are being gobbled up by a co-existing digital world. Late this summer the operator's toll boards (may they rest in peace) will start to give way to computerized cordless boards. Gone will be the clocks, stamps, tickets, ink pens, cords, lights and jacks. They'll all become binary bits shuffling around in time slots at nano-second speeds deep within the bowels of DSS. For us switchmen, the problems that were once as real and tangible will also become digital. We'll most likely have to start thinking digital. Yes, I'd say the world is going to bits."

Employees waxed ecstatic about the new TRS-D, the first of its kind installed in the U.S., and its mother unit, the digital switching system (DSS). Larry Hubbard described the differences between old and new in the October 1981 *Line Chatter*:

"TRS-D will be tied into our network via the DSS office, located in the Roseville central office ... I guess the best way to compare the difference between the old system and how it works is simply to compare the old movie, 'How the West Was Won', and a new one, 'Something Out of Star Wars.'"

Debbie Uribe wrote about the first cut-over in November 1981. "Our TRS-D equipment cut-over has finally arrived! We will now be able to provide our customers the best possible service. People will be able to direct-dial collect calls, credit cards, billed to third-party numbers and overseas. Our customers will be answered faster and more efficiently than ever before. Well, so long cordboards, we'll miss you. Hello TRS-D!"

For some operators, however, TRS-D meant it was time to leave. "I thought the company lost some if its family character about the time we moved downstairs and went computer," said Betty Dosher, who first worked at the company in 1949. "There were new operators coming in and others had gone out of the traffic department. Some of the older operators said they were getting burned out and that's kind of the way I felt, too."

Certainly, the new technology created a different environment in operator services. But there was no doubting the efficiencies resulting from technology. Less than a year after TRS-D was installed at Roseville Telephone, operators were hailed for their productivity. The following appeared in the September 1982 *Line Chatter*:

"Congratulations to Lisa Sanders. She is the first operator to handle over 1,000 calls during a regular shift since we placed in service our new TRS-D operator services system. She handled 1,115 calls during her regular shift on Aug. 9. This averages 148 calls per hour working a position that was arranged to accept toll calls and directory assistance calls. Close behind Lisa are Rainey Vigil, Gail Morillas, Angel Correia, Connie Lenz, Terri Martinez and Mary Ellen Robles. Each of these operators have had shifts where they averaged over 900 calls."

In contrast, during the late 1950s, a good operator was expected to handle 60-to-75 calls per hour, according to Bernice Moser. That translates to 480 calls to 600 calls per regular shift.

Walter Gordon concluded his article in *Telephony* by extolling the virtues of planning:

"Roseville Telephone has put a great deal of effort into meeting the opportunities offered by technology and planning their smooth implementation. It's an approach that works."

There was no doubt the company's approach was working. By 1984, all yardsticks pointed to exceptional progress. Revenue rose to $36,161,000 and net income jumped to $7.5 million. Telephone plant in service rose to $92.6 million. Shareholder ranks climbed to 9,743 land the number of access lines approached 51,000. The full-time employee count, however, dropped from 372 at the end of 1980 to only 326 at the end of 1984. This decline resulted both from improved efficiencies derived from technology and from management's decision to make more use of temporary employees.

The computerization of operator services helped to bring to a close the highly-successful Regional Occupational Program (ROP) at the company. This program enabled high school students to receive on-the-job training at area employers. Debbie Uribe was the company's second ROP student in January 1973; she was hired full-time in May, 1973.

Tim Fritts checks the equipment in Roseville Telephone's first CEV (controlled environmental vault), an installation that brings digital switching power closer to customers.
Roseville Press-Tribune, August 1985

"A friend had heard about the program," said Uribe, who attended Oakmont High School. "She said you work three hours, which meant you didn't go to school for three hours. As a senior, I thought, 'Wow, that sounds like fun.' Once I was into the program, I realized how lucky I was to be given the training. I had no idea I was going to be hired. I remember I was making $2.83 an hour when I started and that was a phenomenal amount of money. My friends were working at the fast food restaurants for $1.50 an hour. And that was just my basic rate. If we worked past 7 p.m., we earned more. So the money was incredible."

ROP was a noteworthy success at Roseville Telephone. From April 1973 through August 1981, the company hired 128 former ROP participants in temporary, part-time or full-time capacities. Many of the ROP students started in the traffic department as operators. ROP employees also worked in the business office, accounting, plant service, assignment, marketing and splicing. Virtually all departments had ROP participation at one time or another.

The program worked well for the student and the company. Nearly half of the ROP participants hired by the company eventually became full-time employees. Many former "ROP-ers," as they were called, hold highly responsible positions today. Debbie Uribe, for example, is the customer services manager of the central alarm station. But the complexity and costs of training operators in a computerized environment doomed the program. It wasn't economically feasible to invest so much time and resources in high school students who would likely not work for the company. This was particularly true in 1981 when the economy was slowing down. The following year, the company had its first and only layoff.

"The program itself is still in the schools, but it's not here at the telephone company," Uribe said. "It stopped in traffic because we went to computerized terminals instead of cordboards. However, it was an important part of Roseville Telephone during those years and I'm only one of many who are sure happy it was around back then."

In 1982, deregulation prompted a major change in accounting for service statistics. Instead of reporting the number of telephones in service, as had been standard since the company began in 1914, the company was only to report the total number of primary access lines it provided. Extensions were not included in the count. This resulted from the "unbundling" of telephone services into separate dial tone service and station apparatus components. Since customers could now buy and install their own equipment, telephone companies no longer could keep an accurate count of stations in service.

The change in reporting access lines came in November 1982 in *Line Chatter*. In October, the employee newsletter reported that the company served 78,216 telephones; in November, the company served 46,304 *access lines*. No, the company was not going backward; it only seemed that way.

Another technological first was achieved in early 1982. Roseville Telephone opened the first 911 emergency reporting system in the Sacramento metropolitan area when Roseville Police went on-line with the new service.

Jay Kinder gave some details about 911 in the March 1982 *Line Chatter*:

"Telephone companies have been working steadfastly behind the scene for several years planning, designing, ordering and installing the necessary central office equipment to meet state guidelines and also satisfy any local requirements. Roseville's system, which is unique in some respects, is designed to identify city residents and trunk them to the city's PSAP (public safety answering point) when they dial 911. Residents of Placer County and Sacramento County who dial 911 are presently routed to a recording which advises them that 911 is not available in their area at this time. On Feb. 8-9, the city of Roseville held press conferences to announce the 911 system. Police Captain Robert Leighty used every opportunity to praise the efforts of RTC in making available to the city of Roseville the first 911 system in the Sacramento metropolitan area."

The torrent of progress in the 1980s was clearly technology-driven. New equipment and new systems created faster and better ways to serve customers.

## NEW EQUIPMENT, TECHNOLOGY INTRODUCED

Roseville Telephone got its first personal computer, which was called a microcomputer then, in June 1983 when an IBM-PC XT was uncrated and set up in data processing. Chuck Spooner marked the occasion with a short item in the following month's *Line Chatter*:

"Plant accounting and marketing have been sharing the system, going through the tutorials and generally getting familiar. In addition, other prospective micro users have dropped by to get some hands-on experience. The program the users have concentrated on initially is Lotus 1-2-3. This is an electronic spreadsheet with graphics and data management capability. We are really impressed with the progress that marketing and plant accounting have made. They are already solving real business problems."

In March 1984, as PCs found their way into other departments, Cheryl Maffei in splicing commented on her new "baby:"

"We are trying to get computer smart with our newest arrival. He's a darling little microcomputer named PC (seems to be a popular name these days). PC's delivery was an unpredictable as they can be. But with the expertise of our well-qualified staff, we were able to avoid any major complications. Once the delivery and installation was finally over, PC checked out with all the right parts. It wasn't long before he began taking in data by leaps and bounds. (Although, at times, he will reject certain data he doesn't like). But it seems that every day he is getting bigger and bigger. Before long we'll need to add to the family and give PC a little brother or sister. Whoever heard of an 'only microcomputer.' They get very lonely, you know."

Donna Hood summed up the fast pace of those years in the March 1984 *Line Chatter*. A new digital switch, the GTD #5, had just been installed in Citrus Heights: "The word of this month is LEARN, LEARN, LEARN. Any time you have a new switch you have new terms, new equipment and new procedures."

In late 1984, a new acronym was introduced to employees — the CEV — which stood for "controlled environmental vault." It was explained in the October 1984 *Line Chatter*:

"The company is looking at serving the area west of Antelope Road by using a controlled environmental vault which meets the concerns of nearby residents

*George Campbell became a director in 1972, replacing Walter Hanisch, who died. Campbell served on the Board of Directors until September 1987, when he became an advisory board member.*

since it is aesthetically appealing. We will use it to house a remote switching unit which will serve this area. Plant from our central office to the 'CEV' will be fiber optics and from the remote location to the subscribers, we will use normal copper wire.

"Basically, this unit will serve the same function as a mini-substation, but will be underground and therefore does not detract from homes in the neighborhood."

Ned Kindelt explained the CEV in more detail in a late 1985 article in *Line Chatter*.

"A CEV is a central office located underneath the ground. The equipment vault is 10-feet, six inches wide and 24-feet long, and will contain a remote switch unit with a fiber optic link to the GTD 5 in Citrus Heights for control. The remote switch unit will be wired for 4,608 lines."

In addition, the CEV had air conditioning, a dehumidifier, an automatic sump pump and an alarm system.

The use of CEVs was pioneered by Roseville Telephone in California. The state's first one was placed on Lichen Drive in Citrus Heights in late 1986. The engineering, splicing and installation was a long, arduous process, according to project director, splicer Jim Hood. He reported in the October 1986 *Line Chatter*.

*Ralph Hoeper became a director in September 1987, replacing George Campbell who retired. Hoeper is president of Foresthill Telephone Company.*

"Our first CEV is almost past history. This has been a very difficult project for many departments. This vault is powered from the Citrus Heights central office by our first fiber optic cable. Our second vault, already a work-day reality for some departments, will be located on Antelope Road near the Foothill Christian Center. To say that this has been a learning experience is being tactful."

That first CEV may have been challenging, but the concept was a lifesaver for Roseville Telephone. Faced with an aggressive expansion of residential housing in the Antelope area of Citrus Heights, the company's conduit capacity to run copper cable from its Citrus Heights central office under Interstate 80 was insufficient for the long term. Had there been no other option, the company would have faced costly construction to increase its underground conduit system.

The CEV approach solved this. Rather than making the conduit system larger, the use of fiber optics resulted in the cable bundle running through the conduits being smaller in diameter. Thin, very high-capacity fiber optics connected the central office and the CEV. The far thicker copper cable ran from the CEV to the customer. Fiber optics enabled much more information to be transmitted through a much smaller bundle of wires. Leon Bower, director of outside plant engineering, explained to fellow employees why CEVs and fiber optics made sense in the fall of 1985:

"If you read local papers, you are aware that the area roughly north of Antelope Road, between the railroad and Watt Avenue in Sacramento County, is about to be developed. They are projecting between 13,000 and 14,000 new homes in the Antelope Urban Reserve in the next 20 years. For the area west of the freeway we are projecting a requirement of 16,000 lines for that 20-year period.

"To serve this area with conventional copper cables would require an investment of some $3.5 million at today's costs in outside plant alone. Underground conduit systems would have to be reinforced, at a very high cost, to accommodate the 14 1500-pair, 24-gauge feeder cables needed. A fiber cable will cost us about $102,000."

After a lengthy explanation of the technical details of how the CEV works, Bower closed by musing about the first call through the new unit. "Wouldn't it be nice if the inaugural call is made from somewhere in Antelope through the remote switch unit over the fiber cable on a light beam, into the cellular switch, out over the air waves to Mr. Doyle in his car as he is coming to work some morning?"

Since 1986, 12 more CEVs scattered evenly throughout the company's service area have placed impressive digital switching power and data transmission capacity close to the users at an economical price. Moreover, all but one of the company's 13 operating CEVs at the end of 1994 were located inside utility right-of-ways. The company did not have to buy the site of the CEV or obtain permits to put them in the ground. Most people are not even aware where the CEVs are placed.

In early 1986 the company reached another milestone when its switching became 100 percent electronic. Rulon Blackburn noted the occasion with a recap of the 12-year conversion to electronic in the February 1986 *Line Chatter*:

"An era has ended. On Jan. 8, 1986, Brian Hubley cut the last 782 line from the SXS (step by step) office in Roseville. That completed the transition from electromechanical to electronic switching for the Roseville Telephone Company.

"Our first venture into electronic switching was #1 EAX in Citrus Heights. It was cut into service in 1974. The next office was Folsom Lake when a #2 EAX was cut into service in December 1977. Then came the first Digital Switching System (DSS). It was an ITT North DSS (later designated 1210) system. Installation was started in August of 1979, and cut into service in February 1980. The system replaced the 786 office in the Roseville central office.

"In July 1984, we cut into service a 1210-64 and, at that time, we moved all of the existing service from the 1210-32, and also cut the 783 office code into the 1210. That left just over 3,000 782 SXS lines remaining. Also in 1984, the GTD 5 was cut into service in the Citrus Heights exchange. The equipment for a 6,222-line addition to the 1210-64 arrived in September 1985. It was installed

*Roseville Telephone engineer Leon Bower compares conventional phone cable, right, with the fiber optic type. Optical cable can carry up to 96,000 calls, while the larger copper wire can handle only 3,000.*

Roseville Press-Tribune, September 1985

and tested between September and the middle of December. We started the 782 cut Dec. 17 and completed it Jan. 8."

In 1987, the lengthy process to replace existing trunk copper cable with fiber optic cable was in full swing. The goal was to have fiber coursing throughout the switching network, connecting all central offices and remote switching units. The quicker the fiber was in place, the better, because growth was again accelerating in the company's territory. Developers were eager to get their projects in the ground quickly to take advantage of declining interest rates. Doug Knowlton reported in *Line Chatter* on the area's growth outlook in March 1987.

"Interest rates are down and home value is up. One developer informed me of a change in his construction plans. Initially, he planned to build out a four-phase subdivision in approximately three years; now his plans are to start in the spring of 1987 and build out in 18 months. There is a demand for housing in California and this area is one of the hot spots.

"The flow of commercial and residential plans coming into the engineering office is starting to increase as spring draws near. We are attempting to engineer and draft as many projects as possible before the big push this summer. We hope we'll be ready.

"The tentative future of our service area is on paper. Where there are presently rolling hills, grassy fields and orchards, on paper this area has been converted to major roadways, giving access to industrial areas, shopping centers and sprawling residential subdivisions. We are meeting these development proposals with engineering forecasting, feeder cable (both copper and fiber) planning, and major underground conduit design. Our clerical, estimating, and records ladies will be the frosting on the cake; they put it all together and get it out to the field forces, where physical work begins."

Through the heavy periods of work, work, work and change, change, and more change, employees kept their sense of humor. Dick Bell talked about the nuances of splicing fiber optic strands:

"I suppose the main thing we are known for in splicing is our ability to connect telephone cable together. We still do that, but now in addition to splicing cables made of copper wire our "Copper Conductor Connecting Engineers" (splicers) must splice cables made up of glass fibers. It takes a lot more patience, concentration and a steady hand to splice a fiber optic cable. (One little mistake and all that light leaks out the end of the fiber and gets all over your clothes!)"

On the deregulated side of the company's business, RTC Communications, more commonly called RCC, scored some major victories. A big one came in 1987 when RCC made another major communications system sale to an old customer — Kaiser-Permanente. Phil Germond wrote about the victory and how much work it took to snare it in the October 1987 *Line Chatter*:

"September 14 was a very big day for RTC/RCC. At precisely 8:30 a.m, the new ROLM CBX II 9000 officially cut-over and was providing service to the Kaiser-Permanente facility in Roseville. If this is news to you, we're not surprised: hardly anyone realized that anything had changed. The transition from the old ROLM to the new ROLM was the smoothest that I have ever been associated with and many other people have expressed the same feeling.

"The project began in July 1986 when RCC received Kaiser's official Request For Proposal (RFP). We had approximately 30 days to respond to the request which in itself was no easy task. On Aug. 29, 1986, our system proposal was submitted to Kaiser. Two companies were being considered: ROLM-Northern California and RCC. The decision on who the successful vendor would be was to be made in October 1986. Unfortunately Kaiser employees voted to strike and the decision on the new telecommunication system was tabled until the strike was over. Finally, in January 1987 Kaiser's Corporate Tele-communications group began reviewing the two proposals. There were many anxious moments as questions were asked, clarifications requested and rumors were passed as to which company would be selected.

"On March 4, 1987, seven months after the proposal was submitted, word came that RCC had been selected as the successful vendor. There was a brief celebration and then reality set in — there was a monumental task to complete. Equipment had to be ordered. There were weeks and weeks of technical training to be scheduled and completed. Coordination meetings with Kaiser, Pac Bell, ROLM, Muzak, Honeywell, etc., etc., had to be scheduled. The tentative cutover date was set as Sept. 14, 1987.

"Major components for the installation began arriving in May, but RTC personnel had already been busy installing a new 900-pair cable from the new telecommunications building to the old terminal room. On June 12, 1987, the new ROLM CBX was powered up and database programming began.

"There was a lot that transpired between June and September such as station reviews, cabling and jacking all the new phone locations, programming, earth-quake restraint testing, installing new feeder cables, writing service orders, training Kaiser personnel on the use of the new phones, installing telephones, trunk testing, installing tie lines, database and route testing and verification and weekly coordination and progress meetings."

The 1987 ROLM installation at Kaiser generated many technical "firsts" for Roseville Telephone, which helped the company compete for large contracts that came up afterward.

## COMPANY ENTERS ALARM MONITORING BUSINESS

Ever since telephone companies have been able to enter deregulated businesses in addition to the traditional regulated telephone business, Bob Doyle's attitude has been, "If we can make a good profit at it, we'll consider doing it."

It was with that in mind in 1984 that Roseville Telephone entered the alarm systems business. As the story goes, Doyle was watching an installer putting in an alarm system in the executive offices when it came to him: "We can do that, too." He figured not only could the company sell and service alarm systems, but it could monitor alarms, too. He reasoned that crime was a growth business, so a bright future lay ahead. But in 1987, it became obvious that alarm companies could do the job cheaper, so Roseville Telephone abandoned it after three years.

In 1988, however, it occurred to Doyle and his team that just monitoring alarms only might make a prosperous business because the company's existing equipment and personnel could be adapted to it. The May 1988 *Line Chatter* announced that the "alarm monitoring project," as it was called, was a go:

"We are in the process of purchasing and installing new equipment to monitor alarm systems for alarm companies. We have 13 Sacramento-area alarm companies that have signed letters of intent. These 13 companies represent over 3,000 accounts which will get us off to a good start. We estimate to be on line in June.

"The monitoring center is UL-listed and is located in operator services and staffed by their personnel. Ernie Bogs will be in charge of the design and engineering of the monitoring center. His knowledge of computers has been a definite asset in the project. If you notice the additions in operator services area now, you'll know what it is."

By the end of 1994, the alarm monitoring division was doing business with 165 alarm dealers throughout the country and servicing in excess of 18,000 accounts. The business is profitable and has excellent prospects for continued growth.

*Roseville Police Chief, Jim Hall, gets alarm demonstration kit for use from Bob Doyle, President of Roseville Telephone.*

Photo by Jim Denman
Roseville Press-Tribune, May 19, 1986

The heady growth of Roseville Telephone in the mid-1980s spawned internal reorganization by the summer of 1988. The marketing and planning department was broadened to include products and services, and sales. Al Johnson made the announcements in the September 1988 *Line Chatter*. He also discussed the importance of marketing in an increasingly technology-driven industry.

"Effective September 4, 1988, RCC and CEES will be integrated into our Marketing and Planning Department. There will be three sections in this department:

- PRODUCTS AND SERVICES SECTION. Headed up by Phil Germond, its primary functions will be to recommend the products and services we offer and provide technical support for these products and services including training of our personnel.

- RATES AND TARIFF SECTION. Headed by Ron Miller, it will be responsible for the pricing of all of our products and services whether they are regulated or non-regulated and to monitor and analyze our sales programs for profitability.

- SALES SECTION. With Duane Reeves as sales manager, it will handle all sales activity of our company. This will include inside sales (marketing representatives), outside sales (communication consultants), a new tele-marketing function and the development of sales programs for our services to be offered our residential customers as well as our business customers.

"Jay Kinder will continue as manager of the marketing and planning department.

"The telecommunications industry is entering a new era of the information age. Roseville Telephone Company will be 100-percent digital switching by the second quarter, 1989. At that time, all of our customers will be served from central offices equipped with digital-type switching systems. We have all of our central offices tied together with fiber optic cables. We are continuing our program to located CEV (controlled environment vaults) with digital remote switching equipment in our exchange plant. This enables us to provide the very latest telecommunication services to our customers.

"Some of these services are as follows: Centrex with customer control of their service, high-speed, broad-band data services, voice mail, Custom Local Area Signal Services (CLASS), multi-line variety package (big business services for the small business), Integrated Services Digital Network (ISDN), voice, data and image switching on same facility, Enhanced Custom Calling Services, Open Network Architecture (ONA) selling network services to Enhanced Service Providers (ESP) who in turn sell to end users.

"This new era of telecommunication services are services provided by the network consisting of the central office switch and facilities to the customer and to the nationwide network. We will have competition for many if not all of these services from other vendors. It is imperative we have a strong, aggressive sales force to pursue the marketplace for the sale of these new services. We will continue to sell our existing products and services such as Business Telephone Systems, Paging, PA Systems, Key Telephone Systems, Customer Custom Calling Services and Single Line Telephone sets, Lease and Maintenance."

## STRONG FINANCIAL PERFORMANCE CLOSES 1980s

By the end of the 1980s, Roseville Telephone was an extraordinarily strong company. Revenue in 1989 had climbed nearly four-fold since the end of the previous decade, jumping to $61,293,000 from only $16,771,000 in 1979. Profit growth was even more impressive, reaching $14.7 million in 1989, nearly five times the $3.1 million net profit generated in 1979. Gross plant investment rose to $144 million at the end of 1989, more than twice the $61.6 million in gross plant investment in 1979.

This sterling growth was driven by major increases in population in its service territory. Citrus Heights added more than 50,000 residents from 1975 to 1989, jumping from 56,232 in 1975 to 107,439 at the end of 1989. Roseville grew even faster as a percentage, more than doubling from 20,050 residents in 1975 to 44,685 in 1990.

It's interesting to note that at the end of 1989 Roseville Telephone had 372 employees, the exact number of employees it had at the end of 1980. More than anything else, this fact illustrates the incredible productivity increases resulting from the company's intensive capital investment programs during the 1980s.

It's an impressive accomplishment that a company could generate a four-fold increase in revenue and a five-fold increase in profit with the same number of employees and only double the asset base. Moreover, the company's long-term debt had declined from $20.1 million at the end of 1979 to only $6.4 million a decade later. In the same time frame, shareholders' equity nearly tripled to $90.7 million from $32.3 million at the end of 1979.

Clearly, the 1980s was a decade to remember at Roseville Telephone. It was nothing short of fabulous from nearly any perspective.

# 1989-1994: Leadership Change; Wireless

## COMPANY CELEBRATES ANNIVERSARIES

*"You've got to invest to keep up with the pace of growth and to stay ahead of what may be the competition. So we've been plowing farther throughout our territory, building for the future."*
— Brian Strom, President and CEO

Anniversary celebrations and open houses are carefully planned marketing events at Roseville Telephone. Since the first open house in 1955, their primary purpose has been public relations. Bob Doyle has always believed it is important to show shareholders their investment is sound. Equally important in Doyle's view is the need to demonstrate to customers the progress Roseville Telephone has made in order to serve them better.

Another important consideration is the positive effect on employees who get a chance to show off their company to visitors. Furthermore, employees themselves learn a great deal about other departments and how the company's mission demands that all departments work as a team. It's an education for all involved.

The company's 75th anniversary open house in September 1989 celebrated several noteworthy achievements. One was the company's transition to digital switching. Only a few years earlier, the company had phased out its last electro-mechanical equipment. In 1989, Roseville Telephone was the first telephone company of its size to have 100-percent digital switching, as the last analog computer switching equipment was removed. Digital switching paved the way for improved interconnect traffic signaling, called Signaling System 7 (SS7), which improved trunking efficiencies and response time connections with other carriers.

The opening of the company's new historical museum was also a highlight of the 75th anniversary celebration. What first began as an idea for a table display of antique telephones and equipment grew into a beautiful museum exhibit in the basement of the company's equipment building on Vernon Street in Roseville. The contrast between the antique equipment of yesteryear and the whiz-bang equipment of 1989 offered an interesting perspective. The 5,000 visitors who braved the unusually rainy mid-September weather to attend the three-day event could see first hand the progress of their telephone company.

*Dennis Cordeiro, the company's manager of safety and environmental affairs, headed up the committee for the very successful 80th anniversary open house in June 1994.*

Company vendors and suppliers were important and welcome participants in the 1989 open house. Their booths and displays gave visitors a wider view of the telecommunications industry. Visitors learned the important role of these industry-associated companies. Live music, free hot dogs and refreshments, raffles and other giveaways added to the festive atmosphere. As in earlier open house events, visitors came away feeling very good about Roseville Telephone, its technology and its role in the community.

Employees expressed their enthusiasm about the open house. Rob DeKeyrel wrote in the October 1989 *Line Chatter*:

"When I got home Sunday night after the open house, I couldn't help but think of all the employees I saw during the weekend working. We all had our best clothes and smiles on. It allowed us to see each other in a different light. It also presented us with the opportunity to see the different skills and talents that we all have. We get conditioned to seeing each other as assigners, splicers, operators, etc. It was a unique opportunity this weekend for all of us to work together as one big team. No separate departments or sections, just Roseville Telephone."

Kate Mitchell, who in 1989 worked in outside plant engineering, shared her thoughts in the same newsletter:

"Overall, an impressive, confusing, surprising, fun, exhausting, wonderful experience, with an incredible amount of CLASS, and I'm not just talking telephone features. The feelings that have been most evident in talking to people about the open house are that there was nothing about it that wasn't first rate, that everyone put out that extra effort, and that the public responded to it; (there was) amazement at the talents of our employees, and their ability to project themselves and handle the public professionally and with good humor."

In a poll after the 1989 event, employees indicated a desire to have an open house every five to 10 years. Since the following years saw continued technological and financial advances at the company, it was determined an open house in 1994 was justified. The cornerstones of the celebration were the formal grand opening of the new Industrial Avenue complex, which opened in late 1993, and the company's 80th anniversary in 1994.

The 1994 open house, under the direction of Dennis Cordeiro, the company's manager of safety and environmental affairs, was by far the company's largest and most elaborate affair ever. Planning commenced about six months before the event. Nearly all the employees were involved over four days, including the opening night special festivities at the Industrial Avenue complex. This open house had two venues, downtown Roseville and Industrial Avenue. The downtown site featured live music, hot dogs, refreshments and guided tours through company offices and facilities, including the administration and equipment buildings on Vernon Street.

Once again, a highlight of the open house was the opening of the museum. This time, it was the grand opening of the museum's well-appointed new quarters at 106 Vernon St. The museum's opening received significant media coverage throughout the Sacramento region. Since the museum was now at street level, it was opened regularly for tours. Finally, the company's treasures of telephone antiquity could be viewed by the public.

The focus at Industrial Avenue was on the technical aspects of serving customers. The company's products and services personnel displayed the wide variety of custom-calling features and high-tech configurations that can increase efficiency and save money for residential and business customers. In addition, the company's large fleet of specially-equipped vehicles was on view. It was an impressive display of technological might.

*"Whatever It Takes" was the theme of the 1994 open house and the construction of the Roseville Telephone museum. Bob Doyle joins the staff of the property and maintenance department in front of the museum.*

Photo by Steve Yeater

Accolades and congratulatory plaques and speeches accented the pre-open house special events for invited guests during both anniversaries. In 1994, Sacramento media personality Tom Sullivan was the emcee of a VIP evening that attracted more than 700 guests, including a virtual "Who's Who" of Roseville and Placer County.

A special commendation was given to Bob Doyle, sent by Roy Neel, president of the United States Telephone Association (USTA) in Washington, D.C. Neel had visited Roseville Telephone two months earlier. It was his first visit to a member telephone company after becoming president of the association in early 1994. Neel's decision to make Roseville Telephone the first visit of his tenure reflected the stature of Roseville Telephone in its industry.

Another leading industry official, Barry Ross, executive director of the California Telephone Association, was on hand to present a commendation from that organization.

*Bob Doyle and Congressman John Doolittle chat during a break at the 80th anniversary open house in June 1994.*

Photo by Steve Yeater

Congratulatory remarks also were offered by political figures in the region. Rep. John Doolittle, a leading Republican, read a letter signed by him and two fellow congressmen, Democrats Robert Matsui and Vic Fazio. State Sen. Tim

Leslie presented Doyle with a resolution from the Senate. Mayor Mel Hamel of Roseville lauded the company's exemplary service to its community, with particular emphasis on Roseville Telephone's commitment to revitalizing the downtown area.

An enormous undertaking, the open house created a bond of pride among employees as they showed the 8,000-plus visitors their company's technological sophistication.

## NEW BORROWING PREPARES FOR GROWTH

*Bob Doyle offers remarks at the 80th anniversary open house in June 1994.*
Photo by Steve Yeater

Roseville Telephone markedly stepped up its capital spending in the late 1980s and early 1990s to prepare for the anticipated significant growth ahead. This major investment cycle began in 1988, when capital spending more than doubled that of any previous year. The company invested $25.7 million in property, plant and equipment in 1988, up from $10.7 million in 1987. The heaviest capital spending prior to that time was in 1981 when the company committed $12.6 million to new plant and equipment.

*Mike Doyle explains Roseville Telephone's high-tech services to visitors at the 1994 open house in June 1994.*
Photo by Steve Yeater

"Capital spending went up so much in those years because we needed to build infrastructure in areas that had never been developed," Al Johnson explained. "We had received maps from developers indicating they intended to build on acreage that previously had been either farm land or vacant land. There was no infrastructure — roads, sewer, gas, electric or anything. So we had to engineer and build new conduits, CEVs (controlled environmental vaults), fiber routes, and supply copper cabling throughout the new areas. It wasn't just upgrading existing infrastructure. It was very costly."

But 1988 was only the beginning. In the following year, $24.1 million was invested in new facilities and equipment. The same scale of investment was made in the years 1991-1993, when capital spending was $25.9 million, $22.6 million and $35.5 million, respectively. This expanded service to nearly a third of the company's service territory, vast parcels that had not yet been developed. The big capital item in 1993, of course, was the construction of the 135,000-square-foot Industrial Avenue complex that cost $18 million to build. In 1994, capital spending came back down to $21.3 million.

Although the company's earnings during this period were excellent, profits alone were not enough to finance the heavy capital requirements. Additional financing would be needed. The options were to sell more stock or borrow. Since the company enjoyed a strong capital position — $100 million in equity and only $5.6 million in long-term debt at the end of 1990 — borrowing appeared the better choice. In late 1991, the directors passed a resolution authorizing the company to seek $40 million in long-term debt. Brian Strom remembered discussions related to financing at board meetings.

"In early 1992, we told Bob that we were going to have to borrow $15 million then, and that a little later, before the end of 1992, we'd need to borrow another $10 million. He said, 'The rates are low, let's borrow the whole $25 million right now and have some excess money on hand.' I told the directors that based upon my recent conversations with investment bankers and insurance company people, it appeared interest rates were likely to go up by the fall. Bob and the directors said, 'Hey, we've been through this before, we know rates will go up by this fall because they always seem to rise in the fall. Rates won't get lower, so let's get the money right now.'

*Company president Brian Strom and his wife, Doris, enjoy a light moment during the 80th anniversary open house.*

Photo by Steve Yeater

"So we got $25 million at 8.25 percent, historically a very good rate, and since we were paying about 9 percent at that time, it was a good move," Strom said. "This money enabled us to continue with our aggressive capital spending. You've got to invest to keep up with the pace of growth and to stay ahead of what may be the competition. So we've been plowing farther throughout our territory, building for the future."

The full debt commitment from the Bank of America was $40 million, the amount authorized by the PUC in February 1992. This put the company in excellent position to finance capital expenditures. Doyle felt the timing was excellent.

*Media personality Tom Sullivan tries out the company's old switchboard during a visit to the telephone museum. Sullivan was emcee of the opening night festivities at the 1994 open house.*

Photo by Steve Yeater

"I said we ought to tie up the money, because the rate was a low one and we were going to need it," said Doyle. "It turned out the timing was good."

The $130 million in capital spending during 1988-1994 kept Roseville Telephone at the cutting edge of technology and enabled it to handle explosive residential, commercial and industrial growth. Customers enjoy the efficiency and reliability of a fiber-optic network backbone. The sophisticated network enables customers to work at home in telecommuting programs that are becoming more popular with employees at high-technology companies, in particular. Telecommuters transmit and receive digitized voice, data and video information through their telephone wires via the so-called "information superhighway."

These service amenities would not be possible had not the telephone company invested in digital switching equipment and fiber optic-capable transmission facilities. From the company's point of view, each new service carries the potential for additional revenue and profit, thus justifying the investment.

As aptly stated in the 1993 annual report — "Is it still true, 'You have to spend money to make money?'" The answer is obvious — "We think so, and our reinvestment of shareholder earnings over the years has yielded consistent results." The report went on to say, "More aggressively than most telecommunications companies, we have chosen to reinvest a significant portion of company earnings. On average, over the last 40 years the company has reinvested 60 percent of earnings into new plant and equipment." Investment in plant and equipment reached $242.5 million at the end of 1994.

## INDUSTRIAL AVENUE COMPLEX POINTS TO THE FUTURE

*Courtney Smith, 3, enjoys the fanfare at the 1994 open house.*

Photo by Steve Yeater

The focal point of Roseville Telephone's commitment to the future is the spacious and beautiful Industrial Avenue complex. Its three buildings house outside plant engineering, marketing and planning, products and services, project coordination, vehicle, construction, warehouse, customer equipment services and splicing. These departments had been scattered in offices throughout Roseville and Citrus Heights. Outside plant personnel were located at 99 Yosemite St., 300 Tahoe Ave. and on Old Auburn Road in Citrus Heights. The complex also includes covered parking for company vehicles and a storage yard for cable reels, poles, conduits, pre-cast boxes and a wide assortment of construction materials.

Nearly 200 of the company's 500 employees work at Industrial Avenue. Current buildings occupy only about a third of the 44 acres owned by the company at the intersection of Industrial Avenue and Washington Boulevard north of downtown Roseville. There is plenty of space for future needs.

"In the mid-1980s, I thought we probably had all the land we needed, but even then I don't think I realized just how big this company was going to get," said Bob Doyle. "Out at Industrial, we started by buying a 17-acre parcel. Then a piece became available on one side of it at the same price, so we picked it up. Not long after, the piece on the other side became available, so we bought that one, too. And then the last piece on the corner became available and we bought it. After starting out with 17 acres, we ended up with 44.

"But it's good property at a good location for a good price," Doyle said. "Having more land than we currently need protects us. First, the land is not going to go down in value, if for some reason we want to sell it in the future. Second, if we decide to sell it, we can dictate who our neighbor is. And, of course, there are any number of activities the company might be getting into in the future that may require more acreage and buildings, so it's a good long-term investment."

Although the new complex has few neighbors, the fact that companies such as Wal-Mart have built nearby — during the worst economic conditions in California since the Great Depression — bodes well for the future of the area.

"These big companies are not investing millions out there because they think this area is a loser," Doyle said. "There are going to be some big things happen in that industrial tract. You've got railroad access, good access to major highways, and the Lincoln Airport nearby. In the future, we're going to be sitting pretty, right in the middle of the action."

*Roseville Telephone moved into its new Industrial Avenue complex in November 1993. Several departments that had been spread out in offices in Roseville and Citrus Heights were consolidated at Industrial Avenue.*
Photo by Ed Asmus
Courtesy of Williams & Paddon

*Courtyard at Industrial Avenue complex.*

Photo by Ed Asmus
Courtesy of Williams & Paddon

## STROM NAMED PRESIDENT AND CEO;
## BOARD RESTRUCTURED

The Industrial Avenue complex prepared Roseville Telephone for its future physical needs. In December 1993, only a month after the new buildings opened, it was time for Doyle to prepare for the company's future management needs. After many months — perhaps even years — contemplating his own succession and that of his aging Board of Directors, Bob Doyle developed a plan for restructuring top management and the Board of Directors that laid the foundation for taking the company into the next decade, century and millennium. It was a difficult task for Doyle because he had to take into account a multitude of considerations.

Doyle announced his succession strategy at the Board of Directors meeting two days before Christmas Eve 1993. Brian Strom would become president and chief executive officer, succeeding Doyle, who had held these positions for nearly 40 years. Doyle would remain a working chairman of the board and maintain his daily routine, fielding questions from shareholders and employees, and offering counsel to Strom. Al Johnson would be promoted to executive vice president and chief operating officer. In January 1994, Michael D. Campbell, a long-time consultant to the company, would come aboard as vice president and chief financial officer.

*The company's new vehicle shop at Industrial Avenue has the latest equipment to keep the company's 100-plus vehicles running smoothly.*

Photo by Ed Asmus
Courtesy of Williams & Paddon

At the board level, Doyle announced that Bill P. Sheppard and C. Doulton Burner had agreed to serve as advisory board members. Doyle congratulated them and thanked them for their combined 43 years of service. Strom was elected to fill one vacant board position and John R. Roberts III was elected the fifth board member. Roberts was well known in the Sacramento region for his success in heading up the Sacramento Area Commerce and Trade Organization. Roberts is currently executive director of the California Rice Industry Association.

The process of planning his own succession was a delicate one for Bob Doyle.

"It wasn't easy because I had to make sure I was picking the right person to replace me, and at the same time I had to find replacements for two individuals who had been on the board for a long time," Doyle said. "Of course, Brian Strom would fill one board slot, but I needed another good candidate, too. I pored over the stockholders' list several times looking for the right person to be on the board. It wasn't easy finding someone with all the right qualities.

"First, you had to get somebody who was fairly young, or you're defeating your purpose. And I had to find somebody with a substantial amount of stock, not just a few hundred shares. So I looked through the list and wrote down names of possible candidates," Doyle explained. "Out of the 9,500 stockholders, probably 9,000 of them want to be on the Board of Directors. But the main thing was to try to get a person that everybody would agree on, including board members, the management team, other employees, and most importantly, the stockholders.

"So when I was going through the list, I saw his name — John Roberts III. He had been with SACTO, the Sacramento Chamber of Commerce and the California Rice Industry Association. He knows a lot of people, is well liked, smart, and in his early 40s. And he had a significant number of shares.

"Most of the people in Roseville didn't know him, which was probably good," Doyle said. "When you get local people everyone knows, and you've known each other for years, somebody's always going to say, 'Why did Doyle ask so-and-so and not me?' I didn't want that to happen. So I figured Roberts would be a good choice, if he was willing to do it."

Doyle's decision to recommend that Brian Strom succeed him as president and chief executive officer was easier.

"I hired Brian in 1989 to take Mark Shull's place as our chief accountant. At the same time, I had an eye out for somebody to eventually take my place. We have a lot of good employees here, but to hire from among employees a person that everybody could agree on was not an easy thing to do. But I didn't want to go outside the company to get somebody.

"So I watched Brian for a long time. I knew he had purchased some stock himself and was in the savings plan. And, in my own way, I was inquiring about him all the time because, as the chief financial officer, Brian interacted with all the different departments. I didn't find anyone who said they didn't like him," Doyle said.

"So I finally figured out who would replace me and who would replace the directors. And I knew the two of them would get along fine because Brian was with Arthur Young before I hired him and his firm was SACTO's auditor when John Roberts was there. I knew they got along real well," Doyle said. "I moved pretty fast once I got the ball rolling. I had already talked to Al and he was fine with my choices. First of all, I mentioned it to Brian in a roundabout way, but asked him not to breathe a word because this couldn't get out until I made sure on the other board member. I didn't know if Roberts would be able to become a director. I had to find out if the association he worked for had a policy against employees being on boards.

"So I called John Roberts up and said, 'The rice association isn't against the Auburn Dam, is it?' And he said, 'Hell, no.' And I said, 'You know, I'm the vice-chairman of the board for the Auburn Dam, and it could be that we might need a new board member. Would you be available?' He said, 'Bob, I would be, but I just don't have the time.' That answered my question. I knew John could be on the telephone company board.

"So then the one guy I have to make sure agrees with all this is my brother, Tom. As a director, he knew it was time to put some younger members on the board. We agreed it was the right thing for the company. So I told him that I was thinking about Brian as a director and he didn't frown on that. I also told him I was thinking about making the changes at the December meeting of the board. Tom agreed that would be the right time.

"Then I told him I was going to step down as president and wanted Brian to succeed me. I told him I had been watching Brian for several years and I

*Brian Strom became Roseville Telephone's president and chief executive officer in late 1993.*

Photo by Sirlin Studios

thought he could do a good job. He agreed. And Tom also knew John Roberts from the period when I was on the board of SACTO, and John had helped us locate some businesses up here," Doyle continued. "I told Tom I had been working on this plan for a long time and had been through the stock book I don't know how many times before I came across John Roberts' name. Tom didn't suggest anybody; he said OK.

"So I called Roberts up and asked him to go to lunch with Tom and me. We were at lunch and I told John we were going to be making some changes at the company. I told him I was going to step down as the president and asked him if he knew Brian Strom. He said he did," Doyle said. "I told him I was going to put Brian in my place and that I was still going to stay on as chairman of the board. I said I thought the older stockholders would like me to hang around a while — after all, we had not had a stock sale in more than 10 years and I was the one who sold them stock. Brian wasn't here yet to do it.

"Roberts said, 'I think that's smart and Brian will do a good job.' I told him I had another problem, I had two board positions and Brian will take one.

"In the meantime, before that happened, the waitress comes up, and Roberts asked, 'What kind of soup do you have?' She said, 'Corn chowder.' He said, 'Is it good?' and she said, 'It's excellent.' He said, 'OK, I'll have a cup of corn chowder,' and he ordered a sandwich.

*Roseville Telephone's management team includes, from left to right, A.A. Johnson, Michael Campbell, Bob Doyle and Brian Strom.*

Photo by Rudy Meyers
Courtesy of Comstock's Magazine

"So I started talking again and said I had a hell of a time trying to find somebody who was not way up in age, had a fair amount of stock, and was somebody I wouldn't find fault with. I went through those records many times. He had just taken a bite of his sandwich when I said, 'John, the one we picked is you.' He said, 'You've got to be kidding.' I said, 'I'm not kidding one goddamned bit. I think you'd do a good job. You've always liked the Roseville Telephone Company.' He said, 'I don't know what to say. It's the biggest honor I've ever had.'

"Tom and I kept eating our lunch and Roberts just sat there, stunned. He turned as white as a sheet of paper. When the waitress came, his corn chowder was untouched and he'd taken only one bite out of that sandwich. She asked, 'Was there something wrong with your lunch?' and I said, 'No, I told him something that turned his stomach.'

"My next move was to talk to Shep and Doulton. I told Tom I didn't know whether to talk to them individually or do it at the board meeting. In the meantime, I'm not sleeping," Doyle said. "I dreaded talking to them worse than anything, because Sheppard had been on the board 26 years and Doulton 17 years, and they just literally loved the Roseville Telephone Company."

In the meantime, Doyle called the other director, Ralph Hoeper, and informed him of his plans. "I didn't want it to come as a complete surprise. Hoeper agreed it was the proper thing to do. Meanwhile, the stress of the whole thing was killing me and I just wanted to get it over.

"Anyway, the board meeting starts and I went clear through the whole meeting before saying anything about my plans. Tom and Hoeper were sitting there wondering, 'When's this son of a bitch going to say something?'

*Director John Roberts and Bob Doyle visit during the 1994 open house.*

Photo by Steve Yeater

"So I said to Sheppard and Burner, 'Before you guys leave, I want to tell you something. There are going to be some big changes made at the Roseville Telephone Company. I'm going to step down as the president and Brian is going to be president and CEO. There's only one problem. I've got to replace two directors. So, Doulton and Bill, I'm going to ask you guys to step down from the Board of Directors and stay on as advisory board members. This is just something that has to be done.' I told them Brian was going to replace one of them and the other new director was John Roberts. They both knew Roberts because our directors used to go to the SACTO annual meetings. I said, 'I'm asking you.' They agreed.

"Of course, it came as a complete surprise. But I couldn't do it any other way. I didn't want somebody else to tell them."

Doyle made it clear to the two long-time directors the changes affected him, too.

" 'You're not the only guys that are sacrificing here,' I told them. 'I'm sacrificing, too. I'm not going to be the president and CEO anymore, so I'm giving up two important titles. But I'm only trying to be fair to the employees and the stockholders, and after all, we owe them. You guys have been on the board for a hell of a long time and you've done a good job.' They had to admit it wasn't easy for me either.

"So anyway, I talked until I was black and blue and everybody seemed to be happy when they left," Doyle said. "As far as I'm concerned, it was without a doubt ... out of the entire time I've been with the Roseville Telephone Company ... this had to be the hardest thing I ever did."

Doyle was relieved. His loyalty to associates is well known. At the same time, Doyle does what's right. "I'm sure sleeping better," he said a month later.

"At least the idea to make changes was my own," Doyle said. "Nobody forced me, but it's not the easiest thing to do. I knew I had to make changes because if I didn't, I wouldn't be doing what's right by the stockholders, by the employees or anybody else. Everybody's at ease now. Nobody's even wondering what's going to happen in the future. It just makes things run a hell of a lot better.

"It ended up working perfectly," Doyle added. "We had a guy (Brian Strom) who was already with the company and we hired a guy (Mike Campbell) in his place who really is one hell of a guy. It just worked real well.

"And, most importantly, the employees know that Brian doesn't want to sell the company, so when I'm gone, the company will just keep right on going."

*Doulton Burner served as a director from 1976 to 1993 when he became an advisory member of the Board of Directors.*

## FACTORS AFFECTING STOCK PRICE

Shareholders holding stock over the long-term have enjoyed significant appreciation. Those who were lucky enough to buy the stock early on have earned exceptional returns. Those who purchased stock during the last sale ending in 1983 have done well, too, seeing their investment jump more than four-fold. The company has paid 5 percent stock dividends in every year from 1983 through 1994, except 1988, when a 10 percent stock dividend was paid. In addition, the price of the shares has risen from $10 in 1983 to $24 at the end of 1994.

During most of the years since 1953, when the stock was first sold to the public, the price was determined by the previous stock sale. The going price at any given time — defined as the price which the employees' savings plan bought shares — was pegged to the previous stock sale, adjusted for any stock splits.

*Rulon Blackburn became the company's director of network and property management department in the spring of 1994.*

That approach worked well through the decades because the company sold new issues of stock regularly. This gave a market currency to the price.

In recent years, however, the price the retirement supplement plan pays for shares is determined by a committee, which takes into account numerous factors. Brian Strom discussed the background and current process that determines the price the employees' plan pays for shares.

"Each quarter the administrative committee makes a determination of the stock's value so that when employees retire, we can calculate the number of shares they receive. Since the retirement supplement plan is made up largely of company stock, you've got to have a pretty reasonable determination of what the price should be," Strom explained.

"A number of years back, in about 1989, the Bank of America trustee asked how the committee went about making the determination of price. We said it was based on what we knew of local trading, which at the time was around $10 a share. But then the newspaper might report that somebody's trying to buy and sell at $12 a share. The B of A people got nervous about that differential so they decided to get into the stock valuation business themselves.

"They started to use a process where they would call four brokerage firms who were known to handle our stock and ask them what our shares were worth. They'd get varying figures — for example, let's assume $12.50 a share, $14 a share, $16 a share, and $18 a share. Their approach was to add the prices up, divide by four, and say that number was the value," Strom said. "The administrative committee didn't agree with that methodology. It asked, 'How can that be the value? Have these brokers traded any shares?' They said, 'No, not necessarily.' The committee decided that approach wouldn't be acceptable in valuing the stock in the employees' plan. It creates too much volatility.'

"As a result, a process was developed, assisted by the valuation group at Ernst & Young, and valuation consultants from another major accounting firm, Arthur Andersen, to effect a quarterly valuation for the employees' retirement plan. A number of valuation measures are taken into account. One is called the comparative market multiple, which takes into account a net income factor, a future net income factor, a revenue factor, an earnings-before-income tax factor, and a book-value factor for Roseville Telephone. Those are all numbers that can be obtained from our own books. Our multiple is compared to multiples of similar telephone companies in the United States," Strom said.

"There are not many similar telephone companies. Rochester (N.Y.) Telephone, Southern New England Telephone and Lincoln (Neb.) Telephone are three of the best comparables that we have. They're all publicly held. We also throw in relevant facts, numbers and ratios from a few of the large companies. We take into account those factors, compare them to market multiples and come up with a weighted average share price. A couple of other factors are also considered, such as a present value estimate of debt-free cash flow. It's another technical thing the valuation consultants love to play with. There is also a dividend factor, which essentially compares Roseville's dividends to the other companies' dividends.

"Those are the three main areas where Roseville Telephone is compared with other telephone companies. One is the comparative market, the next is the cash flow and the third is the dividend. A fourth factor looked at is stock trading within that quarter. After figuring in all these components, the committee comes up with a fair share price, which most recently has been an average of $24 a share. The committee has the methodology verified by Ernst & Young and then finally by Arthur Andersen. That's how the committee gets to the price the retirement supplement plan will offer to purchase shares.

"It's a technical way of approaching it, if you will, a mathematical way. There are other valuation approaches. Our approach is done specifically for the retirement supplement plan."

Shares also trade through solicitations by buyers and sellers in the *Roseville Press-Tribune's* classified advertising section. Most sales through newspaper ads and brokerage firms are for fairly small trades, very seldom a large block.

"We are comfortable with how the price is determined," Strom added. "These people at Arthur Andersen and Ernst & Young — their full-time job is the valuation of businesses. That's all they do. They're not tax people, they're not auditors ... they're valuation specialists. They're good at what they do."

The share price was $15 in June 1989 when the retirement supplement plan bought 500,000 newly-issued shares for $7.5 million. In February 1991, using the valuation analysis developed by outside consultants, the stock price offered by the plan rose to $20 per share. Later in 1991, the per share price was pegged at $22. It went to $23 in February 1993, and to $24 in October 1993. In September 1994, the retirement supplement plan bought another block of 400,000 newly-issued shares at $24 per share for a total price of $9.6 million.

## 1989-1994: VERY GOOD YEARS

The higher stock price of recent years reflected the company's improved results during those years plus its future prospects. Roseville Telephone's earnings in 1989 through 1994 were fueled by strong residential and commercial growth and excellent employee productivity. It was the same recipe for success that has defined the company for more than 40 years.

Revenue in 1994 reached the $100 million level for the first time and net profit exceeded $20 million. At the end of 1994, total access lines served jumped to 94,646. In 1989, revenue was $61.3 million and the company served 71,937 access lines.

Once again, major population increases fueled growth. Roseville grew about 25 percent, to 56,036 residents at the start of 1994, up from 44,685 only four years earlier. According to the Citrus Heights Chamber of Commerce, Citrus Heights' population exceeded 138,000 at the end of 1994, up from 107,439 at end of 1989.

Business accounts amounted to approximately 30 percent of the total, up from only about 10 percent in the early 1970s. This healthy business component contributes greatly to Roseville Telephone's exceptional revenue and profitability per access line, compared to similarly-sized telephone companies.

For example, according to the 1994 edition of *Phonefacts*, the United States Telephone Association's annual handbook, North State Telephone in High Point, N.C., had 96,429 access lines at the end of 1993, with revenue of $47.7 million. Roseville Telephone's revenue for the same year was $93.3 million, almost double that of North State Telephone's, although Roseville served 6,000 fewer access lines.

Another comparison of note is Anchorage Telephone Utility in Alaska, which had 140,924 access lines generating revenue of $98.3 million in 1993. Roseville's revenue for that year was only $5 million less even though it had 50,000 fewer access lines.

These statistics reflect the impressive growth and quality of companies moving and expanding into Roseville Telephone's service territory in recent years. Companies such as Hewlett-Packard and NEC place many more long-distance calls than do small, local businesses. Roseville Telephone has benefited from the international stature of these companies because it shares in toll revenue.

Competition has changed the mix of revenue sources in recent years. In 1988, for example, toll and operator services agreements with AT&T provided 25 percent of Roseville Telephone's consolidated operating revenue. The next year AT&T agreements generated 19 percent of the company's total revenue. At the end of 1994, AT&T accounted for only 10 percent of the Roseville Telephone's revenue.

Profitability was also enhanced by the company's continuous investment in labor-saving equipment and switching technology. In the five years through 1994, the number of controlled environmental vaults in service jumped to 13 from seven. Throughout the company, new systems were introduced to increase productivity. Ron Miller, the affable and able manager of the rates and tariffs department, gave a glimpse of the high-tech environment at the company in his March 1989 article in *Line Chatter:*

"Projects, Projects, Projects," Miller wrote, "Equal Access, Centrex, ISDN, Tri-Vista, 39-1-1, PNS, COMLS, OTTO II, Taxes and Surcharges, AT&T changes, CCCS, CLASS, Enhanced Custom Calling, FEX changes, BRCS, Timelines, Cellular Data Requests, COPT, Training ... etc."

In early 1990, Fred Arcuri reminisced in *Line Chatter* about 1989:

"In the years ahead, people who will look at Roseville Telephone Company and its accomplishments will view 1989 as one of RTC's finest.

"Installation of equipment making us entirely digital, an unbelievably successful 75th anniversary celebration, implementation of new network services such as ISDN, installation of outside plant facilities to keep up with a staggering growth rate, a successful cut over to Equal Access, all of this and more while undergoing some of the most ambitious remodeling and new construction the company has ever undertaken.

"Words like enthusiasm and pride will be used to describe RTC employees. When all is said and done, 1989 will be looked upon as a pivotal year in explaining Roseville Telephone Company's success in the 1990s and beyond."

Gene Cornthwaite of outside plant engineering was similarly nostalgic in March 1990 when he penned the following remarks in *Line Chatter*:

*Michael D. Campbell joined Roseville Telephone in early 1994 as vice president and chief financial officer.*
Photo by Rudy Meyers

"As I sit here trying to decide what to say in this article, I start to reflect on the past 20 some odd years I have been at RTC. All the changes I have seen, all the friends I have made, and all the different jobs that each of us has learned. This huge machine known as 'The Company' (some nuts, some live wires, some loose screws, and some 'wheels') — I think it is truly amazing how this all comes together.

"From the time a developer informs us of his plans to start tearing up one of the last parcels of undisturbed land in what used to be a remote part of our service area, all the way through this machine until someone in their home hears, 'Number, please' (or should I say, 'Roseville Recording #38')... I have heard lots of crying and complaining, and have seen lots of great ideas materialize.

"I know there are some better, higher-paying places to work in this world. But I would have to say to anyone, there is no company I would be more proud to be a part of than this one, with all of you! ... And now that you are all in tears, there is one more person we need to mention, the one man who has kept this amazing collection on the road all this time, Bob Doyle. He deserves a pat on the back from everyone here."

When Mother Nature decides to show her strength, the telephone company gets the message, feels the jolt and takes the heat. On Oct. 17, 1989, at 5:04 p.m. Pacific Daylight Time, an earthquake toppled buildings and bridges in San Francisco and tied up Roseville Telephone. Bill DeMuth recounted in November 1989's *Line Chatter* how the the Loma Prieta earthquake affected Roseville Telephone:

"A few minutes after the Bay Area earthquake, people all over Northern California began complaining about 'NO DIAL TONE.' Customers of Roseville Telephone were no exception. No! Our switches weren't damaged. No! The switches weren't 'down' or locked up. They were simply overloaded.

*Bill DeMuth, manager of central office maintenance, worked furiously to get all lines open in the hours after the 1989 earthquake in the Bay Area.*

"Moments after the earthquake, thousands of subscribers throughout our service area began picking up their phones and calling out to spread the news about the earthquake or to check on friends and relatives in the Bay Area. Many of them discovered that they did not have any dial tone, or if they had dial tone, that they reached 'All Circuits Busy' recordings after dialing. Many people called the operators to complain of no dial tone or asked for assistance in calling the Bay Area. Quickly, the switching systems, the operators, and the trunks between offices became overloaded.

"Hazel Snider and many of her operators and supervisors came into work to handle the increased volume of calls. RTC has over 950 trunks between its toll office and AT&T's switch in Sacramento, but they were continually in use, so even the operators couldn't place calls to the Bay Area or other parts of the country.

"Craig Mosca, Walter Gordon and I came back to work to inspect the central offices to see if anything could be done to improve the situation. Mike Jarvis was already at the Citrus Heights C.O. and kept them informed of that switch's status. Robert Gregory and Vern Roberson from customer services also came in to try and assist with the troubles. It was soon determined that the switching equipment was running properly at its designed limits.

"On a typical day between 5-6 p.m., the Roseville 1210 local office handles approximately 25,000-30,000 calls; the toll office about 20,000-25,000 calls. The evening of the earthquake between 5-6 p.m., there were 138,000 call attempts in the local office and 191,000 in the toll office. The local 1210 switch was engineered for a maximum of 50,000 calls per hour and the toll office for a maximum of 75,000 calls per hour. So, as you can see, the switches were stressed past their capabilities.

"If there is a lesson to be learned from all of this, it would be to remember that during major disasters or emergency situations, DON'T USE YOUR PHONE UNLESS IT IS ABSOLUTELY NECESSARY. Don't tie up the network when people need to use their phones to call police or fire departments. Also, if you do need to make an emergency call, just come off hook and wait for dial tone. There may be over a minute delay for dial tone, but hopefully it will eventually be there. Don't continually keep going on and off hook with your phone. It will just cause more of a load on the system."

The strong financial performance of recent years created opportunities at the company and hiring has been robust for the five years through 1994. At the end of 1989 there were 372 full-time employees. This increased to 501 at the end of 1994.

Moreover, Roseville Telephone has taken advantage of increasing competition in the telecommunications industry and depressed economic conditions, particularly in California, to strengthen its already talented work force. Many telephone companies, including Pacific Bell and AT&T, in recent years have

trimmed their work forces —
through attrition, layoffs and early
retirements. Consequently, Roseville
Telephone has attracted many experienced telephone people to satisfy
its needs. These hires not only offer
the company immediate expertise,
but they also help temper the company's long-term obligations, since
many are older and will not work
enough years to qualify for the
highest levels of pension benefits.
Previous employers will shoulder the
bulk of their retirement benefits. It
would be wrong, however, to infer
that the company is exploiting these
older workers. On the contrary, they
are delighted to be a part of Roseville
Telephone.

Randy Wright typifies the new, but
experienced employee. His article,
"A Few Words From The New Kid
On The Block," appeared in the
April 1990 *Line Chatter:*

"I first became familiar with RTC
about a year and a half ago when
working for AT&T. I supervised the
installation of the 5ESS equipment.
At that time I mentioned to my wife,
Mary, that Roseville Telephone
seemed like a good company to work for. Little did I know I would soon find
out for myself.

"At the end of last year AT&T made a one-time-only, early-retirement offer to
its management employees, and I took advantage of it. As of Dec. 30, 1989, I
was unemployed. All went well until around February when my wife said:

  • 'You are too young to retire.'

  • 'I married you for better or for worse, not for lunch.'

  • 'Get a JOB!'

"Luckily for me, there was an opening here at RTC, and I am once again gain-
fully employed. Of course my duties here in Buildings and Grounds are about
as far as you can get from my former work, but I am greatly enjoying the

*The company's truck fleet has come
a long way from the old "Army rig"
of the 1950s.*
Photo by Sirlin Studios

*Barbara Fletcher is revenue accounting manager at Roseville Telephone. She's joined the company in 1970 after 8 years with two major California banks.*

differences. Being new, I'm pretty busy learning all the ins and outs of B&G; definitely a variety. All the way from learning to do spreadsheets to fork-lift training and a whole lot in between.

"Everyone has been most helpful and very welcoming. As I start my 'second' career, I'm happy it's as a member of the RTC family, and I look forward to spending many productive years working with all of you. Yes, Mary, this is going to be a good place to work."

Technical achievements at Roseville Telephone continued to wow the industry. In 1990, the Citrus Heights central office added equipment to handle another 5,600 lines through its digital switch, the GTD-5. No other GTD-5 in the world handled more access lines. Continuous installation of controlled environmental vaults connected by fiber-optic transmission facilities gives the company one of the most impressive communications networks anywhere.

The company's continuous investment in equipment enabled it to offer the latest services, often before other telephone companies. Roseville Telephone was the first company in California to offer voice mail to all its customers and the first to enable its customers to block unwanted "information services" numbers (900/976). The company was also first to offer Centrex and ISDN capabilities to all its customers.

New services spawned related services. For instance, one popular service, "Homework Hotline," is a variation of voice mail. JanNetta Hance explained this service in October 1992's *Line Chatter*:

"This is set up as a voice mail box that allows the students or their parents to check what homework assignments are due in all their classes. The goal is to improve communication between parents, students, and teachers. We also offer 'Bulletin Board.' This allows schools to set up a voice mail box with information such as upcoming school events, lunch menus, and a line for reporting absences."

The decades of progress did not go unnoticed. In March 1991, a month before the company surpassed the milestone of 80,000 access lines, Bob Doyle's peers in California recognized his achievements by presenting him with the California Telephone Association's "Distinguished Service Award." A decade earlier, Doyle had been inducted into the association's Hall of Fame.

One of the most press-worthy stories of 1991 was Roseville Telephone's opposition to the regulatory mandate ordering it to double its local pay phone charge from 10 cents to 20 cents. Other telephone companies had long charged the 20-cent rate. Mark Shull, the company's long-time controller, told the *Roseville Press-Tribune* in August 1989 that there was no reason to increase the price at that time.

"We feel the company is fairly profitable and see no reason to change our public phone rates. It has been a dime forever."

The pay phone rate for local calls was a nickel until 1953, when it jumped to a dime, remaining at 10 cents for nearly 40 years. But the "dime call" became history in California on June 1, 1991, when Roseville Telephone's pay stations went to the Public Utilities Commission-mandated 20-cent rate.

About the same time the dime call became history, Ron Miller gave *Line Chatter's* April 1991 readers a glimpse at the future:

"You must have noticed all the trenching and cable work along the railroad tracks by 99 Yosemite St. Well, that's MCI at work, running its cables right down the Southern Pacific right-of-way. MCI has asked for a fiber connection to RTC facilities, which we should be beginning soon. This is our first FCC filing for this type of service. We learn something every day, like it or not."

Roseville Telephone, of course, was not standing still as competitors were preparing for the future. The construction crew made news in early 1992 when it installed the longest cable in the company's history. Splicer Doug Giles reported the event in the August 1992 *Line Chatter*:

"Hats off to construction for the unbelievable task of pulling one continual length of fiber optics cable (10,000 feet) to the Citrus Heights central office. This, along with the splicing expertise of Max Clanton, Bob Flynn, Steve Addiego and Tony Nolasco, completed a fiber optics cable system which will serve the company well for many years to come. This system replaces an outdated T-Carrier span which linked us, as a trunk cable, to Pacific Bell."

The company's superior digital network and switching equipment played a big role in winning a major contract from the state of California in the spring of 1993. Several months earlier, the state had expanded and consolidated some of its operations in Roseville. This created a Centrex group of about 200 lines. Karen Rose of the marketing and planning department explained in the April 1993 *Line Chatter* how that led to more business:

"With this consolidation, the state decided to expand its CALNET network into the Roseville area to accommodate these offices. CALNET is the state's private network which carries all of its telephone traffic via circuit, eliminating long-distance dialing.

"The significance of this decision is immeasurable, for it makes Roseville an even more attractive option for relocation of state offices from Sacramento. The state is currently implementing a plan to establish satellite offices and move employees closer to where they reside. Telecommuting is also being encouraged wherever possible — the perfect application for our Centrex and ISDN services!

"In conjunction with CALNET, Roseville Telephone Company's most significant accomplishment was the ability to provide ANI (Automatic Number Identification), which means that although all of their telephone traffic travels across a private facility, RTC made it possible to provide the state with an

*Ron Miller is manager of the rates and tariffs department and a frequent contributor to Line Chatter.*

**Roseville Telephone Company**

*Annual Report 1992*

*1992 Annual Report Cover*

itemization of all call traffic. Keep in mind, ANI over a private facility is not something that we've ever provided in the past and, even more important, neither Pacific Bell nor General Telephone are currently able to provide this service."

The company received a thank you letter from Marianne G. Sutter, a telecommunications systems analyst for the state, upon completion of the job. Excerpts include:

"I would like to express my sincere gratitude for Roseville Telephone Company's part in the conversion of the new General Services Consolidated Centrex in Roseville. There were many firsts for both Roseville Telephone and General Services (for example, ANI service for CALNET, which is not being provided in any of our other Centrexes)."

Listeners to Tom Sullivan's popular afternoon radio talk show on Sacramento's KFBK-AM learned a lot about Roseville Telephone's technological prowess on April 28, 1993. Sullivan had spent that morning touring the company's facilities with expert guides Bob Doyle, Bob Parsons and Al Johnson, about whom Sullivan remarked, "They have forgotten more about telephones than most other telephone companies' people will ever learn." Sullivan was impressed.

"This is fascinating stuff," Sullivan told the radio audience. "I know Roseville Telephone has come a long way from where they used to be, but these guys are so far ahead of Pacific Bell in technology … in fact, do you know that Roseville is basically circled and crisscrossed with fiber optics?

"It was fun and exciting to see the state-of-the-art, next generation of equipment that we will all be using. And Roseville Telephone, much to a lot of people's surprise and certainly to mine, is way ahead in technology. They say they have fiber density for their customers that Pacific Bell won't have until 2005."

KFBK's traffic reporter and "eye in the sky," Commander Bill Eveland, piped in during one of his reports: "I'll tell you one thing, too. If you had bought some of their stock about 10 years ago, you wouldn't be on KFBK, you'd retire!"

*Tom Sullivan, a stockbroker and popular radio personality at KFBK-Sacramento.*

Courtesy of KFBK

Building employee morale has always been a hallmark of Roseville Telephone in the Bob Doyle years. Hard work and planning that pay off in visible progress — duly noted by management — make for satisfied and productive employees.

To illustrate: Perry Allen of the operations information systems department complimented his staff in an October 1993 *Line Chatter* article entitled "A Measure Of Excellence:"

"I want to declare up front that I think I have one of the best jobs in the entire world! Having said that, I expect a significant number of you will skip on to the next page, dismissing this one as yet another product of my reputed eccentricity. Fine! Skip on! This publication is growing to the size of the Sunday paper anyway, and there's plenty of other stuff to read.

"For the patient, I'll explain. This is not meant to be a 'feel-good, breast-beating, self-indulgent, departmental self-pat-on-the-back,' but rather an opportunity to 'publicly' express the magnitude of my respect and admiration for the people who work in my group.

"Charles, Craig, Ed, Jim, James, Joyce, Karen, Lynn, Mason, and Rob. Each of them and all of them view the work they do at RTC as their elected profession, their chosen field of endeavor, their prideful craft. For each of these people, the definition of quality and its importance is not something that comes from meetings, pep talks, or from any preaching on my part. It is an inherent part of their character. It is the cornerstone of their very personality.

"It seems never to occur to any of them that anything less than perfection is acceptable. Their own personal work ethic stands as a baseline for the level of performance they bring to the job. They know no limits. The clock doesn't control what time they leave at the end of the day, and they rarely leave on time. They will often think over problems or methods for improvement while at home. Their commitment to their work is a 24-hour-a-day practice.

"No, they are not 'propeller heads.' Their home lives are diverse and fulfilling. They are all team players who understand and practice the kind of esprit de corps that insures that no accomplishment is beyond their possibilities.

"And what else they have is something that in these times is even less common. They all have the sense that they are working on something for the greater good. That rather old-fashioned idea and ideal that by doing all they can to make their company the best it can be they are doing the right thing for themselves as well.

"It is people like this who will insure that this company will survive, prosper, and make an even bigger name for itself as we approach the challenges of the changes that are coming. I am thoroughly proud of each one of them, and the privilege of my association with them is the underlying reason that I can say that I do have the best job in the world."

Teresa Overbey in the business services marketing group reported in early 1994 that a customer had asked her "if niceness was a prerequisite to work at RTC." In a deregulated, competitive environment, it certainly helps, she concluded.

Another sign of a good company is one that earns repeat business. This is particularly important when the repeat customer is one of your largest. And so it was with much fanfare that Phil Germond announced in November 1993 that Roseville Telephone was a prime contender for the "BIG ONE," another large contract from Kaiser-Permanente. The large HMO was building a new hospital in Roseville and Germond hoped Roseville Telephone would win the contract again, as it had done in 1980 and 1987. It would be several months later when Kaiser's decision would be announced. In the April 1994 *Line Chatter*, Germond reported a victory under the headline, "RTC HITS A GRAND SLAM!!!"

"On March 9, shortly after 1 p.m., Colleen Avery received a telephone call, 'I have the signed contracts and I will deliver them to you shortly.' The voice on the line was that of Ron Duran with Kaiser-Permanente. A few moments before 3 p.m., Ron handed Colleen the contracts, signed, sealed, and delivered. This consummated and brought to a close Roseville Telephone Company's negotiations for a $2.6 million telecommunications system that began over a year ago for their new hospital/medical office building being constructed at Douglas Boulevard and Rocky Ridge and a system upgrade at their Riverside facility."

Germond went on to thank all the various departments and employees for their help in securing the contract. And in the spirit of the 1990s, Germond added:

"If anyone thought that we weren't in a competitive environment, let me assure you that any time a $2.6 million deal is in the works, there are others who are interested. We treated this as a very competitive situation until 3 p.m. on March 9. Our feeling is that it isn't a done deal until the ink is drying on the paper."

The company was also faring well in the competitive alarm monitoring business. Formally established in 1988 after an earlier unsuccessful attempt in the alarm business itself, alarm monitoring has grown into a profitable, stand-alone business. The division, under the direction of Dick Bell and

*Phil Germond is manager of the products and services department.*

*Roseville Telephone's alarm monitoring division serves customers nationwide.*

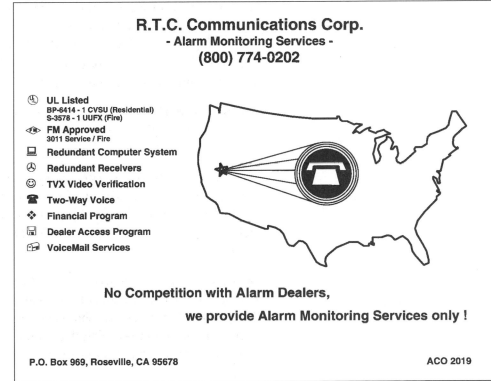

**R.T.C. Communications Corp.**
- Alarm Monitoring Services -
**(800) 774-0202**

**UL Listed**
BP-6414 - 1 CVSU (Residential)
S-3578 - 1 UUFX (Fire)

**FM Approved**
3011 Service / Fire

**Redundant Computer System**

**Redundant Receivers**

**TVX Video Verification**

**Two-Way Voice**

**Financial Program**

**Dealer Access Program**

**VoiceMail Services**

**No Competition with Alarm Dealers,**

**we provide Alarm Monitoring Services only !**

P.O. Box 969, Roseville, CA 95678          ACO 2019

Tim Sproul, had contracts with 165 alarm dealers and monitored more than 18,000 accounts throughout the United states at year-end 1994. The growing interest in alarm monitoring activities earned a front-page slot in every *Line Chatter*, beginning in September 1991. New account activity joined "access lines" as an important company statistic charted and published each month.

Tim Sproul, manager of alarm monitoring services, generated good publicity for the company in late 1994 when he was awarded the first Parker Maurie Memorial Award by the Sacramento Area Alarm Association. Sproul was recognized for his efforts and support of the association members and the alarm industry as a whole.

The sales and service of newly-developed communications technologies represents another line of unregulated business for the company. For example, Roseville Telephone has a Sacramento-area license to market PictureTel video conferencing systems. This system allows users to conduct meetings "attended" by people from different locations. They are connected over ISDN telephone lines plugged into video monitors. Participants can see and talk to each other as if in a meeting. The savings in travel expenses and time justifies the cost of the equipment. The extension of this technology, bringing conferencing to desktop computer monitors, is already catching on in high-tech circles.

Roseville Telephone's continual stream of technological achievements has earned the admiration of even the biggest players in telecommunications. T.Alec Edge, national sales director of AT&T Network Systems, visited Roseville Telephone in March 1994 and later sent Brian Strom a thank you letter:

"Last week's visit with you, Bob, and Al and the tour of Roseville's new facility further convinced me that your company is the premier local exchange company in the country. The tour of your central offices and outside plant last year had clearly shown Roseville's technology prowess and strategic focus. I cannot think of any one company better poised to meet the challenges of the emerging markets in the coming years.

"I've been in the telecommunications business for 35 years, and have always believed that technology is only one element of a successful company. The pride displayed by your employees firmly demonstrates the other element for success."

## WIRELESS: THE FUTURE IS NOW

In 1994, the management team — led by Brian Strom and Michael Campbell — worked hard investigating opportunities important for the future of Roseville Telephone. A major effort was put forth to investigate and analyze the prospects for an upcoming wireless communications service called PCS, or personal communications services.

PCS is the next generation of wireless communications and has been defined as "a family of communications services that allows digital communications, independent of location." It is intended to help meet society's growing demand for "on-the-go" communications. PCS devices will include small, lightweight, multi-functional portable phones, portable fax and other imaging devices and new types of multi-channel cordless phones, and advanced paging devices with two-way data capabilities. These devices should significantly improve the flexibility and functionality of all telecommunications networks and will make possible the availability of communications anytime, anywhere to anyone.

It's anticipated that PCS will bring wireless communications to the mass market through lower-priced equipment and service charges. PCS signals are transmitted along "microcells," similar to conventional cellular transmitters, but smaller and more closely spaced. This means PCS devices can be less powerful and therefore are expected to cost less than current cellular devices. PCS is designed for walk-around use and more local mobile use.

Consider the analogy of a high-powered sports car compared to an economy-sized car. Cellular is akin to the sports car, built to be easily capable of speeding 160 mph. PCS is analogous to the economy car built with functionality in mind, to carry passengers at average speeds. While the economy car does not have the capabilities of the sports car, it also costs a lot less. And so will PCS. Current cellular communications abilities outstrip the average person's requirements.

Less than 10 percent of us now have cellular phones. Cost is the main reason for the relatively low penetration of cellular. PCS should be much more affordable.

PCS will be more versatile than cellular, too, because it will be fully digital from the outset. PCS is designed for sending data as well as voice. Most current cellular networks are based on older analog-based radio technologies.

Under the auspices of the Federal Communications Commission (FCC), auctions for PCS licenses were under way in late 1994 and 1995 as companies vied to win the rights to provide PCS in Major Trading Areas (MTAs) and Business Trading Areas (BTAs). Telecommunications companies throughout America — including telephone companies, cable companies and others — have committed billions of dollars in their quest to eventually garner a share of the PCS business.

Roseville Telephone announced on in mid-1994 that it was exploring the idea of forming a partnership to evaluate the prospects of entry into PCS. Roseville Telephone and prospective partners conducted feasibility studies to operate a PCS network in the geographical region including Central California and Western Washington. They were also talking to other substantial communications companies about joining in the venture.

"If our partnership group is successful in acquiring the licenses we desire, we anticipate it would take about two years before we 'turn up' the PCS network," said Brian Strom.

Strom projected that the initial capital requirements for PCS would approximate $100 million in the California areas involved and another $75 million in Western Washington. The partners would share the cost according to their eventual percentages.

Although Roseville Telephone's role in PCS is not determined as this is written, the company's position has always been that it should be able to offer customers all telecommunications services when they become available. And as competition heats up in the traditional wireline telephone business, the ability to offer PCS represents an opportunity for Roseville Telephone to replace some of the revenue that the traditional telephone business may not provide in the future.

# Employees Create And Share The Success

· · · · · · · · · · · · · · · · · · · · · · ·

AFTER DOYLE TOOK OVER, AN EMPLOYEE-DRIVEN COMPANY

*"My first dividend check was enough to buy an all-day sucker. Later on the dividend became big enough for me to buy a tank of gas. Now I could make a mortgage payment with it."*
—Betty Dosher, retired operator

Employee involvement is a popular buzzword in management circles, but creating a true working partnership between management and employees remains an elusive goal at most large companies. Although there have been strides made in improving management/employee relations over the years, at most companies the "us vs. them" attitude still prevails.

On the other hand, employee relations have been a strength at Roseville Telephone since the day Bob Doyle walked in the door on Aug. 15, 1953. His personal style — an easy rapport with fellow employees, a straightforward manner, a sense of fair play and humor — made him immediately popular with employees.

"When Bob started, I kind of felt sorry for him," said Carl Andree, who joined the company two weeks after Bob Doyle. "He was low-key, just learning. He struck me as a real nice person, but other than that, he was just a coin collector. He didn't act like he was the president's son or anything."

"The atmosphere was entirely different with Bob than it was with the Hanisches," added Bernice Moser, an operator at the time. "Bob was always very curious about what was going on. He just set himself busy getting all the information he could from everybody. He was interested in you and it made us feel pretty good."

Marjie Albrecht, a long-time employee who died in September 1994, remembered that Bob would bring in hamburgers with onions to give to the women in the business office.

"I may have done that once, but it wasn't a regular thing," Doyle commented on Albrecht's recollection. "We did have doughnuts and coffee, though."

From the outset of his presidency, Bob Doyle was the employees' top supporter in receiving necessary fringe benefits such as pension, disability, health and life insurance plans. His vow to treat employees well was fulfilled throughout the

ROSEVILLE TELEPHONE COMPANY

ROSEVILLE, CALIFORNIA

July 1, 1955

To Our Employees:

For some time the Company has given careful consideration and study to the adoption of a Pension Plan that will help you attain a measure of security and financial independence after you have retired from active service with our organization.

We have arranged with The Travelers Insurance Company for the purchase of a Group Annuity Contract which became effective July 1, 1955, covering regular employees and designed to supplement the benefits payable under the Federal Social Security Act. The Company will bear the entire cost of the Plan. While this involves the expenditure of a considerable sum of money, we feel that the expense is fully justified by the benefits that will accrue to you.

The amount of pension that you will receive is based on your length of service with the Company and your basic annual earnings while included in the Plan. As a guide in estimating your monthly retirement income, an illustrative chart is included on the last pages of the booklet.

If you have any questions about the Plan after reading the booklet, we shall be glad to discuss them with you so that you will fully understand its advantages.

ROBERT L. DOYLE
President-Manager

*The first fringe benefit, a pension plan, was introduced in July 1955, more than 40 years after Roseville Telephone was founded.*

years by a consistent upgrading of wages and benefits. He promised his employees better wages, fringes and working conditions, and he delivered on his promises.

Doyle's approach to compensation has been straightforward. Through the years Roseville has followed the lead of Pacific Telephone. When Pacific adjusted its compensation for the many classifications in its sprawling enterprise, Roseville would follow suit. After all, the job classifications were the same or very similar. Since Pacific Telephone determined its compensation packages through collective bargaining with the various unions representing its workers, Roseville Telephone employees in effect received the benefits of union representation without being members. Doyle made sure Roseville's compensation packages were the equal of Pacific's Sacramento-area employees. This formula has worked well.

Under Doyle, however, the positive management/employee environment at Roseville Telephone has a lot to do with non-financial issues. In Doyle's view, the employees do not just work at the company — they are the company. And they do not simply do what is asked of them … they usually are the ones who come up with the new ideas and/or better ways of doing something. This goes back to the earliest days of Doyle's presidency.

"As I've said, I hire people smarter than me and expect them to do the job," Doyle said. "I may not know a hell of a lot about telephones, but I do know about hiring people."

It has been this willingness to allow employees to express their ideas that has engendered fierce loyalty to Doyle and Roseville Telephone. Doyle learned a long time ago that for most people, wages are not necessarily the most important component of job satisfaction. Respect from their peers and superiors is equally as important. If they are doing a good job and the company is doing well, the money side will take care of itself.

Roseville Telephone has been an employee-driven company for four decades. As Doyle will attest, his role has been to let those under him have the leeway to test their ideas. "I've always had an open door for employees to give me their ideas. More often than not, I'd say let's try it."

That willingness to allow employees to succeed — and sometimes fail — developed unusual employee loyalty.

"You could always talk to Bob and tell him what you wanted to do," said Gladys (Ellis) Ross, the long-time chief operator. "He listened. That was one characteristic we all loved about him. He listened."

Doyle's commitment to employees has been unfailing. After those first few years, when the company's primary focus was on catching up, Doyle made every effort to provide employees with excellent equipment, plant and working conditions. Doyle abhors turnover. It doesn't make sense to him to invest in extensive employee training only to let another company reap the benefits. A better strategy is to hire good people and keep them.

Roseville Telephone has always been a company where the workload has been heavy. Emerson Gunning remembered what he told his installation crew in the early 1960s: "I told those who worked under me that it's job security to be a little short of people. You work a little harder maybe, but you have your job. If you hire more people than you really need, eventually you'll have to let one go. On the other hand, it feels good to say to an employee, 'You're going to have a few more dollars in your check next week,' because he had to work overtime. That beats saying, 'There's not enough work so we're not going to need you any

1. Marketing Manager and Staff
2. Outside Plant Engineering Staff
3. Customer Services Facilities Administration
4. Revenue Accounting Supervisor and Staff
5. Construction Supervisor and Secretary
6. Employment Counselor and Assistant

*Since 1960, when Roseville Telephone published its first formal annual report, all employees photos have been included in each year's report. This is an example from the 1983 report.*

more.' That's not a happy thing, and I'm proud to say in my 20 years at the company we never had a layoff."

Another piece of Doyle's strategy of fostering employee fulfillment and satisfaction was for them to become stockholders. He preached, cajoled, insinuated ... and did just about anything he could think of to impress upon employees that they should become stockholders. Payroll deduction for stock purchases has been available during every offering since the second one in 1957. And for 30 years Doyle kept lists of employees who wanted shares so that when stock came in, he could re-sell shares to them. Later on, the savings plan and 401-k plans enabled employees to purchase telephone stock with the company matching 50 cents on the dollar. With these opportunities to purchase stock, employee-investors have been able to build considerable holdings.

"My pitch was the same," Doyle recalled. "I told the employees if they didn't have the money in their pockets in the first place, they wouldn't even miss it. I also said that this company would grow and that I felt their investment would be worth a lot more over time."

The annual report is another manifestation of the company's high regard for its employees. Each one since the first one in 1960 has included photos of all employees, not only the officers and directors.

"Most annual reports picture a group of big, old men sitting there at the table, you know, the president and the other directors," Doyle said. "Yes, we have photos of our five directors, all local people, but we also have photos of every employee. Just about all of them are shareholders and they have relatives who are shareholders, too. It makes them feel good to say, 'That's my nephew there, or there's my daughter's picture.' And employees keep the reports. It's a kick to see what they looked like 10 or 20 years ago. Other companies don't go to the expense and effort, but we think it's worthwhile. It is the best public relations thing that I can think of."

Even though Doyle cannot today say he knows every employee, as he did in years past, he's every bit as proud of employees in the 1990s as he was in the early years.

"I love to take visitors through our offices," Doyle said. "Sure, I tell them about how sophisticated our equipment is, but most of all I tell them to observe the employees. You can buy the greatest of equipment in the world, but if you don't have good employees, it ain't going to work. Or you could buy cheap equipment, but even if you've got good employees, that's not going to work either. If you have both good employees and good equipment — which we have — then you've got it. Our employees are so enthusiastic you think they own the place, and they do own a lot of it.

"We're especially proud that here we do most everything ourselves. We engineer our own equipment, install it, and maintain it. In other words, we're a complete telephone company. Most telephone companies, even the independents, depend on somebody else to do their work. It's that ability to control our own destiny that makes employees proud of their company. They know management has confidence in them. You tell them they can do it, and if you tell somebody they can do it, they can do it.

"Even so, we're not good enough yet. We have to get better, and that's the secret. Any time you think that your company is OK, you're on the downhill grade because it's never OK. You can always do better and this is what you have to instill in your people."

*Tommy Apostolos, second from right, and his construction crew in the early 1960s. From the left are Ed Gardetto, Wayne Hitchcock and next to Apostolos, Dick Kimball.*

Courtesy of John Apostolos

## EARLY EMPLOYEES BUILD FOUNDATION, TRAIN SUCCESSORS

Immediately upon joining Roseville Telephone, Bob Doyle recognized that the company faced a shortage of telephone operating expertise. While David and Walter Hanisch were extremely knowledgeable about the pre-dial telephone equipment and systems, the dial system, with its highly mechanized step-by-step switching technology, was much more complex.

Ned Kindelt, now retired, was one of the many long-time employees whose "can do" attitude was instrumental in the company's success.

Doyle's recognition of the lack of central office expertise led to the early hiring of Emerson Gunning from Mare Island Naval Base. Gunning, along with the other early hires, including Page Ellis, Fred Spring, Tom Trimble and Mark Shull, joined by Doc Harrington who had been hired earlier, formed a nucleus to build upon in the early years. Other experienced telephone people joined the company during the 1950s, including Bob Sharples, Ned Kindelt and Walter Gordon. In the early 1960s, Warren Tinker, George Minasian, Leon Bower, Rulon Blackburn and John Jones came aboard, adding even more expertise to the fast-growing company.

Roseville Telephone, although small and unsophisticated in those years, was an attractive option for a certain type of telephone worker. Since the industry was heavily unionized, compensation levels at the various telephone companies were relatively equivalent. What mattered most to the employees was the "corporate culture," the management's relationship with employees and the outlook for the individual company. Another consideration was the location. Weighing these factors, Roseville Telephone was a good place to work for the career telephone person.

Ned Kindelt spent nearly four years working for General Telephone in Southern California before joining Roseville Telephone in 1957.

"I started in the Ocean Park office, but I ended up working out of all their offices down there," Kindelt said. "I was part of a work group that traveled to General's central offices, doing maintenance and other routine work on the switching equipment. It was like the Army, and seniority counted in determining schedules. As a low man on the totem pole, I got the worst shifts. Also, it was a hard job because you would work at one location for three or four months, then you'd go to another for a few more months. That went on for about a year before I went back to my own central office."

Working conditions such as Kindelt's enabled Roseville to attract experienced people. Another help was an agreement between Pacific Telephone and General Telephone during those years that was designed to minimize employees jumping from one company to the other. The two telephone giants agreed not to hire each other's employees for a minimum of six months after the employee left.

Jens Jensen, another ex-General Telephone employee, explained how this agreement resulted in his coming to Roseville Telephone.

"It was in 1968 and another fellow and I left General Telephone in Southern California. First, our wives moved up here to find jobs ahead of time. Then we moved up with the idea of working for Pacific Telephone," Jensen explained. "Unbeknownst to us, Pacific and General apparently had an agreement that you couldn't quit one company and join the other until you had been out of that first company for a six-month period. So I went to an employment agency to check what I could pick up for six months to get my waiting period out of the way. It was then I heard that Walter Gordon at a small independent telephone company in Roseville might be hiring. My friend and I both applied, but I got the job as a switch man in the central office."

Immediately, Jensen recognized the value of working at a smaller company vs. a large one. "The difference here was that it was small so that everyone knew each other and everyone helped each other. Employees worked together better than at General where you maybe worked with the people in your office real well, but when you got into the other satellite offices, you'd realize it wasn't one company, but a lot of little companies."

Although virtually all the earliest experienced employees hired by Doyle were eager to share their knowledge, Fred Spring stood out as a teacher. His knowledge of construction techniques was legend and he excelled at sharing his expertise with the younger employees.

Merle Ruggles joined the company in 1956 and for many years headed up the purchasing department.

"He really enjoyed being a teacher," said Ed Gardetto of Spring. "He showed us the easy way to do things up on the pole, how to tie those knots up there and move around. We were doing things the hard way. And Fred would help anyone. I remember his going to Lincoln to help the farmers on their lines, both after work and on weekends. He just loved telephone work."

Spring's speciality was dynamiting. "Fred could set that dynamite and know exactly where the dirt and rock would land," remembered Doyle. "He was an artist, really, when it came to construction of any kind."

Another outstanding teacher was Tom Trimble, another retired Pacific employee. His speciality was splicing, the meticulous task of ensuring that the thousands of wire strands coursing through the company's cable network went to the proper places. He taught the company's young hires how to manage the river of wires that fanned throughout the growing underground and overhead system.

Although the tenures of Spring, Trimble and Harrington were all short — all three died in 1959 — their contributions were large. They helped lay the foundation of expertise upon which the company grew.

## COMPANY HELPS EMPLOYEES ACQUIRE WEALTH

Aside from the competitive wages and good working conditions, perhaps the most important benefit Roseville Telephone bestowed upon its employees was the opportunity to acquire shares in the company. Through payroll deduction and the savings and 401-k retirement plans, participating employees have acquired significant stakes over time. Numerous long-time employees retired with sizable nest eggs, substantial enough to enjoy their retirement years without money worries.

Mark Shull was the company's first "financial man," joining Roseville Telephone in early 1957 after working for a small telephone company in Kansas.

Bob Doyle has always believed that an employee who also was an owner would be a better employee. "When you own the place, you look after the little things," he said. "You care and it shows. We've been fortunate that most of our employees have bought stock. Hell, we've made it available, that's for sure, and with the company matching 50 cents on the dollar, you don't have to be too bright to figure out it's a good deal."

Since the second stock sale in 1957, new shares have been allotted for employee payroll deduction plans. In 1967, the company established its savings plan, which allowed employees to put up to 6 percent of their salary into purchasing the company's common stock. And the company would contribute 50 cents for each employee dollar.

In 1983, the 401-k retirement plan was introduced. Under the 401-k plan, employees could contribute up to 10 percent of their pre-tax wages to the plan. Again, the company matches this 50 cents on the dollar. Although there is a federally-mandated ceiling on contributions in a year, the 401-k plan has enabled participants to accumulate a considerable number of shares over time. The opportunity to acquire shares, along with price appreciation and numerous stock dividends, created substantial wealth for quite a few lucky retirees. Walter Gordon, who retired in 1994 at age 55, was one of those fortunate employees who bought stock early and kept buying it through the years.

"I can remember when I bought two shares for $12 each in 1958 shortly after I came to the company," Gordon said. "The quarterly dividend was 15 cents a share so my first dividend check was for 30 cents. My wife said, 'Why in the world did you buy that? What are you going to do with 30 cents? It's worthless. You might as well throw that check away.'

"I told her, 'It's the company I work for and if they gave me a job, I should be willing to invest in the company,'" Gordon recalled. "And the longer I worked here, the more I saw it was a good company with good potential. I feel if you don't believe enough in your company to invest in it, you're working for the wrong company."

When Gordon received raises, he'd take half the raise and buy more shares. When the savings plan started, he reinvested a portion of his raises into increased plan contributions. He continually bought shares. "I figured if I never saw the money, I'd never miss it."

Doyle would tell young employees, "If you eat hamburgers today, you'll be able to eat steak tomorrow." Employees couldn't help but get the message.

Betty Dosher bought her first 10 shares in 1958 and had to spread the payment over two paydays. From then on, she would buy one or two shares each payday in the early years and then participated in the savings plan when it became available. This "tortoise" approach to investing enabled her to build a healthy stake when she retired in March 1985.

"My first dividend check was enough to buy an all-day sucker," she said. "Later on the dividend became big enough for me to buy a tank of gas. Now I could make a mortgage payment with it."

Bernice Moser, another retired operator, said she bought her first shares "because it was the thing to do. I really didn't know much about it, but Bob Doyle said it would grow over time and help supplement our retirement. When I came in 1952, the company didn't have a retirement plan at all."

Ned Kindelt's portfolio of company stock allowed him to retire early. He credited his heavy participation in the savings and 401-k plans for his good fortune.

*Long-time operator Betty Dosher.*

"Actually, I'd say it's not good fortune, but just smart investing. When someone will give me 50 cents on the dollar, I can't turn that down," said Kindelt. "When I became computer-familiar, I did some projections about my retirement situation and it just boggled my mind. I could see it wouldn't be too many years ahead before I could retire. In my first projections in the early '80s, I calculated I'd have to work until age 62. But the stock did so well, I was able to retire at 59."

Most employees took advantage of the opportunity to buy shares. Many wish they had bought more shares earlier in their career when stock was readily available.

"When you're young and raising a family, it was tough to buy a lot of shares," said Dennis Cordeiro, an employee since 1973. "Even today when I see Bob Doyle I say to him, 'Go ahead, Bob, kick me in the butt. I deserve it for not buying shares 20 years ago.'"

Younger employees have benefited greatly from participating in the savings and 401-k plans. Debbie Uribe, who manages the company's alarm monitoring center, knows that when she retires she'll own a sizable block of shares.

"Most friends my age don't have a significant savings or retirement fund, but because of the telephone company, I have a nice nest egg that's growing all the time," Uribe said. "And I still have a good 20 years to go at least, so it's fantastic. I was naive about the stock at the beginning, but I learned as I got older what a good deal it is."

"We constantly encourage our employees to get involved," Doyle said. "We tell them to get some, even if it's five shares. It's nice to say that you own part of the company you work for. We keep pounding this into people."

Not so subtle hints appeared routinely in the *Line Chatter*. In the September 1962 edition, for example, there was a short item about payroll deduction. "We presently have 655 shares on the present payroll stock offering. This is a favorable increase over the last subscription and we are happy to see employees taking advantage of this excellent means of investment." Another regular *Line Chatter* reminder went like this: "This would be a good opportunity to increase your present holdings." That same sentence appeared in scores of *Line Chatters*.

Employees who didn't purchase shares have only themselves to blame. Those who did invest in their own company, however, are eternally grateful to the company and Bob Doyle. One retired operator, Dorothea Jacobs, was particularly effusive in her praise.

"As far as I'm concerned there are two gods in the world," she said at a gathering of the retired operators. "One is God and the other is Bob Doyle. He has made me rich!" "Rich" may be a relative term, but Jacobs' share ownership has allowed her to live comfortably in retirement. Many retired people are not so fortunate.

Doyle, too, is delighted with the success of the savings and 401-k plans.

"Yeah, it's amazing what that stock has done, but who could you do it better for than your own employees. It's nice when retirees come in and say to me, 'Doyle, I'm sure glad I've got telephone stock.' It makes you feel good."

Since 1967, when the savings plan was established, it has become huge. At the close of 1994, the savings plan owned 10 percent of the company's shares worth in excess of $30 million. "And the savings plan doesn't count what the employees own outside of the plan, nor does it account for the retirees' stock either," Doyle is quick to point out. "One thing about our employees, once they buy, they never sell. Our stock is in good hands."

## BENEFITS GROW THROUGH THE YEARS

Employee benefits did not exist at Roseville Telephone during the first 40 years. It wasn't until July 1, 1955, more than a year after Bob Doyle became president, that the first pension plan was introduced. In a letter to employees, Doyle said, "Adoption of a pension plan ... will help you maintain a measure of security and financial independence after you have retired from active service with our organization."

Doyle was proud that the company paid the entire cost of the pension plan. This plan, which was administered by The Travelers Insurance Company, amounted to $8,388 in 1956. It would be nearly a decade before any employee eligible for a pension retired.

The company added fringe benefits as it could afford them. In 1958, the first group health plan was introduced. Doyle's letter to employees said:

"The company is making this plan available and paying the total employee cost in the hope that you will have a feeling of security and initiative to continue as an employee of the Roseville Telephone Company.

"Although it is our hope that none of our employees will have the misfortune to have accidents or become sick, we feel that this plan will be invaluable to them if and when it is needed."

A succession of new and improved fringe benefit packages were given employees over the years. By 1973, the total amount spent on fringe benefits had climbed to $548,700, or $2,888 per employee.

In January 1981, a letter in the *Line Chatter* expressed the genuine sincerity the employees feel for their leadership:

"We, the employees of Roseville Telephone Company, would like to take this opportunity to thank Mr. Robert L. Doyle and the Board of Directors for all of the generous benefits we have received this year. Having a 2 1/2 day holiday for Christmas is just really fantastic and we really appreciate that gift very much. It's a great Christmas bonus. And the delicious Christmas dinner/dance was lots of fun (steaks

*Merry Lou Pratt was in charge of personnel for many years before retiring in 1991. She is flanked by Carol Arcuri, left, and Susan Perkins.*

were great). This on top of all of the increased benefits and improvements made to the 'Company Practices' have made Roseville Telephone Company a very good company to work for.

"We all have you to thank Mr. Doyle, when we have to take the kids to the dentist and the company insurance picks up most of the bill, or the kids are sick and we have to take them to Kaiser, or FHP, or Roseville Community, or the wife needs new glasses, or one of us retires and we've got that little bit extra from the change in the Social Security-retirement improvements, or when our supervisor picked up some good tips on improving office management at the managers training seminar, or any of the other improvements that we have received this past year. We thank you very much, Mr. Doyle, and we wish you and all of your family a very Merry Christmas and Happy New Year."

Today's Roseville Telephone employee is fortunate to receive a package of fringe benefits the equal of any large corporation. In addition, employees enjoy some benefits that may not be common elsewhere.

For example, employees receive four Excused Work Days (EWD) per year that enable them to take care of personal errands and matters that come up during the course of a year. Moreover, EWDs can be taken in hourly increments, a great help for working parents who are juggling family and work responsibilities. In addition, employees receive paid time off for such necessary occurrences as jury duty, witness duty, voting time and school visits. Bereavement leave can be up to five days.

The company sometimes conducts self-help programs, including smoking cessation classes, and in certain instances the company will help pay for outside classes that relate to an employee's job. Another benefit unique to telephone companies is what's termed "Telephone Concession Services." Roseville Telephone employees receive a 50 percent discount off the monthly basic service charge if they live in the company's service territory. Employees living outside the territory receive a rebate on a portion of their telephone company's basic fees.

Another uncommon benefit is reimbursement for unused, accrued sick leave of more than 1,040 hours, after which the employee may earn $5 per unused hour. As a final fringe, retiring employees receive a bonus check totaling $25 for each year of service to the company.

Other benefits of working at Roseville Telephone are not so obvious, but very real. Dick Bell, manager of purchasing, describes these:

"Under Bob Doyle, the employees have always had the best and safest equipment to work with," said Bell, who joined the company in 1971 as a cable splicer. "That means a great deal to those employees working in the outside plant, in particular, where the work can be strenuous and dangerous.

"At our company, the equipment is tested first by those employees who are going to end up being the users. They are the ones to ask the questions and they determine if the equipment is good or not," he added. "It's not like at my former employer where a management committee somewhere selects the equipment to be used in the field even though they've never done the work. As the company's purchasing agent, I tell suppliers to give samples or demonstrations of what they're trying to sell to the employees themselves. If they believe it's worth buying, then we'll likely get it."

A.A. "Al" Johnson, the chief operating officer, sums up why employees find their jobs at Roseville Telephone rewarding:

"The employees are well taken care of," Johnson said. "You won't find a company anyplace where the employees have our wage structure, the employee benefits we have and so forth. We've got people who are retiring and walking away with nearly a million dollars in their pockets. And often these were local kids who were hired off the street without an education other than high school maybe. They just grew up with the company. They have an excellent pension, too. No doubt, the exceptional employee package has been a strong motivator for our employees."

## TRAINING, TRAINING AND MORE TRAINING

For an executive who succeeded without management training, Bob Doyle never had qualms about his employees receiving as much training as they felt was necessary.

"We're constantly sending employees to classes because what a person is doing today might be obsolete in a couple of years," Doyle explained. "Unless the employee keeps up on what's going on technically, you're behind the eight ball.

"The supervisor doesn't necessarily need to go to these schools, but he or she sees that the ones doing the technical work go," he added. "In other words, I never go to a seminar. Why should I go to a seminar? I'm wasting the company's money. I'd go to a seminar and sit there with my mouth open wondering what the hell they're talking about. The persons that should be at that seminar are the ones you've just hired, really. When they come back, give 'em a pat on the back, and let 'em go ahead and do it."

In the *Line Chatter* reports, the references to training sessions are many. In a technical industry that is rapidly evolving, constant training is a must. Otherwise, as Doyle indicated, you fall behind.

"In the early days of electronic switching, the training programs were sometimes up to nine months long," said Al Johnson. "They sent people back to Chicago, and they'd come home every six weeks or so. This situation was not

*Sandy Frazer, right, has been Al Johnson's secretary for years.*

unique to Roseville Telephone. Any company getting into the electronic age of switching equipment faced similar grueling training periods. Electronic switching was a completely new concept.

"Today there are places where people can get that same type of education, but years ago, the only place that knowledge was available was from the manufacturer of the equipment," Johnson added. "You couldn't go to Harvard or Yale or Berkeley or Sierra College. But you had to have that knowledge, because if you're going to invest a million dollars in the equipment, you have to have somebody to take care of it and there's no way they could learn it any other place."

Jens Jensen is amazed at all the training he's received in his nearly 30 years with the company.

"I've had a lot of training, probably more than most people. There wasn't so much in the central office, but when I got outside into splicing, being as I had had some switch room and some electronics experience, it opened me up for schools for outside plant that maybe other people couldn't qualify for or wouldn't have understood as easily," Jensen said. "I have also had some extremely talented people working with me. John Jones, for one, he's the head of our splicing department, is a very capable electronics person. He knows telephone, electronics, equipment. I worked with him closely for about five years and learned a vast amount. Then I started going to outside plant schools, some digital carrier schools, fiber schools, cable schools and such. I'd estimate I've spent a full year, at least 52 weeks, in schools, seminars and group meetings. The company has invested a lot in its employees and I think that's why we're ahead of other telephone companies in so many departments."

Training hasn't been limited to any one department in the company. As new, more sophisticated equipment was installed, training inevitably followed. Retired operator Bernice Moser underwent hundreds of hours of training and in turn passed along her knowledge to other operators.

"There were always new things to learn from the time I came in 1952," Moser said. "Soon after I came we went to dial. Then when we moved upstairs in 1959, we had a new switchboard and other new equipment to track toll calls, things like that. It seemed like every year there was something new to learn because the technology was changing all the time."

In 1981, the operators "moved downstairs" when the operator and information functions were computerized. It was called TRS-D, for "Traffic Room System-Digital." The old cord board operator stations were replaced by computer terminals and keyboards. It was the end of an era. For long-time operators such as Moser and Betty Dosher, the retirement of familiar equipment and old ways of doing things brought a realization that it was time for youth to be served.

Every department, from the executive office to the mailroom, participated in the constant march of technology. In 1976, executive secretary Virginia Amick led the effort to introduce "word processing" to Roseville Telephone. In data processing, Chuck Spooner and his crew marveled at the new-fangled "PC." The company's first personal computers, the IBM PC-XTs, were hailed as incredible aids in productivity. After that, PCs gave way to microcomputers and microprocessors, which even later were joined together in "LANs," or Local Area Networks. The company's mainframe computers were upgraded in capacity and speed to handle the increasing size and sophistication of the customer base. Later, redundancy was incorporated into the system to make them "fail-safe" systems.

Fiber optics, cable pressurization, computer-aided mapping — these are only a few of the innovations introduced to employees through the years. And all required extensive training to make them effective.

In the 1980s, when the deregulated environment came to telephone companies across the land, the excellent training standards at Roseville Telephone paid off in enhanced revenue. When the company competed for large system contracts, whether for lease or sale, its reputation for training frequently made the difference, even though competitors may have come in with lower bids. Well-planned and coordinated presentations by teams of company personnel consistently were able to win large system sales. Decisions typically were made weighing key factors including equipment, service and training. Training continues to be a long suit of the company.

Few companies have embraced computerization as avidly as Roseville Telephone, and no department has been untouched. As one project to enhance productivity is ending, another one is already under way. Progress has been non-stop. This environment of continuous upgrading has kept employees motivated and challenged. It's never dull.

"You can't stand still in this business," Doyle is fond of saying, "because you'll be obsolete in no time."

Ongoing in-house training and the availability of paid outside schooling are also important factors in retaining key employees.

"Bob helped the young kids who joined the company when he initiated the program where you could go to a college or junior college and get further training at company expense as long as it was job-oriented," said Bernice Moser. "He took young, promising employees and made sure they were trained. If training hadn't been important to him, we would have had to have gone outside of the company to get them. Training helps develop loyalty, too, because you feel that if the company has spent all this money on you, you should give back to the company all you've got."

## UNIONIZING EFFORTS UNSUCCESSFUL

Through the years there have been several efforts to unionize workers at Roseville Telephone. All were unsuccessful. The reasons unions haven't succeeded in gaining a foothold are easily explained.

The major telephone workers' union, the giant Communications Workers of America (originally the National Federation of Telephone Workers), didn't gain nationwide strength until the late 1940s and 1950s. In the 1940s, Roseville Telephone was a small, provincial company with few employees other than the operators. The union was concentrating on the giant Bell companies. And as has been mentioned, the operators under chief operator Gladys (Ellis) Ross were quite happy to have one of the few decent jobs in Roseville available for women. It's unlikely that any of them would have sought union representation. And if Gladys had caught wind of any union movement, there would have been hell to pay.

Gladys was beloved by her operators, but she was a company woman through and through. She was loyal to Walter Hanisch and then to Bob Doyle after he became the manager. There is no evidence, however, that any company employee was ever discriminated against for union activities during this period or any other.

In the 1950s and 1960s, however, the threat of union activity was heightened, for a couple of reasons. After decades of slow growth, Roseville Telephone was beginning to grow rapidly. As Bob Doyle sold stock and borrowed to invest in expanding plant and equipment, he was also hiring new employees, many of whom had worked for Bell companies or larger independents. These experienced telephone employees were accustomed to union representation.

It was Doyle's intelligent approach to employee relations that minimized the opportunities union representation had at Roseville Telephone. His promise to his first employees were "... the pay might not be great right now, but trust me, because later on when we build this into a hell of a phone company, I'll take care of myself and I'll take care of you, too." This was no empty promise.

In the minutes of board meetings throughout the years, the board used the pay schedules at Pacific Telephone as a guideline. If management pay was scheduled to rise 7 percent at Pacific on a certain date, invariably Roseville Telephone's board would decide to match or beat that increase in every situation. The same held for hourly workers. Their pay increases were tied to increases won by the unionized workers at the Pacific company. This compensation-matching strategy kept Roseville's employees on a par with their Bell counterparts from the early Bob Doyle years. In truth, though, Roseville's employees had it even better because they didn't have to pony up union dues. This meant Roseville's "equal pay and benefits" strategy was even better than equal. Who could argue with that?

Of course, unionism and worker representation encompass more than just compensation. Unions also protect members from undue harassment from superiors and historically have been successful in opening up dialogue between management and employees. Today this is called "communication," and even excellent pay and benefits don't guarantee there is good communication at a company, even Roseville Telephone.

One of the more active employees in pushing for improved communication between employees and management was Jens Jensen. Having worked as a frame man, central office installer and maintenance technician for General Telephone in Southern California for almost three years before joining Roseville Telephone in the fall of 1968, Jensen was accustomed to a union shop and was not afraid to speak up if he felt something was wrong. In a company that treated its employees paternalistically, Jensen represented a new wrinkle.

He was viewed with some suspicion at the time. He recalls his first few years at Roseville Telephone.

Director of Human Resources, Barbara Nussbaum, left, and Controller, Laurel Dismukes, are two of the company's key personnel.

"My observations were not pay- or benefits-related. We always were treated well in that regard. But I saw some issues I felt needed to be addressed," Jensen explained. "My main objective in my unionizing efforts was to open up some lines of communications."

Jensen recalls that his fellow workers were not wholeheartedly against a union at that time. They were interested in listening, even if they weren't yet ready to vote affirmatively on formal representation. But, as may be expected, the idea of a union didn't sit well in the corporate office.

"Of course," recalled Jensen, "I had negative response from management. I was right up front with Bob Doyle and told him what I was doing. He gave me his opinions and I told him mine and we disagreed for a time. I told him I felt the company needed a way for an hourly worker to discuss a problem he or she was having with management without the fear of repercussions."

As a practitioner of the open door policy, Doyle did discuss the union situation with Jensen. But he clearly didn't like the idea of a union at Roseville Telephone and said so.

"I told those workers who were interested that if they voted for the union, fine, then we'd follow every single union rule to the exact dotted "i" and crossed "t" with no exceptions," he remembered. "I just wanted them to know how things would be. They certainly would be different."

Doyle's opposition to a union at Roseville Telephone, then and now, is rooted in three primary beliefs. First, he feels the company's benevolent treatment of employees, validated by excellent wages and benefits plus opportunities to own stock in the company, means employees share directly in the company's success. Second, he believes that any significant union participation could not help but foster an "us vs. them" attitude. And third, for decades Doyle has observed how one of Roseville's biggest employers, the heavily unionized railroad, has been in decline. In Doyle's view, the traditional acrimonious relationship between the railroad and and its employees is the result of unions.

"Of course, Roseville has been a railroad town forever and you have to remember the first people I hired here were local kids, most of them right out of high school," Doyle recalled. "Their fathers worked at the railroad and were union, and they didn't like to see anything that wasn't union around. So it was natural that the kids would think there needed to be a union.

"In those days, it was the railroad and the telephone company, and that was about it in Roseville," Doyle chuckled, recalling the early years. "I made sure that I got the phone bills out to coincide with payday for Southern Pacific; otherwise you didn't get your money, because it ended up in the bars or the whorehouses. But if you happened to get the phone bill to them in time, you might get your money."

Doyle spent time in bars during the early years and it infuriated him to hear railroad workers publicly complaining about their employer. The workers would lament that they were mistreated and tell anybody who wanted to listen how they hated to go to work.

"I thought to myself, 'Is that any way to run a railroad ... your employees hate every minute being there? It didn't make sense.' So I knew I wanted our employees at Roseville Telephone to be proud of working there. I didn't want them in the bars bad-mouthing the company."

A little more than six years after Jensen joined Roseville Telephone, the Employee Company Relations Committee, later to be called Employee Relations Committee (ERC), was formed. According to a report in the November 1974 *Line Chatter*, the purpose of the ERC was two-fold — to represent the hourly employee and to improve communication within the company. Larry Hubbard was the first chairman of the ERC with Dick Bell the alternate. The first meeting, on Nov. 6, 1974, set up a process for employee grievances to be addressed. Changing the pay dates was also discussed.

Both employees and management were complimentary of each other after the first meeting. Hubbard said the monthly meetings showed that management was interested in feedback from employees. And Doyle told *Line Chatter* he felt the new ERC would work well, and that he is "happy when he knows that the employees are happy."

Jensen remembers that relations improved immediately upon formation of the ERC.

"That open channel of communication is what I personally wanted out of a union. The ERC opened that channel of communication very fast and very fairly. It went right into that type of deal where if a per diem person had a gripe, he could present it to the Employee Relations Committee and it would take it to management."

Several years later, when Jensen moved to the splicing department, he became president of the ERC. "I got a chance to work with Al Johnson; Doug Knowlton was a very important part of it, too, at that time. They were always willing to listen and in some cases helped us out quite a bit. In other cases, we helped them out by not pursuing something that wouldn't have done any of us any good."

A serious union challenge came in 1980 when the Communications Workers of America (CWA) tried to unionize all outside plant employees. It was defeated by a 2-to-1 margin. Interesting enough, however, a "Company Practices Quiz" made the front page of every *Line Chatter* from 1980 for about three years. The quiz listed questions related to company benefits. Any employee who dutifully worked on the quiz could not help but conclude the company's benefits were outstanding. The quiz format was a not-so-subtle way of reminding employees how fortunate they were to be working at Roseville Telephone.

In July 1986, another attempt failed. The International Brotherhood of Electrical Workers (IBEW) attempted to unionize hourly workers in plant service, splicing and construction. It went down to defeat, 47-6.

Bob Doyle sent a letter to each employee who participated in the election. A portion of it read:

"I want to thank all employees for voting and expressing their views on union representation. I know we can do a better job without this outside interference. As I mentioned in our group meetings, I plan to meet with you on a regular basis to insure I know your concerns and problems. This election was very costly for our company with unnecessary legal fees incurred, lost time by many key people, as well as a general uneasiness I believe we all experienced. By opening the lines of communications within the company to insure upper management is aware of what's bothering you, your concerns can be addressed promptly, foregoing outside interference and cost."

Jensen said his involvement with the ERC eventually led to a broader understanding of the company. "I changed my outlook on the company during those

*Greg Gierczak is Roseville Telephone's director of regulatory affairs, succeeding Mark Shull who retired in 1990.*

years because I was learning about the whole company. When I first joined, I only knew about my own departments."

Nonetheless, Jensen's union activities didn't sit all that well with Bob Doyle. "But he was fair," Jensen added. "I think a lot of the problem was that he never really heard about the problems we used to have."

Today, Jensen is a supervisor in the splicing department — he's a part of management. His progress through the years not only has made Jensen happy, but it heartens Doyle, too.

"At our 75th anniversary open house in September 1989, one of the first persons to volunteer to be a tour leader in his group was Jens Jensen," Doyle recalled. "Here he was, a guy that 20 years earlier was trying to get the union into our company. Now he's proud as punch about Roseville Telephone and telling all our visitors what a great company he works for. I mean to tell you, if that doesn't make somebody like me feel good, I don't know what does. Seeing Jensen be a tour leader was very special to me. I'll never forget that."

Employees at Roseville Telephone, past and present, sang a similar refrain when asked about unions. "Why would we want a union? We already get the same pay and benefits as other telephone workers and we don't have to strike to get them. Plus, most of us have stock in the company. What's good for Roseville Telephone is good for the employees so why would we want to change that?"

When employees have that attitude, unions have very little chance of making an inroad.

# Roseville's No. 1 Corporate Citizen

EMPLOYEES GENEROUS WITH TIME, MONEY

*"Some of us might find it difficult to give up a portion of our income. However, when you stop to consider how many of your neighbors benefit from your gift, the giving becomes worthwhile."*
— Bob Doyle

Each issue of *Line Chatter* includes thank you letters to Roseville Telephone for the wide variety of community activities supported by employee organizations and individuals. This long history of community involvement is an outgrowth of Bob Doyle's belief that the telephone company is an integral part of the communities it serves.

It would be difficult to list all the activities in which Roseville Telephone aids the people in its territory because there are so many. For example, since 1971 patients in Roseville Hospital receive the *Roseville Press-Tribune* compliments of Roseville Telephone. In addition to direct corporate support, various employee groups contribute time and money. And Doyle himself has been a consistent financial supporter of certain programs, particularly youth baseball and softball leagues. Doyle sometimes supports programs anonymously.

Through the years the company has been a major supporter of the Greater Sacramento United Way campaign. When the annual campaign kicked off, Doyle would write a letter to employees expressing the company's support of United Way. He strongly encouraged participation since he viewed the campaign as a statement of the company's generosity. Employees got the message that "giving the United Way" was a very good thing to do. Moreover, total contributions and participation levels by department were published in *Line Chatter*, so it was clear where the weak links were. Excerpts of Doyle's letter to employees in the Sept. 30, 1975, newsletter reflect his interest.

*The Roseville Telephone Foundation presents the Placer County Search and Rescue with new equipment that was purchased with RTF's contribution in March 1994.*

Photo by Stewart Brown

"Roseville Telephone Company has always made every endeavor to support the United Way. We are proud to report that at the close of last year's campaign, company contributions increased 44.6 percent over the prior year's. The combined company and employee gift amounted to $5,707.50.

"Some of us might find it difficult to give up a portion of our income, especially with today's inflated prices. However, when you stop to consider how many of your neighbors benefit from your gift, the giving becomes worthwhile. Remember, no one is immune to the misfortunes of life. While the company endorses the idea of 'fair share' giving, we feel that the decision to give or not to give is an individual choice. I urge your consideration of a 'fair share' gift as appropriate thanks for your own good fortune. Your company provides payroll deduction as an easy, convenient way to lend a helping hand to the community in which you live.

"I would like to take this opportunity to extend my sincere appreciation to Jim Phelps for the tremendous job he has done as Roseville Telephone's representative on the (United Way) Advisory Committee for the past three years. While I was honored to accept a merit award on behalf of the company last year, Jim really deserves most of the credit. Through his efforts, 16.1 percent of the total moneys raised in our community was donated by Roseville Telephone Company.

"While Jim has done an outstanding job, I feel that after this campaign has concluded, the position on the advisory committee should be turned over to another department. To generate some enthusiasm among those departments where participation was very low, I have decided to select next year's company representative from the department with the lowest participation average.

"Again, let me state the decision 'to give or not to give' is an individual choice which is entirely up to you. However, your gift, no matter how small, helps our community in a big way. I urge you to give 'The United Way.'"

This letter is typical of Doyle's approach. He commends employees for their past giving, sets a goal for the future and issues a challenge to those who haven't participated to his satisfaction in the past. It obviously worked, because by 1992 the company's United Way contribution grew to $50,000.

## THE GIFT OF LIFE

"The gift of life" — donating blood — has a long tradition at Roseville Telephone. In the November 1961 *Line Chatter*, 14 employees were acknowledged for donating 15 pints of blood. Bob Doyle led the way by donating two pints. The newsletter included this tongue-in-cheek comment, "Mr. Doyle is setting an example by donating twice. It seems his blood is more rare than others." How many other company presidents are blood donors?

*Jim Phelps, supervisor of fixed asset management, was very successful in heading up the company's United Way campaign in the mid-1970s.*

But the individual most active in establishing the company's blood bank program is Donna Hood, who retired in January 1994 after 33 years with the company. Through her leadership, a blood bank program was developed that to this day remains a highly successful and well-supported effort. Hood first became involved to help a fellow employee's daughter.

"She faced critical surgery and would need transfusions, but the blood banking system as we know it today didn't exist in Roseville yet," Hood explained. "So we needed to find 10 people, and match them to 'O' positive, who would donate for the blood to be on hand during her surgery. When a need like this affects someone in your family or a friend's family, it hits home. It has been a very worthwhile program."

Hood's compassion for those in need went even further when she underwent major surgery to donate bone marrow to help save the life of a young Arkansas girl in October 1991. Hood explained in the November 1991 *Line Chatter* how the process worked.

"Following the surgery, the marrow was placed in a six-pack type container and given to another volunteer with airline reservations to the donation site. Seven to ten days prior to my surgery, the patient began chemotherapy and/or radiation to destroy her own marrow. Because her immune system is also destroyed, she will remain in isolation for four to six weeks until it can be determined that the procedure worked."

A letter to Bob Doyle from the Sacramento Blood Center expressed gratitude for allowing Hood the time necessary to be a donor.

"We wish to express our appreciation for the support you have given to Donna Hood before, during, and after her marrow donation. Through the generous gift of her time as well as her bone marrow, Donna has given another person a real chance of survival."

*Donna Hood, now retired, was very active at blood drives in the company. Hood, standing in back, was also on the original Board of Directors of the Roseville Telephone Foundation along with Ophelia Martinez, left, Imelda Ruiz, right, and Hazel Snider, the first president of the foundation.*

Photo by Stewart Brown

The bone marrow transplant was a success. More than a year later, Hood was invited to a reunion of four bone marrow donors and recipients at Children's Hospital of Wisconsin in Milwaukee. On Dec. 4, 1992, Hood met Sunshine Runyon, 10, the recipient, and her family. It was a special moment for Hood, the heart-warming culmination of three decades of giving.

"At the time of the donation, I only knew that the recipient was an 8-year-old girl," Hood said. "It was wonderful that more than a year later I was able to meet her and give her a big hug."

In March 1993, another employee, Allen Norton, was cited by the Sacramento Blood Center for being an "apheresis" donor. In these procedures, which often take several hours, platelets and white blood cells are taken from the donor to be transfused to seriously ill patients, often leukemia victims, who desperately need these specific blood products to survive. Dr. Leonor Fernando of the Sacramento Medical Foundation said the success of this program "requires a dedicated and highly motivated donor and an understanding and compassionate employer" who would allow "flexibility in making Allen available for this important donation."

Also in 1993, Teri Powell was given a plaque by the Sacramento Blood Center for reaching the three-gallon milestone.

## ITPA, TOMMY APOSTOLOS FUND SPREAD GOOD WORKS

In addition to individual volunteer efforts, employee organizations have been founded to spearhead charitable contributions for specific purposes.

In January 1978, the organizational meeting of the Mother Lode Chapter of the Independent Telephone Pioneers Association (ITPA) was held. The membership included more than 50 employees and retirees of Roseville Telephone, Foresthill Telephone and Citizens Utilities in Elk Grove. To qualify, members must have had 15 years or more of service in telephone or related work. The first officers — all Roseville Telephone employees — were Doug Knowlton, president; Jack Morris, 1st vice president; Jay Kinder, 2nd vice president; Donna Hood, secretary; and Lila Mettler, treasurer.

The purpose of the ITPA is to preserve history, traditions and ideals; promote fellowship; and provide community service. It regularly sponsors money-raising events, such as breakfasts, lunches, dinners, bake sales, blanket crocheting, chili cookoffs and walk-a-thons, candy sales, event and restaurant coupon book sales, t-shirt sales and furniture sales. ITPA has staged hundreds of events since 1978. Its members join other employees to sing Christmas carols to cheer up residents in area convalescent homes.

ITPA is constantly developing creative fund-raising activities to aid individuals and organizations throughout the area. Much of its success can be attributed to non-member employees who generously support ITPA activities.

A letter from Jennifer Schwen, whose daughter, Annelyce, received help from the ITPA, is representative of hundreds of such letters received through the years. It appeared in the November 1992 *Line Chatter*:

"Annelyce and I would like to express our sincere gratitude for your gifts of love which came our way from Roseville Telephone Company employees. I wasn't aware that such generosity and love existed anymore until my daughter got sick. When I needed support at that tragic time, total strangers came to our aid. Your gifts not only smoothed the way for Annelyce's recovery, but renewed my faith in my fellow man.

"Among other things, the money purchased a brace for Annelyce's weak leg, an answering machine so I wouldn't miss any calls from her doctors, some development toys to support recovery, and financed a trip to San Francisco for a second opinion. ... Roseville is a lucky community to have such people as you all living here!"

ITPA is not only successful because of the funds it raises for needy causes, but its members have learned to have fun as they help other people. It's a recipe that works to everyone's benefit.

Another company-affiliated volunteer organization is the Tommy Apostolos Fund. It was founded in 1988 in memory of the highly popular, long-time construction boss who joined the company in January 1951. In commenting on Apostolos' passing in the August 1988 *Line Chatter*, Jack Poulsen called Apostolos "a great person and a real asset to Roseville Telephone. He was a very rare individual."

In the March 1991 *Line Chatter*, Tom Firchau said this about Apostolos: "When God made Tommy, he broke the mold (that's what he used to say). Tommy always had a way of spicing up a room and was never long on words. I consider it a privilege to be so fortunate to have known him."

Apostolos was a giant of a man with a gentle demeanor. He was a kind, caring individual who loved children. In his honor, the Tommy Apostolos Fund raises funds each year to finance a holiday "clothing spree" for needy children in the Roseville Telephone service territory. In 1989, enough money was raised to send 10 children on their "spree" at Mervyn's Department Store in Roseville. Each year the number of children participating has increased. In 1994, the fund raised about $30,000 and nearly 200 children received $150 each to spend on clothing, shoes and other necessities.

The Apostolos Fund was formed in concert with the Apostolos family, Roseville Police Association, Placer County Law Enforcement Chaplaincy and Roseville Telephone. The chaplaincy works with local school officials to determine which children will be invited to participate. The police association helps with the annual dinner that raises most of the money to finance the clothing spree. Mervyn's gives the children discounts of up to 40 percent. Roseville Telephone employees make a sizable contribution through the Roseville Telephone Foundation and help the children select their clothing at the spree.

*The late Tommy Apostolos was the company's construction foreman for about 30 years. He's shown here with his wife, Peggy. After his death in 1988, family and friends formed an organization in his honor that raises funds to purchase clothing for needy children.*

Photo courtesy of John Apostolos

*John Apostolos gives Ophelia Martinez of the Roseville Telephone Foundation a plaque recognizing the foundation's success in raising funds for the Tommy Apostolos Fund.*

Photo by Stewart Brown

"It's a wonderful program that has helped a lot of kids get warm clothing and shoes right before the weather begins to get cold," said John Apostolos, Tommy's son, who works in the regulatory department at the telephone company. "The employees are unbelievable in the way they support it. Not only does the foundation make a substantial donation, but the dinner is well-attended by the employees."

Benefit events are publicized in-house with flyers put on billboards. Since employees are constantly being asked to give, occasionally a touch of humor helps. For example, on the bright green flyer promoting the 1995 Apostolos dinner dance, there was also scribbled: "Guess who has tickets? — That's right — Victor 'in yer pocket again' Esparza!"

## ROSEVILLE TELEPHONE FOUNDATION

A hallmark of Roseville Telephone has been its desire to control its own destiny in every way possible. With Bob Doyle's encouragement, all departments continually look for ways to do things themselves. It follows from Doyle's all-inclusive philosophy that "... not only can we do it ourselves, but we can do it better."

So it was not surprising that in late 1992 Doyle decided the same principle of "do it ourselves" would work for the company's charitable programs. Hazel Snider, the chief operator and long-time volunteer, explains how the Roseville Telephone Foundation came about.

"Bob called me one day in 1992 and said he wanted to run an idea past me," Snider explained. "He said our United Way contribution had become substantial — it was $50,000 in 1992 — but maybe the local communities in our territory would be better served if we formed our own organization to manage our charitable giving. 'I just think it'd be a hell of an idea if we formed our own organization,' is what Doyle told me.

"I said it would be nice if we could do it, and he said, 'Hell, we can do it.' I didn't think much more about it until a couple of months later when I received a call from Brian Strom, and he tells me, 'Mr. Doyle has appointed you the president of the Roseville Telephone Foundation.' I said, 'What?' But that's how it started."

On Nov. 4, 1992, Doyle announced the creation of the organization:

"I am pleased to announce the formation of the Roseville Telephone Foundation, a non-profit corporation organized by the company for the purpose of meeting the charitable needs of residents living primarily in Roseville Telephone's service area."

Legally chartered as a non-profit organization, the foundation, according to Doyle, "is able to help those living right here in and around our service area … and we know where every nickel goes."

Donor participation increased when the employees saw they were contributing to their own in-house charity. In 1993, the foundation collected $64,000. In 1994, the figure jumped to $80,000. With fewer than 500 employees on average in 1994, the per employee contribution approximates $150. That is well above average for corporate employee contributions.

"The man talks about it, decides to do it, does it, and it's a success," Snider said of Doyle. "It's incredible. You've got to respect someone who can do that."

Organizations receiving help through 1994 included: American Red Cross; Salvation Army; Boys Scouts of America; Sierra Council; Child Abuse Council; Sierra Family Services; March of Dimes; Tommy Apostolos Fund; Mother Lode Campfire Girls; PRIDE Industries; Start-A-Heart/Save-Your-Heart; Association for Retarded Citizens; Mental Health Association; Placer Extends A Caring Environment For Families In Crisis (P.E.A.C.E.); Community Resources Council; Sierra Council On Alcoholism And Drug Dependence; Volunteer Center Of Placer County; California Veterans Advocacy Corp., St. Vincent DePaul Society; College For Kids/Sierra College Foundation; Teenage Pregnancy And Parenting Program; Historical Society Amtrak Fund; Roseville Arts Center; Placer County Search & Rescue and United Cerebral Palsy.

The *Line Chatter* carries letters each month from organizations thanking the Roseville Telephone Foundation. The first such letter appeared in May 1993. It was written by Michael Ziegler, president and chief executive officer of PRIDE Industries, the first local non-profit organization to receive a check from the foundation. The check for $2,263 was presented on April 7, 1993.

"On behalf of all of us at PRIDE Industries, I totally appreciate your generous gift to our program. All of your donation will go directly to provide services for people with disabilities who reside in Placer County.

"I think it is wonderful that the employees of Roseville Telephone created a foundation to collect funds to help social programs in Placer County. I applaud your efforts and thank you for selecting PRIDE as one of your recipients."

As Doyle anticipated, the foundation has promoted exceptional pride among employees. When employees see their contributions going specifically to aid organizations in the

*Hazel Snider, first president of the Roseville Telephone Foundation, presented Pride Industries' Michael Ziegler with the foundation's first check on April 7, 1993. The foundation raised more than $80,000 in 1994 to help worthwhile local charities.*

Photos by Stewart Brown

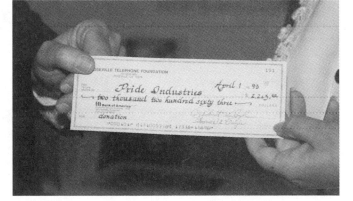

communities where they live, it heightens their positive feelings about giving. The Roseville Telephone Foundation is the employees' ongoing commitment to bettering their community.

## ROSEVILLE TELEPHONE MUSEUM, A TREASURE TROVE

In addition to the hundreds of thousands of dollars donated to good causes by Roseville Telephone and its employees through the years, the company recently gave the community a new treasure, the Roseville Telephone Museum. This extraordinary collection of antique telephone equipment and corporate history is a cultural jewel for the city of Roseville and one of the outstanding telephone collections in the United States.

The museum had an unlikely beginning. It was never planned, but evolved. The coincidence of events that led to the development of the museum began in 1985 with Bob Parsons' desire to keep older telephone equipment of the company intact. It was then that the last of the old, reliable step-by-step switching equipment in the Roseville central office was being torn down and replaced by electronic switching equipment. As the step-by-step equipment was being dismantled, Walter Gordon asked Parsons if he wanted to keep any of the old line finders, connectors, automatic ticketers, and other step-by-step components. Otherwise, Gordon said, they'd be tossed into the trash bin. To long-time employees such as Parsons, there was considerable nostalgia associated with the "steppers" because they represented an era of telephony soon to disappear. The old equipment wasn't junk to Parsons; it was history.

"As we replaced that equipment, I felt it was important to keep something from the old days, especially if I was familiar with it and understood how it all worked," recalled Parsons. From then on, Parsons informally began collecting equipment that was put out of service as new equipment was installed.

*In 1989, Roseville Telephone established a museum to display historic equipment and corporate documents. The museum expanded in time for the 1994 80th anniversary opening house.*

Photo by Sirlin Studios

Four years later, during the planning sessions for the 75th anniversary open house in September of 1989, Parsons and Doyle decided a historical display would be interesting.

"When we started cleaning up for the 1989 open house, it occurred to me that we had a lot of older telephone equipment stuck away here and there and that rather than throw the stuff away, it might make a nice display for the open house," recalled Doyle. "In 1989, we had just gone to all digital switching, so I felt visitors might like to see how we used to do things. That's how it started out; we initially planned to have a display. About that time Gene Lippincott of Spokane, Wash., heard about our historical display. So he called and said he had been collecting old telephone equipment for years and inquired if we'd be interested in buying some of it. We knew Lippincott because in the years before the Bell System breakup, we owned our phones and customers leased. In those years, we sent phones to Lippincott who would recondition, sterilize and return them in like-new condition."

One of the scores of beautiful and historic wall phones on display at the Roseville Telephone Museum.

Parsons remembers being excited when he first saw pictures of Lippincott's telephone collection. "He had a couple hundred of them. He sent pictures to me and I showed them to Bob Doyle," Parsons said. "Unfortunately, we hadn't kept any telephones to speak of in any quantity or variety from the past. I don't think many telephone companies did because you were constantly turning in old phone sets for better and faster sets. So you threw old phones away. There were these few people, the true collectors, who would stash them away in a barn or warehouse. Lippincott sent 10 or 12 pictures of his collection. The telephones were crowded in a display case ... you couldn't really see them, only that there were lots of them, at least 200.

"After seeing the photos and thinking about it for a while, Bob Doyle warmed up to the idea of pursuing the collection," Parsons added. "He said, 'If we had these telephones along with all the equipment we have plus any of the other stuff that has Roseville Telephone on it, we could have a complete display like a telephone company should have.' Here was a chance to pick up some of the equipment and telephones we should have saved. So Doyle sent Merle Ruggles and me to Spokane to negotiate with Lippincott."

Parsons and Ruggles went to Spokane in August 1989, only a month before the scheduled 75th anniversary open house. Time was tight. Negotiations started slowly since neither side wanted to tip its hand. Parsons remembered that session.

"Merle and I met with Lippincott in the morning and looked over his collection. After lunch, we started to talk price. It was one of those things ... 'How much do you have to have for them,' and 'How much do you want for them,' and 'How much will you give?' Nobody was willing to make the first move," Parsons recalled. "Each side was afraid of being too high or too low. After an hour of this, it was clear we weren't going to progress at this rate. So Lippincott sat at the desk and put his head in his hands like he's thinking something telepathic or something. Then he says, 'I see a number. Let me try this. How's this sound? $50,000.' I thought that was a good price because it was for everything — all those phones, display cases, a phone booth with everything buffed, real spit and polish. It was beautiful and all we had to do was ship it to Roseville and put it on display.

 "So I said, 'I don't know how Bob Doyle's going to react to that.' We didn't really go there with a preconceived number, although Bob had his numbers as I think he always does when he's going to negotiate. I think it's one of his secrets, that he always has an upper and a lower number in mind so he can work on it. I told Lippincott I'd have to get Bob on the phone.

"Lippincott left the room while Ruggles talked with Doyle. Bob asked a lot of questions. Did the equipment look as good as in the photos? What were our impressions? Could we get it to Roseville in time for the open house? After discussing it at some length, he asked to talk to Lippincott. They sealed the deal right on the phone," Parsons said. "Merle and I got a list of items in the collection and wrapped up as much of the deal as we could during that visit. We came home that evening from Spokane. It was probably the most exciting deal that I have been on, because of what it was and the way it was handled. Here were two old-time telephone business guys, Doyle and Lippincott, getting in there, not BS-ing each other, but just getting down to brass tacks. It was very rewarding to me, because we came home with the bacon, so to speak."

*Stewart Brown of the company's customer service department shows museum visitors how the "step by step" switching equipment worked.*

So it was the Lippincott collection that provided the bulk of the original History of Telephony display at the 75th anniversary open house in 1989. Getting the new museum ready for the open house was no small task.

Stewart Brown, who along with Parsons is an unofficial historian, curator and tour guide for the museum, remembers how it came together.

"Bob Parsons was selected as the coordinator to assemble the museum and get it together. He, in turn, recruited several employees to help. The main committee consisted of Bob Doyle, Al Johnson, Bob Parsons, Walter Gordon and Leon Bower. It was basically these people who made sure all the components of this big job got done in time," recalled Brown.

Committee members and employees worked furiously to get the museum ready. A site in the basement of the main equipment building in Roseville was the only place large enough to fit the display. Workers quickly renovated the 1,500-square-foot space to make a handsome museum.

The historical display also involved long-time employees and retirees. When they heard about the company's desire to locate old, used equipment, several stepped forward to donate items they had at home. They freely contributed equipment in the spirit of making the historical exhibit the best it could be. It was another example of teamwork of employees, past and present.

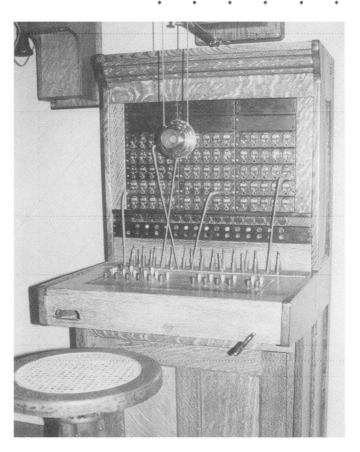

*Antique switchboards such as this one are on display at Roseville Telephone's museum.*

Visitors gave the exhibit rave reviews at the 1989 open house. Many sent letters much like the following, which came from Paul Stokestad, president of Pasco Scientific:

"My compliments on an excellent museum. Not only do you have an extensive collection, but the displays are beautifully done."

The museum's popularity heightened Doyle's and Parsons' desire to continue to build the collection. Lippincott's connections led to more opportunities to acquire telephony collectibles. For example, Lippincott was a consultant to a Wisconsin collector who apparently owned equipment complementary to the items already acquired by Roseville Telephone. Lippincott's introduction resulted in Parsons adding about 100 more pieces to the company's collection.

Later on, when Parsons was getting display cases refinished, the craftsman doing the work told Parsons about a woman whose father, Louis Smith of Vassar, Kan., had telephone equipment to sell. Parsons immediately called Smith to request photos of his collection and soon therafter went to Kansas to inspect it.

"To go there is the only way you can really communicate and see if the pieces are different from ours," Parsons said. "Smith had over 200 pieces. It's interesting how he arrived at his asking price — it was the amount he owed on his mortgage. His wife had died several months earlier and he wanted enough to pay the note off. It bothered him to be in debt."

In June of 1991, Parsons and Stewart Brown headed to Kansas to supervise the boxing and moving of Smith's telephone collectibles. "He was a suspicious old guy, it seemed to us," recalled Parsons. "He wanted to get right to the bank with his check and pay his note off and make sure the money was good. I guess he didn't trust us.

"At lunch, Smith told us about another town in Kansas — Coffeyville — where he had gone some years earlier to find parts. About two or three months after our trip to Vassar, I found the name 'Watts' in a collector's catalogue. It turned out that Oral Watts of Coffeyville was member #1A with the American Telephone Collectors Association, ATCA, and his wife, Malone Watts, was #1B. We had just become a member and our number was almost 2,000, so I knew the Watts had to be very serious collectors."

Parsons called Malone Watts in Coffeyville, who said her husband had died a few years earlier. Most of the collection was still intact and she told Parsons she'd be willing to sell it because she didn't want to be bothered with it any more. Without her husband, she had lost interest.

"The Watts had about the largest collection of phones, magnetos, telephone parts and pieces you'd ever find, so we went ahead and acquired it in 1992," Parsons said. "After that, collectors from Everett, Wash., who knew Lippincott, sent photos of items they had. We selected a few pieces we didn't have already, including an old telephone booth."

The company's collection currently includes more than 2,000 pieces representing over 100 years of telephony. About 80 percent of the collection is stored in a company warehouse at its Barton Road switching office. Despite the size of the collection, there are few duplicates.

"You might look at a candlestick-style telephone and think they're all the same, but they aren't," Parsons said. "There were so many different manufacturers and each phone it seemed had different little gimmicks and features. Some, for example, had a little 'mother-in-law' receiver on the back, so as you're talking, your mother-in-law could listen in. The phones then were mostly hand-crafted and made to last, so they were quite sturdy."

Parsons lauds Doyle's interest in collecting old equipment and establishing a museum. "A collection such as ours preserves an important part of American history and that of our phone company, too," he said.

One of the many highlights of the museum is the original magneto switchboard used at Roseville Telephone from its founding in 1914. It was put back into working order so visitors can make calls through it on antique wall telephones in the museum. The original switchboard found its way back home in a roundabout fashion.

In the 1930s, a fire destroyed the switchboard at Colfax Telephone, east of Roseville. Since the original switchboard in Roseville had been replaced in the early 1920s, Walter Hanisch gave Colfax the old switchboard to help the exchange get back into service quickly. The switchboard stayed in use until Colfax converted to dial many years later. It was then placed in storage where it stayed until Continental Telephone bought the Colfax Telephone exchange in the 1970s. Soon thereafter, the old board was shipped to storage at Continental's western regional headquarters office in Bakersfield. Later, it was pulled out of storage again by Dick Crowe, a Contel executive, who used it as decorative furniture in his office.

"When Crowe heard that we were getting together our museum, he had the switchboard packed up and shipped to us because he felt it rightfully belonged back in Roseville," said Doyle. "We refurbished it and got it working again. We're real happy to have it back."

The museum features old telephones of virtually every type. There are beautiful candlestick-style phones, crank wall phones and desk sets. There's also a display of color phones that were particularly popular in the 1960s. One section is devoted to switchboards. On one side is the original switchboard. On the other side is a section of working, step-by-step switching equipment.

Another section of the museum is devoted to outside plant equipment and gear showing a cut-a-way exhibit of telephone cable in a manhole complete with displays of cable splicing. There are also displays of colorful glass insulators used on telephone poles to prevent wires from grounding. Another corner of the museum is devoted to corporate history. It includes photos of former and current corporate directors, including the founders of the company. There also are old telephone directories and important corporate papers, including the original Articles of Incorporation drawn up in 1914.

The company owns one of the largest collections of novelty phones in existence. For instance, the company owns telephones in the shape of Mickey Mouse, Kermit the Frog, Star Trek's U.S.S. Enterprise, Superman and Snoopy, to name only a few. There are more than a hundred such novelty phones in all. They are not yet on display at the museum, but will be eventually.

How good is the Roseville Telephone collection? In November 1991, Barry Lambergam, an attorney from Washington, D.C., sent a letter to Bob Doyle, which was later reprinted in *Line Chatter*. The following are excerpts:

"Although we have never had occasion to speak, you may be aware that I am with the Washington, D.C., law firm which represents Roseville Telephone before the Federal Communications Commission. Last week, I had the opportunity to visit

*Roseville Telephone's museum has one of the finest displays of antique telephones.*

Roseville Telephone and the pleasure of finally meeting some of the RTC employees with whom I have been working these past few years. Although we are in a technology-driven business, it still takes good people to make a company successful. With the kind of people you have at RTC, it comes as no surprise to me that RTC has made such a smooth and rapid transition into the digital age!

"The reason for my letter, however, is more about RTC's past than its future. I wanted you to know how much I enjoyed touring your telephone museum with Ron Miller and Stewart Brown. Living in Washington, I can honestly tell you that your exhibits are of Smithsonian caliber.

"You are to be commended for your foresight in not discarding what many others would have considered junk and for your efforts in preserving over 75 years of telephone history. I hope the museum will continue to grow with RTC."

The latest important development at the museum occurred just prior to the 1994 80th anniversary open house when Doyle directed that the museum be relocated from its awkward, out-of-the-way and cramped quarters in the basement of the Roseville central switching office to a newly-renovated, larger space at 106/110 Vernon Street. The museum's new quarters had been home to plant engineering before this group moved to the newly-opened Industrial Avenue complex. The decision to move the telephone museum illustrates how employees turn a problem into an opportunity … in a hurry.

The company intended to tear down the old, vacated buildings at 106 and 110 Vernon Street in downtown Roseville to make room for additional employee parking. This plan ran into a hitch when the estimate to remove the old structures came in at the unexpectedly high cost of nearly $400,000. Doyle winced at that price to tear down two buildings … it just didn't seem to make sense.

Al Johnson offered Doyle another option, originally put forth by Tim Fritts of the company's property and maintenance department. "Instead of removing the buildings, why not renovate them and move the museum there," Johnson told Doyle.

Fritts had made the suggestion during a discussion with Johnson about the high cost of tearing down the buildings. "Al was rightfully questioning the price of it, and as we talked it over, I said there are other alternatives," Fritts remembered. "For one, I said we could move the museum there since I knew the company eventually wanted to get the museum to a street-level location where parking and accessibility would be better. It made sense to me and it made sense to Al."

Shortly thereafter, Fritts received a call from Doyle who asked if it could really be done. Fritts and Russ Kelley, his boss, conferred and told Doyle, yes, they believed it was feasible. Within a few days, Doyle received approval from the

It was Tim Fritts, a supervisor in the property and maintenance department, who came up with the idea to move the museum to its current street-level location in Roseville.

Board of Directors and the project got the go-ahead in mid-April 1994, less than two months before the open house in early June.

"I thought it was a hell of an idea," recalled Doyle. "It will turn a problem into a solution! We'd finally get our museum to street level where it belongs and have more room for display, too. Plus, we'd save a lot of money and wouldn't need to tear down those old buildings. How can it be better than that?"

The museum renovation became a focal point of the 80th anniversary open house because it was going to be a major endeavor to have the museum ready by early June. There was an incredible amount of work to be done. The museum renovation inspired the theme for the 1994 open house — "Whatever It Takes" — and that is exactly how the museum came together. A Herculean effort by the company's employees — particularly Bob Parsons, Stewart Brown and their customer services department, along with "decorator" Laurel Dismukes, the company's controller — helped get the monumental job done in time. Also, contractor Harbison Mahoney Higgins put an equally prodigious effort into finishing the job on time. Work continued until the morning of the open house when the finishing touches were done in the outside plant display area.

Since 1989, Doyle had been hoping to figure out a cost-effective way of opening up the museum to the general public on a regular basis. Finally, thanks to an employee's good idea, Doyle's wish came true. Certainly, no one is prouder of the museum than Doyle or Johnson, two telephone industry veterans who are committed to preserving the colorful history of their company and industry.

"The museum may belong to the Roseville Telephone Company, but it's a community thing as far as I'm concerned," Doyle said. "It's Roseville's museum. I think over a period of time it will attract a lot of visitors, which will be good for the town. There is a lot of payback in history. I think our museum will eventually be viewed as a Western asset."

Presently, the museum is open weekdays to groups of seven or more. On Saturdays, it is open to the general public for a nominal charge. As visitation grows, hours will be expanded.

Doyle admits that not everyone thought it was worthwhile to establish a telephone museum, "but when they saw visitors come and rave about it ... well, that changed everything," Doyle said. "Now there's not a person here who isn't proud of the museum. It's a part of the company, something a lot of telephone companies don't take the trouble to do. Not only are we taking the trouble to collect old equipment, but we're taking the trouble to make the stuff work. I'm convinced it's worth it."

Doyle feels the same about the *History Of The Roseville Telephone Company*. It's worthwhile, in his view, to chronicle the history of a company that went from being a backward, tiny, much-maligned telephone exchange to a highly-

*When it was decided the museum should locate to new quarters in time for the 1994 open house, Russ Kelley and his hard working crew in property and maintenance made it happen.*

sophisticated, highly-regarded telecommunications company that along the way has greatly benefited its owners, employees and community.

"It's been a great story, but what makes it worth it is that the employees who made it happen are still here," Doyle said. "If they had all died already, it wouldn't make much sense. But most of them are still around here and remember how terrible we were 40 years ago. It's a living history."

The book will be given to employees and, in Doyle's opinion, beats the typical selection of employee gifts at most companies.

"I told the Board of Directors that a lot of companies give employees a turkey for Christmas. That's fine, but when the turkey is eaten, there's nothing to show for it. On the other hand, you give an employee a book, and he or she has something to be proud of. It makes them feel real good because it's a story about their own company."

# Telephony's Most Independent Executive

## A HARD LIFE GROWING UP ON THE FARM

*"My dad was witty and could keep you in stitches ... not always the cleanest language you'd ever heard. He had a saying for everything, more or less all on the shady side."*
— Bob Doyle

Robert L. Doyle was born on a cold winter day on Feb. 11, 1919, on the old Doyle ranch in Roseville, the second son of William J. and Hazel (Wright) Doyle. Bob was 13 months younger than his brother William J. Doyle, Jr., who was called Jack.

"Our family was like two families, you might say," Bob Doyle said. "First, there was Jack and myself and then it was Marjorie, who was eight years younger than me. Tom was 10 years younger than me and Betty, the youngest, was 11 years younger than me. So there was only a couple of years difference between the three of them, but eight years between Marjorie and me and 10 years between Tom and me. Well, in those days, that was quite a difference. Because they didn't have babysitters, you just took care of your own. And with your mother out there doing the farming and handling everything with the house, it was up to the oldest ones to take care of the kids."

Those early years were typical of farm families in the early decades of the century. When the children weren't in school, they toiled around the farm, the boys helping their father in the fields and the daughters helping with household work. When Bill Doyle wasn't in his vineyards or tending to his other crops or livestock elsewhere on his 400-acre ranch, he could be found on his porch reading or talking with a visitor. Many current residents remember seeing "Old Man Doyle," as they called him, out and about. The Doyles lived in a big farmhouse on the bend of Folsom Road

*The Doyle ranch house on Folsom Road.*
Courtesy of Robert L. Doyle

*Robert L. Doyle as a toddler. Born on Feb. 11, 1919, he was Bill and Hazel Doyle's second child.*

Courtesy of Robert L. Doyle

just south of downtown Roseville. It was a large, sturdy house with a large porch around it. The house was set back about 20 yards south of the intersection of present day Folsom Road and Estates Drive. It's where the administrative office of Park Roseville, a retirement housing development, is currently located.

The Doyle ranch roughly was bounded by what today is East Roseville Parkway, Douglas Boulevard (which was then called Rocky Ridge Road), Folsom Road on the north and Dry Creek on the east. The Roseville Square shopping plaza is on former Doyle ranch acreage as are the Payless Drug and Mervyn's department stores. Interstate 80 cuts right through the former ranch property.

Although Bill Doyle was among the more prosperous farmers in the area, his tastes were simple and his manner straightforward. He was as unpretentious as one could be. In an age of rugged individuals and in a town known for its characters, Bill Doyle was remarkable for his independence.

By the time Bill Doyle married in 1916 at age 41, he was well established. His father, "Lucky Jack" Doyle, had died in 1910, leaving his son the farm and other property and buildings. Bill Doyle's investment in the telephone company was solid, returning a 10-percent dividend nearly every year. Long hours on the ranch developed in Bill Doyle an appreciation for the leisurely card games he enjoyed with his pals in town. But in an era of hard drinkers and roustabouts, Bill Doyle lived a rather clean life.

"My dad never smoked and never drank," said Bob Doyle. "The reason he didn't drink was because evidently when his father came to town from the ranch out there, my father would often have to come and get him. I guess my grandfather would drink too much and get into fights, raise a lot of hell. It made my dad think there's no way he was going to be like that. So he just didn't, period."

Although his exterior was gruff and his formal education limited, Bill Doyle was an avid reader and was worldly in his knowledge, if not in his experiences. Bob Doyle recalled how captivating his dad could be:

"He seemed to remember everything he read. He knew about geography and history, all kinds of things that he had read about, and he was one of those people who, when he read a book, he could tell you exactly what was in there … not like some people who read a book and 15 minutes later don't even know the title. He retained what he read. People would come over to our house just to sit down and talk to my dad because he was interesting. Here was a guy that didn't even go all the way through grammar school, because in those days, hell, if you're a farmer, school didn't mean that much. But there was something about him, he seemed to know so many things. He was just an intelligent person."

Anybody traveling east or north through Roseville went right past the Doyle house. Many remember seeing the elder Doyle as they passed the house. Ron

Amick grew up nearby and went to school with the younger Doyle children.

"Mr. Doyle was a real character. He wore these green pants and boots, and striped shirts. He was always out on the farm," Amick recalled. "About the time I went to high school, somebody told me that he was the main owner of the telephone company. I couldn't ever picture Mr. Doyle being involved in the telephone business. That's the last thing I would have expected him to be involved in."

Bill Sheppard first met Bill Doyle in the late 1940s when he rented a barn from him. "He was a pistol. He cussed, but he didn't smoke or drink. He'd come to my feed store, sit there for an hour or two talking with some of the other big growers who would come in. He wore boots up to his knees, winter time and summer time."

Bill Doyle's appearance belied his wealth. Ed Gardetto remembered the senior Doyle playing cards with his cronies at a downtown cigar store. "Old man Doyle had on his big old boots with his pant legs tucked in them, and one of his friends said to him, 'All the money you got, don't you ever dress up, for Chrissakes.' Mr. Doyle just looked at him and said, 'With my money, I can dress up any way I want.' That's the way he was."

*Bob Doyle tools around in his first little car as brother Jack looks on.*
Courtesy of Robert L. Doyle

Bob Doyle remembered his father being irritated when townspeople gave him flak about his appearance.

"He said to me, 'These goddamned people have to go out and buy all these fancy clothes to be seen. All I have to do to be noticed is wash my face and the whole damn town's talking about it.' He had an answer for everybody, and I mean a good answer. In truth, my dad took a bath every night and used to shave regularly with a straight razor. He wore clothing for farming, but he was anything but dirty. He was real clean."

One time, Bill Doyle decided he wanted new rain gutters put on his house. He wanted them to last a long time so he chose copper gutters, very heavy and very expensive.

"Apparently the guy he picked to put in the gutters was a little suspicious because my dad didn't give the appearance he could afford copper," Bob Doyle recalled. "When he called the bank to inquire about my father, the man was told, 'If Mr. Doyle wants copper gutters on his house, you put copper gutters on his house.'"

Gladys (Ellis) Ross, the longtime chief operator, admitted being apprehensive when Bill Doyle came into the telephone office.

"He looked like a rough, tough man and he'd come in with his farm clothes on," she recalled. "But he was always kind to us and I always had respect for him. Sometimes, though, I was almost a little afraid of Mr. Doyle, but he was good, he really was."

Bill Doyle, like his sons Bob and Tom, was known to be blunt. He didn't hedge his comments; he said exactly what was on his mind. He wouldn't suffer fools.

The elder Doyle's mannerisms, philosophies and style rubbed off on his three sons. Bob Doyle remembers learning from his father's business dealings.

"He would say, 'If you learn to keep your mouth shut, then nobody will ever learn how dumb you are.' There's a lot to that. Let's say a guy goes to a meeting and does a lot of talking. Then there's the guy who doesn't say much, only nods his head once in a while. When the meeting's over, the others in the meeting think that second guy was pretty damn smart because they can't think of anything he said wrong. But the guy who was doing all the talking, they say, 'Hell, he didn't know what he was talking about.' A lot of my dad's thinking rubbed off on me."

Bob Doyle also remembers his father's aversion to "riding on 'ships' of various kinds." Doyle explains: "My dad would say, 'Relationship is a damn poor ship to travel on,' which meant, of course, it's not a good idea to have business dealings with your family. He said the same thing about partnerships.

*Bill and Hazel Doyle, hard-working farmers.*
Courtesy of Robert L. Doyle

"My dad was witty and could keep you in stitches … not always the cleanest language you'd ever heard, of course, and he had a saying for everything. I don't care what it was. And his sayings were more or less all on the shady side."

Hazel Wright Doyle was a hardy, much younger woman, whose family hailed from the Capay Valley, west of Woodland. It isn't known how she met Bill Doyle, but it's believed they may have met when her family came to Roseville to sell their farm produce. It may have been that Bill Doyle realized that if he didn't have a family, the Doyle name would die out. His sister Winifred had already married the prominent rancher, William Kaseberg.

After marrying in 1916, Hazel Doyle settled into the rigorous life of a farm family. She did the chores and raised the children while her husband tended to the ranch. She also was a turkey farmer in her own right and wasn't afraid to tackle anything that needed doing on the ranch.

"She was just a good hard-working farm woman," Bob Doyle remembered. "She milked cows, chopped wood and did whatever else was needed to be done back then. In those days, that's what a farmer's wife did."

Myron McIntyre remembers Hazel Doyle as a very independent and strong woman.

"She was a Democrat and she wasn't afraid to tell you what she thought about Republicans. She had a big garden and a big porch that went all the way around the house. And I tell you, it was just like a nursery. She was a not a person who talked about things ... she did them. Family was extremely important to her."

The children knew little about their father's involvement and ownership in the local telephone company. Unlike Walter Hanisch's son, David, and Leroy Etzel's daughters, Betty and Marguerite, the Doyle children didn't work at the telephone company in the summers, nor did they hang around the office. Although their father was an owner, he didn't work there, so they had no reason to be at the telephone office.

The Doyles grew up with an intimate familiarity with the land that was to serve the brothers well in the future. Jack, Bob and Tom Doyle learned early on that working a farm was hard work. Jack was the natural farmer. There wasn't anything he couldn't fix. Bob preferred baseball to farm work, but he put in his time on the ranch. Being 10 years younger, Tom was still a kid when his brothers were already working hard on the farm helping their dad.

As kids growing up in the Depression, their days were filled with chores and simple fun. Hunting was a favorite sport of all three brothers and Bob and Tom hunted regularly into the 1960s. Merle Ruggles was one of Tom Doyle's boyhood friends and spent a lot of time there, particularly on the weekends.

"I'll never forget Bob had this old goose called 'Joe' and that thing was better than a watchdog," Ruggles recalled. "If the goose didn't want you on the property, you didn't go. One day I was out there and Bob yells it's all clear, that Joe wasn't there. I started down the stairs to leave and all of a sudden out of nowhere comes Joe, the goose. He nailed me good and finally Bob had to get him off me. I still have scars from where old Joe pinched me. Finally, Bob had to give the goose away, he got so mean. His meanness finally did him in. Joe would peck at car tires and eventually got run over."

Bob and Jack Doyle, although only a year apart, had different interests.

"Jack and I were close, but we weren't necessarily best friends, mostly because he didn't play sports. I played basically all the sports, particularly basketball and baseball, but Jack spent his time fixing things around the ranch while I was out jolly jacking around in the outfield," Bob Doyle explained. "I tried to get Jack to come down and see our ball team play. Once in a great while I talked him into it, but he just didn't like it."

On the whole, the Doyles were an ordinary Roseville ranch family. Keeping up with the cattle, sheep, turkeys, grapes, almonds, and grain crops kept Bill and Hazel Doyle and their five children close to the land in those years. They didn't vacation or socialize to any great extent. They enjoyed a typical small-town, farm lifestyle.

Myron McIntyre doubts anybody was real close to Bill Doyle and his family in those days. "Bill Doyle wasn't just a farmer, but he stayed on the land and that was his life."

## BASEBALL, BASEBALL, BASEBALL

Baseball was America's national pastime in the Depression years and nobody loved the sport more than Bob Doyle. "I was lucky because my dad loved baseball, too. That's the reason I got to play; otherwise, he wanted me to work on the farm. But for baseball, he'd let me go."

The desire to play sports is what kept Bob Doyle in school. He had no scholarly or career ambitions, because he knew he'd be working on the farm after school.

"When I was young I'd be the shag boy for some of the players, that is, I'd shag fly balls," Doyle said. "I got to be real good chasing down fly balls because I did it so much. I just loved it."

Doyle's experience shagging flies paid off as he became one of the area's top outfielders. His strengths were his foot speed and great anticipation in catching fly balls. Few balls got past him. He was also a good hitter. Doyle's baseball prowess might have resulted in his attending college, had it not been for his father's narrowly-focused thinking.

*Bob Doyle was one of the area's best baseball players in the late 1930s and early 1940s.*

Courtesy of Robert L. Doyle

"When I was still a junior in high school, I played on a softball team that was playing in Davis," Doyle remembered. "We had a hell of a ball game down there and I had made a lot of good catches. This guy came to me afterward and asked, 'Do you play hardball?' I said, 'Yes,' and he said, "When you get out of high school, you come down and see me.' He was the baseball coach for the college in Davis."

"I told my dad what the coach had said, that I could probably play at Davis. Since Davis had a farming program, it seemed like a reasonable thing. But he said, 'The hell with them. Those bastards down there, they're farming in good ground; it's not like the hard pan we have here. You go down and listen to them, and try to farm that way here, and you'll go broke, flat on your ass.'

"Obviously, he didn't encourage me to go to college. If he would have said, 'I think it's a good idea,' I would have probably gone to Davis and I'd have a college education. But it didn't bother me that much, because I knew I was going to be a farmer. That's what my life was going to be."

After high school Doyle became one of the better players in the Auburn-Placer semi-pro baseball circuit. He was good enough that in the fall of 1941, he was invited to Yuba City to try out for the Cincinnati Redlegs, a National League team. He got through the first set of tryouts and was prepared for the second set, a 10-day tryout. Then, his baseball career was interrupted forever. The Japanese bombed Pearl Harbor on Dec. 7, 1941, torpedoing Doyle's and thousands of other baseball players' hopes for a shot in the "bigs."

## LEARNING THE ARMY WAY

Bob Doyle's high school career was uneventful, but in addition to learning about baseball, which became the foundation of his management style, he learned how to type. It's interesting how a simple, clerical function such as typing aided him in his career.

"One of the exercises was to learn how to type the alphabet backwards. Even to this day, I can recite it backwards — z, y, x, w, v, u, t, s, r, q, p, o, n, m, l, k, j, i, h, g, f, e, d, c, b, a. I thought at the time, 'By god, that's pretty good,'" Doyle said. "It was typing ability that enabled me to maneuver my way around the Army."

In January 1942, Bob Doyle was drafted. He remembered those first days.

"When I went in the service, I was sent to Monterey. There were a couple of guys that I'd played semi-pro baseball with here and I thought we were all going to go together. We got on this damn troop train and it takes off. We get going and not too much later I looked back ... and they had dropped some cars off and my buddies are gone. My part of the train kept going and I end up at Camp Grant, Ill., about four miles out of Rockford. This is in January 1942. It was colder than a well digger's ass in Idaho.

"I got off that troop train and found out I was assigned to the medical corps. I wondered how I got into it? In the testing beforehand, I told them I had driven tractors and trucks and everything else. I figured I'd probably be in a tank. I sure as hell didn't think I'd be in the medical corps.

"Well, the medical corps didn't sound too interesting. So immediately, I said, 'I'm sure as hell not going to pack a bedpan in the hospital or run around, get my ass shot off and I can't shoot back, you know.' So I ended up going to be a cook in baker's school. Well, I didn't like that at all."

Doyle's next stop was Fort Thomas, Ky., across the river from Cincinnati. It was there Doyle convinced his superiors that cooking was not for him. Since his typing skills were in demand, he avoided the bedpans and sauce pans.

Doyle's next stop was in a detachment squad sent to Huntington, W. Va. He was assigned to a captain who examined men coming into the service. Doyle was

*During an Army leave in 1943, Bob Doyle visits with his brother Jack on the steps of the old Doyle homestead. Their sister Marjorie is crouching in the background.*

Courtesy of Robert L. Doyle

the captain's clerk. He asked medical history questions of the recruits. "I'd ask about operations, broken bones, stuff like that. I even had to check for hemorrhoids. But the point was that basically if that guy was warm, he was in. We didn't disqualify very many fellows, that's for sure."

The Army provided Doyle's first travel experiences. He was getting to see and experience parts of the country he'd only read about before.

"In West Virginia, they'd bring those coal miners out of the mountains. It was something. They had never been to school and hardly knew their own names. When they were old enough, they went right down into the mines. It was pitiful."

After a stint in West Virginia, Doyle went back to Fort Thomas and was relocated to Walter Reed Hospital in Washington, D.C., the Army's medical center.

"At Walter Reed, we handled soldiers coming back from the front with all sorts of terrible injuries … amputees, burned guys with their faces all scarred. Everything you could imagine."

In addition to wounded soldiers, Doyle faced superiors who enjoyed flexing their authority over greenhorns like Doyle. It was in the Army, Doyle says, that he learned how not to do things.

His next stop was San Francisco, where he earned the rank of corporal. Doyle was happy because he was close enough to home that he felt he could work a deal to play baseball in Roseville on the weekends. He was there about a year before being transferred to Santa Monica. Wounded soldiers from the Pacific theater were treated at a hospital in Pasadena. Then Doyle was shipped to Seattle and then on to Hawaii, where he joined a unit called the "School of Preventive Medicine."

"And so we're waiting to go overseas as the School of Preventive Medicine and I have no idea what I'm going to do," Doyle remembered. "I expected I'd be a doctor's assistant, but nobody ever told me. Finally, they put us on this hospital boat and we headed for Manila."

As their ship plowed through the the Pacific en route to Manila, the war ended. Doyle's military career was nearing a close. When the ship arrived in Manila, Doyle witnessed a mass of American humanity that had only one goal in mind — to get home. But it took time to process the soldiers and pack them on the old pot-bellied Liberty ships for the long trip back home.

"We were staying in Manila in some huge old buildings that had been all shot to pieces. Everybody wanted to go home … it was something, guys getting drunker than hell on coconut wine. It was about seven months before I got my orders to go home.

"Finally, after a number of delays, we got on this damn Liberty ship to go home with probably three times as many people on it as should be. I'll bet half of them were sea sick. You never saw anything like it. You didn't dare go down stairs ... down in the hold, because everybody was heavin' in their helmets. Half of them couldn't eat. It took 22 days from Manila to San Pedro in Los Angeles. Half of those poor bastards didn't eat. I mean, I don't know how the hell they ever lived."

Corporal Robert L. Doyle had no designs on furthering his career in the armed forces. Upon being discharged — honorably, of course — Doyle was asked if he wanted to join the Army Reserves. "I told them, 'The hell I will. You got four years and that's all you're going to get out of me.' Thank God, because the guys who joined the reserves went to Korea."

Four years to the month, in January 1946, Doyle returned to Roseville and immediately began farming with his father and his brothers, Jack and Tom.

Although Doyle's Army career featured no notable achievements, four years away from Roseville meeting people from all walks of life helped prepare him for a career path he had no idea at that time existed for him. One of Doyle's core traits is his ability to observe and to learn from what happens around him. There's no doubt that being in the Army gave him tools, likely hidden ones, that helped him succeed in his career at Roseville Telephone.

"I'm sure, I got a hell of lot more out of the service than I thought I did even though I never got above a corporal or made any money," Doyle said. "I saw a lot of things I wouldn't have seen if I had never left Roseville. I think it also taught me a lot about people."

*Bob Doyle served in the Army Medical Corps from January 1942 through January 1946. He started out making $21 a month and ended up making $66 a month.*

Courtesy of Robert L. Doyle

## FARMING WITH THE DOYLE BROTHERS

Back in Roseville, 26-year-old Bob Doyle was a single young man with no money. "You didn't even make $100 a month in the Army, so I had nothing when I got back. I joined my brother in farming for my father."

Bob Doyle was essentially an employee on his dad's farm. He would put in long hours — often from dawn to dusk — and each week his dad would leave his pay in an envelope taped to the inside of the office door. The Doyle boys would not get rich working for their father, that was clear. Moreover, the elder Doyle was hard-nosed when it came to paying his employees, including his sons. Inevitably, there was a clash between father and son.

"After a year or two working my ass off, I got real sick for a few days and couldn't work. I found I was docked for the time I had missed," Doyle recalled. "I went right to my father and asked him what was going on. He said if I didn't work, I didn't get paid. Period.

"I became very angry and I pointed my finger at his face and called him a so-and-so. I told him we had been working our asses off for him at low pay and didn't deserve to be treated that way. I told him where to stick it."

Later, after he had calmed down, Bob Doyle asked his father if he would stake his three sons to some acreage so they could farm together and no longer work for him. In essence, Bob negotiated for some of his inheritance so the brothers could get a head start in farming.

"We didn't ask him for any money or anything else, just the land so we could farm it ourselves. He agreed."

It marked the beginnings of the Doyle Brothers, owned by partners Jack, Bob and Tom Doyle. Their objective was to farm their own land and other owners' acreage on a lease/share basis.

"We originally farmed 2,000 acres of grain a year. Part of it was property that we owned and part of it was property that we leased on a share basis," Doyle explained. "In other words, we would give the owner 25 percent of the gross income from the crop. We did all the work, putting on fertilizer, seeding, harvesting and everything else."

In addition to doing their own farming, the brothers still helped with their father's almonds and grapes. In addition to the Doyle ranch, which was about 400 acres, the brothers farmed about 800 acres they owned west of town, where Base Line Road and Crowder Lane are now.

"Also, we asked our Uncle Will (Kaseberg) if we could plow his land," Bob Doyle said. "It was all sheep pasture and was virgin soil for farming."

The Doyle Brothers' first year was successful. The weather cooperated beautifully and they had bumper crops. It's good that they did because the brothers had gone deep into debt to buy equipment to farm on a relatively large scale. It was a good lesson for Bob Doyle to learn how prudent borrowing could enhance business success. He was to put that into effect later when running the telephone company.

"After my dad gave us the OK to farm on our own, we needed to borrow $28,000 to buy the farm equipment we'd need," Bob Doyle remembered. "I talked to the Bank of America and the Citizens Bank of Roseville. Joe Royer ran Citizens back then. I went to him first and told him we wanted to borrow $28,000 and that we wanted his best deal ... we weren't going to come back and negotiate. I told him I'd go across to the Bank of America and also talk to them.

"Royer told me he had known my dad for years and had lent him money, all that kind of stuff, to warm me up," Doyle continued. "He offered me the $28,000, but said we'd have to borrow the whole thing up front.

"Across the street at the Bank of America, I was offered the $28,000 on a credit line ... in other words, we didn't have to borrow it all — and pay interest on it all — right from the start. We could borrow as we needed. So we went with the Bank of America and Royer was not happy, to say the least. But I had told him to offer us his best deal and he didn't. Later on he became a big shareholder, though, so I guess he got over it."

In the Doyle Brothers partnership, Bob was the bookkeeper. Jack was the best farmer of the three and Tom was a real good farmer, too. The brothers worked night and day to get ahead.

"We'd run the tractor 24 hours a day, stopping it only to refuel. I remember sometimes I'd plow ground from 6 at night until 6 in the morning," remembered Bob Doyle.

The Doyle Brothers were known as extremely hard workers and their business kept growing. The brothers didn't make a lot of money in those early years; instead they plowed their profits back into the business.

"Jack was always mechanically inclined and could fix anything. It just came natural," remembered Bob Doyle. "He'd get an old Model T, put an old block

*The Doyle Brothers, Jack, Bob and Tom, pose with their father Bill Doyle.*
Courtesy of Robert L. Doyle

and tackle deal on those big trees we had and pull the motor out. Then he'd take it apart, fix it, and put it all together again. I always wondered how the hell he did that. And it didn't matter what broke, the tractor, the harvester or even a washing machine ... anything, he could fix it, whether it involved welding or anything. He never went to school to learn that stuff, he just knew how to do it. Jack was one hell of a farmer and was the backbone of the Doyle Brothers."

Merle Ruggles recalled the Doyle Brothers' farming days. "They had their monthly meetings of what they had to do. They'd all pull down their own shifts when it come plowing time. One would work night shifts, one would work day, and so on. If they had a breakdown, Jack normally was the mechanic. And on the weekends, I'd go down and drive at night or during the day if they had other things to do, because they had almonds at that time, and grapes," Ruggles said. "Across the street from me were grape vineyards. They had about 90 acres of grapes plus they had grapes down the other end, down towards the creek. And then their dad raised turkeys. They had a few cows. They had to work real hard."

The brothers farmed together until the summer of 1953 when, at his father's behest, Bob Doyle agreed to join Roseville Telephone. At the outset, the brothers agreed that Bob's stint at the telephone company would be treated as a leave of absence. Once Bob got matters straightened out at the telephone company, he'd come back to Doyle Brothers. That was the plan. But the future held a different course, for both Bob and his brothers.

## FATHER ASKS BOB DOYLE TO 'CLEAN UP THE PHONE COMPANY'

By 1953, Bill Doyle was nearing 80 years old and had been president of Roseville Telephone for 36 years. His telephone company was straining to grow despite the wishes of its elderly owners that it stay small. Technology was changing rapidly and the area served by the company was growing. It was time for Bill Doyle to pass the torch to another family member. The patriarch chose his middle son, 34-year-old Bob.

"I'm sure my dad asked me to go to the company because he knew Jack was really the best farmer and Tom was too young, even though he had become a director the year before. Since I had been in the service, my dad figured I knew a lot more about office work than my brothers. It made sense that I would be the one to go," Doyle said. "He must have thought he had only one choice, that was me, since he probably figured I wasn't good for anything else."

On Aug. 15, 1953, Bob Doyle made his last career move. He went from being a self-employed, up-and-coming farmer to a "commercial representative" in the business office of a tiny telephone company. He didn't plan on being there long.

"When my father came to me in 1953, it was out of a clear blue sky. The Public Utilities Commission had told the board of directors of the telephone company — and it wasn't the first time — 'You either get somebody in there for some public relations and to try to straighten that company out or we're going to take it away from you.' It was that serious," Doyle recollected. "The management, which was Walter Hanisch and his son, wanted to go down south and get somebody to run the company. But my dad asked me. I said, 'I don't know a damn thing about the telephone business, but I'll do the best I can. I'll see if I can find somebody who knows something about running it. And I'll hire that person and when he gets the company going, I'll go back to farming with my brothers.' That was the understanding. I told my brothers I'd take care of dad's interest in the telephone company and then I'd be back."

As an owner, Bob remained a part of the Doyle Brothers' operation at the outset and contributed his $200 monthly salary to the partnership as income. Even Tom Doyle's $25 monthly stipend for being a Roseville Telephone director was thrown in the kitty to be divided among the three brothers. "Yeah," said Tom Doyle. "I put my $25 into the partnership and got back $8.33 as my share. Such a good deal."

It didn't take long for Bob Doyle to figure out what was wrong at the telephone company. The service was atrocious and the management and owners were insensitive to the needs of the customers. It was a dire situation that he found himself in. As a successful farmer, he had already learned that when the owners invest in the future, the business will grow and prosper. It worked in farming and he felt it could work in the telephone business, too, even though he knew nothing about the industry at that time.

"Conditions were horrible. We were all in the one little building and the construction yard was down the street. That's all the company owned in 40 years. They had never bought any property for the future and hardly improved their plant ... they just didn't do anything. The money they earned was mostly all paid in cash dividends to the few stockholders who owned the company. They never sold any stock to the public. If they wanted to do something, they had to come up with money from themselves. Whoever had the most stock was the president. Well, it was my dad."

"After being there a little while, it appeared to me that the management had no right to be in the telephone business because they certainly weren't taking care of even what they had. It was a crime."

It didn't take Bob Doyle long to decide, whether consciously or not, that he relished the challenge of revamping and building his father's telephone company. He stayed on because he wanted to safeguard his family's long-time investment and he hadn't found anybody else to lead the company. "I guess that somebody turned out to be me," he would say later.

*Young Bob Doyle becomes president of Roseville Telephone in late January 1954.*

## THE FIRST MONTHS AS 'THE JANITOR'

His first months were spent learning about the business operations of the company. For one, he collected coins from the few coin pay stations that existed then. He sifted the coins in the three-decker wooden coin screen sorter that separated nickels, dimes and quarters. The sorter is now in the Roseville Telephone Museum. The coins were rolled and taken to the bank. This was one of Bob Doyle's first jobs.

"When I first went to work — I called myself the janitor — we had maybe four or five pay phones in the whole area. In those days there was no place to put pay phones. There were no businesses to put the pay stations at. I can remember later on when something would come along like a Kentucky Fried Chicken, we'd say, 'Hey, there is a good place to put a pay phone.' We would run down there and put a pay phone in."

In the early 1950s, the telephone company's best-earning pay phone was across the tracks from its office, in Roseville's "old town." Although its image as a man's town was beginning to erode as the 1950s came, "old town" was still lively.

"They still had houses of ill-repute, gambling and lots of bars in old town then. There were taxi cabs coming up from Sacramento constantly," Doyle remembered. "The pay phones were being used all the time. There was an old pay phone at the Barker Hotel, and if I didn't get over there and empty that thing at least once a week, it was plugged. There was a big box for coins in those old pay phones, but it would fill up fast. We fixed up that old booth and it's now in our museum."

Although the early emphasis was on Citrus Heights, the company needed to serve expanding areas of Roseville, too. But in Doyle's earliest days at the company, Walter Hanisch was still the manager and had authority. When a new subdivision was going into Roseville with about 50 units, the ultraconservative Hanisch did not believe it was cost-justified to put in fixed plant to serve the new homes. He believed the development would fail and the homes would remain vacant.

"They started to build these houses, a bunch of flat tops, and Walter said, 'Nobody is going to live in those houses. You can take a cat and throw it right through the wall and they would get up and walk away.' This was the attitude he had and it was a big reason nothing happened at the company for so many years.

"But I said, 'We've got to have some kind of telephone service down there.' I knew a guy who was going to live there and I asked if we could put a pay phone on his front lawn. That way residents in this subdivision would have some place to go to make a call. I figured this was a better solution than nothing, at least until we could put in facilities to serve the houses themselves. And that is exactly what we did."

Had it not been for Bob Doyle's strong sense of loyalty to his dad and family, it would have been easy to throw up his hands and recommend that the company be sold.

"I think it was good I didn't know anything," Doyle said about the first year at the company. "If I had really known all the pitfalls, I probably would have been scared to death. But I just knew that something had to be done. I didn't want the Roseville Telephone Company to have to sell out to anybody."

## BUILDING A COMPANY AND HAVING FUN DOING IT

Bob Doyle can often be a hard-charging and impatient boss, but he also understands the value of humor in the work place. Whether it be during a serious meeting, or during a social outing, you can count on Doyle telling a funny story or joke in addition to his long list of colorful expressions, many adopted from his father. And when he laughs, it's a full, belly laugh that makes his eyes twinkle, particularly if he's putting one over on somebody.

Dan McGrath, a columnist for the *Sacramento Bee*, captured Bob Doyle's persona in a June 1994 article.

"His silver-gray hair is 'styled' in one of the world's most enduring crew cuts, and his lively blue eyes dance with mischief. His weathered, craggy features bespeak wisdom and experience, life lived to its fullest …"

Barbara Sande Dimmitt profiled Roseville Telephone in the November 1994 edition of *Comstock's* magazine. Her opening paragraph is vintage Bob Doyle:

"'One thing that helps Roseville is that we're right next to the capital … You see, Sacramento's a suburb of Roseville. You probably didn't know that, but it is. Roseville has got a lot of things to offer. But basically, people come here for the telephone service.' His craggy face crinkles with a smile, and he laughs from the belly. Wise eyes watch for your reaction. It's a joke you think — or is it?"

In almost 40 years, Bob Doyle has had only two secretaries, Ellen Lynn, who became his secretary in 1957, and Virginia Amick, who took over from Lynn when she retired in 1984. They have seen more of Bob Doyle than anybody else other than his family. His door is usually open so the secretaries in the executive offices often can hear his conversations because his voice carries.

"Bob always answers his own phone if he doesn't have somebody in there with him," said Amick. "That alone catches callers off guard because how many places can you call the chairman of the company direct without going through a secretary? Probably nowhere else, but that's Bob.

*Bob Doyle served as Sheriff Bob "Deadeye" Doyle during Roseville's Centennial Days in 1964.*

Courtesy of Robert L. Doyle

"One time a telephone subscriber called him and apparently said to him, 'When are you going to get out here and fix this telephone?' Well, Bob thought it was one of the board members at that time, Bill Sheppard, trying to pull a fast one on him," Amick remembered. "So Bob replies, 'Why in the hell don't you fix your own goddamn phone?' This goes on for a bit and Bob finally says, 'What do you want me to do ... do you want me to climb the pole for you?' Then it occurred to Bob that the caller was a real customer, not Bill Sheppard. It was the funniest thing in the whole world to watch Bob back out of that. I remember him laughing a lot and apologizing. 'I really thought you were someone else,' he told the caller, and then added, 'We'll take care of this problem right away.' And it did get top priority."

Recently retired Vern Roberson recalled a time when he faced an angry woman wielding a shotgun while he tried to trim a tree in Citrus Heights. He called Doyle to the rescue. It's called the "But Lady" episode and occurred in 1956, according to Roberson.

"I was out on Oak Avenue and had Merle Ruggles with me. He was just starting with the company and was with me on the job to learn about the company," Roberson said. "We had open wire then, and when trees get in the wires, the phone service was the devil. So we went out there and asked a homeowner if we could trim his tree to clear the branches from the wires. He said go ahead.

"So we're trimming some branches and out comes a woman next door with a double-barreled shotgun. Apparently, she rented from the man next door who let us trim his tree. So she says to us, 'What are you doing?' I said, 'Trimming a tree, ma'am,' and she said, 'Oh, no, you're not. You don't cut no limb off the tree.' I said, 'Yes, ma'am, I got to.' She said, 'I'll shoot you if you do.' I had no desire to be shot, but I told her the owner had given me permission. She said, 'Don't give me that crap, I'll just shoot you.' Of course, Merle ... he's petrified. So I said, 'OK, lady.'

"So I went over and got my spurs off the truck, and she said, 'What are you going to do?' I said, 'I'm going to climb that pole and call my boss and tell him I have a problem here.' She said, 'Oh, no, you can't climb that pole.' I said, 'Yes, ma'am, I can. You watch me.'

"I climbed that pole as fast as any monkey. I clipped into the telephone line, called in and got Doyle. I said, 'Mr. Doyle, I've got a slight problem on my hands. I've got a lady out here wanting to shoot me.' He said, 'What in hell for?' So I told him the story, and then said, 'I'm up the pole and she's got the shotgun aiming right square at my butt. I can't talk to her.' He said, 'Don't do a thing, don't get her excited. You just sit down there in the shade and mind your own business. I'll be right there and I'll talk to her.' I said, 'Mr. Doyle, you can't talk to her.' He said, 'You stay there, I'll talk to her.'

"So I came down the pole, took my belt hooks to the truck, and Merle says, 'What are you going to do?' I said, 'Mr. Doyle said to wait right here and he'd be right here.' The lady mumbled something and went back into the house after a bit. She asked me if I was going, and I said, 'Lady, I ain't about to leave. I'm going to be right here. My boss is coming to talk to you. I ain't going nowhere.' So Doyle pulled up and said, 'Where's that woman at?' And I said, 'Right there in that house, Bob. But I'll tell you, you can't talk to her.' He said, 'Come on, we'll go talk to her.' So we went up and he knocked on the door, and boy, she just about shoved that door in his face, and out she comes with that double-barreled shotgun. She said, 'Yes, and by god, I'll shoot you too.'

"Doyle just said, 'I'm Bob Doyle of Roseville Telephone Company.' And she said, 'I don't care who you are.' She's cussing and carrying on. And Bob said 'But, lady...' and that's all he'd ever get out, 'But, lady … but, lady …' And this went on for I don't know how long. Finally, Doyle had it. He looked at her and said, 'Go to hell, you crazy old witch. You're about three bricks short of a load.'

"I was dying laughing. If she had shot me, I'd have died happy. If she'd have killed us all, I still would have been laughing. So Bob finally said, 'Let's go.' I really didn't know if we were going to get shot in the back or not. She was crazy, you didn't know. And Merle was over there scared as hell, and if you'd said 'Boo!' he'd have died of a heart attack. If a car had come by and backfired right about then, we would have buried Merle, that's no joke. He was shaking."

For the time being, the tree in question remained untrimmed. "Next time," Roberson thought to himself as he and Ruggles drove off.

In his early years at the company, Doyle was the boss, yes, but he was one of the boys, too. In addition to the infamous Friday night meetings of his managers, he'd often have a brew with other employees and business associates. One of Bob Doyle's closest associates through the years has been insurance broker Richard "Dick" Wise. He remembers meeting Doyle in the mid-1960s when his father, Nathan Wise, made a sales pitch to Doyle for the company's insurance business.

"I was just kind of a neophyte in the insurance business when my dad and a fellow who worked for my dad called on Bob and made a presentation. The other fellow was doing most of the talking, and my dad was kind of listening and supervising, if you will," Wise said. "My dad was in his sixties at that time. So about half way through the presentation, Bob looked over at my dad and quipped, 'Evidently Nate is not overwhelmed by this whole presentation because he seems to be resting pretty well.' My dad had fallen asleep. So they woke him up and finished the proposal. Bob had to present it to the board, and he said, 'Why don't you wait outside while we discuss the proposal.' We waited about 10 minutes. Then Bob came out and asked my dad if it was worth a drink for the board if we got the deal. My dad said, 'You bet your life.' Bob smiled, 'You've already got the deal.' So they went over and celebrated, and that's how we started."

During the 1960s Doyle and his managers worked hard and played hard. A frequent companion of Doyle's was George Minasian, the business office manager who retired in 1990.

"Yes, we did drink a lot back then. I mean Bob and Tom, Gunning and me and Merle … Mark Shull was not so much included in our group at that time in the same sense that Gunning, Merle and I were, and even Tinker. We were loud and profane and that would get us thrown out of saloons. Of course, that would never happen to Bob now, but in those days, we just didn't care. That was our early life. We've all toned down since then. Bob is a lot more reserved now, and I think he considers himself above that sort of behavior. But it didn't matter in those days. As people have looked upon the success of the company, Bob straightened out his act quite a bit."

Clarice Gunning admits she was concerned during those years. "My first impression was that Bob Doyle was honest, above board, a heavy drinker and a lot of fun. I thought for a period there he was leading my husband down the road to alcoholism, but fortunately that didn't occur, and Bob's OK, too."

In 1964, during the City of Roseville's Centennial Days, Doyle's company cronies participated to the fullest in the days long, Wild West-themed celebration. The honorary sheriff was none other than "Deadeye" Doyle, who helped string up the criminals of the day, ably assisted by deputies Em Gunning and Merle Ruggles. The lawmen wore western outfits and all grew beards for the celebration. One can imagine the hard partying that occurred in those years.

Wise admits to a lot of partying with Bob and Tom Doyle in the '60s and early '70s.

"It was a different lifestyle then. It was much more accepted. I don't drink at all any more and I used to drink lots. I don't think Bob drinks much any more either. But it was a different time, a different environment. Bob never had short arms and deep pockets. He was a hell of a host and always fun to be with. His sayings were … well, ribald is an understatement," Wise remembered. "My dad used to play piano in a whorehouse in Chicago. He played by ear. Between Bob and him, they probably knew every dirty song that was ever sung.

"Even though we did a lot of partying in those years, when the bell rang, Bob was always there. He never let a hangover or the fact that he was partying the night before have anything to do with the way he ran the company. The guy had a constitution like a bull. He could pack it away and feel good the next day. I didn't, but he did."

Humor is not restricted to drinking bouts, however. To this day, Bob Doyle enjoys a good story, joke and loves to banter, seeing if he can one-up you. Bob Parsons is a frequent lunch partner of Bob Doyle's and the two have come to be good friends. Perhaps no one experiences the humorous side of Bob Doyle more than Parsons.

*Richard "Dick" Wise has been Roseville Telephone's insurance broker for 30 years.*

Photo by Rob Wilcox

"I remember one time we were talking and he started to tell me something — and just the way he looks, when he goes to set up a joke or imitate somebody — he gets that look in his eyes, and I start to laugh before he gets to the part that's funny," Parsons said. "Then he starts to laugh and before he even gets to the punch line, we're both laughing. By the time he gets to the punch line, we're both in tears. Now here's two grown men sitting there laughing hysterically, but it's just the way one thing plays off of another."

Stewart Brown, a supervisor under Parsons, has observed his boss and Bob Doyle humorously skirmish in their attempts to one-up each other.

"A few years ago we were setting up a phone bank for volunteers to call in support of the Auburn Dam. I was with Bob Parsons and Mr. Doyle where the phone bank was to be set up — the phones hadn't actually been set up yet. On the way back, Bob Parsons said something to Bob Doyle about getting the phones up and Parsons said, in his quiet, dry way, 'I think we ought to put in rotary dial …'

"Of course, dial phones are long gone by this time and we've got push button phones all over the place. Parsons made the comment just to be funny," Brown remembered. "So Doyle looks at him with that twinkle in his eye, 'Yeah … pay stations.' We cracked up. Imagine a group of volunteers using rotary dial pay stations in this day and age?"

Dick Wise recalled Bob Doyle's acceptance speech when honored as the "Man of the Year" during a "Roseville on the Go" a few years ago.

"Most people get up when honored and are like humble pie. They say, 'I really don't deserve this,' or 'I'm thankful,' something like that. But not Bob. Eli Broad had talked first, and everybody gave polite applause, and here comes Doyle who has been named the 'Man of the Year.' He stands up and says, 'I know a lot of people might stand up here and say they didn't deserve this honor. But I think that's a slap in the face to the people who voted for me. These people obviously knew what the hell they were doing and I'm not going to do anything to discredit them. They obviously made a wonderful choice.' He went on and on as only he can and the whole place just roared. There are damned few people who could get away with that. But Bob is really secure in himself, he doesn't care what people think."

Aside from his great sense of humor, Doyle is probably best known for his colorful expressions and his innocent profanities.

## PROFANITY — A LONG-TIME DOYLE TRADITION

*(Editor's note: The following text includes expressions that could offend some readers. It must be understood that the Doyles, particularly William J. Doyle and his sons Bob and Tom, always spoke bluntly and colorfully. The way the Doyles use profanity, however, differs from most people, because they do not speak with malice. It's simply the colorful way they talk. Readers who do not understand this approach should skip this subchapter, if they choose. But no history about the Doyles and the Roseville Telephone Company would be complete without mentioning their colorful language and bawdy humor.)*

In profiling Bob Doyle for his June 3, 1994, column in the *Sacramento Bee*, Dan McGrath described his subject's vocabulary as "... well, salty enough to hold the floor at a longshoreman's hall."

Bob Doyle remembers one of the first times he noticed that his dad used colorful language around the household.

"My mother had some ladies in the house there one time and my dad came in. The women were talking about this and that and bitching about this and that, and the old man said, 'Just keep a stiff upper lip and a tight asshole, and everything will be all right.' He was just talking, you know, and, of course, my mother's ready to fall through the floor. But nobody seemed to pay any attention. This was the way he was.

"My grandmother was really a strict Catholic. So the priest used to come over to get money and my dad would be sitting out there and they'd talk and laugh a lot. He was using cuss words all the time. It was the funniest thing you ever saw. Some people can get away with that and some people can't get away with that. Just because my dad did it doesn't mean that everybody can do it. For some reason, my whole family seems to think that they should do like the old man did. And some of the time we botch it up pretty good, which is bad. I try to be careful, especially around women. You've got to know who they are. But sometimes it's bad and embarrassing to everybody."

Bob and Tom Doyle have always used profanity in their everyday language and those around them just know that's the way they talk. They don't take offense.

Gladys Ross, the former chief operator, was nearly 50 when Bob Doyle joined the company in 1953. Having grown up in old Roseville, where over the years thousands of railroaders spent many a night in saloons and local brothels, Bob's language didn't shock Gladys.

"Well, he was loose in language and all that, but that didn't bother anybody too much because of the way he was," Gladys remembered. "To me, it added to his ability and charm, really. Now nobody else could do it respectfully, but he always called me 'Happy Bottom.' Of course you couldn't do that today."

*Bob Sharples was in charge of property and maintenance before retiring. He was Bob Doyle's "Mr. Fix It" for many years.*

Bob Doyle laughs when that nickname is brought up. "Yeah, I called her 'Happy Bottom' because her name was Gladys — you know, 'Glad Ass.'"

Gladys added: "You couldn't get mad at him for the way he did it because you always knew it wasn't meant to harm. I think it's a secret the way he can talk like that with people."

Mark Shull remembered that, ironically, Bob Doyle's salty language helped him command respect during the early days of dealing with the California Public Utilities Commission staff.

"I can remember in particular we used to go down there and one of the staffers in the commission office particularly enjoyed getting Bob all upset. There would be a lot of table pounding on both sides and Bob would state our position in no uncertain terms. He'd make full use of his language skills. By the time we left, we usually had accomplished what we wanted to," Shull said.

Bill Sheppard knew Bob Doyle's dad and was familiar with the family language.

"Bob just grew up talking that way because that's just the way his dad was," Sheppard said. "He can get away with swearing where he doesn't mean it. It's like my wife says about me. 'If Shep says you're a son of a bitch, it means he likes you.' It's the same with Bob. He doesn't intend to offend anybody. And he says it in such a way nowadays that I don't think he does. Most people love him and take it in stride."

Bob Doyle's family got used to his ways years ago. This is not to say that his wife, Carmen, or children, Carol and Mike, embrace his rough language, but they understand that it's his way.

"They are not really wild and crazy guys, particularly nowadays," said Carmen Doyle about Bob and Tom Doyle. "They just have big voices. And the more they drink the louder their voices get.

"I know Bob's father didn't drink or smoke, but I understand that he was a character. Almost every other word was a cuss word. So Bob and Tom grew up with it," Carmen Doyle continued. "But I told Bob I didn't want my kids to learn all that and he really did try to control it at home. Sometimes he just couldn't help it, but usually he was pretty good about it."

*Bob Doyle in "period" clothing during a Southern Pacific celebration in the early 1960s.*

Courtesy of Robert L. Doyle

The Doyle children, Mike Doyle and Carol Smith, are not unduly judgmental about their dad's profanity. Neither swear to any extent, but they accept that profanity is part of their father's persona. But Carol would get embarrassed if her father was profane around her friends. That attitude continues.

Virginia Amick gave an example of how Bob Doyle uses his salty language to loosen up visitors.

"I remember when Alan Ewen, at the time the head of SACTO, would come to visit him," she said. "He was quite formal, especially compared to Bob. But it wouldn't be long before you'd hear the two of them in there telling stories and cussing. Bob does that a lot, especially when he doesn't know someone. He starts slowly but he'll be a little more loose to break the ice a little. That's how it worked with Alan Ewen and they had a good relationship."

As might be expected, Bob Parsons — with his interest in history — has taken it upon himself to chronicle as many of Bob Doyle's expressions as he can. Parsons is not only interested in preserving history; it's also because he is an ardent admirer of his long-time boss. Parsons at one time or another has heard just about every colorful expression Doyle has uttered in the last 20 years.

"I started jotting down some of his most common expressions so I wouldn't forget them," Parsons explained. "Like when someone is busy, he'd say 'He's busier than a one-armed paper hanger.' When you think about that, a guy hanging paper with one arm ... he's a busy man. Bob may use a one-armed paper hanger this week, but he'll switch to something else because he has that sense that maybe he's used that one a lot and he'll get another one. And that's what makes the guy unique.

"With all his expressions," says Parsons, "I don't know of any one person who has ever used all of these. They're his little quips and colloquial things that he says…and, of course, delivery is everything."

Parsons' partial list of "Doylisms" includes:

- *We had to lift the urinals to keep them on their toes.*

- *He waits until the bill comes to go to the rest room; he has short arms and deep pockets.*

- *He's tighter than a bull's ass at fly time.*

- *He doesn't have sense enough to pour piss out of a boot if the directions were written on the heel.*

- *He can't find his ass with both hands.*

- *Happier than a little kid with two peters.*

- *Keep a stiff upper lip and a tight asshole, and everything will be OK.*

- *He wouldn't spend 10 cents to see a piss-ant eat a bale of hay.*

- *The rain was coming down like a cow pissing on a flat rock.*

- *He reminds me of a horse turd floating down the river saying, "Look at us apples float!"*

- *He tried, that's all a steer can do.*

- *He got what the eagle left on the rock.*

- *It's so quiet, you can hear the zippers in the men's room.*

- *If you follow him, you'll be wearing horse turds as big as diamonds.*

- *He is as nervous as a prostitute in church.*

- *He was shaking like a dog shitting peach seeds.*

- *I've gained so much weight that only my tie fits.*

- *It's colder than a well digger's ass in Idaho.*

- *He'd charge hell with one bucket of water.*

- *It's cold enough to freeze the balls off a pool table.*

- *He was as gritty as the white end of a hen's turd.*

- *That went over like a turd in a punch bowl.*

- *We stand behind everything but the fertilizer spreader.*

- *It's the greatest thing since the zipper.*

- *How come there are so many more horses' asses than there are horses?*

*Bob Parsons, left, with secretary Terri Esparza. Parsons, director of customer services, is a frequent lunch partner of Bob Doyle's.*

Somehow Bob Doyle manages to intersperse these expressions, and quite a few more, into his everyday conversation without offending others. It's truly an art, probably not one to be emulated, however.

Not all Doyle's profanity is innocent fun, of course. He's a man who can be quick to anger and on those occasions, his profanities are direct and fully carry the intended meaning. Anyone who's been around him will attest that when he's upset, everyone within listening distance will know it. Doyle's fuse can be short, particularly when the target of his anger lingers in his office or on the telephone.

Over the years, one topic that could be guaranteed to rile Doyle is the idea of another telephone company taking over Roseville Telephone. Potential buyers have felt Doyle's wrath at its hottest.

# WARDING OFF POTENTIAL ACQUIRERS

Nearly every independent telephone company larger than Roseville Telephone has shown an interest in acquiring the company at one time or another. Their approaches have ranged from the low-key approach of gingerly pursuing a friendly acquisition to the blunt approach of those who told Bob Doyle point blank they wanted Roseville Telephone. To all suitors, Doyle has been unequivocal in telling them where to go. Roseville Telephone is not for sale, never has been, and as far as Doyle is concerned, never will be.

Doyle's defense against potential takeover artists was well-developed from the earliest days of selling stock to the public. He knew that consolidation was going to be a fact of life in the telephone industry as larger companies sought to grow by systematically snapping up local telephone exchanges. When Doyle joined Roseville Telephone in 1953, there were more than 60 telephone companies in California. By 1994, there were only 22. Acquisition fever was particularly heated in the 1960s when Continental Telephone and General Telephone were especially voracious.

"From the time we sold that first stock issue, I knew it was important to know who held the stock," said Doyle. "That's why I didn't want to use stockbrokers to market our shares. If we could do it ourselves, it would give us our best shot at keeping the shares in the community. People that live here enjoy the benefits of owning a stake in the company. Every day they see what Roseville Telephone means to the community, in terms of payroll, our commitment to use local vendors, and all that the company and employees give back to the community."

Doyle has encountered numerous "feelers" from companies hoping to acquire Roseville Telephone. Some attempts have been subtle, others not so subtle. No approach has ever been serious or formal enough to require a review by the company's board. Any potential acquiring company understood it would need the full support of Bob and Tom Doyle for any bid to be successful. And the chances of convincing the brothers to support a sale of Roseville Telephone are very long indeed.

"I never ever had any thoughts about selling, even though I knew that there were a lot of people who'd like to buy us and give us a lot of money," said Tom Doyle. "But I figured, my dad's always been in there, and I felt loyal to all the other directors and our employees and the stockholders. I'm not going to sell anybody down the river for personal gain."

Attorney Bob Raymer said Bob Doyle has been very shrewd in avoiding takeover attempts.

"He's very analytical about this business of keeping independent. He started out years ago to see to it that the stock was distributed locally and that the principal stockholders were people who were closely allied with him or the community," Raymer explained. "Of course, there's no way that he can control what a stockholder does — the stockholder can sell it to a stranger and, of course, to a degree, that's been done. But I think that control of the company is still very comfortably within the local community. If Bob had elected to do the more usual thing and to go to a securities underwriter to distribute his stock, it's very likely that he could not have kept control of the company."

The current president and chief executive officer, Brian Strom, explained the likely impact on the employees and community if Roseville Telephone were to be acquired.

"Any new owner would make the company somewhat of a satellite office," Strom said. "Probably a third of our work force would go, including virtually all the administrative staff, and the higher-up supervisors, engineers and central office guys. That, of course, would include me, because I'd be replaced by someone less expensive, or I wouldn't be replaced at all. A new owner would just stop in once a month to see if the switches were still turned on.

"It would be a gore to the community, of course, because of the much lower payroll, lost jobs, lost business that we do here and less community involvement. I think it would be hard to duplicate our company's stature in the Roseville community if it was a branch office with the headquarters in New York City, Chicago or some other place. I think our shareholders are smart enough to know that this company has been, and will continue to be, a good investment for the long haul."

Companies interested in acquiring Roseville Telephone have faced an immovable force in Bob Doyle. As is his nature, potential buyers have been summarily dismissed, often in a less-than-cordial way. Doyle recalls some of the acquisition forays he's fielded through the years. The companies' names are not disclosed, for reasons of privacy.

In one instance, the chief executive of a particularly aggressive company called Bob Doyle to say he wanted to visit. He told Bob he'd fly his own plane to Sacramento's Executive Airport and asked Bob to pick him up there.

"I knew what he was going to do, but I picked him up anyway. This was quite a ways back," Doyle recalled. "So I got him in my car and drove about five blocks. There was a great big tree by the road, so I just parked under the tree and asked, 'What do you want?' He said, 'Well, you know, you're not making enough money.' I said, 'Is that right?' He said, 'Yeah, if we could get Roseville to come along with us, I could do this and I could do that.' I said, 'I'm doing great as far as I'm concerned. I think they're paying me more than I'm worth. But, you know, our company isn't for sale. I've told everybody that, but I don't think some people believe me. It isn't for sale under any circumstances.'

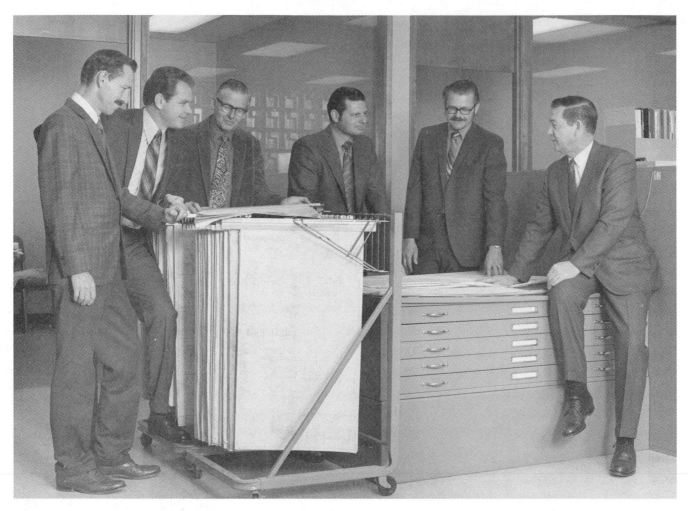

*The company's outside plant engineering head Warren Tinker, right, with his staff in 1971-72. From the left are Leon Bower, Doug Knowlton, Wes Risley, Doug Reed, and Jack Poulsen.*

"This occurred during the years this company was really aggressive, swallowing up a lot of the small independent companies. He was intent on getting us," Doyle continued. "So he looks straight at me and said, 'I want the Roseville Telephone Company. I want it and I'll tell you what I'm going to do, I'm going to come up here, advertise in the newspaper and offer to buy shares at a premium, a hell of a lot more than it's worth. I'll get the stock. I'm serious.' I said, 'I want to tell you something, I'm going to take you back to your goddamn plane right now, and go ahead, you get your ass up here and try to buy the stock. But this is one time you're going to get screwed, because it ain't going to work.'

"Then I took him back and told him to get his ass out of my car and said, 'I don't want anything to do with you from now on. When we go to a convention, you stay on your side of the room and I'll stay on my side. You're no good and you're a detriment to anybody in the goddamn telephone business. In the meantime, I'll be waiting for you. You come up to Roseville and let's just see what the hell you can do. But you're not going to succeed because I sold the stock and I know where the bodies are buried.' He never came."

A popular ploy of acquiring companies was to secretly gain control of a block of stock and then bid a premium price to secure the remaining shares. For those independent companies where founding families controlled the stock, it wasn't too difficult for large, publicly-traded companies to offer their highly liquid stock in exchange for the relatively illiquid stock positions held by controlling families. Roseville Telephone, however, presents a much more difficult challenge for a potential acquirer. Although its shares are publicly-held, buyers and sellers negotiate transactions directly rather than through the more customary stock exchange channels. The absence of significant brokerage company participation makes it difficult for one owner to accumulate a sizable block of shares.

Moreover, Roseville Telephone has always been its own stock transfer agent. This means it cancels stock certificates and issues new ones when shares change ownership. Bob Raymer explains the significance of the transfer agent. "A lot of companies of this size let a bank be the transfer agent. It isn't simple to be your own transfer agent, you've got a tremendous number of compliance issues. The SEC regulates this area. You need equipment, you need people, you need compliance, but Roseville Telephone wants to know who owns the stock because of the control of the company. They don't want the stock to be nibbled away."

Even Doyle's best efforts to resist takeovers would likely fail, however, if the stockholders were unhappy. Clearly, they're not. Shareholders give Doyle and his management team an overwhelming vote of confidence year after year.

"If a company wants to buy us and starts looking into it, they'll find that we often get 95-to-96 percent of the proxy votes represented either in person or by proxy. That high a percentage proxy vote is unheard of. Once a company sees that, they forget it," Doyle explained. "I have made it a point every year, and I've never slacked off, to make sure I get those proxies in. That's a top priority to me. I've got the big holders trained now to a point where I get a better than 50 percent response from the first mail out. I call right after they go out and tell them not to screw around and get those damn proxies in. I tell them I don't want to have to call them next time. So each year, it seems, I have fewer people to call.

"There are always those people who might want to ignore it, figuring their proxy vote won't make a difference. But they know if they don't send it in, that bastard Doyle will call, so they send it in," Doyle said. "They know I'm not going to ask somebody else from here to call ... it's going to be me. That usually moves them to act."

Doyle learned the importance of getting proxy votes during the first public sale of shares in 1953. "L.C. Anderson, our attorney and a director back then, drilled into me that if there was one thing I could do to keep the company (in local hands), it was to get those proxies in every year. L.C. Anderson gave me a lot of good advice ... he was one smart guy, good people, really.

*L.C. Anderson, an attorney and director of Roseville Telephone, gave Bob Doyle a lot of good advice in 1953-54.*

Courtesy of Jack Anderson

"I'm still asked why after all these years I worry so much about getting the proxy votes in. Well, I know it would be almost impossible for a company to get hold of Roseville Telephone without us wanting that to happen, but I'm not so stupid to say it's impossible ... anything is possible. So I'll continue to make it a top priority to get those proxies in as long as I'm here."

Insurance broker Dick Wise sums up the situation for an acquirer:

"If anyone has any ideas of taking over Roseville Telephone, they've sure as heck got their work cut out for them because I don't think Doyle's ever been under 93-94 percent of the proxies."

Doyle has been approached with a variety of propositions to pique his interest in selling. For instance, one company offered to relocate its headquarters to Roseville as an inducement to keep the combined companies "local."

"I told that guy Roseville Telephone is not for sale and that he'd better not continue to torment me about it or, if we ever decided to sell, it sure as hell wouldn't be to him."

One time the president and a vice president of a large company dropped in unannounced "to see how the company is doing," they told Doyle. Always suspicious, Doyle told the two before they sat down, "We can talk about anything you want or see anything you'd like, but if you're here to talk about buying the Roseville Telephone Company, you can get your ass out of here right now."

Another time, the president of another large telephone company wanted to have lunch with Doyle to talk about the possibility of a merger. Doyle's response was blunt.

"I told him I've always considered his company the shittiest telephone company in the United States. I said, 'You treat your employees terribly and your service isn't first-class. On the other hand, I've always considered Roseville Telephone the best telephone company in the country ... so who do you think would gain from a merger?'"

Yet another company president angled hard on one occasion to sit next to Doyle at a telephone convention dinner sponsored by an equipment manufacturer. Doyle caught wind of the executive's tactics. Doyle ate elsewhere that evening. "I can afford to buy my own dinner," he said at the time.

"There are any number of large companies out there that would love to own the Roseville Telephone Company. We're a cherry. But our people know that if this company were sold, heads would roll," Doyle said. "Sure, I take every opportunity to tell employees the advantages they have as an independent company. For one, they don't have to worry about being transferred. The farthest I can transfer them is to Citrus Heights and if I transfer them in the morning, if they walk fast, they can be there for lunch. Now that's what I call job security. You work for any other company of any size at all and they can ship you any place they want to. You might end up in Fresno, or in Needles.

"Our employees and retirees are all stockholders, and many of them are pretty big stockholders. If you take the savings plan, which holds 10 percent of the stock, and then you take individual holdings of employees and retirees, you can see it would be hard to get a big enough stake to get on our board," Doyle said. "With more than 14 million shares outstanding, it would take more than 700,000 shares to get even a 5 percent ownership. Even that wouldn't be enough shares to guarantee a seat on the Board of Directors."

Although Roseville Telephone shares are not listed, some trading activity is conducted through stockbrokers. The one broker who has been most involved in trading Roseville Telephone shares through the years is Bill Baxter of Prudential Securities. For many years prior to joining Prudential, Baxter was with Dean Witter. His insight into Doyle's ability to keep the company independent is revealing.

"It's a rags to riches story, yes, but Roseville Telephone has earned its success. The company has cared about the stockholder. Its top managers don't have stock options, limousines, executive dining rooms, country club memberships and the other perks identified with corporate America," Baxter said. "Sure, Bob Doyle always lived well, but he's never drawn a huge salary. In fact, for many, many years his salary was peanuts, well under what other executives at similar size companies were making.

"But more than anything else," Baxter added, "I think it's been the long-term, tax-deferred accumulation of wealth by the shareholders that keeps Roseville Telephone independent. Long-term shareholders have seen the company grow and prosper and along with that, their shares have appreciated. That's exactly what a stockbroker tries to achieve for clients — build long-term value in an investment. Bob has done that for his shareholders, and consequently, they continue to support the company's management."

Major players in the telephone industry have gotten the message over the years: Roseville Telephone is not for sale.

## SELLING STOCK AT ALL TIMES

Selling stock and taking care of the shareholders have been Bob Doyle's principal duties for more than 40 years. Although he directed operations for more than 20 years before Al Johnson came aboard in 1977, operational responsibilities were delegated to managers. Doyle was almost always involved in selling a new issue of stock until 1983, the last of the 10 stock offerings in 30 years. Even when he wasn't selling new stock, until recent years Doyle helped place stock that became available from existing shareholders.

*Stockbroker Bill Baxter has been instrumental in making a market in Roseville Telephone's stock.*

Current Securities and Exchange Commission (SEC) regulations no longer allow Doyle or any employee of the company to be involved in stock transactions. Those who inquire with the corporate office about selling shares are instructed of the alternatives available to them. They can sell their shares to the company's employee retirement supplement plan at the price quoted at that time. Or they can advertise that they have shares to sell — typically in the classified section of the *Roseville Press-Tribune*. Another option is to sell their shares through a stockbroker.

"In recent years, the stock has sold at a premium because we don't have any stock for sale. When we receive calls from those interested in buying shares, we say the only way is from present stockholders," Doyle explained. "When a present stockholder wants to sell shares, if he brings it in here, the company doesn't purchase the stock. It's the employee plan that buys the stock through its trustee, which is the trust department at the Bank of America. So we tell them that if they want to leave their shares here, they'll get a certified check for whatever the price is with no brokerage fee, no nothing. But we also advise them if they want to sell shares themselves, they should find a buyer, negotiate a price, exchange the money and then bring the certificate here when it's done. We transfer shares from the old owner to the new owner at no charge. We don't get involved in anything but the transfer."

In the past, however, Doyle was unquestionably the No. 1 salesman of Roseville Telephone stock. It was a rare day when he wasn't somehow involved in selling shares. Bob Parsons remembers many lunches when Doyle was selling.

"For about 10 years there in the '70s and early '80s, he was selling whatever stock we sold," Parsons said. "I was on some of those trips with him, and it could make for what you'd call a very interesting day. I'd listen to all these different angles, new ways he's trying out to get people enthused about the company to buy some more stock. It was amazing to me how many different local characters we'd meet. They were not characters to him, just businessmen with a different approach. He has the ability to talk to one person and then to a completely different character without being rude. He is a unique individual in that respect. He doesn't try being a salesman, but he's just so natural. That's why people buy from him."

*The company's stock transfer department includes, from the left, Ophelia Martinez, Virginia Amick and Lila Mettler. Amick has been Bob Doyle's secretary since 1984.*

Whether it was lunch at various eateries in Roseville and Sacramento, or dinner at Stroh's Neptune Table in South Land Park in Sacramento, Doyle was always hustling to sell stock in Roseville Telephone.

"That was his thing," said Ellen Lynn, Doyle's long-time secretary. "Selling stock, that was his field. He was involved all the time, either selling stock or making contacts to sell stock."

"If he went on a vacation anywhere, Bob Doyle would sell stock if he were able to," added Virginia Amick, his current secretary. "It made no difference where he was, he sold stock."

There are few leaders and shakers in the Roseville area who do not own — or have owned — Roseville Telephone stock. When Bob Doyle puts the arm on you to buy stock, he's a hard man to turn down. At times, public officials' ownership of telephone stock has caused controversy, particularly when city and/or county leaders faced important issues that one side might construe to benefit Roseville Telephone. In some instances, public officials have had to sell their shares to appease critics.

Doyle's sales efforts reached all corners of his world, but nowhere does he press harder than with employees. He didn't force any of them to buy stock nor did he give any ultimatums. Nonetheless, because he believed in the company so much, at every turn he urged employees to buy shares.

One of his first sales targets was the first manager he hired, Emerson Gunning.

"Bob was always on me to buy stock," Gunning said. "He'd say he has five shares of stock and do I want them? At that time I had money in the bank, so I'd call my wife, and she'd say, 'You don't want more stock?' I said, 'I got a chance to get them, I might as well do it. That's how I kept buying shares. I don't think I ever refused him when offered. He was on my back all the time. But I wasn't alone; he bugged me because he knew I took a good cut, and he knew what I wanted out of life. This is why he did it."

Doyle recalled working hard to get Gunning to buy stock.

"When Gunning, came to work here, I went to work on him trying to sell him stock. I said, 'People come in and want to sell like four or five shares. If you're interested, pick them up.' He said his wife's father had lost a lot of money in stocks during the Depression. He said, 'We have government bonds. That's the only thing that she'll have anything to do with.' I told him those bonds are all right, but you'll never make a lot of money on them. I said, 'This stock has got a chance to really do something.' Then I urged him to get involved in payroll deduction.

"He did get involved in the payroll deduction, but every now and then I'd call him and say, 'Gunning, I've got four shares or five more shares that have come in — Do you want them? If you don't, I'll call somebody else.' He'd say, 'Could you wait until tomorrow morning?' Invariably, he'd buy them. I never knew if he'd tell his wife or not, but he'd buy them. He's a big shareholder now even though he's been retired for more than 20 years."

Virginia Amick remembered Doyle using his sales spiel on her in 1976, only a few days after coming back to Roseville Telephone after a 21-year absence.

"I think about the third day I was here, I ran into him in the hall and he came up to me and said, 'Virginia, welcome to Roseville Telephone Company. When are you going to join the savings plan?' At the time, I didn't realize what he was doing, but he knew I couldn't join the plan until I'd been here a year. But he planted the seed. He said, 'By god, when you get into the savings plan … I know you can't do it now, but when you do, you go full bore. You get in there at 6 percent.' So when my year came due, I got in at 6 percent with his encouragement and there was no reason for me not to," Amick said. "He also has this sixth sense of knowing when you have money and when you don't, because a few months later he called me and said, 'I've got a few shares of stock, Virginia, how about buying them?' Several years later, when the 401-k plan came in, he said, 'By god, you take that at 10 percent.' I said to myself, 'That's 16 percent with savings and 401-k! At the time, my husband had lost his job so I was the sole support of my family. On the other hand, I can't walk in there and one of these days, Bob's going to ask me, 'What kind of percentage are you taking?' because he would not be shy to ask. I couldn't lie to him, and I knew if I said 5 percent, he'd go 'Oh,' so I did the 10 percent for a total of 16 percent between the two. I will be forever indebted to that man because when I leave this company, I expect to be financially secure. He's made that possible for the employees."

Although never a condition, it was an unwritten rule that if you bought stock from Doyle, you kept it. This was a crucial component of Doyle's long-term strategy — to place shares in long-term hands. Doyle would look askance at anybody he knew — particularly an employee — selling telephone stock. To him, selling stock was tantamount to treason. The exception was for true emergencies, but even then, he often advised the stockholder not to sell shares, but instead use them as collateral for a bank loan.

"There isn't anybody he comes into contact with who doesn't buy stock," said Dick Wise. "If you're a warm body, you're going to get stock. If you sell the stock, it's as if you disavowed God or something. Buying stock from Doyle is like a forced savings plan. I'd rather sell something out of my pension plan than sell telephone stock. Hell, the IRS is easier on you than Bob Doyle. He's murder. He is unmerciful, but he's made a lot of people a lot of money and he's caused them to keep it because they don't want to face his wrath. Who the hell needs it?"

George Minasian gives an idea of how it was for an employee who wanted to sell stock.

"Bob would do anything to keep you from selling it, especially the employees. In the old days, particularly when we had a stock sale going, he could get pretty bitter about an employee coming here and selling stock," Minasian explained.

"Employees just didn't go to Bob and tell him you wanted to sell your stock. If you could get somebody in your family to buy it or transfer it yourself, that's no problem, but if you couldn't do that, forget it. I bought stock for my kids when I first came here. Years later, when one of them had to sell stock to buy a house, I said I'd buy the stock. I said, 'You're not going to tell Bob you're selling stock because he's going to jump all over me.'"

Another employee summed up the situation succinctly, saying, "We were so afraid to sell our stock, he literally forced us to get rich."

Long-time shareholder Eleanor Owen received a call a few years ago from Doyle because he noticed she had sold some shares. "I explained to Bob that I had told a friend that if he ever wanted to sell his shares, I'd buy them. When he took me up on the offer, I wasn't in a position really to buy the shares. But I bought them anyway and immediately resold them to my next door neighbors who had always wanted telephone stock. I didn't make a profit on it. Bob understood; he watches that stock like a hawk."

"Nothing upsets Bob more than somebody who wants to sell their stock," said stockbroker Bill Baxter. "I can't think of anything other than a death in the family that would have upset Bob more than somebody wanting to sell their stock."

But Doyle understands that emergencies do occur. Bernice (Harris) Moser faced just such a situation when her husband suffered from cancer in the late 1960s. Health insurance didn't cover the $110 per day treatments he was undergoing. She was forced to sell stock she had been gradually acquiring since the second offering in 1957. As Doyle watched her liquidate her stock position, he suggested she not sell all of it, but take out a bank loan instead.

"He called over to Citizens Bank and I borrowed several thousand dollars, using my telephone stock as collateral. I told Bob I couldn't afford to pay interest, but he said, 'Don't worry about it, the stock dividend will be enough to pay your interest. When you get it paid off, you'll still have your stock.' So I did that and I had to even borrow a second time, but I got it all paid back and kept my stock. I think he knew the stock was going to do well in the future and that's why he urged me not to sell any more."

In the years after her husband's death, Moser was able to rebuild her stake in the company and had a comfortable nest egg of telephone stock when she retired in 1984.

Borrowing against stock was frequently Doyle's suggestion to employees who had stock positions, but needed cash quickly. He loathed employees selling their shares.

"I figured it was my job to first, sell stock, and second, to try to convince people to keep their stock," Doyle explained. "Certainly, when people would come in here wanting to sell their stock, I'd try to talk them out of it. Sometimes, though, I wasn't successful and they sold their shares. After all, it is their stock and their money. I'd give it my best effort, but if they still wanted to sell shares, they did. I never held it against them."

Board members were natural targets for his sales pitch. Not only did they accumulate large stock positions over time, but Doyle leaned on them to help him sell the stock, too.

Doulton Burner bought stock in every offering from the very first time in 1953 when Bob Doyle climbed the stairs to Burner's second-story Vernon Street office to sell him 50 shares. Now an advisory board member, Burner is one of the company's largest individual shareholders.

"No matter where we were, Bob was always selling stock," Burner said. "We'd go to lunch some place and the owner would buy a little stock wherever we went. Bob always had his salesman hat on."

Family social outings became sales opportunities as well. Carmen Doyle recalls many dinners when Bob sold stock.

"We use to go down to Hank Stroh's Neptune's Table in Sacramento," Carmen recalled. "No sooner would we get in there than Bob would take off and go to all the tables. Hank Stroh would introduce Bob and help him sell the stock. I would tell Bob, 'The next time we go there, don't you dare get up. We are going out to enjoy ourselves.' But then the minute we would get there, Hank is all over the restaurant introducing Bob to guests. Bob would say, 'I can't help it. He wants me to sell.'"

Another favorite dinner spot of the Doyles was Aldo's in Town and Country Village in Sacramento. Carmen Doyle said the proprietor, Aldo Bovero, would get upset at Bob's persistence in trying to sell stock.

"One time I remember Aldo was very upset with Bob. He said, 'You come here to have a good time. I'm busy and I don't have time to talk about stock. If I want to know more about it, I'll call you. Don't bring it up anymore.' At a later time we went there for dinner and were waiting at the bar. Then I said, 'Here comes Aldo. Now don't you dare bring up stock because he was so upset last time.' Well, this time Aldo greets us with a big smile, 'Oh Mr. Doyle, how are you?' The next thing he said was, 'I want to buy some stock.' He must have heard the stock was good."

Bill Sheppard, a long-time director and substantial shareholder, remembers Doyle pushing him to buy stock in 1959.

"He made me buy $600 worth that first time. I think it was $12 per share so I bought 50," Sheppard recalled. "After that I got interested in the damned thing and I never will forget one time I went over to the bank and borrowed $30,000 to buy telephone stock. Damn, that was a lot of stock."

When long-time director Leroy Etzel died in 1965 and his wife followed him four years later, their daughters Marguerite Smart and Betty Benedetti inherited Roseville Telephone shares and also their parents' beautiful home overlooking Lake Merritt in Oakland. It was prime property, worth holding.

"But we also faced a considerable estate tax bill," Marguerite Smart remembered. "We intended to keep the house in Oakland and sell Roseville Telephone shares to pay the taxes, but Bob Doyle talked us out of it. He said, 'You don't need to re-roof your stock and you don't pay taxes on it every year. You should keep the stock and sell the house.' That's what we did and we're eternally grateful that Bob talked us out of selling our shares. The house has gone up in value a lot, but not nearly as much as our shares in telephone stock."

"It got to where Marguerite and Larry (Smart) didn't want to see me when they came in to try and sell their stock," said Doyle. "That's because a couple of times I talked them out of it ... but they've been thanking me ever since."

Although the minutes of Roseville Telephone's monthly board meetings are brief, typically only one page, one can imagine the discussions that took place during some of the meetings. In the June 1974 board meeting, Doyle suggested the directors use their fees to acquire additional shares of company stock. A stock sale at $20 per share was in progress at the time — it started the previous September and was going slowly. The minutes said: "After some discussion, board members reported they supported the plan and would use their fees to buy stock as soon as PUC permission was received."

One can imagine how that meeting went. Surely Bob Doyle ranted and raved, challenging the directors to buy more shares. If they wouldn't buy the stock, why should the rest of the public? But Doyle's pressure paid off for his "victims," as the shares appreciated handsomely through the years.

Dick Wise is delighted that Bob Doyle intimidated him into holding onto his Roseville Telephone stock for decades.

"Of course, if I had sold stock, I wouldn't be his insurance agent any more. That was part of his control. Which is good, because in spite of myself, it's been very good. It's probably worth 20 times what I originally paid for it. It's been unbelievable."

Even though almost every business and professional person in Roseville has at one time or another been pitched by Bob Doyle to buy stock, he is most gratified that the employees, from top managers to the lowest-paid employees in the company, have been able to prosper from owning company stock. Bill Baxter summed up Doyle's stock-selling efforts at the 1993 shareholders' meeting.

*Bob Doyle received a special commemorative plaque from the United States Telephone Association during the 80th anniversary open house in 1994.*

Photo by Steve Yeater

*Roy Neel, president of the United States Telephone Association, visited Roseville Telephone in April 1994, his first visit to a local telephone company upon becoming president of the powerful Washington D.C.-based group.*

Courtesy of the Roseville Press-Tribune

"I can speak for all the stockbrokers in town that we tip our caps to the best stockbroker in the Sacramento Valley, and that's Bob Doyle," Baxter said. "That's a fact. Not only has he made a lot of the employees rich, he's also made a lot of people in the Sacramento Valley rich. He's got a hell of a fan club."

## DOYLE'S MANAGEMENT STYLE AND PHILOSOPHY

*"The best executive is the one who has sense enough to pick good men to do what he wants done, and self-restraint enough to keep from meddling with them while they do it."*
— Theodore Roosevelt

"Telephone company, Bob Doyle speaking."

That has been Bob Doyle's greeting to callers for more than 40 years. Even though the company generates more than $100 million in revenue and earns in excess of $20 million annually, the Chairman of the Board answers his own phone. Always has and always will.

"It kind of catches people off guard when I answer the phone," Doyle explains. "Callers don't expect that. But I don't hide from people like most executives. I don't have the secretary telling the caller I'm busy or on another line if I'm sitting in my office twiddling my thumbs."

Answering his own phone is only one of the habits that gives Doyle an executive style all his own. He adheres to certain rules and does not waver from them. Doyle has developed a management philosophy that is simple and extremely effective. It's based upon faith and confidence that his managers and employees will always try to do what's right. And he leads by example.

"My doors are open. If somebody wants to come in here and talk, they can. That's what it is all about. The minute I am too good to listen to an employee — hell, they usually have ideas a hell of a lot better than mine — I'm the loser. That's because if I don't listen, that employee will never come back again. He or she will say, 'Well, that smart son of a bitch, let him learn it for himself.'"

Doyle eschews the popular management style of intimidation.

"You're not supposed to have people running around afraid that if they make a mistake, they can't report it to their boss because he's going to bad mouth them. That's the worst thing a manager can do," Doyle said. "You have to encourage your people to want to do things and not be afraid of you."

Mistakes should be learning experiences, according to Doyle. "You've got to have it so that if an employee makes a mistake, he will come to you and say, 'I've just screwed up.' The manager then should say, 'I'm glad you told me.' I mean that's the way we learn. You treat an employee right and he's going to bust his hump for you because he thinks you're a good guy. If you chew him out, and say, 'Anybody should know better than that,' the employee won't respond."

Of course, according to Doyle, the secret to effective management is hiring smart people who can make their boss look good.

"I tell the supervisors, 'You are no different than I am. If you have your people working hard, you're going to have a successful department. If you don't, your department is going to go to pot. The only way you're going to have a successful department is to hire people smarter than you are,'" Doyle explained. "'Don't be afraid that they're going to take your job. The best way you can keep somebody from taking your job is to have a good department. And the way to get a good department is to hire people smarter than you are. And give them credit. Even tell them they're smarter than you are. It won't hurt you. You sleep better at night because you know it already.'"

Doyle's baseball management style has already been mentioned. "Put the right people in the right place and you try to make sure they get along, but you leave them alone. Don't keep after them. If there's something wrong, you try to find out what it is.

"And if somebody calls up and asks me about something I don't know anything about, I just tell him I don't know," Doyle continued. "I'm not afraid to say I don't know. People think because I'm the chairman I should know everything. Hell, if I'd climb a pole, I'd slip and fall right on my ass. That's not what I'm here for. I'm here to get somebody to see that they crawl up that pole, and it's not the supervisor. The supervisor is there to make sure somebody crawls up that pole. But I'm here to get the supervisor and to stay out of everybody's way."

Doyle doesn't rely upon scads of written reports to keep informed. He makes excellent use of the tool of his trade — the telephone. When he calls managers, his approach is simple, but very effective. "What's going on," is how he begins almost every conversation. His way of asking the question forces one to tell him everything going on because one never knows how much Doyle knows, or doesn't know. It's Doyle's way of keeping tabs on all that's going on at the company. It's a very effective approach for gathering information.

While Doyle respects higher education, it's no substitute for common sense and leadership.

"I always tried to get good, honest people. I don't necessarily look for somebody who has been to college. It doesn't mean a damn thing. Most of our supervisors have never seen a college, but they've got good common horse sense, and that you can't learn out of a book," Doyle said. "You can get straight A's, but you take the book away and he's going to be a failure without that book to go to. You have to know how to handle people. If you don't, you're not going to get results."

*Leon Bower, director of outside plant engineering, holds a fiber-optic cable. A hallmark of Roseville Telephone has been its continued investment in the latest technologies to provide the best possible service.*

A central theme in Doyle's management scheme has been to continually invest in the latest equipment.

"There is no possible way I know right now when we buy equipment how long it will be good for, but I know we'd better get it installed in a hurry because it could be obsolete even as it is installed, in some cases. That's because there's new equipment coming out all the time. If you've got the old equipment, you're falling farther and farther behind. In the telephone business, you have to keep up or you'll soon be out of business."

Doyle isn't shy about looking at new lines of business. He wanted to be involved in cable television in the mid-1960s until the FCC ruled telephone companies couldn't enter that industry. The company's large cellular stake is a testament to Doyle's belief in getting into new businesses as is the company's large and growing stake in alarm monitoring and the upcoming personal communications services (PCS) business.

"You have to grab on to something, and if you see it isn't going to work, then you can let it go. But if you don't grab on to it and let somebody else get it, you'll never get it back," Doyle explained. "I know I'll make some mistakes because you can't win them all. But you can't be successful if you don't make a mistake once in a while. If you're afraid to take a chance, you're not going to get to first base. You've had it. If it doesn't pan out, you bail out."

Even though Roseville Telephone is known for its prodigious technological and financial achievements through the years, employees know not to rest on their laurels.

"Any time you think you're doing good enough, you're on the downhill grade. You're never doing good enough," Doyle preaches. "Even with what we've done, we can always do better. That has to be your aim. As long as you have that attitude, nobody is going to outmaneuver you. Once you think you're doing OK and no one's going to do it any better, you're in big trouble, because somebody will do it better."

In addition to welcoming ideas and suggestions from employees, one of Doyle's cardinal rules is to back up employees' decisions. This was illustrated one day when he ran into a business customer in front of the company's executive office. The customer knew Bob and asked that his required deposit on new phone service be waived. Doyle refused. He told the customer to pay the deposit.

"I have to back up my employees. If I would have OK'd that, the employee in the business office would have said, 'Isn't that something, that customer is not going to pay the bill and Doyle OK'd it.' The only way I would have approved his request would have been to bring him and our employee here and get both sides of the story. Maybe other bosses would let a friend get away with special consideration, but not me.

"The only exception was when my mother was alive," Doyle continued. "If for some reason her phone bill was overdue, I said call me before disconnecting it because I'll pay the bill. But I'm not going to pay for my brothers, sisters, in-laws and outlaws, because how could I sit here and tell our employees not to disconnect my sister or brother, but you should disconnect all your relatives if they don't pay? I'm not built that way."

One of Doyle's strengths is his decision-making. He generally takes his time and is thorough, studying the issue from all angles.

"Sometimes decisions look easy, but I've learned there's always another side to any decision. If you just make a snap decision and it's wrong, the damage is done. It's pretty hard to go back. I'm not the kind of guy who runs around saying, 'I'm sorry, we shouldn't have done this.' Not that we don't make mistakes anyway, but I believe you have to try hard to make sure you don't make mistakes."

Delegating authority is perhaps Doyle's greatest strength. His confidence has inspired employees to take reasonable risks. They know that he'll generally support their analyses. "I expect anybody with a proposal for me pretty well has it figured out before they offer it," says Doyle.

Al Johnson said Doyle's trust in his employees stems from the earliest days at the company.

"He had retired Bell people who had lots of experience, but one of the reasons they liked working here was because Bob gave them free rein. They could almost do anything they wanted … within reason, of course. But make no mistake about it, Bob always made the final decisions."

*NEC Electronics USA Inc. has grown to become one of the area's largest employers.*
Courtesy of the City of Roseville

Brian Strom said the nature of the decision makes a difference in how quickly Bob Doyle responds.

"A good example is how quickly he would sometimes act to approve certain investments in telephone plant and new technology. Bob's right on top of that. For example, if Walter Gordon came up to Al Johnson and said, 'We need this new switch,' and Al walked into Bob and said, 'We need a new switch,' Bob would say, 'Done.' But with people and compensation decisions — ones he knows don't need to be made overnight — he'll take his time and warm up to the idea."

## ROLE IN CREATING REGIONAL GROWTH

Roseville Telephone has benefited from being in the path of regional progress. The migration from the cities to the suburbs has brought continuous growth to Roseville and Citrus Heights. Through the 1950s, 1960s and most of the 1970s, the growth was primarily residential. But residents brought businesses to service a growing population. In the late 1970s and early 1980s, beginning with Shugart Associates and Kaiser-Permanente, followed quickly by Hewlett-Packard and NEC, Roseville Telephone's service area began to attract major manufacturing, medical and industrial development.

An item of conjecture remains how important a role did Bob Doyle and Roseville Telephone play in stimulating the impressive growth. Would these heavyweight companies have located here if Roseville Telephone had not been at the leading edge of telecommunications technology? How influential was Doyle personally in attracting the companies? Was it the "team approach" to selling large companies that differentiated Roseville Telephone from the others?

"Whenever he could, he would make improvements in equipment and acquire facilities that would permit the company to do more and more than it was presently doing," said Bob Raymer. "He always had this vision that the telephone company would need to be much larger, and he was always getting ready for it. Of course, the growth of the community had a lot to do with it. On the other hand, in almost any other community in the country, independent telephone companies handled growth by selling out to bigger companies. What's unique in Roseville is that it is a very fine leading-edge company that's able to handle these big projects alone."

In 1974, the Sacramento Area Commerce and Trade Organization (SACTO) was founded to attract quality companies to the greater Sacramento region. It was in early 1976 that SACTO's executive director, Alan Ewen, called Doyle to request a meeting. It was the beginning of what was to be a long, fruitful relationship between SACTO and the company.

"I didn't know him," Ewen said. "All I knew was that he was president of the telephone company. So I decided I would call and ask for an appointment. Lo and behold, he answers the phone. I was pleasantly surprised by that and I expressed that. He said, 'Well, what the hell, I haven't got anything else to do.' Right then, I knew I was going to like him."

The next day Ewen drove to Roseville to meet Doyle. "I went in and here is this guy with a crew cut. I introduced myself and explained SACTO's purpose. So he says, 'Welcome to the park. Nobody's been able to do anything with that kind of a job.' After talking about how he got into the telephone business, we talked about growth in South Placer County, what he envisioned for its future, and I told him how we were approaching companies. There was an incipient trust right at the beginning, person-to-person. I knew I could say things to him in confidence. I did ask him for help in introducing me to Roseville people who might be interested in what SACTO was doing."

The two stayed in touch and helped each other. Ewen told Doyle he was talking to many large companies — some Japanese — who were looking at the

Sacramento region for expansion. Ewen asked Doyle if Roseville Telephone could handle the needs of a big industrial customer.

"It appeared the telephone company in 1976 was already on its way to becoming fully modern, but I sensed that after I told Doyle how important telecommunications issues are to large companies seeking sites, he really got on top of it. That was in 1976," Ewen said. "Of course, the following year Al Johnson came aboard with all his expertise in equipment and systems. I think from about that point on, Roseville could offer anything any other company could offer."

*Hewlett-Packard is the Roseville area's largest employer.*
Courtesy of the City of Roseville

In 1977, Ewen was courting a number of companies who had shown interest in the Sacramento region. It was fortuitous that Roseville Telephone had redoubled its efforts to achieve technological parity, later superiority, with the Bell companies, because SACTO's grand plan in the 1970s called for most of the development in the upcoming years to occur along the Interstate 80 corridor, including Roseville. In the 1980s, the focus would shift to Highway 50 followed by Highway 99 and Interstate 5 in the south part of the region by the 1990s. It was a plan to add businesses in an organized, balanced fashion.

The prize catch in the 1970s was Hewlett-Packard. Its decision in 1979 to acquire acreage and build in the industrial tract north of downtown Roseville has had huge ramifications for Roseville and, consequently, the telephone company. Ewen remembers answering questions from H-P's site selection committee.

"David Packard himself asked me about telephone service and I told him we had an independent in Roseville that was modernizing. I said I was confident Roseville Telephone was able to handle their load in every way and suggested the site selection committee visit the company and discuss their needs. They did, and later I was told they were satisfied Roseville could handle their requirements."

Ewen told Doyle that H-P's decision to build in Roseville was very important because other large companies would likely follow H-P's lead. Not long afterward, NEC announced it would build in Roseville, just down the road from H-P.

"It was very interesting how NEC came," Ewen said. "It was all very hush, hush. NEC originally was interested in the Folsom area, near Scott Road and Highway 50. In the final analysis, however, NEC didn't want to be alone, but wanted to be near someone doing similar work. At that time, there was only H-P."

In the years SACTO was headed by Ewen and his successor, John Roberts, Doyle was an active SACTO member. He was vice president for a time and also on the SACTO board. Ewen and Roberts could rely upon Doyle to give visiting site selection contingents a thorough tour of what South Placer County had to offer. Other than selling stock, no part of Doyle's work routine is more satisfying to him than to talk up the merits of Roseville and the surrounding area. Certainly, no one was more knowledgeable about development in the region.

Nonetheless, when Roberts first met Doyle, he was prepared for the worst. Roberts grew up in Kansas and worked for 10 years in economic development in Texas. Both states have many independent telephone companies. Roberts' experience with independents had not been good.

"When I came to Sacramento and started to get the lay of the land, I heard about an independent telephone company in Roseville. My first reaction was that Roseville was a beautiful community, but it was too bad they had an independent company. But people kept telling me, 'You've got to learn more about Roseville Telephone because it's different.' I thought, 'Oh, sure.'"

It wasn't long afterward that Roberts had a prospect decide to relocate in Roseville.

"We came to Roseville, met with a lot of engineering people at the company, met with various committees of the chamber of commerce, and others," Roberts said. "Afterward, the prospect said to me, 'If this company is half of what they say they are, we could be happy in Roseville.' We then visited other companies — Hewlett-Packard being one of them — and they said the telephone service was superior. As we started talking to more prospects about locating in Roseville, there were more and more favorable comments about the telephone company. Over a period of years, my impressions evolved from being very doubtful at first to one of being absolutely sold that this company and its leadership were different and better. The quality of the telephone company evolved into a recruitment tool. In this age when telecommunications is critical, many companies found Roseville's location to be superior largely because of the phone service.

"A good example of a company that moved to Roseville because of the telecommunications issue is Dana Commercial Credit Corp., which is based in Michigan. They're one of the 100 best companies to work for in America, and they insist on absolute quality," Roberts said. "And their first requirement was top-rate telecommunications services. Dana did a thorough study of it. Dana is in Roseville now and wouldn't be happier anywhere else in California, and it was just because of what Roseville Telephone had to offer.

"So I think that's really remarkable that an independent outsider with no biases in his views about this region comes here from Texas and evolves over a period of 12-to-24 months from a Doubting Thomas to 'This is the best sales tool that we have for this region.' That was how I got to know Roseville Telephone."

Development brings progress and progress brings development … and more telephones into service. It's a formula that has enabled the company to grow.

*John Roberts was impressed with Roseville Telephone when he was an executive recruiting companies to the Sacramento area in the 1980s. He is now a Roseville Telephone director.*

Photo by Rudy Meyers

"He just loves watching dirt being moved. He's like a little kid with his Tonka toys," said Mike Doyle, Bob's son. "He watches these earth movers and that's music to his ears. He loves to see progress."

Doyle's pitch to visitors is familiar. He talks about the importance of Interstate 80. "Hell, you can go to the East Coast on the same road and it's easy to go north and south, too. That other road (Highway 50) — hell, when you get to Lake Tahoe, it's the end of the road, plus it's closed all winter with landslides."

The industrial tract north of Roseville is one of the largest in California. "There's plenty of room out there for more companies to buy and expand," Doyle boasts. "We show visitors the different housing options available, from modest homes to the higher-end ones meant for executives. We can show them Folsom Lake. And most of them don't know about Lincoln Airport. Hewlett-Packard has several flights a day going into the Lincoln Airport. I know every inch of this damn area, the good things and the bad things. I show both because you have to be honest, but I'll tell you, I can make a strong case why this is a good area to locate a plant."

In addition to his upfront work on behalf of recruiting companies to South Placer, Al Johnson credits Doyle for numerous behind-the-scenes efforts to help facilitate quality growth in the region.

"I knew he was behind pushing one of the largest bond issues ever proposed in the area to finance the construction of sewage treatment facilities to handle growth," Johnson said. "Also, he was among the local leaders who persuaded Shugart Associates to come back. Shugart was ready to drop all its plans of coming to Roseville, but Doyle got business leaders together and they assured the Shugart people of support. Shugart, a disk drive manufacturer, was the first sizable industrial firm to come to Roseville. About the same time Kaiser came here with its out-patient clinic. Then, H-P came and NEC followed later."

More recently, the much-publicized Sun City development in Roseville may not have occurred had it not been for intervention and extra effort from Doyle. Although Del Webb Corp. had acquired an option on acreage in West Roseville in 1988, the Phoenix-based developer of high-quality, active adult communities had grown increasingly frustrated with the planning cycle in Roseville. Webb's other communities — in Phoenix, Tucson and Las Vegas — had not encountered nearly as many obstacles as there were in Roseville. Sun City Palm Springs, the company's only other California project, had faced an easier route. Webb was ready to fold its plans to come to Roseville when Doyle called a meeting of Webb's local executives and chief executive officer at the telephone company's office.

"I told them that despite what they thought, the local community was in full support of their development and that they should hang in there, it'll come in time," said Doyle. "They were ready to bag the whole project."

Phil Dion, Webb's president and chief executive officer, agreed the meeting with Doyle was a factor. "I can't say that meeting alone convinced us to stay on track, but certainly Mr. Doyle's influence and interest in having us build in Roseville helped us eventually to resolve the issues we faced. His assurances that the community was in support of our project was very welcome at the time."

Doyle's support of Del Webb will pay off. Sun City Roseville residents will enjoy "fiber to the curb" from Roseville Telephone, which gives them the capability to transmit video, voice and data over their telephone lines. Residents will have access to the latest telecommunications services offered.

In Alan Ewen's view, Roseville Telephone's commitment to high technology is a vitally important ingredient in attracting companies. "What the telephone company could offer companies was, next to power, the most important aspect of the demand by big companies. I know it was important to Herman Miller's eventually building its large manufacturing facility in Roseville."

Doyle was also a forceful supporter of the Route 65 bypass, a necessity if large industrial users were to locate in the industrial tract. Finally, after years of work, the bypass, named after the late congressman, Harold "Bizz" Johnson, became reality in 1987. It strengthened Doyle's argument that companies should consider locating in the industrial tract.

Doyle has also been a strong supporter of the proposed Auburn Dam. "Build It, Dam It" is a bumper sticker Doyle has on his car and on his desk to give to visitors. And he's mentioned the importance of the proposed dam in several annual reports. Doyle supports a multiple-purpose dam that would offer recreation, ensure water supplies to the region and greatly enhance the flood protection plan already in place to protect the Sacramento region from potentially disastrous floods.

"He's long impressed me with his political sensitivity," added Ewen. "Doyle is loyal to his constituency, but he also knows how the hen eats the feed, and is willing to take a role in political campaigns financially. He'll find good candidates that he thinks are for the long-term betterment of Roseville and he'll back them. He's done that unfailingly. Some of his haven't been the favorites and some of his haven't won, but I can think of numerous times that he would call me on the phone and say, 'Joe Baloney is running for so-and-so. If you know of anybody who has some money that can help in his campaign, I'd appreciate it.' I'd scramble around and find somebody.

"I think it's fair to say that he's played a quiet, unsung role behind many important projects, and that's particularly true in the drive for Auburn Dam. He's been a consistent political contributor, and good to civic causes. He is not afraid to support what he believes in."

*Alan Ewen, an early president of the Sacramento Area Commerce and Trade Organization (SACTO), helped recruit Hewlett-Packard to south Placer County.*

Photo by Gittings

## ROSEVILLE'S NO. 1 SUPPORTER

Doyle does not support growth for growth's sake. As a lifetime Roseville resident with family roots of 135 years in the town, he's acutely sensitive to the quality of the growth. Virginia Amick recounts an episode when a businessman visited Doyle about a proposed development in Roseville.

"Bob did not like it because he sensed this outside developer was just coming in to do his project, take his money and run. Bob told him in no uncertain terms to leave," Amick said. "Bob doesn't like anyone to come in and take advantage of Roseville, because not only does he love Roseville Telephone, he loves Roseville. He doesn't want to see growth that would be bad for our community. That's why he likes companies like Hewlett-Packard and NEC. It's clean development. Of course, he is pro-growth, but his throwing that man out was an eye-opener for me. After a point, he didn't want anything else to do with him."

"Bob likes to know who's looking at what property," said Mike Doyle. "He wants to know what businesses might be coming in, because he's not just pro-growth. He wants the right people to be coming in. He doesn't want something that in 10 years is going to go down hill. To my dad, it's Roseville, Roseville, Roseville. In his mind, this is the best place to live in the world and he aims to keep it that way."

The generosity of Roseville Telephone and Bob Doyle is well known, but there's even more behind the scenes. Virginia Amick is in the best position to know all the little things the company and Doyle do for the community which do not get credit.

"I think people who have lived here for years do not know that he loves Roseville as much as he does. They make the presumption he's just doing it for Roseville Telephone Company, but I think he does a lot of things because of Roseville," she said. "I don't think that the community really realizes how much money is put back in the community. We have people coming in a couple of times a week asking for donations. Not everybody gets a donation, because there's no way you could possibly do it, but we give lots of money to the community, and, of course, now with the Foundation, we're even giving more. He also gives a lot himself."

Dick Wise calls Doyle "the No. 1 booster in Roseville. He loves the town. A lot of people may not know it, and I'm not sure they appreciate it, but he always does what's best for Roseville."

## A COUNTRY SLICKER

Bob Doyle is one of the most unassuming, unpretentious persons one is likely to meet. People almost always underestimate Doyle's knowledge, intuitive abilities and grasp of about any situation on first impression. Until he's comfortable with a visitor, he plays his cards close to the vest. Even after he knows you, expect him to continue to throw you off guard with his comments and opinions. Long-time attorney Bob Raymer has viewed Doyle in both business and personal situations. He's as attuned to Doyle's personality and mannerisms as any non-family member. Raymer affectionately refers to Doyle as a "country slicker."

"I have a biologist friend who got interested in forest genetics and spent a lot of time up in the Sierra. After being up there and getting to know the people who lived in the mountains, he coined the word 'country slicker,'" Raymer said. "It was his experience that people who could survive in the country were a lot smarter than the so-called 'city slicker' types. So he called them 'country slickers.' Bob Doyle is one who came from the land, but by his intuition, enthusiasm and natural leadership, he instinctively knows how to address problems. That doesn't mean he's technically attuned to every regulatory or technological nuance, but he's a natural leader to the degree that he's brought in good people to help him with those technical aspects, and he has the facility for identifying good people. As I observed him through the years, again and again he demonstrated the ability to inspire people and get control of situations and to make true many of the rosy predictions that he made. It didn't make any difference whether things were going well or going ill, he never doubted for a minute that Roseville Telephone Company was, and would be, the finest telephone company anywhere."

Since Doyle answers his own phone, he frequently receives solicitation calls from stockbrokers and other salesman trying to pitch him on the latest "great deal." When salespeople call, Doyle will occasionally toy with them. One day a stockbroker from New York City called Doyle at his office to interest him in an investment. Doyle listened patiently for a few minutes, nodding his head and uttering "Uh huh ... yeah ... uh huh" every 10-to-15 seconds. Finally, he stops the pitch. "Excuse me," Doyle said, "but may I ask you a question? Have you got any family, relatives or good friends? ... You do! Well, good. Then why don't you let *them* in on this great deal. After all, you don't even know me. If it's so good, sell it them and make them rich."

He followed the conversation with a vintage Doyle comment. "What does that guy think I am, stupid or something? Can you imagine him trying to sell me something and I don't even know him? Let him sell it to his friends ... I'll bet he didn't expect me to say that."

## A FAMILY MAN

While Bob Doyle is best known as the boisterous, straight-shooting president of the telephone company, his private life is active and full. His wife Carmen and their two adult children, Mike Doyle and Carol Smith, have been his life away from the office. Granddaughter Courtney Smith, 3, is the most recent addition to the family and she'll be joined by a brother or sister in the spring of 1995.

As the patriarch of the Doyle family in Roseville, Bob takes his role seriously. In nearly every public pronouncement dealing with major policy issues or projected development in the area, Doyle speaks from two perspectives. As the elder representative of the pioneering Doyle family, with roots in Roseville going back to 1860, Doyle is attentive to the traditions of the past. As the senior member of the current Doyle clan, his aim is to ensure that Roseville remains an excellent place to live and work for his children and their children. He is outspoken about local issues and takes the uncompromising position that progress must be first-class, whether it be at Roseville Telephone, community development in general, or in his personal undertakings. He is adamant about quality.

Away from business, Bob Doyle is a surprisingly private person. Through 40 years as president and chief executive officer, he carried his worries home. Carmen Doyle calls her husband completely devoted to his work, a man whose waking hours are primarily focused on Roseville Telephone Company.

"He's always been a hundred percent for the company and employees. He's a company man," Carmen Doyle said. "Sometimes, especially in the earlier days, he would come home and would be extra quiet. It's not easy for him to talk about his work, and in those instances, you just have to figure it's best to leave him alone, because you know he's got something important on his mind."

Although work occupied much of his time through the years, Bob Doyle rarely missed his daughter's dance performances or his son's ball games. And he regularly chauffeured daughter Carol to school along with her classmates from the neighborhood. Carol remembers her dad as a dutiful parent who made the time to be there when something important in her life happened.

"Some people might believe my father was the type of company man who completely ignored his children, but that's not the way I remember it," said Carol. "In fact, he and my mother made it such that our house was the center of my friends' activities. On the weekends, the kids were playing or swimming at our house. When there were sleepovers, they were usually at our house, and I don't think it was because we had the biggest house; I think it was more my parents' way to keep us close by so they could keep track of us."

*Newlyweds Bob and Carmen Doyle.*

*Family man Bob Doyle with children Carol and Mike.*

When the children were young, Carmen Doyle didn't drive. This left to her husband many household chores, such as getting the groceries. "Every night I'd have a list of things to get," Doyle explained. "It wasn't until Carol was 5 or so before Carmen went to driving school and learned. She's a damn good driver now."

On occasion, Doyle dragged his two children to the office on a Saturday. Mike Doyle recalled these infrequent outings.

"We wanted to be out running around with friends and playing ball, but on weekends, he would bring us down here and he would open up the mail and stock and whatever he wanted to catch up on, so we'd hang around for a little while," Mike Doyle said. "When he'd bring us here during the work week, I remember we'd play hide-and-seek in his office. When his first secretary, Ellen Lynn, was there, I remember hiding under her desk when she was working. So we had fun."

As important as the telephone company was to him, Doyle was known frequently to put his children first. Virginia Amick recalled an instance when three executives came from the East Coast to have a meeting with Doyle.

"Just as the meeting began, the telephone rang and it was his son, Michael, calling from school. He was sick and needed to be picked up. Mark Shull was in the meeting, too. So Bob said, 'Excuse me. He can take care of you. My son is sick and I'm going to pick him up.' That type of thing happened on numerous occasions."

At home, Doyle's link to the company and its employees continued. Through the years Doyle typically relied upon at least one company employee who was unofficially designated to be his handyman since Doyle's own skills in attending to routine household maintenance and repairs were minimal to non-existent. He delegated these duties. For many years, Emerson Gunning was the fix-it man. He spent many Saturdays at the Doyle household.

"Yes, I used to do a lot of stuff for him," said Gunning. "Bob can't fix anything, but that never bothered me because his skill was to guide others to do the right things. Some people are good with tools and others aren't. He wasn't good at things like that."

After Gunning retired in 1974, Bob Sharples, another long-time employee, filled the gap. Sharples was in charge of buildings and grounds for the company.

One Saturday, Sharples and Gunning were at the telephone company fixing some electronic clocks. Doyle was at his desk, catching up on paper work. Sharples recalled the day. It illustrated a typical situation when Doyle needed help with a chore around the house.

"Bob asked me where could he get a water pump because he needed to empty his swimming pool. Apparently, he was going to have it sealed. I told him I knew where I could get a pump. It would do about 300-to-400 gallons a minute, so it would take a while to empty his pool."

Later in the morning, the three of them went to Doyle's home. Sharples and Gunning rigged up the pump and hoses and started pumping.

"It was getting close to noon and here comes Carmen with hamburgers and the fixings, and then Bob carts out a jug of wine. As we sat there waiting for the pool to empty, we drank a bunch of that damned wine … got all smoked up. When poor old Gunning went down to move the hose, he slipped and banged his butt and his head on the bottom of the pool. If he hadn't been gassed, the fall probably would have killed him."

Those Saturday escapades were tolerated, but not always enjoyed in the Doyle household. Monday through Friday, work ruled Bob Doyle. On the weekends and holidays, though, Carmen expected Bob's attention to be focused on the family.

During the Christmas season when the children were young, Doyle was Santa to his children. He owned his own Santa suit. Finally one Christmas, Carol exhibited that knowing look that "Santa" was somebody she knew very well. On the next day, a new Santa showed up, but there was no fooling young Carol. "Mr. Gunning!" she said in her youthful accusatory tone.

"Santa" Doyle was also known for giving his children shares in Roseville Telephone every chance he could.

"I remember especially at Christmas time, we would get maybe five shares of stock. He would put it in a big stock envelope on the Christmas tree, and of course, we knew what that present was," Mike Doyle said. "Carol and I would stand there and go, 'Oh, no, not more Roseville Telephone stock.' Of course, we were kids, we didn't know. At Easter sometimes we'd get five shares, too, so we'd get shares here and there. It adds up over time. Now that I'm working at the company, I can look behind the scenes and see not only how it's grown over the years, but also I have a good idea about the future of Roseville Telephone. I just don't see how anyone would want to invest any place else."

Carol and Mike Doyle enjoyed playing hide and seek when they visited their father's office at Roseville Telephone.

*Bob Doyle reprises his "Santa" role for Bob Parsons' granddaughter, Justine. For many years, Doyle was a "Santa" for handicapped children in Newcastle.*

For many years, Doyle was Santa Claus for physically and mentally handicapped children in Newcastle. He made time for those individuals, particularly children, who needed a lift during the holidays. In 1992, Doyle donned a new Santa outfit for a cameo appearance at Bob Parsons' daughter's house.

"It was very cold and my daughter wasn't sure she could get all four of her children to see Santa," Parsons said. "One of them had a cold. So on Christmas Eve — we usually work a half day — I was telling Bob about my daughter's problem. Then he said, 'Well, if you want to take me home, I'll change and come back here to her condo.' And he came in dressed as Santa. I had never seen Bob do that, and as you can imagine, he did one of the best Santa Claus routines that you're going to see any guy do. I set it up and told the kids, 'Here comes Santa.' He has these bells and he rings them at the door. He was so good. It's just another example of his breadth. There's a lot to Bob Doyle, a lot more than most people might think."

On occasion, family and business intertwined. An example occurred in November 1991 when Mike Doyle agreed to take up his father's invitation to join Roseville Telephone. It was a career move Mike hadn't necessarily counted on.

"I had worked at a health club for about five years and was going to Sierra College, but like most people in their early 20s, I wasn't sure what I wanted to be," Mike Doyle explained. "I didn't even think about working for Roseville Telephone Company, basically because it's been my dad's career. It's been his baby and I just didn't feel I would get a square opportunity to prove myself here, so I didn't think about it. But he approached me one day and asked if I had ever thought about working for Roseville Telephone, and I basically told him no."

At that point, Mike's knowledge of the company was limited to what he had heard at shareholder meetings and what his father talked about at home. Mike declined his father's initial feelers about joining the company.

"I explained my reasons and he accepted them. About a year later, he approached me again and wanted to know in general what my life plans were, did I have any goals, had I decided yet what I wanted out of life. I still hadn't made a decision," Mike Doyle continued. "He asked if I had a couple of minutes to go over a few things with me. We sat down and out comes the Roseville Telephone folder again. 'Maybe I didn't explain myself correctly the first time,' he told me. 'I understand that there are no courses in college on telephony where you can go take it and learn about it. You can take basic courses in accounting or computer classes which would affect certain departments, if you were interested.' I told him I really didn't know all the various departments that made up the company so I didn't know which courses would help.

"So he went through and covered the basics, everything from the mail department to outside plant. He had it on a piece of paper and broke it down from department to department. Then he said, 'Why don't you think about it and see if maybe we can't put something together. Of course, being my son, I've had a chance to see your personality, see your work ethics, and I just feel as an employer and as your dad that you would be beneficial to Roseville Telephone.' A week later, he got back to me and said, 'I've talked it over with Al and Brian and what we'd like to do, if you're willing, is to put you through kind of a tour in the company, working in maybe six or seven different departments, one every three-to-six months. After a couple of years, you can see how you like it. Like any new employee, if you get there and you decide that's not what you want to do for 30 or 40 years, or if the company doesn't gain anything by having you, then at least it will look good on a resume.' When I thought of the opportunity that way, I decided it was worth a try."

After gaining experience in several departments over nearly three years, Mike Doyle decided to pursue a career in the products and services side of the business. He's happy in his work and well thought of by his peers. Mike's success and popularity at the company come as no surprise to his father.

*Mike Doyle works in the products and services department at Roseville Telephone and looks to a long career at the company.*

"In the years before I talked to him, I watched him closely," Bob Doyle said of Mike. "I concluded that he has the right stuff and would be a benefit to the company. He's a good kid and his personality fits well with the other employees. Of course, he knows he's behind the 8-ball because of me, that everybody's watching him. He works hard, but he would have anyway. That's the kind of kid he is. If I didn't think he'd work hard, I wouldn't have asked him to join the company in the first place, because it would have been embarrassing to him and to me."

Although Bob Doyle is — and was — a better father and husband than many may think, Carmen Doyle is credited with being a major positive influence in his life. They met when she worked in the business office at the company. Bob Raymer offered this opinion on Carmen Doyle:

"I think it's been an excellent marriage and they have two really fine children. Carmen really has been an important factor in Bob's life, and probably in more ways than he recognizes. She is a lovely person and very bright woman. She did a marvelous job of bringing up their children and has been the kind of wife to Bob that really advanced his situation more than he knows. She was, and is, a very handsome woman, but there is much, much more to her, and the attraction she had for Bob is on several levels. I don't think he could have accomplished as much as he has without her stability."

Bill Sheppard is blunt in his admiration for Carmen Doyle. "She is a hell of a woman and has been good for Bob. He's been lucky, by god."

Socially, the Doyles are an easy couple to be with, according to Brian Strom. "I found out early that it didn't matter that you weren't the same age as Bob, you could get along with Bob and Carmen socially very well. They're a delightful couple to be with. They don't pull the old folks/young folks, rich folks/poor folks thing at all. They're real comfortable to be with."

Bill Duarte, Carmen's son by her first marriage, called Bob an excellent husband and father. "We always had a great respect for each other and he helped me stay on the straight and narrow when I was growing up as a teen in the 1960s," said Duarte, now electric utility director for the City of Healdsburg. "And my mother is a great lady who's always been there for any of us kids — she didn't play any favorites. She's very generous. Bob and my mom have had a really good marriage."

*Bob and Carmen Doyle enjoy a visit to the Roseville Telephone Museum with their daughter, Carol Smith, her husband, Mike, and daughter, Courtney.*

Photo by Steve Yeater

One of the Doyles' favorite outings is going to dinner. Over the years, they frequented the finest dining spots in the greater Sacramento area. Bob Doyle, however, never was the type to use his position as a prominent executive to curry favors.

"When we go out, he doesn't tell people what he does," said Carmen Doyle. "If they ask, he just tells them he works for the Roseville Telephone Company. It's rare that he ever tells someone what he is at the company. As he's leaving — if he likes somebody — he may give a person his card, but he never, ever says, 'I'm the Chairman of the Board of Roseville Telephone or the President or anything like that.' People there might find out later who he is from somebody else, but they won't from him."

Of Bob Doyle's business/family relationships, clearly the most important is with his brother, Tom. No Doyle has been involved with the company longer than Tom Doyle — he became a director in 1952 and corporate secretary in 1965. And as a substantial stockholder — he and Bob are the two largest individual shareholders — Tom's opinion carries weight with his brother. Through the years, Tom attended many conventions, loan signings and significant corporate events.

"Tom has been an ally of Bob's in most respects," said Bob Raymer, who has watched the Doyle brothers interact for 30 years. "I think Tom's support of what Bob has wanted to do has been important. Obviously, they don't always agree, but they work it out."

Others who see Tom and Bob Doyle together agree with Raymer's assessment. While both brothers are strong-willed, they usually can shut the door and resolve their differences privately. Tom is no rubber stamp, but both brothers understand it's important that they be united on major issues. Even when they disagree, their loyalty to their father's legacy and the Doyle family eventually brings them together. Blood runs thick in the Doyles.

"None of us always agree" is long-time director Doulton Burner's view of Tom and Bob Doyle's relationship. "But they always end up doing what they believe to be the best course of action for the Roseville Telephone Company. To me, that's what counts."

## QUALITIES OF COMMON SENSE, LOYALTY, INTEGRITY

When Bob Doyle is asked what quality is most important in determining success in business, he answers, "To be a good businessman, you don't have to be too smart, you just have to have good common horse sense."

What exactly does this blend of common horse sense really mean as it relates to Bob Doyle's success? "Good common horse sense" is only one of the qualities that describe Doyle.

Other qualities frequently mentioned when Doyle's name comes up are vision, honesty, integrity, loyalty, leadership and persistence. Each of these qualities is deeply ingrained in Bob Doyle. He's an individual one does not easily forget.

Through the years, the most distinguishing of Doyle's qualities has been his uncanny ability to anticipate community growth, particularly as it relates to development within Roseville Telephone's service territory. By its very nature, long-term planning is only as good as the assumptions underlying it. In a business that requires important and expensive decisions to be made several years in advance, Doyle's hunches about the future usually have been right on target. For decades, he held that actual growth would outstrip the best estimates developed by his engineering staff and directed his management team to build infrastructure capable of servicing his expectations of growth.

Doyle's belief in the growth of the area was a no-brainer to him. "I felt we had to grow considering how people were moving to California, plus the fact that our service territory had Interstate 80 going right through us. And we also had Folsom Lake."

Emerson Gunning remembers Doyle talking up growth in the area as early as 1954. "Bob's got a sight for the future, there's no doubt about it," Gunning said. "When he took me out that first time, he said Rocky Ridge, now Douglas Boulevard, would eventually look like Fulton Avenue in Sacramento, I thought he was off his rocker. But he was right. He also said then, 40 years ago, that the territory had room for over 250,000 telephones — the company had only about 2,500 at the time. You know what, the company serves more phones than that now. Who'd ever have thought we'd have this many people right now?"

*Bob Doyle, one of the telecommunications most successful executives.*

Photo by Sirlin Studios

In 1965, when Bob Raymer first visited Roseville Telephone, he noted that Bob Doyle had an extraordinarily bullish view of what was going to happen to the community.

"Just as he does now, he somehow realized, and he was correct about it, that the community was about to undergo or continue to undergo major growth," Raymer said. "So early on I got the feeling that indeed he was an enthusiastic telephone manager and was doing good things. He was stretching even then to get modern equipment and to prepare himself for what he felt in his gut was going to happen. I guess it was more than a gut feeling, he had lived in that community all his life."

Walter Gordon remembers offering his growth estimates to Doyle in the early 1960s.

"We'd figure out what we thought we'd need to handle expected growth and then go ask Bob Doyle what he thought," Gordon recollected. "He'd always say, 'Take what you have come up with and put about a 50 percent increase on top of it.' He was always adding about 50 percent. But he was usually right because he knew what was going on in the area. He was always driving around in the area and talking with builders, financial people and the like."

Leon Bower can remember Doyle urging the outside plant people not to scrimp. "He'd always say to us, 'When you place cable, you place it big enough, I don't want you going back there in a couple of years and doing it again.' He wanted it done right the first time."

As head of operations since arriving in Roseville in 1977, it's been Al Johnson's job to make recommendations about capital spending to Doyle and the Board of Directors. Doyle typically instructed Johnson to plan for even more growth than internal estimates showed. "He almost always wanted us to put in larger cables than I recommended," remembered Al Johnson. "He'd tell me, 'I know what the growth is; I know what's going to happen.' And, by god, he was right."

In addition to beefing up infrastructure capacity, Doyle always insisted on quality equipment and materials.

"He has always been first-class equipment-wise, facility-wise, building-wise. He never cut corners and never tried to get more for less," Johnson said. "Bob wanted to get his money's worth, of course, but he wanted the best products, the best system. Sometimes the cost was higher initially, but in the long run he saved the company a hell of a lot of money. We didn't have to go back in areas to expand capacity to accommodate faster-than-expected growth.

"Of course, his insistence on quality came from the fact that he wanted customers to have the best telephone service possible," Johnson added. "At the same time, the company's major investments in technology enabled us to keep control of labor costs, too."

To keep ahead of the growth required the company to build infrastructure — and invest lots of money — long before the anticipated revenue stream from new customers would begin. In the early years of Doyle's presidency, the company's appetite for debt was large compared to the size of the operation. In other words, if Doyle's instincts about growth were wrong, the company would have had excess plant in place for prospective customers who didn't come. Fortunately, Doyle's vision of rapid growth became reality.

Doyle's closest associate in the early days was Mark Shull. As the company's top financial executive for more than 30 years, it was Shull's responsibility to reconcile Doyle's sanguine view of growth prospects with the company's ability to finance the growth. Shull has the utmost respect for his former boss' clairvoyance.

"To me," said Shull, "Bob's best assets are his uncommon common sense and his ability to see the future. I don't know how he did it, but he has almost always predicted the future to a tee. And if he said he was going to do something, whether it was to buy a piece of land or sell millions of dollars of stock, he did it."

Doyle's rosy predictions were not idle chit chat in the office or in closed board meetings. His opinion about future growth permeated his annual report messages. Consider the following excerpts from early annuals:

*1961 Annual Report* — "Our state population will increase by an estimated 600,000 during 1962. The population growth in Northern and Central California during 1962 is estimated at 272,000. This would approximate 745 new residents per day in the Northern area ... Your company has planned ahead and will be ready to serve the future residents of our area ... We presently serve about 11,000 telephones. Based upon a study, when our area is fully populated, we expect to serve approximately 250,000 telephones ... "

*1962 Annual Report* — "We had a net gain of 1,502 telephones in 1962, approximately 14 percent over 1961. Our working stations at year end were 12,295 ... The growth is only beginning and our future looks very bright indeed."

*1966 Annual Report* — "Our state continues to grow, and with it your company. California is first in agriculture, leads the nation as a space and defense contractor, leads all states in retail sales, and is first in total personal income. Our own growth and that of our area continues, although somewhat more slowly than in other years. The temporary slowdown gave us the opportunity we needed to prepare ourselves for the expected growth period ahead."

*1969 Annual Report* — "Population in the area served by your company continued to grow at an estimated rate of 1.4 percent over 1968. Although this increase was less than that recorded in the early 1960s, the rate was still above the national average. Looking back, one sees that the population in the counties we serve is up substantially over the 1960 census: Placer County, 46 percent, and Sacramento County, 30 percent. Our future is very bright."

*1971 Annual Report* — "With the completion of the Sunrise Shopping Center and other developments in our operating area we expect that 1972 will be a year of progress for your company. Our longer-range prospects also appear to promise continuing growth and an exciting and eventful future."

*1975 Annual Report* — "Our management is projecting continued significant growth in 1976. A number of residential subdivisions are presently under construction in our operating territory. Still others are in various stages of planning. Moreover, a large commercial shopping center is under construction and we anticipate that it will increase the demand for telephone service in the southern part of our area. Because of these and other projected developments, the company is prepared to install more than 5,000 new stations in 1976."

In later years, Doyle has been even more bullish, and as this book is printed, he believes growth prospects for Roseville Telephone are stronger than ever, particularly in the relatively undeveloped western area of the company's service territory.

Another outstanding quality of Doyle's is his honesty. He tells it like it is — good and bad. His up-front nature catches many off guard, but those who deal with him regularly appreciate his directness. There is no hidden agenda.

"You know where you stand and you'd better be honest with him at all times," says Virginia Amick, his secretary. "There's no way I'd ever try to keep anything from him. If you give him an honest answer, he may not like it, but still he's got it and he will be fair about it."

Bob Parsons has frequent meetings with Doyle. "He's going to tell you his true feelings every time," Parsons said. "That's one quality I always appreciate about Bob ... you don't leave a meeting with him wondering. He makes it clear what you might want to think about or do."

Mike Doyle respects his dad's direct style:

"He doesn't beat around the bush, that's for sure," his son said. "If there's something my dad wants, or if he's got a question or something's wrong, he just comes right out and tells you. They know where he stands, they know what he expects of them. If it doesn't work out, he deals with it."

For the past 15 years, first as the company's outside accountant, and now as president and chief executive officer, Brian Strom has worked closely with Doyle.

"Occasionally, I'd have to bring him news he didn't particularly like, but he's never been one to dodge an issue," Strom said. "Hit him between the eyes with the bad news as opposed to hiding it or sweeping it under the rug. Even when he doesn't like it, he respects you for telling him bad news."

Ron Amick, the retired Pacific Telephone executive, is even more blunt about the need to be honest with Doyle.

"He's smart, he listens, he perceives and he knows what the hell is going on, so never try to pull any crap on him, because if you do you'll find yourself out the door damned fast," is how Amick put it.

The current manager of the company's 100-plus vehicle fleet, Tom Andrade, an employee since 1968, explains Doyle's view on quality and mistakes.

"While Robert wants nothing but the best in equipment, he doesn't want to get burned on anything. The philosophy he instilled in me when I took this job was this: 'Just remember this, if you make a mistake, it's a mistake. If it happens again, it's your fault.' I always think about that. It makes sense. That's the way he is. He runs a tight ship. You don't lie to the man. You do what he expects you to do."

Along with honesty, Doyle exudes old-fashioned integrity. His core values and principles have not changed over the decades.

"Hell, look at that puss on him. You know he can't lie," said Bill Sheppard, who's known Doyle for more than 40 years. "There isn't any amount of money that could get him, entice him into anything that is not up and above board."

Alan Ewen, the former SACTO executive director, lauds Doyle's qualities.

"With all the humor that's presented by his character, he's got an unfailing integrity, and he has that great way to manage his people. He doesn't interfere and micromanage; he's smart enough to let knowledgeable people have their run, and he has the courage to allow others to fail," Ewen said. "And, of course, he's very straightforward. He doesn't harbor anything or hold anything. He's not shadowy. I look upon him as a guy of my generation who is solid gold. You can count on his values. That's so important today when you can't count on very many people's values."

One of Doyle's most obvious qualities is his persistence. He doesn't give up on something he wants to do. Perhaps nowhere was this characteristic more apparent than during his stock-selling days. While some stock issues sold easily, others didn't. He had to keep hammering away at it.

"There were days I'd throw my hands up and wonder how we were going to do it," confessed Doyle, "and if I had known how hard it was going to be, maybe I wouldn't have done it. But there was no way I wasn't going to finish something I started. I'm not built that way."

*The company's vehicle manager, Tom Andrade, and his secretary, Mary Dillingham. Andrade's department keeps the company's vehicles in tip-top shape.*

The final stock sale that concluded in August 1983 was his most arduous. Faced with sky-high interest rates — the prime rate peaked at 21 1/2 percent in the early 1980s — Doyle not only had a difficult time selling new stock, but he had to re-sell shares sold by existing shareholders as well. He was scrambling, no doubt about it. In mid-1983, however, interest rates had come down from their peaks, and the company's appetite for capital was lower than anticipated. This meant the company didn't need to completely sell out that issue, if it didn't want to, because it had enough capital on hand to satisfy anticipated spending.

Nonetheless, Doyle pushed on until all the shares in the issue were sold.

"No way I wasn't going to complete selling all that issue," Doyle said. "I had never sold less than the full amount and I wasn't going to start then."

Another core Doyle value is loyalty. He is extremely loyal on both a business and personal level. Vendors who have served the company well through the years with quality service and products have typically retained their business with the company. The company has had the same attorneys, insurance broker, accountants and financial adviser for 30 years. And whenever feasible, Doyle urges his managers to do business locally.

"He is extremely loyal and that's a rare trait to have the kind of commitment to another person or another business that he has," said Dick Wise. "He'll really go the extra mile to do what's right and that's rare. You can't do handshake deals with very many people, but Bob Doyle happens to be one of them."

Doyle's loyalty to vendors and professionals doing business with the company is not blind, of course. As a former outside consultant to the company, Brian Strom understands how vendors think in dealing with the company.

"Vendors and consultants recognize that they'd rather have a good association in hand for a lot of years than to just rake in a lot of money for a couple of years and then be gone," Strom said. "If vendors treat Bob fair, he'll keep them around."

Perhaps nowhere are the advantages of loyalty more apparent than the relationship between Doyle and company employees. The mutual respect is enormous. Strom gives his view of it.

"I certainly can't speak for the whole company because I'm in a privileged relationship, so to speak, but all the employees I know look at Bob as the best thing since sliced bread. He's been real fair to them. He's got some strict guidelines, but if you play by his rules and treat the company well, he'll treat you well."

Marketing director Jay Kinder agrees.

"Bob commands a lot of loyalty. When he stands up and says this is a great company because of the employees, and when you realize what he's done for us, you believe it."

Doyle's loyalty from employees is also derived from his willingness to compliment employees on a job well done. He received a letter from a customer who commented on how clean and uncluttered the company cars are compared to other official vehicles she had seen. The customer was particularly impressed that there was nothing on the dashboards of the company cars. Doyle immediately sent a copy of the letter to Tom Andrade at the vehicle shop and made sure the letter was printed in the *Line Chatter*. Doyle is always patting employees on the back when it is deserved.

Wise offers this description of Doyle's strengths as a person, which also make him an unusually successful executive.

"In one way, he's a simple kind of guy, but on the other hand he's probably one of the most complex simple kind of guys imaginable, because his simplicity is in his integrity, his honesty and his commitment. He has a straightforward sense of values ... a really strong, strong commitment to values.

"His common sense is something else, too. For instance, in negotiations, he deals fairly, but I think he always leaves a little edge for the other guy so everybody can walk away from the deal feeling good. You don't feel like you've just been beat to death and there's nothing left and you think, 'Good God, who needs to do business with this guy?' He always leaves a little for you, but he gets a great deal for the telephone company. And that's a real art."

Beyond his qualities as a businessman and family man, Wise said being a friend of Doyle's is special.

"Bob Doyle is one of the half dozen real friends I have. He's the kind of guy that if you really needed something, I don't care what it was, he would do it," Wise said. "I don't care if it was money, or whatever, he would do it. I don't think he'd ever turn his back on anybody.

"It's because he really likes people. You've really got to be four kinds of a jerk to be on Bob Doyle's bad side. He'll give you every break in the world. All you have to do is be a regular person. And if you don't put on airs and you're genuine, you've got him," Wise continued. "He will not abide anybody who is phony and he won't abide anybody who's not honest. If you're just straightforward with the guy, he's just a very easy person to know. You get in a car with him and every goddamned telephone truck that goes by he waves at. He knows everybody in the company and a lot of them don't recognize what they've got. He's a rare individual."

Carmen Doyle supports Wise's contention that her husband is an easy person to talk to, even though some characterize him as being gruff.

"When we were first married and I started meeting some of the sales people that came through, they'd tell me they were all scared to go in and talk to Bob. I'd say, 'Why? He would love to talk to you.' They'd say, 'Oh, no. Everyone tells us we've got to stay away from him because of this and that.' I told them that was so wrong. 'The next time you are in town, you go and just say hello. If he doesn't want to talk a lot of business, that's fine. But go in and talk to him.' And we became friends with a lot of them because they started doing that."

*Jay Kinder started with Roseville Telephone while attending high school. He's now director of marketing and planning.*

# A Bright Future

## PROJECTIONS POINT TO GROWTH

*"I may not be here to see it all happen, but in not too many years people won't even recognize the area out west of town. It's a sleeper if there ever was a sleeper."*
— Bob Doyle

Recession wracked California in the first half of the 1990s, but bleak economic conditions elsewhere in the state hardly slowed growth around Roseville. In fact, the city's population grew about 7 percent annually in those years, to 56,036 residents at the start of 1994, up from 44,685 only four years earlier.

Top retailing companies, including Pace Warehouse, Home Depot and Wal-Mart, built large stores in the local market. Average sales per retail outlet in Roseville exceeded $1 million a year compared to the national average of $600,000. Albertson's grocery chain built a huge distribution center down the street from Hewlett-Packard's industrial campus.

Also, Kaiser-Permanente expanded its Roseville facilities, and the Sutter Health group, owner of Roseville Community Hospital, is building a major medical center on 56 acres. Related medical service industries are cropping up, too, including a large Foundation Health Corp. complex. And 15 auto dealers joined together to open the 90-acre Roseville Automall, one of the nation's largest.

*Del Webb Corporation's Sun City Roseville is the region's largest real estate development with 3,500 residences to be built over a 10-year period. Roseville Telephone is making "fiber to the curb" a reality for the residents of Sun City Roseville.*

Courtesy of Del Webb Corporation

Home building is under way all around Roseville. The giant of the projects is Del Webb Corporation's Sun City Roseville, taking shape on the former Fiddyment Ranch west of Roseville. When fully developed in about 10 years, there will be 3,500 homes on 1,200 acres. Upscale residential developments such as Tree Lake Village and Wexford are attracting executives and professionals into the area. At the end of 1994, there were

more than 20 residential subdivisions under construction around Roseville and many more are in the planning stages.

One of the region's major developments, Highland Reserve, is near Roseville Telephone's new Industrial Avenue complex. This 1,900-acre master planned community will mix quality residential and commercial development with a major shopping center. Roseville's two biggest employers, Hewlett-Packard and NEC, continue to expand and hire more skilled — and well-paid — workers.

All this growth has not escaped Bob Doyle, who for many years has held a grand vision of Roseville's future. The scope of the area's recent growth may even outstrip Doyle's lofty predictions.

*Sam's Club, the membership ware-house division of the giant Wal-Mart retail chain, is one example of the company's faith in prospects for retail sales in Roseville.*

Courtesy of the City of Roseville

"There are certain things you have to understand," Doyle said. "For example, those three big stores — Pace, Home Depot and Wal-Mart — were built after the recession was already under way, not before. Who's going to build such great big stores during a recession unless they think the area has a great future? If they had built them before the recession, then you could say, 'Poor bastards, they built the stores and now they've got to suffer with the rest of us.' But that's not what's happened. They came in and said, 'We're going to build a great big store and we'll show you what's going to happen down the road.'

"And it wasn't just one retailer thinking that way. There were quite a few of them. Plus, you've got Kaiser expanding here, putting nothing but money into the area, and Prudential Securities recently opened a big office. Now, they're not moving these people here because they think it's going to go down hill. They all think Roseville is the future, and I think the same goddamned thing … I don't think we've seen anything yet."

Although Doyle is generally optimistic about growth throughout Roseville Telephone's service area, he is most bullish about the area west of Roseville.

"I may not be here to see it all happen, but I can say that in not too many years from now people won't even recognize the area out west of town. It's a sleeper if there ever was a sleeper. That's where Del Webb is building and a lot of other housing is going in there, too.

"Base Line Road is the only road that goes clear through to the Sacramento River, all the way to El Centro Road to get to the Sacramento airport. If you stood in Roseville and had a rifle that would carry to the river, you could stand on Base Line Road and that bullet would never leave the road … it would go all the way to the river, that's how straight it is. It's two-lane now, but I'm sure it will be widened; it has to be.

"You take any other road going west and you run into a subdivision or something," Doyle said. "I predict you're going to see the same scale of development on Base Line Road that you now see happening on Douglas Boulevard, only it will probably be even bigger. You have major roadways such as Walerga Road and Watt Avenue feeding into Base Line. You're going to see shopping centers because that's where the people are going to be."

Doyle predicts major hotel and restaurant facilities will eventually be built in Roseville.

"We don't have a convention center or even any large hotels. When people come to these hospitals to visit patients, where are they going to stay? They've got to go to Sacramento because there's no place to stay," Doyle said. "And there's no place — really nice place, that is — for service club meetings, corporate meetings, things like that. We're going to need these as the population grows."

Doyle is quick to point out that growth will clearly benefit Roseville Telephone. "In the future, we'll have high-rise buildings. Instead of a house that has two phones, maybe we'll have a hotel with 2,000 phones."

Not everybody agrees with Doyle's projections, but he describes his detractors as "people who can't see beyond their nose."

"I talk about my ideas of what's going to happen, especially out west of town, and sometimes people laugh at me," Doyle said. "But I let them laugh because over the 40 years that I have been predicting things around here, look at what's happened. And I don't think it's going to stop now.

"Most of the old timers — I'm talking about those my age who were born and raised here — they can't see the growth. The people who really see it are the new ones who moved in more recently. The guy who just moved in from San Francisco or Los Angeles — out here trying to buy a piece of ground — he can see a hell of a lot more than the one who's been here all this time. All I can say is that it's going to be something."

## ALWAYS ON THE CUSP OF TECHNOLOGY

Technology continues to propel the telecommunications industry as miniaturization and increasing computer power become available at affordable prices. Walter Gordon talked about the tremendous advances taking place in the industry.

"Broad-band switching will be the next quantum leap in technology for telephone companies," Gordon said. "In narrow-band, our first digital carriers, called T1 carriers, carried 1.544 megabits of information per second. That was our first digital carrier and we bought lots of them. Then we went into fiber optics with 45-megabit fiber. This could carry 45 million bits of information per second. That's still narrow band.

Kaiser-Permanente has been an important employer in Roseville since 1980 when it opened its first outpatient facilities near Riverside Boulevard and Cirby Way in Roseville. The giant HMO is just finishing a beautiful, new medical complex to be ready in the spring of 1995.

Courtesy of the City of Roseville

"We then bought 90-megabit fiber, which was starting to enter into the broad-band range. After that, we bought 560-megabit fiber ... that is broad-band. They have fiber today that's 2.4 gigabits. A gigabit is a billion bits of information. As you continue on, it's thought that the limit that can be transmitted will be about 6 terabits. At that rate, you'll be doing what is called photon switching. Light is made up of photons. When you look at light, you're looking at photons that are coming to you. When you measure the light level, you're actually measuring the amount of photons that strike a particular surface. Six terabits is 6 trillion bits of information per second."

Future broad-band capabilities in the telephone industry will mean that more of the information carried on telephone lines will be non-voice data and video information, rather than voice.

"Video to us is only information," Gordon explained. "That's really all it is. If you have a particular video that you want to carry (over the lines), you just encode it as information in a digital stream and then transmit. If I have a computer file that I want to transmit, that's information, too. If a doctor takes an x-ray and wants to send that information, it is digitized, encoded and transmitted. In many instances, files are compressed before being transmitted. That is a big factor today. Compression takes all the superfluous information out of it."

Roseville Telephone's heavy investments in the latest transmission and digital technologies are designed to eventually enable every customer in the service area to have access to the "information superhighway" connecting users to resources available to them throughout the world.

"We talk about fiber to the curb, but eventually we need to be able to have fiber to every home, and then inside every home," said Al Johnson. "These new products coming around — such as the digital television — depend on fiber not just to the curb, but right to the TV set. These devices can do wonderful things, but they depend on digital information carried at tremendously high speeds."

The future holds marvelous opportunities in a digital world. Members of a properly-equipped household will enjoy access to visual, data and voice transmissions that have myriad applications in medicine, education, business, entertainment and personal communications.

The transmission capacity of fiber optic cable is incredible compared to copper cable. For example, two optical fibers (a pair) can transmit 24,000 telephone calls simultaneously. Current copper pairs can transmit only 24 calls. And fiber optic cable can transmit voice, data and video signals — or a combination of all three — simultaneously at the speed of light.

"Once you have fiber to the customer premises and inside, then you've got a virtual Utopia because it offers so many possibilities," Johnson added. "But you have to have broad-band capabilities throughout or none of this futuristic stuff will work."

While it's clearly within the technical capabilities of Roseville Telephone and others to place fiber to the curb, to the customer's premises, and inside the premises, the cost is a hurdle. Telecommunications today is market-driven. Will the demand for such futuristic options justify the enormous capital expense required to make them available?

In the past, regulatory authorities may well have mandated that over a certain period of time telephone companies should provide digital-capable outlets all the way into the customer's premises. Then regulators could have allowed the utility companies to charge rates sufficient to earn a fair return on the capital investments. In today's competitive environment, however, there is more financial risk to the companies.

"We know there is competition coming, but we do not know if it will be immediate or gradual," Johnson said. "We also don't know if the competitive playing field will be level or not. It makes it real hard deciding whether to commit the capital to do all these things."

"That's the real question — competition," said Bob Doyle. "If the rules are the same for us and for competitors, we feel we have as a good a chance as the next guy to keep our existing customers and add new ones. But if competitors can do things and we can't, well that's a different story. That just isn't right and you better believe we'll fight it."

Roseville Telephone is already investigating the possibilities of getting into new businesses. Guidelines will be much the same as the company used in assessing the feasibility of entering the cellular telephone and alarm monitoring businesses.

"As more competition comes in, we need to explore other potential business opportunities, whether it's cable or even having our own long distance company," said Brian Strom. "We will have to make investments in areas where we currently haven't invested any moneys. Hopefully, any new business ventures we undertake will grow and provide a good return as the cellular company does. Cable TV and PCS are prime examples of new businesses we might enter."

In the past, telephone companies have been prohibited from operating a cable television business, but court cases and regulations proposed by the Federal Communications Commission (FCC) in early 1995 will allow companies such as Roseville Telephone to enter the business. Michael Campbell, vice president/chief financial officer, said the company's advanced infrastructure makes it likely it will be a player in cable.

There are several possible scenarios related to entering the cable business, according to Campbell. The company could acquire an existing cable business or it could start its own cable company. This would involve purchasing programming content from existing providers, constructing earth stations to capture the video signals off satellites and then distributing the signal to cable customers who are already telephone customers. Another alternative is to simply be the carrier of video programming for one or more competing cable companies. The alternatives are under consideration.

"There are a number of businesses we could enter, but the common denominator for us is to match any new business with our existing skill set," Campbell explained. "For example, we are highly skilled in the area of operator services and alarm monitoring, so it would make sense to expand our businesses related to those areas.

"Another factor is that these skills — I'm referring to operator services and alarm monitoring — are not geographic specific. This means we can operate businesses anywhere in the country without needing to physically be in the places we operate. We want to look into businesses in which we can leverage our substantial investments in skilled labor and advanced technology and grow in a modular fashion."

As far as Bob Doyle is concerned, any business that can make a good return on investment would be considered:

"I see the company getting into anything and everything that's available, if it's worth a damn. We may try a business with the idea of not getting too involved financially, so if we see it's not paying, we can drop it," Doyle said. "But sometimes you don't know if a business can succeed unless you try. I don't believe in leaving any stone unturned. We've got consultants and everybody in this company looking for anything they think we can get into, from CATV to no matter what. If we can make a buck, whether it's in the telephone industry or not, we should look at it. We've got the property and buildings for growth and we've got personnel who are well trained and going to schools constantly. If anybody else can do it, we can do it. If it's something new, we can go to school to learn. Hell, the competitors have to go to school, too, if it's new."

## THE POST-BOB DOYLE PERIOD

Inevitably, the question arises, "What's the Roseville Telephone Company going to be like without Bob Doyle?" Just about everyone has an opinion.

"Bob has many wonderful employees who will continue on with the way that he has always wanted the company to be run," said Ellen Lynn, Doyle's former secretary.

"The company will hardly miss a beat," said Doyle's current secretary, Virginia Amick. "Of course, he'll be greatly missed and he has certainly left his influence on the company. But Bob has built a strong foundation, and Brian Strom has no plans to change things to any degree. Plus, I think all our employees and management will just step in and work that much harder. I think the company will continue on very smoothly."

Chuck Spooner, the manager of the data processing department, believes that Doyle's reign has paved the way for continued excellence in the future.

"While it's hard for me to picture Roseville Telephone without Bob Doyle, there is a strong management team in place here that's certainly going to want to carry on in the direction he set. Under Brian Strom as well as under Bob, one has a very strong sense of security that this is a very healthy company. And just like Bob, Brian is not looking to sell the company to the highest bidder."

The very idea of being acquired is particularly odious to Spooner.

*While Roseville is no longer just a "railroad town" Southern Pacific remains one of the city's largest employers as it has been since arriving in Roseville in 1906.*

"I had a pretty traumatic experience when the previous company I had worked for was involved in a merger," remembered Spooner. "So when I visited Roseville Telephone in September of 1971 and was introduced to Bob Doyle, I asked him what was the possibility that there would be a merger here.

"He gave me about a 10-minute dissertation about how some of the big independents had been in here many times and how he just kicked their butts out of his office. I've always felt very comfortable with the fact that this is a very secure place to work, not one up for sale to the highest bidder," Spooner said. "And I know Brian Strom and the board feel that way, too. We're a good strong company, providing good service, serving our customers, our stockholders and our employees. There's no reason to put the company on the auction block. It feels pretty good."

While no can predict the future, it's a certainty that there will be challenges for Roseville Telephone. As competition barges into its once exclusive turf, the company will need to be as progressive in its marketing, sales and service as it traditionally has been in technology. Company director John Roberts expresses the challenges facing the company:

"How do you take a company that has been highly regulated by the government and interject into its marketplace multiple non-regulated competitors — at the same time the company is still being regulated — then how do you take that company out of the regulated environment to join these unregulated competitors? It's the challenge of going from a regulated environment to one of intense market focus," Roberts said. "As I see the future, we'll need to do a mad dash to get as competitive as fast as we possibly can so we do not lose any market share. I am confident we can do it if we keep our minds on the right issues."

In Roberts' view, the promotion of Brian Strom to president and CEO and the hiring of Mike Campbell added to Roseville Telephone's already strong capability to tackle any challenges in the future.

*Robert L. Doyle — a lifetime dedicated to building the Roseville Telephone Company.*

Photo by Rudy Meyers

"I think Brian's common-sense, level-headedness is what the company needs at this time in its life. I'm also impressed with Mike Campbell — he's a more technical type. When you add Brian and Mike to the long-time management team, led by Al Johnson, a group which has been stable, knowledgeable and imbued with a quality service ethic, you've got a really good crew to help us get through some of these challenges."

Certainly, if there's one person bullish about Roseville Telephone's future, it's Bob Doyle. After more than 40 years building a "hell of a telephone company," Doyle is secure in his outlook for the future.

"I've said it many times in the past and I'll say it again, you ain't seen nothing yet!"

# Appendix A—References

The author's principal sources for the information contained in this book included:

- Annual reports of Roseville Telephone Company to California Railroad Commission and California Public Utilities Commission (CPUC) (1913-1959)

- Railroad Commission and CPUC Decisions, 1913-1994.

- Roseville Telephone annual reports, 1960-1994.

- *Line Chatter* newsletters, 1958-1994.

- Board of Directors minutes, 1963-1994.

- U.S. Census Bureau Statistics.

In addition, the author conducted extensive interviews with approximately 150 retirees, employees, vendors, consultants and others knowledgeable about Roseville Telephone Company and its history.

Other sources of local information were gleaned from archived records at Roseville Telephone which included articles from the *Roseville Register, Roseville Tribune, San Juan Record, Citrus Heights Bulletin, San Juan World, Roseville Press-Tribune, The Sacramento Union, Sacramento Bee, San Francisco Chronicle, Business Journal of Sacramento, Comstock's* magazine, *Telephony* and *Phonefacts.*

The books used for background information included *The Spirit of Independent Telephony* (Charles A. Pleasance, Independent Telephone Books, 1989); *Heritage & Destiny, Reflections On The Bell System In Transition* (Alvin von Auw, Praeger Publishers, 1983); *Good Ole Ma* (Bill Corman, Vantage Press, 1993); *Telephone, The First Hundred Years* (John Brooks, Harper & Row), 1976; *History of Placer and Nevada Counties* (William Lardner and M.J. Brock, Historic Record Company, 1924); and *Profiles Out of the Past* (Leonard M. Davis, Roseville Community Projects, Inc., 1982).

Photos were provided by (in alphabetical order); Jack Anderson, John Apostolos, Ed Asmus/Williams & Paddon, Bill Baxter, Stewart Brown, Steve Chanecka, Comstock's magazine, James J. Cordano Co., Leonard M. Davis Historical Collection, Del Webb Corp., Robert L. Doyle, Gladys Ellis, Alan Ewen/Gittings, Emerson Gunning, KFBK-Sacramento, McClellan Air Force Base History Office, Bill McNabb, Jr., Rudy Meyers, Robert Parsons, Betty Radford, Robert Raymer, City of Roseville, Roseville Press-Tribune, Merle Ruggles, Marguerite Smart, Tim Sproul, Sirlin Studios, U.S. Bureau of Reclamation, Richard Wise, and Steve Yeater.

# Appendix B—Corporate Summary By Year

| Year | Total Plant In Service* | Revenue | Net Income** | Telephones/ Access Lines*** | Fulltime Employees At Year End |
|---|---|---|---|---|---|
| 1914 | $12,000 | $7,600 | $1,682 | 388 | 7 |
| 1915 | $15,192 | $9,130 | $2,081 | 460 | 7 |
| 1916 | $19,444 | $11,207 | $2,72 | 1550 | 8 |
| 1917 | $22,111 | $12,627 | $2,428 | N/A | 9 |
| 1918 | $22,989 | $12,555 | $1,860 | 644 | 9 |
| 1919 | $23,801 | $12,573 | $ 497 | 666 | 8 |
| 1920 | $24,537 | $15,703 | $1,168 | 700 | 11 |
| 1921 | $25,692 | $18,761 | $2,450 | 760 | 12 |
| 1922 | $28,977 | $18,522 | $1,295 | 800 | 11 |
| 1923 | $41,473 | $21,566 | $5,00 | 900 | 12 |
| 1924 | $46,675 | $25,202 | $6,417 | 900 | 12 |
| 1925 | $54,979 | $27,637 | $8,003 | 1,081 | 12 |
| 1926 | $64,378 | $31,185 | $9,147 | 1,250 | 12 |
| 1927 | $65,844 | $32,625 | $9,693 | 1,279 | 12 |
| 1928 | $66,795 | $33,322 | $8,723 | 1,285 | 12 |
| 1929 | $72,255 | $34,343 | $7,958 | 1,285 | 13 |
| 1930 | $80,614 | $34,569 | $8,862 | 1,300 | 12 |
| 1931 | $81,409 | $34,110 | $8,491 | 1,253 | 12 |
| 1932 | $81,752 | $30,392 | $6,620 | 1,105 | 10 |
| 1933 | $81,969 | $27,626 | $5,246 | 1,134 | 10 |
| 1934 | $82,578 | $27,992 | $7,712 | 1,180 | 10 |
| 1935 | $82,944 | $28,934 | $8,338 | N/A | 10 |
| 1936 | $82,990 | $32,130 | $9,215 | 1,200 | 10 |
| 1937 | $88,459 | $34,937 | $9,322 | 1,280 | 11 |
| 1938 | $92,768 | $36,255 | $7,630 | 1,267 | 12 |
| 1939 | $97,991 | $37,830 | $9,516 | 1,308 | 13 |
| 1940 | $101,687 | $39,112 | $8,633 | 1,337 | 14 |
| 1941 | $112,765 | $43,992 | $11,676 | 1,485 | 14 |
| 1942 | $117,492 | $52,341 | $10,422 | 1,580 | 13 |
| 1943 | $120,200 | $56,623 | $12,611 | 1,690 | 14 |
| 1944 | $124,474 | $68,132 | $11,347 | 1,690 | 15 |
| 1945 | $127,037 | $79,924 | $16,559 | 1,756 | 18 |
| 1946 | $138,870 | $90,227 | $21,579 | 1,876 | 21 |
| 1947 | $163,870 | $102,208 | $21,766 | 1,851 | 22 |
| 1948 | $187,382 | $112,459 | $19,685 | 2,308 | 28 |
| 1949 | $260,548 | $125,567 | $22,748 | 2,668 | 28 |
| 1950 | $286,012 | $147,429 | $23,708 | 2,903 | 30 |
| 1951 | $373,884 | $159,663 | $24,015 | 2,851 | 36 |
| 1952 | $501,375 | $175,539 | $25,391 | 3,479 | 40 |
| 1953 | $589,470 | $210,392 | $30,990 | 3,777 | 47 |
| (Robert L. Doyle becomes president in January 1954) | | | | | |
| 1954 | $712,347 | $283,997 | $56,059 | 4,144 | 40 |
| 1955 | $928,890 | $335,433 | $54,950 | 4,921 | 49 |

| Year | Total Plant In Service* | Revenue | Net Income** | Telephones/ Access Lines*** | Fulltime Employees At Year End |
|---|---|---|---|---|---|
| 1956 | $1,195,152 | $427,734 | $75,374 | 5,543 | 53 |
| 1957 | $1,764,614 | $469,505 | $70,782 | 6,153 | 57 |
| 1958 | $2,130,997 | $597,784 | $95,107 | 7,173 | 64 |
| 1959 | $2,737,891 | $967,900 | $163,304 | 8,476 | 86 |
| 1960 | $4,137,046 | $1,271,178 | $161,026 | 9,740 | 108 |
| 1961 | $5,345,640 | $1,420,651 | $182,306 | 10,792 | 110 |
| 1962 | $6,536,547 | $1,681,595 | $290.681 | 12,294 | 116 |
| 1963 | $7,349,918 | $2,071,122 | $398.496 | 13,931 | 122 |
| 1964 | $8,684,127 | $2,310,904 | $412,811 | 15,879 | 127 |
| 1965 | $9,628,746 | $2,690,967 | $457,265 | 17,014 | 132 |
| 1966 | $11,161,857 | $2,887,879 | $456,835 | 18,204 | 140 |
| 1967 | $12,321,304 | $3,215,044 | $443,137 | 19,176 | 144 |
| 1968 | $13,278,618 | $3,725,721 | $535,272 | 20,402 | 147 |
| 1969 | $14,019,887 | $3,896,243 | $578,050 | 21,639 | 146 |
| 1970 | $15,017,915 | $4,326,643 | $744,899 | 23,567 | 148 |
| 1971 | $16,704,575 | $4,368,225 | $583,031 | 26,040 | 160 |
| 1972 | $18,624,817 | $5,215,147 | $785,264 | 29,346 | 176 |
| 1973 | $23,203,750 | $6,018,906 | $1,155,182 | 33,247 | 207 |
| 1974 | $27,225,571 | $7,587,056 | $1,308,518 | 37,150 | 227 |
| 1975 | $30,567,000 | $8,350,000 | $1,445,000 | 41,944 | 240 |
| 1976 | $34,305,000 | $9,729,000 | $1,490,000 | 47,341 | 260 |
| 1977 | $44,448,000 | $11,682,000 | $2,612,000 | 54,955 | 288 |
| 1978 | $50,844,000 | $14,166,000 | $2,718,000 | 63,025 | 325 |
| 1979 | $61,609,000 | $16,771,000 | $3,123,000 | 70,583 | 358 |
| 1980 | $72,387,000 | $21,305,000 | $3,547,000 | 74,588 | 372 |
| 1981 | $83,605,000 | $25,328,000 | $2,576,000 | 77,743/45,288*** | 362 |
| 1982 | $87,088,000 | $30,376,000 | $4,323,000 | 46,435 | 336 |
| 1983 | $91,647,000 | $33,542,000 | $6,053,000 | 48,439 | 331 |
| 1984 | $92,299,000 | $36,161,000 | $7,520,000 | 50,891 | 326 |
| 1985 | $98,980,000 | $39,676,000 | $8,634,000 | 54,029 | 323 |
| 1986 | $101,067,000 | $43,343,000 | $9,432,000 | 57,851 | 332 |
| 1987 | $105,991,000 | $46,044,000 | $11,551,000 | 61,636 | 335 |
| 1988 | $132,907,000 | $48,790,000 | $10,414,000 | 65,741 | 352 |
| 1989 | $144,001,000 | $61,293,000 | $14,740,000 | 71,937 | 372 |
| 1990 | $159,880,000 | $73,629,000 | $16,830,000 | 78,848 | 409 |
| 1991 | $181,552,000 | $88,461,000 | $19,940,000 | 83,010 | 439 |
| 1992 | $203,379,000 | $92,280,000 | $21,816,000 | 86,317 | 456 |
| 1993 | $228,927,000 | $96,280,000 | $22,518,000 | 90,375 | 463 |
| 1994 | $243,774,000 | $102,963,000 | $20,355,000 | 94,646 | 501 |

\* — Total Plant In Service, or Gross Plant Investment, is the total investment in plant and equipment before depreciation.

\*\* — In the early years, net income as reported often didn't include rent expense and interest income, creating inconsistencies.

\*\*\* — Telephone stations include all phones served, including those on extension lines until 1981-1982 when only access lines (the telephone line to the main telephone) were counted.

# Appendix C—Directors, Past And Present

Roseville Telephone Company's directors in order of their starting dates of service:

**William J. Doyle (1914-1954)** — One of the Roseville area's most prominent farmers, Doyle became involved in the telephone business in 1913 when the Roseville Home Telephone Co. faced financial difficulties and was reorganized. He was the largest shareholder and a vice president in the Home Telephone Co. before that group decided to sell out to the Roseville Telephone Company, which was formed by many of the previous owners of the Home Telephone Co. Doyle was vice president of the Roseville Telephone Company upon its founding in 1914 and became president in October 1917 upon Gottlieb Hanisch's death. W.J. "Bill" Doyle remained president until January 1954 when his son, Robert L. Doyle, was elected by the directors to succeed his father.

*William J. Doyle*

**Gottlieb M. Hanisch (1914-1917)** — Hanisch was born in Austria in 1844 and came with his family to San Francisco in 1850. In 1867, he moved to a ranch east of Roseville. In the late 1800s and early 1900s, Hanisch became a prominent businessman in Roseville. He was involved in plumbing and construction and helped organize and was the president of the first locally-owned telephone exchange, the Roseville Home Telephone Co., which acquired the local interests of the Sunset Telephone and Telegraph Co. (Pacific Telephone) in late 1910. When the Home Telephone Co. sold its assets to the newly-formed Roseville Telephone Company in 1914, Hanisch remained president of the new company and remained in that position until he died in 1917. Hanisch was also Roseville's first Volunteer Fire Chief who started the volunteer fire department in 1907.

*Gottlieb M. Hanisch*

**Francis A. (F.A.) Lewis (1914-1957)** — Lewis was an original director of the Roseville Home Telephone Co. and its successor, the Roseville Telephone Company. Lewis was Roseville's first druggist, having moved his business from Rocklin to Roseville when the railroad moved its operations to Roseville. Lewis was elected a vice-president of the Roseville Telephone Company in 1917 upon Gottlieb Hanisch's death. Through the years Lewis was one of the most independent of the directors and challenged management's slow-growth position. Lewis remained on the Board of Directors until his death in 1957.

*Francis A. (F.A.) Lewis*

**Lena A. Etzel (1914-1930)** — A former schoolteacher, Mrs. Etzel arrived in Roseville in 1908 with her husband, carpenter/contractor Chris Etzel. She was a founding director of Roseville Telephone. Lena Etzel was involved in Roseville cultural activities and remained on the Board of Directors until her death in 1930.

*Lena A. Etzel*

*photo not available*

*Charles A. Baker*

*photo not available*

*Leroy Etzel*

**Charles T. (C.T.) McCracken (1914-1923)** — McCracken also was one of the founders of the Roseville Home Telephone Co. who became part of the original ownership and management of the Roseville Telephone Company. McCracken came from Illinois where he was a school teacher for two years and a railroad fireman and locomotive engineer for 10 years before moving to California in 1906 at age 32. McCracken owned a drayage, feed and fuel business in Roseville from 1906 through 1917. From 1918 through 1923, McCracken was assistant manager of Roseville Telephone and helped Walter Hanisch. McCracken left the Board of Directors and sold his shares in 1923 to found one of the area's first auto service stations. McCracken was not associated with the telephone company after 1923. He died in 1949.

**Charles A. Baker (1917-1953)** — Baker was Roseville Telephone's corporate secretary and treasurer from its outset in 1914. He didn't become a member of the Board of Directors until 1917 when he replaced the deceased Gottlieb Hanisch. A native of England, Baker opened up his haberdashery upon arrival to Roseville in 1909 and was known for his austere British demeanor and his frugality. Although he was involved with the telephone company from its very beginning, the parsimonious Baker never owned a telephone in his home. He had no use for modern conveniences — he didn't have a refrigerator nor did he have heat in his home. Foods were kept cool in a basement room where the Baker and guests would retreat during the hot summer months. Baker sold his shop in December 1923 and retired. Baker owned a property next to the original telephone office that housed the "Pall Mall" club and had offices upstairs. Roseville Telephone acquired his property in the 1950s. Baker was a director from 1917 to 1953 when he resigned in favor of attorney L.C. Anderson.

**Hale M. Trevey (1923-1935)** — Trevey was a prominent engineer with the Southern Pacific and an investor. He bought his first stock from Charles McCracken in 1923 and kept acquiring shares. For most of the 10-plus years Trevey was on the Board of Directors, he was the second largest shareholder after W.J. Doyle with an 11 percent ownership of the company. Trevey, a native of Memphis, Tennessee, was schooled in Missouri and became a railroad engineer in 1903. He moved to Roseville in 1907. Trevey was also a shareholder in the Railroad Bank of Roseville and the Roseville Banking Company. Trevey left the board in 1935 and was replaced by Chris Etzel.

**Leroy Etzel (1930-1965)** — Etzel was steeped in Roseville Telephone history as the son of Lena and Chris Etzel. When his mother died in 1930, it was "Roy," as he preferred to be called, who filled his mother's position on the Board of Directors rather than her husband, Chris. Etzel had a successful business career of his own and he rose to become the chief executive of the Pacific Fruit Express, a subsidiary of the Southern Pacific Railroad. Etzel took the train from Oakland to Roseville for the monthly board meetings.

**Chris Etzel (1935-1949)** — The elder Etzel was retired from his carpentry and contracting businesses when he joined the Board of Directors in 1935. The two Etzels, Chris and his son, Roy, together became the second largest shareholders in the company after Trevey died in 1935. Chris Etzel died in 1949 and his position on the Board of Directors was filled by Walter Hanisch.

**Walter D. Hanisch (1949-1972)** — Hanisch grew up in Roseville and joined the Roseville Home Telephone Co. as a lineman in December 1912. Hanisch became manager of the company in 1914, a position he would retain for 40 years. In 1949, Hanisch joined the Board of Directors. After retiring from active management in the Roseville Telephone Company in 1954, Hanisch remained on the board until his death on New Year's Day, 1972. Like his father, Walter Hanisch held a life-long interest in firefighting and was chief of Roseville's volunteer department from many years. Hanisch was also an amateur meteorologist and avid ham radio operator.

**Thomas E. Doyle (1952-Present)** — Doyle joined the Board of Directors in January 1952 and as of April 1995 has been a director longer than any other in company history except F.A. Lewis. When he joined the board he was a farmer with the Doyle Brothers farming partnership. In 1965, he became corporate secretary for Roseville Telephone and still holds that position. Through the years, Tom Doyle has been active in real estate investment and the savings and loan business. He is chairman of the board of Placer Savings Bank.

**A. Stanley Anderson (1952-1967)** — Anderson joined the Board of Directors in January 1952 and with Tom Doyle was the first of the "new wave of directors." Anderson was a large chicken rancher in Rio Linda and, among other things, was responsible for providing the chickens to be barbecued at the festive company picnics in the 1950s and 1960s. Anderson was also a close friend of Jack Doyle, the oldest of the three Doyle brothers, who drowned in 1958. Anderson died in 1967 and was succeeded on the Board of Directors by Bill P. Sheppard.

**Lorenzo C. (L.C.) Anderson (1953-1955)** — No relation to Stan Anderson, L.C. Anderson (he hated his first name) was a long-time Roseville attorney whose offices were above the Pall Mall Club on Lincoln Street next door to the small Roseville Telephone office. Anderson replaced Charles Baker on the Board of Directors in late 1953 and held that position until January 1955 when he died suddenly of a bleeding ulcer. Bob Doyle considered Anderson his key adviser in the early days. It was L.C. Anderson who impressed upon Doyle the importance of retaining local control of the stock. Anderson rented his office suite for $35 a month from Baker, the long-time director. When Anderson told Baker the rent should be more, the frugal Baker replied, "No, we're getting along just fine so we'll keep the rent right where it is."

*Chris Etzel*

*Walter D. Hanisch*

*Thomas E. Doyle*

*A. Stanley Anderson*

*L.C. Anderson*

*Robert L. Doyle*

*Thomas E. Srednik*

*Eugene Garbolino*

*Bill P. Sheppard*

*George Campbell*

**Robert L. Doyle (1954-Present)** — Bob Doyle joined the Board of Directors in January 1954 when he replaced his father, William J. Doyle, as president and chairman of the board of Roseville Telephone. He led the company for 40 years as president and manager of the company until December 1993 when he stepped down from those posts in favor of Brian Strom. Doyle remains a working chairman who maintains a normal work schedule.

**Thomas E. Srednik (1955-1965)** — Srednik was a Roseville attorney who became the company's legal counsel and a director in January 1955 replacing L.C. Anderson, who died. Srednik helped the company craft its second and third stock sales, but resigned from the board in 1965 after a disagreement with Bob Doyle.

**Eugene Garbolino — (1957-1976)** Garbolino was a prominent Roseville businessman who joined the Board of Directors in 1957 upon the death of retired druggist F.A. Lewis, one of the company's founders. Garbolino and his brother Fred were principals in Garbolino Bros. Grape Shippers, a large grape shipping concern. Garbolino also operated Garbolino Furniture and was chairman of the board and president of the Citizens Bank. He died in 1976 and was replaced on the board by Doulton Burner.

**Bill P. Sheppard (1967-1993)** — succeeded Stan Anderson in 1967. Sheppard was the owner of the Roseville Feed Store serving the area's farming interests. Sheppard also became one of the largest turkey farmers in the area and raised several hundred thousand turkeys at ranches in the local area and the San Joaquin Valley. Sheppard remained a board member until December 1993 when he stepped down and became an advisory board member. John Roberts succeeded Sheppard on the Board of Directors.

**George Campbell (1972-1987)** — Campbell succeeded Walter Hanisch on the board in 1972. Campbell was a prominent local businessman who was associated with Standard Oil of California. Campbell was active in political circles and was a former mayor and city councilman in Roseville. He was also an aide to the late congressman Harold T. "Bizz" Johnson. Campbell stepped down from the Board of Directors in 1987 due to health reasons and was replaced by Ralph Hoeper.

**C. Doulton Burner (1976-1993)** — Burner joined the Board of Directors in 1976 upon the death of Eugene Garbolino. Burner was a long-time area businessman who ran the Retail Credit Association bureaus in Roseville and Auburn before retiring. He remained a director until late 1993 when he became an advisory member of the Board of Directors.

*C. Doulton Burner*

**Ralph Hoeper (1987-Present)** — Hoeper is the long-time owner and president of Foresthill Telephone Company in Foresthill, Calif. Hoeper joined the Board of Directors in 1987 succeeding George Campbell who retired. Hoeper is active in the United States Telephone Association and the California Telephone Association.

*Ralph Hoeper*

**Brian Strom (1993-Present)** — Strom was elected to the Board of Directors in December 1993 succeeding Doulton Burner who retired. Strom was a consultant to Roseville Telephone while at Arthur Young & Co. in the early 1980s. He joined Roseville Telephone in 1989 as chief financial officer and was appointed president and chief executive officer in December 1993.

*Brian Strom*

**John R. Roberts III (1993-Present)** — Roberts joined the Board of Directors in December 1993 succeeding Bill P. Sheppard who retired. Roberts came to the Sacramento region from Texas in 1984 and was executive director of the Sacramento Area Commerce and Trade Organization (SACTO) for several years before taking a post with the Sacramento Chamber of Commerce. He is currently executive director of the California Rice Industry Association.

*John R. Roberts III*

# Index